THROUGH THE '80s
THINKING GLOBALLY, ACTING LOCALLY

Edited by
Frank Feather

Foreword by
Edward R. Schreyer
Governor General of Canada

Introduction by
Maurice Strong

Postscript by
Aurelio Peccei

World Future Society
Washington, D.C. • U.S.A.

Editor: Frank Feather

Chairman of Editorial Review Board: Howard F. Didsbury, Jr.

Editorial Review Board: James Crider, Robert Foulon, Frank Snowden Hopkins, Charles H. Little, Theodore J. Maziarski, Andrew A. Spekke

Staff Editors: Edward Cornish, Jerry Richardson

Production Manager: Peter Zuckerman

Editorial Coordinator: Sarah Warner

Editorial Assistants: Jeff Brooks, Dean Haledjian, Jean Hollister, Melinda Katz, JoAnn Zea

Graphic Design: Diane Smirnow

Cover Art: Jane Hurd ©

Typesetting: Unicorn Graphics

Published by:
World Future Society
4916 St. Elmo Avenue
Washington, D.C. 20014 ● U.S.A.

Library of Congress Cataloging in Publication Data

Through the '80s, thinking globally, acting locally.
1. Twentieth century—Forecasts—Addresses, essays, lectures. 2. Civilization, Modern—1950—Addresses, essays, lectures. 3. Forecasting—Addresses, essays, lectures. I. Feather, Frank, 1943-
CB161.T49 304 303.4 80-18540
ISBN O-930242-11-4

Library of Congress Catalog Number: 80-52246

International Standard Book Number: 0-930242-11-4

Printed in the United States of America

Contents

iii

INVENTORYING OUR RESOURCES

THE INTERNATIONAL CONTEXT

ECONOMICS: GETTING DOWN TO BUSINESS

HUMAN VALUES: PERSONAL, SOCIAL, RELIGIOUS

COMMUNICATIONS: CONNECTING OURSELVES TOGETHER

EDUCATION: LEARNING TO MEET TOMORROW

Note

This volume was prepared in conjunction with the First Global Conference on the Future, held in Toronto, Canada, July 20-24, 1980. The conference combined the Third General Assembly of the World Future Society and the fifth annual conference of the Canadian Futures Society.

The papers presented here were selected from the very large number submitted to the conference committee. The committee regrets that space limitations permitted only a small number of papers to be published in this volume. In addition, many papers had to be cut substantially. Footnotes and other scholarly paraphernalia were dispensed with, so that as wide a selection of thoughts as possible could be presented.

Foreword

The Mystery of the Future

From the very dawn of civilization, the future has fascinated mankind and penetrating its mystery has been a constant challenge. The pronouncements of the Delphic oracle, all the way down to today's interest in futurology and computer projections testify to this obsession of man to *know* what lies ahead, to try to shape the whole world's destiny, to dream of an ideal universe.

The technological advances of the twentieth century and the opening of instantaneous global communication channels have brought our planet to an unprecedented state of awareness which makes it impossible for a country or a people to live in isolation. For better or for worse, our destinies are inextricably linked and we must work together to harness our present and future state of knowledge to make it work to the benefit of all the earth's inhabitants. The fate of the very next generation of humanity will be altered tremendously by decisions of this next decade especially as regards energy patterns and dependencies.

We can no longer lie back and let history repeat itself; it has repeated itself too often already. We must heed D.W. Brogan's warning: "Never underestimate the stupidity factor as a determinant of history." The world has suffered more than its share of blunders, whether they were unleashed by satanic minds or happened by accident. Man is the only animal intelligent enough to destroy his planet; conversely, he is also able to save it.

> Edward R. Schreyer
> Governor General of Canada
> Government House
> Ottawa

1

Le Mystère de l'Avenir

Fasciné par le caractère insondable de l'avenir, l'homme a tenté, depuis l'éveil de la civilisation, d'en pénétrer le mystère. L'interprétation de l'oracle de Delphes par les anciens et l'intérêt que suscitent aujourd'hui la futurologie et les projections d'ordinateurs témoignent de cette obsession de l'homme de savoir ce que le futur lui réserve, de ses efforts pour influencer la destinée de l'univers et de son rêve d'un monde idéal.

Grâce aux progrès technologiques du vingtième siècle et à l'installation de réseaux de communication permettant la transmission instantanée de messages, partout dans le monde, notre planète a atteint un niveau de sensibilisation sans précédent qui exclut toute possibilité pour un pays ou un peuple de vivre dans l'isolement. Pour le meilleur ou pour le pire, nos destins sont indissolublement liés; nous devons donc nous efforcer, ensemble, d'exploiter nos connaissances actuelles et futures pour en faire profiter l'humanité tout entière. Le sort de la prochaine génération est étroitement lié aux décisions qui seront prises au cours de la nouvelle décennie, tout particulièrement celles qui auront pour objet les besoins et les interdépendances en matière d'énergie.

Nous ne pouvons plus nous reposer dans la croyance que l'histoire est un éternel recommencement; elle s'est déjà répétée trop souvent. Nous devons tenir compte de la mise en garde de l'historien D. W. Brogan qui nous invite à ne pas sous-estimer le facteur stupidité comme élément déterminant de l'histoire. L'humanité a enduré plus que sa part de sottises qu'elles aient été l'oeuvre d'esprits démoniaques ou le fruit du hasard. L'homme est le seul animal suffisamment intelligent pour détruire sa planète; en revanche, il est également en mesure de la sauver.

Edward R. Schreyer
le Gouverneur-général du Canada
Résidence du Gouverneur-Général
Ottawa

Preface

A Time for Action

by

Maurice F. Strong

It is encouraging to see the broadening concern for futuristic issues. What began as a discussion amongst a relatively small core of scientists, futurists, and public interest groups now engages wide attention. This has fed on our personal experiences with environmental problems and energy shortages. The public concern has inevitably been accompanied by the fears and resentments of those whose lives have been directly affected by shifting patterns of employment, unemployment, inflation, and hazards to their own health or safety. They have also suffered from the impediments, caused by government regulation or public re-action, to the development of enterprises to which their wealth or careers are committed. I doubt if there is a community or family which has not been touched by some aspect of the growing controversy over the future direction of society.

So, today, we have succeeded in creating—albeit at a high level of generality—a high degree of awareness. But, our job is by no means finished. Indeed, it has only just begun, and we are just beginning to see the kind of difficulties we will confront.

For I am persuaded that we are in one of those seminal transition periods in human history. The way in which we deal with the issues will determine the direction in which this transition will take us. At this point, I believe its outcome is not pre-determined. Most of the basic forces which are shaping our future are the result of human actions and human failures. In a very real sense, then, we are today in command of our own evolution.

Maurice F. Strong is a Canadian businessman who served as director of the United Nations Environment Programme. He was chairman of the Stockholm Conference on the Environment and the Vancouver Conference on Habitats.

3

Whatever may be the result, one thing is certain—the period we have now entered will inevitably be one of greater turbulence, uncertainty, and conflict. We have just begun to see the real and deep-seated conflicts that can be engendered—conflicts over scarce resources, conflicts over land and living space, conflicts over the control of ocean resources, even conflicts over the use of the air waves. These conflicts will range from the "local" level to the "global" level.

But whether local or global, the issues must inevitably be perceived within a global framework while being dealt with at the most effectively managed scale and level of decision-making, i.e., locally.

All too often there is a great tendency to try to elevate every issue to the global level for its solution. The danger in talking about problems on a "global" basis is that we will lapse into "thinking" that all solutions to them can only be mounted at the global level. There *are* many global problems in the sense that they can only be fully understood and addressed in their global context; there are few global solutions! Most of the "actions" required to deal with these problems must be taken at the "local" and national levels—within a global context.

The capacity of governments to act depends in the final analysis on the will of people. The transition will only be feasible if it is undergirded by basic changes in the attitudes, values, and expectations of people. This will mean for industrialized societies a virtual cultural revolution. The dominant culture must be one that places highest values on quality rather than quantity, on conservation rather than waste, on cooperation above competition.

Introduction

Transition to Harmonic Globalism

by

Frank Feather

Holistic View

We are all living on a tiny mudball which is spiralling through space. The sooner we all accept this simple but soberingly powerful reality, the better will be the future of the mudball and its various inhabitants.

Multi-Dimensional Perspective

From such an extraterrestrial viewpoint, it is clear that the human future on planet Earth depends crucially on three simple things:

(1) our relationships with our "selves" and each other (the human perspective);

(2) our relationships with the world around us (the global perspective); and

(3) our relationships with the environment and its resources (the managerial perspective).

Interdependent Global Future

The program sessions of the First Global Conference on the Future (Toronto, 1980) were intentionally grouped under these three headings to provide the systemic opportunity for the international delegates to learn more about themselves, each other, and their varying perspectives. In designing the conference format, it was recognized that the viability of human coexistence in an increasingly interdependent world depends on the synergistic awareness of globality.

Opportunity for Action

It is claimed that the world of the early 1980s faces more crises

---

Frank Feather, Chairman and Director-General of the First Global Conference on the Future held in Toronto in 1980, is a career banking executive, editor of Business Tomorrow, *and creator of the universally applicable concept of "harmonic management."*

5

than ever before in its history. It is also fair to say, however, that never before has the human race been blessed with as many resources at its disposal. This paradox is brought out by the varying perspectives expressed in the papers selected for inclusion in this book.

I firmly believe that all global problems are intrinsically solvable—probably, as Maurice Strong points out, by local action as much as by global solution. What is required is a collective wisdom to marshall our resources for collective action. This means that minor disagreements and petty biases have to be put aside—there are more fundamental matters of moment to be addressed.

Human Oneness

If it is to be worthwhile, however, the global future must evolve harmonically. On the human scale this means we have to view each other as members of the same human family—we are one people. There is strength in diversity. We must be prepared to see that minor biological nuances and cultural differences cannot continue to be viewed as divisive. The vivid color of our global mosaic can and must merge together as a harmonious fabric of overlapping and reinforcing perspectives on the collective future of *all* our children. Indeed, the long-term stability of humanity can occur *only* through such globally-oriented determination and will. We must recognize the need for an embracing acceptance of the oneness of our race from which a genuine spirit of "future" will emerge.

Human Brain-Power

It is also important to recognize individual creative potential as highlighted by the relatively new knowledge about the human brain. Most people are still not generally aware of it but each of us has two brains—two symmetrical brains, identical in appearance but very different in the way they function. The significance of this phenomenon has far-reaching and unrecognized implications for the future.

Each brain has its own sphere of consciousness. The left-brain is the rational, objective, and materialistically oriented coordinator of our outwardly directed behavior and movement. It is the verbal, talking brain that perceives and communicates in logical, linear analytical thought processes.

In contrast, the right-brain perceives and expresses itself non-verbally and multi-dimensionally in imagery and feelings. This is the intuitive, creative and innovative side of our head which looks after our internal nervous system.

Left-Brain "Non-Think"

While both brains need each other to operate effectively, Western society has tended to reward left-brain processes of logical analysis. As a result, the creative, intuitive and innovative capacities of the right-brain have been suppressed in most of us. Consequently, Western society has continued down a linear path to self-destruction, sticking to old ways of doing things without regard to the surrounding global environment. Such behavior is totally inappropriate for the future.

Right-Brain "New-Think"

In today's environment, the only constant is change itself and there is no left-brain precedent upon which to base many wide-ranging decisions faced daily by policy-makers and managers. You cannot cope with the new world using values and leadership styles of the industrial era. The Post-Industrial Age will be characterized by decision-makers who set policy based more on intuition and creative insights generated by a more active right-brain.

Post-Industrial Transition to Harmonic Globalism

The global transition from Industrialism to Post-Industrialism is analagous to the emergence of the humanistic right-brain characteristics outlined earlier:

Transition to Harmonic Globalism

	Industrialism (Left-Brain)	Post-Industrialism (Right-Brain)
Human Perspectives	Achievement	Self-Actualization
	Self-Control	Self-Expression
	Responsive	Anticipative
Global Perspectives	Independence	Interdependence
	Separate Goals	Linked Objectives
	Separation	Coordination
Managerial Perspectives	Mechanistic	Organic
	Specific	Comprehensive
	Short-Term	Long-Term

The challenge of the 1980s is to re-orient individuals and their social organizations so that they are capable of continuously and consciously undergoing change and renewal within the global environment of which they are a part. There is no doubt we are capable of gaining a keener awareness of our place together in the global domain. There is also no reason why we cannot operate collectively and in sympathy and harmony with the planet on which we so recently evolved.

The Emergent Global Mind

The potential of our collective brains is probably infinite. In fact, many of us already sense the emergence of a "thinking" and "feeling" futuristic network which seems to be pulsating its way into more and more individual psyches around the globe.

Despite all the apparent problems in the world, the only *real* issue is whether we can all strive for one aim: "To think globally while acting locally." If more of us can learn to "think with one mind," then the transition to "harmonic globalism" is assured. Indeed, it is *essential* if we are to arrive at 1990 in better shape than we now find ourselves in 1980. The Future awaits us—in our collective imaginations.

7

The Trauma
of Change

The Third Wave

by
Alvin Toffler

A new civilization is emerging in our lives, and blind men everywhere are trying to suppress it. This new civilization brings with it new family styles; changed ways of working, loving, and living; a new economy; new political conflicts; and beyond all this an altered consciousness as well. Pieces of this new civilization exist today. Millions are already attuning their lives to the rhythms of tomorrow. Others, terrified of the future, are engaged in a desperate, futile flight into the past and are trying to restore the dying world that gave them birth.

The dawn of this new civilization is the single most explosive fact of our lifetimes.

It is the central event—the key to understanding the years immediately ahead. It is an event as profound as that First Wave of change unleashed ten thousand years ago by the invention of agriculture, or the earthshaking Second Wave of change touched off by the industrial revolution. We are the children of the next transformation, the Third Wave.

We grope for words to describe the full power and reach of this extraordinary change. Some speak of a looming Space Age, Information Age, Electronic Era, or Global Village. Zbigniew Brzezinski has told us we face a "technetronic age." Sociologist Daniel Bell describes the coming of a "post-industrial society." Soviet futurists speak of the S.T.R.—the "scientific-technological revolution." I myself have written extensively about the arrival of a "super-industrial society." Yet none of these terms, including my own, is adequate.

Some of these phrases, by focusing on a single factor, narrow rather than expand our understanding. Others are static, implying that a new society can come into our lives smoothly, without conflict or stress. None of these terms even begins to convey the full force, scope, and dynamism of the changes rushing toward us or of the pressures and conflicts they trigger.

Humanity faces a quantum leap forward. It faces the deepest social upheaval and creative restructuring of all time. Without clearly recognizing it, we are engaged in building a remarkable new civilization from the ground up. This is the meaning of the Third Wave.

Alvin Toffler, widely known for his book Future Shock, *is the author of a new best-seller* The Third Wave, *from which this paper is excerpted.* © *1980 by Alvin Toffler.*

Until now the human race has undergone two great waves of change, each one largely obliterating earlier cultures or civilizations and replacing them with ways of life inconceivable to those who came before. The First Wave of change—the agricultural revolution—took thousands of years to play itself out. The Second Wave—the rise of industrial civilization—took a mere three hundred years. Today history is even more accelerative, and it is likely that the Third Wave will sweep across history and complete itself in a few decades. We who happen to share the planet at this explosive moment will therefore feel the full impact of the Third Wave in our own lifetimes.

Tearing our families apart, rocking our economy, paralyzing our political systems, shattering our values, the Third Wave affects everyone. It challenges all the old power relationships, the privileges and prerogatives of the endangered elites of today, and provides the backdrop against which the key power struggles of tomorrow will be fought.

Much in this emerging civilization contradicts the old traditional industrial civilization. It is, at one and the same time, highly technological and anti-industrial.

The Third Wave brings with it a genuinely new way of life based on diversified, renewable energy sources; on methods of production that make most factory assembly lines obsolete; on new, non-nuclear families; on a novel institution that might be called the "electronic cottage"; and on radically changed schools and corporations of the future. The emergent civilization writes a new code of behavior for us and carries us beyond standardization, synchronization, and centralization, beyond the concentration of energy, money, and power.

This new civilization, as it challenges the old, will topple bureaucracies, reduce the role of the nation-state, and give rise to semiautonomous economies in a postimperialist world. It requires governments that are simpler, more effective, yet more democratic than any we know today. It is a civilization with its own distinctive world outlook, its own ways of dealing with time, space, logic, and causality.

Above all, as we shall see, Third Wave civilization begins to heal the historic breach between producer and consumer, giving rise to the "prosumer" economics of tomorrow. For this reason, among many, it could—with some intelligent help from us—turn out to be the first truly humane civilization in recorded history.

The Revolutionary Premise

Two apparently contrasting images of the future grip the popular imagination today. Most people—to the extent that they bother to think about the future at all—assume the world they know will last indefinitely. They find it difficult to imagine a truly different way of life for themselves, let alone a totally new civilization. Of course they recognize that things are changing. But they assume today's changes will somehow pass them by and that nothing will shake the familiar economic framework and political structure. They confidently expect the future to continue the present.

This straight-line thinking comes in various packages. At one level it appears as an unexamined assumption lying behind the decisions of businessmen, teachers, parents, and politicians. At a more sophisticated level it comes dressed up in statistics, computerized data, and forecasters' jargon. Either way it adds up to a vision of a future world that is essentially "more of the same"—Second Wave industrialism writ even larger and spread over more of this planet.

Recent events have severely shaken this confident image of the future. As crisis after crisis has crackled across the headlines, as Iran erupted, as Mao was de-deified, as oil prices skyrocketed and inflation ran wild, as terrorism spread and governments seemed helpless to stop it, a bleaker vision has become increasingly popular. Thus, large numbers of people—fed on a steady diet of bad news, disaster movies, apocalyptic Bible stories, and nightmare scenarios issued by prestigious think tanks—have apparently concluded that today's society cannot be projected into the future because there is no future. For them, Armageddon is only minutes away. The earth is racing toward its final cataclysmic shudder.

On the surface these two visions of the future seem very different. Yet both produce similar psychological and political effects. For both lead to the paralysis of imagination and will.

If tomorrow's society is simply an enlarged, Cinerama version of the present, there is little we *need* do to prepare for it. If, on the other hand, society is inevitably destined to self-destruct within our lifetime, there is nothing we *can* do about it. In short, both these ways of looking at the future generate privatism and passivity. Both freeze us into inaction.

Yet, in trying to understand what is happening to us, we are not limited to this simpleminded choice between Armageddon and More-of-the-Same. There are many more clarifying and constructive ways to think about tomorrow—ways that prepare us for the future and, more important, help us to change the present.

My book *The Third Wave* is based on what I call the "revolutionary premise." It assumes that, even though the decades immediately ahead are likely to be filled with upheavals, turbulence, perhaps even widespread violence, we will not totally destroy ourselves. It assumes that the jolting changes we are now experiencing are not chaotic or random but that, in fact, they form a sharp, clearly discernible pattern. It assumes, moreover, that these changes are cumulative—that they add up to a giant transformation in the way we live, work, play, and think and that a sane and desirable future is possible. In short, *The Third Wave* begins with the premise that what is happening now is nothing less than a global revolution, a quantum jump in history.

Put differently, *The Third Wave* flows from the assumption that we are the final generation of an old civilization and the first generation of a new one, and that much of our personal confusion, anguish, and disorientation can be traced directly to the conflict within us, and within our political institutions, between the dying Second Wave civilization and the emergent Third Wave civilization that is thundering in to take its place.

The Greatest Evolutionary Jump in History

by

John Platt

I have a somewhat unusual view of the human situation today. I think we are passing through an evolutionary leap of unprecedented magnitude. This can be seen in the accompanying table, A Classification of Major Evolutionary Jumps, which compares our great technological developments since World War II with the largest evolutionary jumps of similar kinds in previous epochs. Many of our jumps in the last 40 years, as shown in the right-hand column, would appear to be comparable to the biggest jumps in the whole 4-billion-year history of life on earth, if judged by their probable long-run consequences, say for the next thousand years or million years or billion years.

So today, nuclear missiles are the most overwhelming weapons ever known. Our new contraceptives are having global effects, but are now overshadowed by recombinant-DNA technology which might be able to create millions of new species. In the long run, solar-electric power may be as important as photosynthesis, which has been our main energy source for 2 billion years. Television is watched for hours every day by half the human race, and is changing the family, the school, commerce, politics, and the development of our brains. This electronic revolution may be a more dramatic extension of our nervous system and vision than the first development of image-forming eyes, 600 million years ago. Electronic data-processing has changed all the operations of science, business, and government, and will knit together every future society. And the possibility of working and living in space is a step whose beginnings today are hardly more than the coming ashore of the lungfish. The simultaneous convergence of all these developments fitting together into a great evolutionary jump, in this short period, is absolutely staggering.

In the world of nature, our activities are also producing a unique evolutionary epoch, with new radioactive wastes, with the peaking and exhaustion of fossil fuels, with possible global changes of climate in the next few decades, and the probable extinction of hundreds of thousands

John Platt is a humanistic scientist now living in Cambridge, Massachusetts. He is the author of The Step to Man, Perception and Change, *and other books.*

A Classification of Major Evolutionary Jumps

Eras	Early life	Multi-cellular	Early human	Post-glacial	Modern	Present transformation
Time (years before present)	4000 M—	1000 M—	3 M—	10,000—	600—	40—
Functional areas						
Genetic mixing and control	SEX-CROSSING	Migration		DOMESTICATION AND BREEDING	DISEASE-CONTROL, CONTRACEPTION	MOLECULAR BIOLOGY, RE-COMBINANT DNA
Energy conversion	PHOTO-SYNTHESIS	PLANT-EATING	FIRE	AGRICULTURE wind, hydro	COAL-STEAM, ELECTRICITY	NUCLEAR FISSION, (FUSION), SOLAR ELECTRIC (SPACE POWER)
Encapsulation and habitats	CELLS ocean niches	Shell, skin, bark LAND	Clothes all climates	CITIES all continents	West "frontier"	SPACE CAPSULES (SETTLEMENTS) Arctic, ocean
Methods of travel	Drift	Fins, feet, wings	Boats	Horses, WHEELS, SHIPS	RAILROAD, AUTO, AIRPLANE	Jet, ROCKET
Tools and weapons	Chemical	Teeth, claws	TOOLS, WEAPONS	METAL	MACHINES, GUNS, EXPLOSIVES	AUTOMATION, ROCKETS, NUCLEAR WEAPONS
Detection and signaling	Chemical	HEARING, VISION, echo-location	SPEECH	WRITING	PRINTING telephone, radio	ELECTROMAGNETIC SPECTRUM—RADAR, Laser, TELEVISION
Problem-solving and storage	DNA CHAINS	NERVOUS SYSTEM AND BRAINS	Oral memory, predic-tion	MATH, SCIENCE, LOGIC	SCIENCE-TECHNOLOGY	ELECTRONIC DATA-PROCESSING FEED-BACK CONTROL
Mechanisms of change	Accident and SELECTION	Foresight, REINFORCE-MENT	THOUGHT	INVENTION	RESEARCH AND DEVELOPMENT	SYSTEMS-ANALYSIS AND DESIGN PROJECTS (Manhattan, Apollo)

of species because of the destruction of their habitats—an event that has had no parallel since the last great extinction 65 million years ago.

For the human race and for life on earth, this all adds up to a "system-break," as Boulding has called it. These order-of-magnitude accelerations in recent epochs and recent decades are like the accelerating changes in the moments just before the fracture of a metal—or the birth of a baby. On a graph, if the time-periods of Table 1 are spread out on a linear scale, the unique evolutionary peak in the last 40 years is like a knife-edge on a knife-edge.

With this simultaneous eruption of great new forces and powers, it is not clear that we can modify or even foresee the future very successfully, even for a 10- to 20-year period. As with the birth of a baby, or the coming ashore of the land animals, there is a combination of inevitability and surprise. As late as 1937, Lord Rutherford, the discoverer of the nucleus of the atom, said that the idea of getting out atomic energy was "moonshine"—when it was only 5 years away; and in the 1960s, hardly a single biologist anticipated the recombinant-DNA developments of 1973. But it is obviously urgent and essential to try to see how much is really inevitable or really surprising and how much is still subject to some human social design and control.

It is especially important, at this moment of global birth, not to waste our energies in resisting or in lamenting or in copying the past. The baby's history in the womb is of very little use to it in its new situation. What the new baby must suddenly do is to learn how to breathe and cry and swallow, and we must likewise find out quickly and successfully how to manage our great new powers in the world ahead, if we are to survive. The difference is that the baby, as the descendant of millions of successful babies, has all the needed information already encoded in its genes. But the human race, in this first attempt to build a global society, with totally new tools, has no such fail-safe mechanism or inherited knowledge of how to do it. It becomes crucial to have adequate look-out and design systems, with forecasting and computer systems-modeling and futures courses and organizations. We will have to use all our commitment and all our skills at anticipatory problem-solving, so as to do it right the first time, or the whole human experiment may come to an end, in any of a dozen ways.

The social design and construction problem is central. As with the Federalists two hundred years ago, with their first social-feedback ideas or "checks and balances," we must think harder than we have ever thought before about how to design and create the components of a self-stabilizing world society. We must generate anticipatory global institutions with adequate powers, and yet find ways of preserving democratic methods of mutual problem-solving and collective self-management in a multicultural world, if our new baby planet is not to tear itself apart.

Evidently we need some major advances in the general principles of anticipatory cybernetic democratic design. Such principles in fact might even be derivable from some of the powerful new developments in social science in the last 40 years, such as systems theory, decision theory, game theory, reinforcement theory, global modeling, the theory of justice, or other social inventions. We might find more subtle and effective democratic feedback concepts and mechanisms that would make it much easier to correct the defects in existing institutions or to devise new self-correcting institutions of novel kinds.

The world of the year 2000 will be far more different from the world of 1980 than the world of 1800 was from 1780, or the world of 1930 was from 1910. And the future beyond that will be almost unimaginably different from the twentieth century.

Homo Obsoletus?

by

Isaac Asimov

I am constantly being asked to peer into the future in this direction or that, and frequently I am asked to consider the future of computers.

I am glad to do this and am quite capable of talking very rapidly on the subject, but sooner or later (usually sooner) I am interrupted in my course of glowing optimism and am asked, "But do you think that human beings may be replaced by the computer? That human beings may become obsolete?"

Do I? Let's consider the matter in orderly progression.

1) *Ought the question to be considered at all or is it just a very human fear and distrust of change, particularly technological change?*

One can imagine the anger, for instance, of early builders when the equivalent of the yardstick came into use.

One can almost hear them mutter, "Of what value then is the keen eye and the cool judgment of the experienced carpenter, if any fool can tell whether a piece of timber will stretch across a doorway by measuring it with that inanimate marked stick? Brains will decay and the human being will become extinct, replaced by wood."

And surely the bards of old must have been horrified at the invention of writing, of a code of markings that eliminated the need for memory. A child of ten, having learned to read, could then recite the "Iliad," though he had never seen it before, simply by following the markings. How the mind would degenerate!

A Spartan monarch on seeing a demonstration of a catapult hurling its heavy rock, cried out, "Oh, Heracles, the valor of man is at an end."

He equated martial valor with hand-to-hand thumping, you see, but if so, he was too late by some thousands of years, for such a cry must have rung out with the invention of the bow-and-arrow.

These fears were wrong every time.

The use of inanimate aids to judgment and memory did not destroy judgment and memory. We use them all the better now for not wasting them in ways that a few marks on a piece of wood or on a piece of paper make unnecessary.

Isaac Asimov is the author of more than 215 books, many of which deal with the future. He lives in New York City.

16

To be sure, it is not easy to find someone nowadays with a memory so trained that he can reel off long epic poems—but it wasn't so easy in ancient times, either, or a good bard would not have been as valued as he was.

And even if our unaided talents had degenerated a little, is the gain not worth the loss? Could the Taj Mahal or the Golden Gate Bridge have been built by eye? How many people would know the plays of Shakespeare or the novels of Tolstoy if we had to depend on finding someone who knew them by heart and was willing to recite them to us?

Came the Industrial Revolution, and its steam-engines, and internal-combustion engines, and explosives, to take the weight of hard labor from the backs of human beings. Steam and gasoline vapor and electric current drag loads no horse could budge. Rocks are shattered in a moment that an array of slaves would take a week to split. Tricks with light and magnetism and subatomic particles are performed that no Scheherezade could imagine.

Did human muscles grow flaccid as a result? Yes, they might, except that they don't have to.

Keeping one's body in shape is the great game of today and people go through the motions of jogging and tennis and push-ups to make up voluntarily for what they no longer need do under the hard grip of enslaved compulsion.

And now we have computers. We even have very cheap, very small, very clever ones; computers that can do all the little tasks about our house and office that till now we had managed to do in our head, or with pen and paper—and which we so often got wrong.

We no longer need our ability to multiply eight and seven in our head and get fifty-six (or is it fifty-four?) and we can discard our talent for making lists and forgetting the crucial item.

Will our brains therefore decay (for the thousandth time in the history of technological advance) and will we become obsolete?

Or will we once again make a virtue of a loss, and use computers as adversaries in games, for instance, that will hone our minds to new acuteness? Will computers do our work while letting us sleep into permanent stupor, or will they free us of disgraceful tasks beneath the level of human ability and allow us to tackle truly creative tasks—so that we may build Taj Mahals in place of mud huts?

It is, in fact, up to us whether to use our tools as cushions or spurs.

But wait, are computers tools? Just tools?

When I am asked whether computers will make human beings obsolete, the questioner does not have in mind a computer that serves simply as a tool, but one that serves as a surrogate-human.

After all, because a computer is a lump of inanimate matter notable only for the speed with which it performs simple arithmetical operations in endless and varied repetition, that does not mean it will stay so forever. At the rate at which computers are advancing and improving, might we not expect that given enough time, computers will become capable of duplicating any feat of the human brain—any feat at all?

And, eventually, if computers can write books, devise poems, compose symphonies, perform research, create new ideas—will they not be as intelligent as human beings, or even more intelligent? And might they not then replace human beings, kill us off as unnecessary excrescences, and take over as the new masters of Earth?

If this is the case, we would have to decide that the human fear of the computer is an entirely new terror and a justified one; and not merely a repetition of a thousand fears of the past. The computer, it could be, differs from earlier technological advances in kind and not in degree only.

So we must consider the possible obsolescence of humanity and put to ourselves a second question—

2) *Why not?*

The history of the evolution of life is the history of the slow alteration of species, or the bodily replacement of one species by quite another, whenever it happens that the change, or replacement, results in a better fit within a particular environmental niche.

In general, we human beings, as spectators of this past drama, tend to cheer on the victors. We think it only right that the vertebrates possessing, as they do, an efficient internal skeleton, should now dominate the world of life, even though they are but the most recently developed of the grand divisions of the animal kingdom.

The conquest of the land is one of the great feats of the ages and we approve as, first, amphibians, then reptiles, and finally the mammals dominate the continents.

It is exciting to see brain-power come into its own. The mammals are brainier than the reptiles they replaced; the placental mammals are brainier than the marsupials; the primates are the brainiest of all (if we ignore the cetaceans, who spoiled everything for themselves by returning to the sea and losing their chance at manipulative appendages).

Even in the last twenty million years we have seen the primates sort themselves out, the hominids finally appear on the scene, and, in climax, *Homo sapiens* come along to establish dominion over the world and to produce a technological civilization through the sheer force of a giant brain.

Of course, part of the fascination of the drama is that we know and approve the ending. We view all the replacements as steps on the road to ourselves—and we are smugly satisfied that we ourselves are the crown and climax of the long trudge up the three-billion-year road.

Our pleasure in ourselves-as-climax makes any notion of a continuation of this play-that-is-over seem in the highest degree unnatural and reprehensible.

Yet the play is not over. It is only the accident of the briefness of our lives in relation to the speed of evolutionary change that makes the pattern of life seem static now; and it is the folly of self-love that leaves us satisfied with that. Actually, evolution continues and there is nothing unnatural in the thought that *Homo sapiens* will be replaced by a modification of itself slowly formed over the coming ages—or even by an entirely different species that better fits the environmental niche we now occupy (or the environmental niche into which our present one will change).

Of course, the brain-power of *Homo sapiens* and the accumulated machine-power of our technology is such that the simple evolutionary change of the past may no longer be in the cards. Human beings are now developing the capacity to engage in genetic engineering so that they may be able to guide their own evolution at a far greater speed than the blind force of hit-and-miss mutation and natural selection could manage in the past.

Human beings are also developing the capacity to create an artificial intelligence comparable to their own.

In either case, it may be that the grand design of evolution includes the slow change from species to species through random factors until, finally, after an extended period, a species is formed that is sufficiently intelligent to direct its own evolution and to create new kinds of intelligence on a non-organic basis.

In that case, the replacement of humanity by either a hyper-humanity or by computers is a natural phenomenon to which we can object only for reasons that, like self-love, are frivolous and irrelevant.

So far, however, I have only been arguing that the replacement of humanity is not necessarily an evil. Can we go farther and say that it is a positive good?

Perhaps.

Look about you and consider what human beings have done and are doing to the world. Consider the manner in which they have brought extinction to other life-forms; unbalanced the ecological relationships of those species that still remain; destroyed the soil; polluted the water and the air; introduced poisons and dangers the planet has never yet seen. Consider further that all these changes for the worse have been going on at an accelerating pace and are still accelerating now.

Viewed in that manner, the succession of a computer-intelligence that is superior to the human variety and that is (perhaps) not associated with the emotions and with the judgmental-incapacity of the latter is something that could be much to be desired. The great fear might be that the computer will not be developed to the point of succession before *Homo sapiens* succeeds in destroying itself and much of the planet as well.

It is with that thought in mind that sometimes, when I am asked if the computer will ever replace the human being, that I answer, "I hope so."

But wait, are we sure that we will be replaced by a superior intelligence, if and when one exists? Let us go on to our third question—

3) *What is a superior intelligence?*

It is entirely too simple to compare qualities as though we were measuring lengths with a ruler. Because we are used to one-dimensional comparisons and understand perfectly what we mean when we say that the distance from New York to San Francisco is greater than the distance from Chicago to San Francisco, we get into the habit of assuming that all things may be so unsubtly compared.

For instance, a zebra can reach a distant point sooner than a bee can, so that we are justified, we think, in saying that a zebra is faster than a bee. And yet a bee is far smaller than a zebra, and it flies through the air, which the zebra does not. Both differences are important in qualifying that "faster."

A bee can fly out of a ditch which holds the zebra helpless; it can fly through the bars of a cage which holds the zebra prisoner. Which is faster now?

If A surpasses B in one quality, B may surpass A in another quality. And, as conditions change, one quality or the other may assume the greater importance.

A human being in an airplane flies more quickly than a bird, but he or she cannot fly as slowly as a bird, and slowness may be very desirable for survival at times.

A human being in a helicopter can fly as slowly as a bird but he or she cannot fly as noiselessly as a bird, and silence may be very desirable for survival at times.

In short, survival requires a complex of characteristics, and no species is replaced by another because of a difference in one characteristic only. And that goes for a simplistic superiority in intelligence, too.

We see this in human affairs often enough. In the stress of an emergency, it is not necessarily the person with the highest IQ who wins out; it could be the one with the greatest resolution; the greatest strength; the greatest capacity for endurance; the greatest wealth; the greatest friendships in high places. Intelligence is important, yes; but it is not all-important.

For that matter, intelligence is not a simply-defined quality; it comes in all varieties. The intensely-trained and super-scholarly professor who is as a child in all matters not pertaining to his specialty is a stereotypical figure of modern folk-lore. Nor would we be in the least surprised at the spectacle of a shrewd businessman who is intelligent enough to guide a billion-dollar organization with a sure touch, and yet who is incapable of learning to speak grammatically.

How then do we compare human intelligence and computer intelligence and what do we mean by "superior" intelligence?

Already, if we wish to define intelligence as the capacity to perform arithmetical operations speedily, the computer is millions of times as intelligent as a human being—and yet we are all confident that the computer is not intelligent at all.

As computers are designed with greater and greater capacities—as they are designed to play chess, to translate languages, to compose music, to imitate the responses of a psychiatrist—it will become more and more difficult, however, to maintain that it is not intelligent.

Remember, though, that the development of intelligence in human beings and in computers took different paths and was driven along by different mechanisms.

The human brain evolved by hit-and-miss, by random mutations, making use of subtle chemical changes, and by a forward drive powered by natural selection and the need to survive in a particular world of given qualities and dangers.

The computer brain evolved by deliberate design as the result of careful human thought, making use of subtle electrical changes, and by a forward drive powered by technological advance and the need to serve particular human requirements.

It would be very odd if, after taking such divergent roads, brains and computers would ever end in such similarity to one another that one of them could be said to be "superior" in intelligence to the other.

It is much more likely that even when the two are "equally" intelligent, the properties of intelligence would be so different in each that no simple comparison could be made. There would always be some activities to which computers would be better adapted and others to which the human brain would be better adapted; and this would be particularly true if genetic engineering makes it possible for human beings to improve the brain as well as the computer.

Indeed, it would be undesirable, perhaps, to try to develop either a computer or a brain to possess "all-round" capacities. The gain in generality would surely involve an inevitable loss in specialized abilities, so that keeping the two forms of intelligence different would remain desirable.

Consequently, the question of replacement is quite likely never to arise. What we would see, instead, would be a matter of complementation. It could be that human-and-computer might form a symbiotic intelligence that would be far greater than either could develop alone; a symbiotic intelligence that would open new horizons and make it possible to achieve new heights.

In fact, it could be the doorway that leads humanity from its isolated infancy to its in-combination adulthood.

The Exhaustion of Liberalism

by

Ruben Nelson

Where there is no vision, the people perish.

–Proverbs

Will the eighties be more or less turbulent, surprising and stressful than the seventies?

When your first child was born, did you expect that your children would have a better life than your own?

Over the last couple of years, as a planning consultant and speaker, I have been putting these questions to scores of audiences in Canada. The answers are disquieting. They give a very different sense of what is on the minds of Canadians than the one inferred by the speeches and ads of our recent election campaign, or by the spate of turn-of-the-year prophecies for the eighties.

About nine out of ten of us, I would say, expect the eighties to be *significantly* more stressful than the seventies. On a scale of 0 to 10, on which 0 indicates tranquility; 5, no change from the seventies; and 10 that all hell will break loose, the average response has been between 7 and 8.5

The answer to the second question swings by age. Fully 85% of those who had children before about 1960 shared the expectation when their first child was born that life would be better for their children. For younger parents the figures are reversed. Only 15% of them expect the future to be better for their children.

The message is clear. Officially we appear content and we act as if we know what we are doing, but a closer look indicates that increasing numbers of us are less and less sure that the directions in which Canada is moving will guarantee the future which we seek for ourselves and for our children.

This explains why we vote without conviction, why all political parties feel the same, and why our leaders are impotent. They do not move us because they distract us from the reality of our experience and

---

Ruben F.W. Nelson is President of Square One Management Ltd., Ottawa, Canada, a future-oriented consulting firm specializing in social futures and social policy. He is immediate past president of the Canadian Association for Futures Studies.

expectations. They deal with us as if life can be lived from the outside, and as if the good life can be captured by strategies and programs and delivered by governments, all without reference to the reality of lived experience.

This is seen in the way our leaders encourage us to think about the energy question. The emphasis from all of them is on what "they" would do to keep prices down, to increase supply and keep our society going. Yet deep within us, we sense that the energy issue is not a matter of price or even supply. We sense we need to deal with energy on the demand side; that the key to the energy crises lies in a change of life style. Yet no political leader is willing to talk to us about the way we live and its relationship to energy.

The concerns of the politicians in the campaign were much the same as those of the decade-end prophets. Most experts and futurists focus on technology, economic statistics, and the shape of the automobile in 2008. They assume that if the Gross National Product and technological invention go well, then so will the nation. They ignore what it will be like to *live* through the future.

Consider all those articles which reviewed the seventies and forecast the eighties—in *Macleans, Fortune, The Globe and Mail* and *Canadian Business.* The focus and tone were the same. Technology and the economy were in the forefront. All assumed that the most critical factors shaping our futures are external.

Life As We Will Live It

The point is, when we as persons look back on our lives or forward to the future, we focus on life as lived and experienced. We do not focus on new innovations in technology, the average increase in the Consumer Price Index, or the Gross National Product. Rather, what is important to us is the quality and rhythms of our relations with those we know and love, including ourselves. We sense that if these things are secure, we can handle anything.

Accordingly, the eighties will not only surprise us, they will stun us.

In the eighties, we will discover the importance of lived experience and re-discover that living well is not a function of "command over goods and services" as our economists tell us, but a function of living well—living life from the inside out with integrity.

We will recognize that all of the talk of change—economic, technological and organizational—has been premised on the unconscious assumption that the fundamental habits of head, heart, and hand which we have been refining for the last 500 years in Western Europe and North America are reliable guides to the future, and therefore can still safely be assumed and acted upon. We will recognize what many of us already suspect—namely, that this is a naive assumption.

We will recognize that the change we are experiencing and are caught in is far more profound than we previously thought, or that our leaders have led us to believe.

Officially, we deny all this. Officially we are still "progressive liberals."

Living well means having more, and, like Avis, trying harder. In the recent election campaign there was no hint from any major party that we face substantial disorientation and distress. The worst that we were offered was pain today for jam tomorrow, and even this was ridiculed by two of three major parties.

Privately, however, we have begun to change. Who among us expects an early return to steady 5% growth, as successive finance ministers promised us through the seventies? Who believes that inflation will be "wrestled to the ground?" Who believes a "no" vote in the Quebec referendum, or even the election of Claude Ryan, will mark "the death of separatism"? Who still believes that there will, or should be, a real increase in purchasing power every year, as a matter of right?

The real challenge of the eighties is not to suppress these discoveries from ourselves. We gain nothing by becoming so repressive that we are fearful of our own experience and that of our neighbor. Humpty Dumpty has already fallen and cannot be put back together, regardless of how oppressive or effective the authority. In short, the eighties will see the death of liberalism.

I am not suggesting that most Canadians—or even most futurists—recognize my vision of the eighties as plausible and likely. Quite the reverse. Presently in Canada there is little sustained public discussion about the need for or the nature of the re-formulations which would enhance our future. The sense that the world is changing around us in ways which are too profound for us to easily understand is dim among us and totally unacceptable as an operating premise in our institutions, be they government departments, hospitals, churches or even our universities. Rather, virtually all our institutions operate on the premise that if only we had a few more man-years, a little more money, a bit more equipment, a few more students, then all would be well. True, the progressives among us recognize that there is need for more and better executive education and staff training, but even they do not suspect that something is fundamentally out of whack, with the possible exception of the fact that we appear to be running out of money.

As a society, we presume that if we have a problem it can be dealt with by more information, by more data, by new techniques, by more schooling, by more education and training. That this is so can be seen in every major institution in Canada, from the types of people we hire, in the forms by which we are organized, in the task forces we appoint, in the experts we consult. But this very activity presumes that the foundations of our lives are secure, and that we are troubled because we have not extended our intelligence consistently enough, with rigor. It is virtually beyond us to consider that the roots of our trouble are very deep within us, that our deepest understandings are inherently deluding, distorting and misshaping. It is beyond us to think that as the old joke goes, if we really do seek a sane society, given the way that we insist on travelling, we can't get there from here. We, like Aristotle, find it beyond our comprehension to consider the clue offered to us by Old Testament prophets—namely, that the deepest source

24

of stress in human life arises from the distortion of our preconscious understanding, from the corruption of our consciousness and our imagination.

Living Our Lives "From the Inside Out"

My point is simple: The messages conveyed by our dominant institutions—the media, our political and business leaders, our universities, and our experts—distract us from understanding the reality and importance of living our lives from the inside out. Even most career planning is becoming the crafty manipulation of one's self and one's life, as if it were an external object, rather than as if one's life is something to be lived. Career success and living well have become disjointed. Even worse, for many, the latter has been collapsed into the former. To test this assertion, consider how seldom the efforts of personnel officers and career counsellors are directed to your genuine psychological independence from the organization, including the capacity to say no to those in authority. As with the Mounties, nobody says no. It could cost you your job. Few notice that we have confused loyalty with the impotence that comes from dependence.

Given our fixation on things that are external and measurable, we are ill-equipped to understand, let alone deal with, the future. This is so because the eighties will be a time of such fundamental shifts of perception that no government will be able to ignore or resist, much less control, their momentum.

One indication that the transformation has already begun may be seen in the way Canadians now complete the sentence: "We live _____ the earth."

One is tempted to fill in the blank with *on*. Twenty years ago this would have been the only answer. Now increasing numbers say *in*, or *with*, or *for*. The change of preposition is revolutionary. It marks the end of liberalism and the industrial age. It marks the end of our sense that we are independent of both the earth and one another. It marks the recognition that, rather than being separate and self-contained entities, with no essential relationship to one another (witness the classic phrase of British empiricism—"a thing is what it is and is no other"), we are inherently relational creatures whose character is a function of the relationships we enter and which enter us.

Today we still plead with each other to "have relationships," as if the are optional. Tomorrow, we will plead with each other to recognize the relationships we have, whether we see them or not.

Once we discover the reality and centrality of relationships as an empirical rather than a moral matter, a liberal and therefore industrial view of life can no longer be sustained.

The shift is even reflected in today's Sunday School hymns. Children used to be taught that they were bade to shine, "you in your small corner and I in mine." The implication is clear: The Holy Spirit works like Adam Smith's guiding hand, bringing wholeness to our individual efforts. Now children sing that they are "drops of water in a mighty ocean," and that they are "sons and daughters of one life."

Our Present Transformation

The transformation we are experiencing can be seen in our present dissatisfaction with government and our willingness to re-evaluate its role in our lives, though none of the systems analysts or policy experts we hired by the truckload in the seventies predicted it. The re-evaluation is driven not by rational argument, but by a gut feeling that our governments are misusing and betraying us. Nothing short of insisting that they stop will do. That liberal intellectuals disdain this passion and anxiety is no reason to disown it. The tragedy is not the so-called neo-conservative feeling, but how little our intellectual opinion leaders help us to understand the changes occurring within us.

The key to understanding the future is to understand that fundamental shifts in orientation change what makes sense to us and what does not. This is the essence of the revolution. Not only our values but our sense of reality is changing. Arguments based on the old realities are not so much invalid as uninteresting. This is true of women's changed perception of their nature, role, and status, of francophone Québecois determination never again to be led or coerced into seeing themselves as a people who need to apologize for their life together, or the assertion by blacks of their rooted character and identity, and of the revolution in Iran.

Iran is pertinent. Our ideas about that society were so superficial that *Time* magazine was assuring us in November of 1978 that the Shah's throne was secure. Three months later he was gone. Leaders and newswriters encouraged us to think of events in Iran as "surprising," "unpredictable," "unreal." Last May, the Planning Executives Institute—the largest organization of corporate planners in North America—was assured at its annual meeting in Montreal that events in Iran were not only surprising, but unpredictable. The implication was clear: no planner could be held accountable for the losses suffered by their firms.

The essential shape of the Iranian revolution, however, was both predictable and in fact predicted. But those who understand what Western influences were doing to Iranian society—our historians of religion—are not persons with whom corporate planners or other experts normally converse.

In Canada in the eighties, I see a significant number of Canadians coming to insist that *their* new sense of the importance of their own experience and of the reality of their relationships to one another, to society, and to the earth be reflected in the way society works. The reworking of all our social forms in these terms is the basic task of the next several generations.

But in the near term, the eighties will have more to do with the exhaustion of the 18th and 19th century notions by which we have lived than with the clear articulation of new notions to replace them. It will be a time of withdrawing belief from established order, rather than of creating new order. We will move into the wilderness—giving up what we have known because it is too painful to stay—without much sense of the shape of the promised land. The eighties will be messy, tumultuous and, for some, dangerous. Our psychological unpreparedness for all this is the main source of the danger. We will be tempted to deny change. We will continue to think that reform does not mean re-forming.

Denial can be seen in the still-common resistance of males to the women's movements. It can be seen in the response to Québec over the last 20 years: to this day, Pierre Elliott Trudeau encourages us to understand the Parti Québécois and René Lévesque as embodiments of evil, a threat, rather than as an understandable expression of a people regaining their self-confidence. He encourages us to believe that calling up the troops can deny this new reality.

I think, in the long run, we will come to the conclusion that our leaders in the sixties and seventies betrayed us by focussing our attention on appeasing Québec—what does Québec want? We in the English-speaking community were not encouraged to understand and wrestle with the changes which were occurring within us, so that we would have a similar experience of transformation and renewal, with its tensions, threats and joy.

True, there is a new realism in the land, a new sobriety. We sense that reality is more resistant to our good will than we had believed. The easy expectations of the early Trudeau years—the notion that all problems could be handled by the application of money, effort, rationality and systems—are now sensed to be unwarranted and naive.

Yet many people have the feeling that not only is the roof falling in—rising energy, food and housing costs—but also the bottom is falling out, with no ground of commitment from which to develop new directions.

No Vision to Guide Us

The thought is occurring among more and more of us that our problem is not merely that we lack able administration, but that we have no common purpose, no common directions, no vision to guide us as we venture into the wilderness. Nothing to which we can commit ourselves, nothing that we can embrace which will make enough sense of our lives to keep us going.

This was vividly caught by Thomas Berry when he said:

It's all a question of story. We are in trouble now because we do not have a good story. We are in between stories. The Old Story—the account of how the world came to be and how we fit into it—is not functioning properly, and we have not learned the New Story. The Old Story sustained us for a long period of time. It shaped our emotional attitudes, provided us with life purpose, energized action, consecrated suffering, integrated knowledge, and guided education. We awoke in the morning and knew where we were. We could answer the questions of our children. We could identify crime, punish criminals. Everything was taken care of because the story was there. It did not make men good. It did not take away the pains and stupidities of life, or make for unfailing warmth in human association, but it did provide a context in which life could function in a meaningful manner.

27

Irving Kristol has made the point that 100 years ago the present juncture would have been called a "spiritual crisis," rather than a "crisis of values." Our common use of the second term gives the sense that the crisis is external to us, that we can make rational decisions about new values and then manipulate our way to the future, without cost to ourselves. But in our spiritual crisis, we are vulnerable in the face of the spirits among us. The specter of Jonestown is a parable of our times. Kristol is pressing us to recognize that we cannot have a vision merely because we see one is needed.

Hence, the absurdity of Pierre Trudeau's proposal that the disorientation which is common among Canadians can be dealt with by an explicit preamble in a new constitution—namely, a statement of goals for Canada. We sense, even if we have not the courage to say it, that such a statement would be like ads for Canada Day—apparently impressive, hard to argue against, but finally not only to no effect but further distracting and corrupting, for it promises us a sense of life without risk and vulnerability.

If I am right, the eighties will be profoundly unsettling. As we enter the eighties, given our present leaders and the present conceptual frameworks within which we work, we are as naked as lambs before wolves. We will find ourselves living without conviction, which, of course, will destroy the possibility of respecting ourselves, let alone our neighbor. In short, we seem to have chosen a strategy which is necessarily self-defeating.

The alternative is not flashy, but it offers some possibility of hope. The alternative is to begin to do now what we have refused to do for the last 20 years. The alternative is to begin to take seriously that the conversations that more and more of us are having with ourselves are not only personally but socially significant. We must learn to face this and to talk with each other.

If one has a deep respect for life as lived from the inside, then no other road is possible. In a time of turmoil, there is no way to put down roots which are sufficiently common and potent other than by learning to talk with each other as people before a fire. After all, what is there to do in the wilderness, except pull up a rock and talk with each other?

It may not appear much, but I know of no other activity which is as revolutionary or as healing as the creation of friendships within which we talk with each other about what really matters to us. The fact that this appears in none of our management manuals or courses on policy analysis may suggest that I am a fool. It may also suggest the depth of the confusion in which we have trapped ourselves.

A Global
Perspective

To Think Globally and Act Locally, Perceive Newly

by

Willis W. Harman

"Thinking globally, acting locally," the inspired theme of the First Global Conference on the Future, Toronto, 1980, immediately provokes two questions:

- How can we think globally when different peoples around the globe have fundamentally different pictures of reality?

- How can we act locally and still avoid the fragmentation of individualism?

How can we get any sort of consensus on the global dealing with global issues when our basic perceptions of reality are as different as those of the Western businessman, the "New Age" environmentalist, the North American Indian, the Islamic leader in a Middle Eastern nation, the Russian bureaucrat, and the Chinese farmer? What is the hope of our ever thinking globally?

I recall a conversation with a North American Indian who told me that understanding the Indian perception of reality is very simple—you just have to remember two things: (1) everything in the universe is alive; (2) we're all relatives. Actually, we in the West have a very similar perception in our past, the so-called "Great Chain of Being" of the Middle Ages. In fact, it turns out that something similar is in the Shinto of Japanese culture and many other traditional religions around the globe. These concepts are surprisingly universal; it is the materialist view of industrial society that is out of step, with its concept of humanity controlling and exploiting an insentient world.

Thus there would seem to be two possible candidate perceptions of reality around which a global order might eventually be constructed. One is the materialist world view implicit in the institutions of modern industrial nations (capitalist, socialist, and communist). The other is closer to the perception of the North American Indian and may be emergent as an ecological perspective in some of the contemporary

Willis W. Harman is Associate Director, Center for the Study of Social Policy, SRI International, Menlo Park, California. He is the author of An Incomplete Guide to the Future *and other works.*

30

social movements around themes like conserver society, development alternative, appropriate technology, holistic health, alternative lifestyles, and so on. The second seems rather impractical and visionary to most of what we call "decision makers" in modern society. It does seem to have the virtue of being the more compatible with a vast diversity of cultures in the Third World.

How can we act locally and yet assure that our actions will somehow add up to wise overall social choices? All decisions shape the future: How can we choose locally and still contribute to the overall choice of a desirable future? This question was addressed by Adam Smith and answered in terms of an "invisible hand," some sort of combination of cultural overlay and collective unconscious, that guides the marketplace choices so they combine with a wisdom not intended by the chooser. But the invisible hand has been noticeably faltering in contemporary capitalist society. The choices of self-seeking individuals in a world of increasingly resource-consuming, environmentally damaging, and powerful technology are not guaranteed to sum to desirable social choices. Is there no alternative to increasingly heavyhanded centralized regulation?

One way in which individual choices have been reconciled with overall social choices is through unconscious identification of the individual with the whole—the *participation mystique* of primitive tribes or the web of tradition in traditional societies, as brought out so vividly in the musical, *Fiddler on the Roof.* But that way is no longer open after the individuation of modern society. The only other way would seem to be through *conscious identification* of the individual with the whole. Perhaps we see the beginning of this development in the grassroots emergence of an ecological ethic.

These two questions, relating to the hope for global thinking and local acting, are very real. They deserve our serious attention. To approach them I need to remind you of two things, one being a peculiarity of modern industrial society and the other a fundamental characteristic of ourselves.

A Peculiarity of Industrial Society

Part of the folklore when I was growing up in the Pacific Northwest was a comparison of the ways of the Indian and the white man. To get warm the Indian builds a little fire and gets up close; the white man builds a big fire and stands way back. The Indian observed this to be rather silly behavior on the part of the white man. Similarly, there are aspects of modern industrial society that could convey a tinge of insanity to the onlooker from another culture. We refer to people in our society not as citizens, but as *consumers*; consumption is a virtue and frugality is bad for the economy. An adequate number of jobs must be provided whether or not they are needed for production, to create demand which the economy requires. No matter that they are featherbedding and makework and basically meaningless. No matter that the created demand translates into social costs associated with the resources consumed and the waste exuded; those very social costs can be the basis for new growth industries in cleaning up the mess.

More and more of total human activity becomes monetized in the mainstream economy. Thus, for example, we stay healthy by courtesy of the health spas and health-care industries; later on we will be in the care of the nursing homes industry, and finally the funeral homes industry. We find it "rational" to have most of our food products embodying more energy from fossil fuel sources than from the sun. We believe in the rationality of a world order in which the most powerful nations in the world consecrate a quarter of their national budgets to a military policy founded on the chilling concept of "mutually assured destruction."

This (and more) all came to seem reasonable by a path which Herman Kahn has labeled "the basic long-term multifold trend of Western civilization." This trend started some 8 to 10 centuries ago in Western Europe, with the gradual secularization of values and the introduction of the concept of material progress. Among its component trends were industrialization of production, growing dominance of economic rationality, development of modern science, and—especially pertinent to our present discussion—increasing linkage between science and technology.

Modern science is generally assumed to be the most trustworthy knowledge available in the world today. It represents the knowledge base of industrial culture. Because modern science developed in an industrializing culture it was shaped, to an increasing extent in recent decades, by the pragmatic utilitarian values of that culture. That science is supported that promises to generate new technology. The methodology of science emphasized prediction and control because those potentialities of knowledge served the technology-focused values of the society, the ability to manipulate the physical universe to serve the ends of human society.

All that seems eminently reasonable. But it has led to an unnoticed bias in the knowledge base of industrial society. The quantifying, measuring, prediction-and-control emphasizing methods of science have brought fantastic gains in knowledge bout the sense-perceived world, and in technologies deriving from that knowledge. Along with these gains there has been an ignoring of, and even a bias against, systematic exploration of the "other half" of human experience—the realm of inner experience of conscious and unconscious mental activities. This is the area of experience which most cultures have valued highly in the form of some sort of religious practice and tradition, and from which all societies have derived their deepest value commitments and most meaningful goals. In ignoring it, industrial society has learned more and more about "know-how," while having less and less consensus about value commitments that decide what is ultimately most worth doing.

The British physicist, Sir Arthur Eddington, wrote once of the ichthyologist who combed the seven seas with a one-inch mesh net and after years of such exploration came to the "scientific" conclusion that there are no marine creatures with a diameter less than one inch! It may seem at first thought inconceivable that the "comb" of scientific methodology applied to human experience could have resulted in a similarly faulty conclusion. Yet such appears to be the case.

A Peculiarity of Us

Of all the findings of modern psychology, one of the most firmly established (and one with the most pervasive implications) is that only the most minute part of our total mental activity is conscious. By far the greater part goes on out of consciousness. There is an immense array of evidence indicating that this unconscious activity covers a vast spectrum ranging through autonomic functioning, reflexes, dreaming, psychodynamic defense mechanisms, habitual behavior, memory search, pattern recognition, conceptualization, "hunches" and intuition, creative imagination, and religious/mystical awareness. Some of this unconscious activity we know about only through inference; some sporadically comes into consciousness and is experienced more directly.

Studies of hypnosis, perception, psychotherapy, and other phenomena related to this unconscious activity make it clear that we are quite capable of fooling ourselves, individually and collectively. The power of expectation and suggestion to influence perception is far greater than is ordinarily considered. We tend to see what we expect to see, what it has been suggested to us we should see; anthropologists find that persons raised in different cultures literally see different realities. On the other hand, we tend not to see some things that would be threatening or that would be in conflict with our deeply held beliefs. Thus we really don't know the extent to which what we perceive, individually or collectively, is a consequence of cultural expectations and suggestions. Even in science the possibility is present that the questions asked, and the manner of exploring them, are affected by the cultural surround. Discomforting as the thought may be, science as we know it is a cultural artifact of industrial society—in a different culture, science would have different emphases, different favored modes of "explanation," different guiding metaphors; it would describe a different reality.

Take for example a question that intrigued the physicist-physiologist Hermann von Helmholtz: How does it happen in the evolutionary process that we ended up with two eyes and binocular vision? Contrast two kinds of explanations. One, totally acceptable in scientific circles, speaks of things like random mutations, the accidental appearance of an organism with rudimentary binocular vision, enhanced survival capabilities because of improved vision, natural selection—and so we all have two eyes! The other kind of explanation speaks of some sort of teleological "pull" in the evolutionary process; of evolution toward increased awareness, complexity, freedom; in short, of evolution *going somewhere*, and the organism developing two eyes because it wanted to see better! This is a totally unacceptable kind of explanation in modern sophisticated circles. Yet it is much more in tune with the metaphysical premises of a large fraction of the world's population, and also more congenial to the sense among a growing group of scientists that consciousness somehow has to be factored into our total picture of the universe.

There has recently appeared some compelling evidence that the equating of mind with brain, as is implied by much of contemporary science, is a limiting and distorting concept. On both sides of the Iron Curtain interest has grown in a phenomenon termed "remote viewing." In a variety of experimental procedures, a remote target is randomly selected and the subject is asked to let his mind travel to that spot and observe what is there, making a sketch which can be compared later with a photograph and scored for accuracy. The ability to accomplish this remarkable feat turns out to be unexpectedly trainable. Most importantly, the training essentially consists in removal of the negative belief that one cannot do it.

Other experimental results indicate that at an unconscious level we "know" what is going on in the minds of others with whom we are in rapport to an extent that cannot be accounted for by any known form of physical communication. Our minds are not separate as we ordinarily take them to be.

This is not the time and place to review the supporting data for such conclusions. There exists by now an impressive amount of anecdotal and experimental evidence that mind is not brain. Mind is extensible in space and time in ways not accountable through a physicalistic model of the brain. Minds are joined in ways not explainable in terms of physical signals, subliminal or otherwise. The abilities of the creative/intuitive mind are not limited in the ways one would expect if mind were "nothing but" a prodigiously complex computer encased within the skull.

We do deceive ourselves through repression and other unconscious defense mechanisms. One part of us lies to another part; one part hides things from another part and distorts our perceptions. We do conceal the unsavory in the depths of the unconscious and then forget how we did it. But most importantly we do, as the American psychologist Abraham Maslow put it, fear and conceal "the godlike in ourselves," and we support this concealment by a materialistic belief system.

The Practicality of the "Perennial Wisdom"

As we contemplate "thinking globally," it is important to examine the global consequences of the materialistic bias of industrial society. Because a consensus was established on how to test and publicly validate the knowledge of the physical sciences, that knowledge tends to be essentially agreed upon around the world. Chemistry, physics, or astronomy are basically identical in India or Iran, Chile or China. The same is more or less true of the biological sciences. But it is not the same with knowledge of human inner experience. Spiritual psychology, so to speak, has an Eastern version, an Islamic version, a North American Indian version, a Christian version, an assortment of so-called "primitive" and animistic versions, all presumably very different. Since this inner experience is the seat of any culture's most fundamental guiding values and deepest commitments, some sort of consensus here would seem essential to any sort of truly stable global order. Thus the issue becomes a vital one, whether in fact the basic premises of these various religious traditions are fundamentally antagonistic to one another, and whether in fact there is an irreconcilable conflict between them and the basic premises inherent in modern science.

Comparative examination of the rich variety of religious traditions in human history leads to an important conclusion which we will state in two parts:

a. The religious beliefs and practices of a culture tend to fall into two parts, an *exoteric* or public version, and an *esoteric* version understood by some inner circle but tending to require for its understanding a rigorous discipline involving some sort of exploration of extraordinary states of consciousness.

b. Although the exoteric versions differ markedly, one from the other, the esoteric versions appear to be essentially the same for all durable religious traditions, East and West, ancient and modern, primitive and sophisticated. Aldous Huxley's book *The Perennial Philosophy* contributed significantly to making this argument publicly available. What the conclusion implies, of course, is that all these traditions are rooted in the same kind of deep inner experience, potentially accessible to all humans.

This "perennial wisdom" at the core of the world's religious traditions includes something like the following propositions:

1. All persons growing up in any particular culture are deeply affected by the suggestions emanating from their cultural surround regarding how they should perceive reality. We are all literally hypnotized from infancy by the culture in which we are immersed. We perceive the world the way we have been hypnotized to perceive it.

2. A prime task of adult life is to become dehypnotized, "enlightened"—to "know thy Self."

3. As this dehypnotization occurs it becomes apparent to the individual that there are potential levels of consciousness far beyond ordinary consciousness in the sense that ordinary consciousness is beyond dreamless sleep. These levels may sporadically become accessible to conscious awareness. They include the creative/intuitive part of the mind, whose contents seep through into consciousness as creative solutions to problems posed, moral insight, or artistic inspiration. Ecological, humane, and spiritual value commitments are all rooted in this realm of human experience.

4. Access to this creative/intuitive mind can be improved by reinforcing one's belief in it, and through practicing non-attachment to all else. In the end, one discovers it to be capable of guiding us far more reliably than the conscious analytical ego-mind.

5. The central understanding coming from this realm of experience is that there is one Mind of which we all partake. Thus mind is in no way limited as a physical model of the brain-mind would suggest—in extensibility in space or time, in separateness from other minds or from nature, in the potentiality of creating effects in the physical world.

6. Thus, at the deepest level, all people share a common interest and a common destiny—a destiny that far transcends the greed and fear, the pain and conflict around which so much of our society is constructed.

There is every reason to assume that as the imbalance is removed from our scientific enterprise and attention is directed to exploring inner experience, in ways congenial to the scientific spirit yet appropriate to the subject matter, the findings of that science will also be compatible with the perennial wisdom. As hinted above, there have already been some major advances in that regard.

Toward Thinking Globally and Acting Locally

And now we see that there is indeed hope of positive answers to the two questions we started with:

1. What is the conceptual foundation on which might be built a truly global order which would honor and safeguard the diversity of existing cultures, and yet give them a basis for consensus on global issues?

2. How can we choose locally and yet contribute to the overall societal choice of a desirable future?

There is, in the "perennial wisdom," a set of premises that is compatible with the many cultures around the globe—East, Mid-East and West; North and South; developed and developing—and is also compatible with the extended science of a trans-industrial society. The premises are completely consistent with the principle in science of public validation of knowledge—with the idea of learning through "inner experiments" comparable with the "outer experiments" of conventional science.

On the foundation of such a set of premises, and on no other, can be built a global order in which the core values of all cultures will be preserved—in which the great juggernaut of the world industrial economy will not ride roughshod over the less materially focused cultures. On this foundation can be built a global understanding of the spirituality of humankind that will avoid the bitter religious conflicts of the past. On this foundation industrial society can evolve toward solution of the dilemma of the alienation, goallessness, and emptiness of a predominantly materialistic society.

This foundation, too, includes the answer to the second question. The "invisible hand" that guides individual microchoices so that they add to societally desirable macrochoices turns out to be in part a cultural overlay of globally shared premises and shared vision, and in part the collective intuitive guidance assumed in the "perennial wisdom."

This proposition, that there *is* a sound basis for thinking globally and acting locally, and for so guiding society's decision-making processes, may sound much too idealistic and impractical for serious consideration. It no doubt seemed impractical to many when, two centuries ago, the Founding Fathers of the United States of America proposed that the new nation be built on precisely this same foundation—that it be a "New Order of the Ages" (*Novus Ordo Seclorum*). In 1782 they chose for the Great Seal a symbol coming out of the Freemasonry-Rosicrucian tradition to which practically all of them belonged, the symbol so familiar from the back of the dollar bill—the unfinished pyramid capped by the All-Seeing Eye, communicating that the structure is not complete unless the divine Vision is in the capstone position.

It is apparent, I believe, that these proposed answers to the twin questions of how to think globally and act locally would imply a drastic change in perception on the part of nearly all—of people in the technologically advanced societies not less than those in the developing world; of those espousing particular religious traditions no less than those of positivistic scientific persuasions.

Thinking Globally, Acting Locally

by

Roy Amara

None of us needs any longer to be convinced that events taking place anywhere in the world can affect, often instantaneously and dramatically, how we live. The threat of nuclear war, the delicate world oil supply/demand balance, developments in the Persian Gulf and Africa, possible effects of increasing fossil fuel burning on worldwide climate changes—these, and many more examples, underline clearly the increasing interconnectedness of nations. And this *fact* of interdependence, of course, is even more deeply felt at a variety of levels below that of nations and regions. From nation to state to local community our lives are inextricably linked on issues of inflation, unemployment, housing, transportation, crime—in short, the whole gamut of human activities that comprise modern-day societies.

What is true geographically is also true temporally. Most issues now confronting us are not only geographically global in extent but also long-term in nature. No "quick fixes" are to be found for inflation, for energy shortages, for failing productivity. Particularly in the U.S., we have been using up our societal "capital reserves": by borrowing from (or "discounting") the future heavily; by undersaving and overconsuming; by failing to develop indigenous energy sources; and by ignoring the obsolescing of much of our physical infrastructure. We have been "short-terming" our choices to the point where it has become abundantly clear that we now have no other choice but to "dig in" for the long pull, if we want to avoid the slow but inevitable dissipation of U.S. (and perhaps world) society as we know it.

Dramatic technological changes, growing populations, and rapid industrial development have brought us, often painfully and reluctantly, into grudging acknowledgement of both increasing *interdependence* and the increasing necessity to think systematically about *long-term* consequences of choices. The reluctance to think globally and long term stems in part from our inability to cope with and comprehend issues at "global" levels. Hopelessness and helplessness easily overtake us when confronted with very complex situations that often seem very much out of control. Neither prior experience, or our most sophisticated ana-

---

Roy C. Amara is President of the Institute for the Future, Menlo Park, California.

lytical tools, or the best of our collective wisdom seem remotely adequate. We know we must think "globally"—because the issues being faced are by nature increasingly global—but we lack global approaches, mechanisms, institutions, and solutions.

Thus, even when the necessity to think globally and long-term is made crystal clear and even accepted intellectually, the difficulties of tying *action to thought* bring us up short. How can global long-term perceptions and perspectives serve as useful guides for action? In more direct terms, we come to two of the most frequently asked non-rhetorical questions about futures planning and research: "So what?" and "But what do I do differently on Monday morning?"

There is much that can—and should—be done differently on Monday morning! Furthermore, even if we could and knew how to act globally, it would probably be unwise to try to do so from a strictly "systems" viewpoint. Why? Because the desirable properties of diversity, adaptability, and stability for complex dynamic systems—whether technological, biological, or social—seem to be best achieved by *informed choice* taking place at *local levels* of system organization. Informed how? Informed spatially (that is, having information about the state of the network) and informed temporally (that is, having information about long-term objectives and consequences). In other words, the strategy that appears to make most sense is one of *local action now* based on the best perceptions of likely consequences in *space* (geographically) and *time* (future-oriented).

But the overriding reasons for choosing a strategy of "thinking globally, acting locally" stem as well from much more pragmatic considerations. The incremental empirical, day-to-day experience that is accumulating from a wide variety of societal sectors—both in the U.S. and elsewhere—is that each of us, as individuals and in small groups, must increasingly *inform ourselves and involve ourselves* more directly to influence societal choices that affect our lives. In fact, participatory movements of all kinds—the world over—are likely to become one of the dominant transforming forces of the remainder of the twentieth century. Let's see how.

In the U.S. the relatively recent growth of "direct action" movements has developed many strands. For example, citizens are increasingly bypassing traditional institutions and processes that they feel have given them little choice or have proved ineffective. At the same time, new or modified processes are being continuously created which provide greater opportunities for the individual to participate directly in societal decision-making. Some have correctly characterized the changes as moving from *representative* to more *participatory* forms of governance. Pragmatically, the changes represent an attempt to restore "human scale," to increase understanding, to get back to basics, to decentralize societal organizations and decision-making. Conceptually, such changes are aimed at addressing the dilemma stated so well recently by Daniel Bell: "The nation-state has become too small for the big problems of life, and too big for the small problems."

And the effects of these changes are being felt everywhere. In the U.S., decentralization, together with the attendant shifts in power, is occurring in the public sector—from President to the Congress, and from the federal to state and local governments. Similarly, in the private sector, we see continued growth of autonomous work groups, more shared decision-making in task-oriented work activities, and more "bottom-up" organizational communication and initiative-taking. We are witnessing, at the same time, the decline or breakup of major institutions—political parties, labor unions, national broadcast networks— that are being augmented, superseded or bypassed by alternative arrangements.

Growing rapidly also is the use of initiatives, devices through which citizens can bring proposed legislation directly to voters for approval at local, state, and ultimately perhaps, at national levels. Another dramatic change that has taken place in the last decade—and destined to continue to exert powerful influences—has been the unprecedented growth of special interest groups of all kinds: public interest law firms; consumer, environmental and conservation groups; public interest lobbies; shareholder groups; political action committees; civic action groups. At the same time, we are becoming much more aware of the need for coping with complexity through "simplification" and "appropriateness" in lifestyles ("voluntary simplicity") and in the development and use of technology ("appropriate technology"). Nowhere are these trends perhaps more apparent than in the growing realization that conservation efforts by each individual represent the only real hope for getting a grip on our energy problems, that intelligent preventative care holds the key to control of spiraling health-care costs, and that direct community involvement is the most vital ingredient of effective educational processes in our schools. What is happening, in short, is that we are beginning to tackle problems at grass-roots levels, restructuring institutions with which we are directly in contact, initiating change from the bottom up.

The process is, however, not without its dangers. The most important of these is that we may act increasingly locally, but forget the other part of our maxim, "thinking globally." *Acting locally without thinking globally is a sure invitation to disaster.* For then we are not dealing with a well-articulated system, but rather a loose collection of uncoordinated individual actions—in the limit resulting in either a "hangup" of the process through the inability to agree on or achieve any objective or, worse still, resulting in chaos from the continuing conflict and strife of opposing interests. Thus, an essential feature of our system must be the capability for achieving *informed* local action, informed by the best available information for making choices. In essence, what we have come to is the concept of a "global village": "global" in the sense that we see issues as "wholes," and "village" in the sense that an adequate set of communication and social networks are put in place. But these are the very capabilities that our technological and social support systems of the late 20th and early 21st century can readily provide! We are on the verge of one of the potentially greatest technological revolutions in the history of mankind: the dramatic diffusion of computer/communications capabilities in the form of communication satellites, cable systems, wideband transmission networks, viewdata, teletext, conferencing systems, videodiscs—permitting information and resources sharing and exchange on an unprecedented scale. This is why our most promising strategy for coping successfully with increasing interdependence and complexity can be no better stated than, "Thinking Globally, Acting Locally . . . Thinking Long-Term, Acting Now."

Management of Complex Systems:
A Growing Societal Challenge

by

Robert Theobald

Each of us tend to look at the world as though our view of it is correct. Today, we are all having increasing problems as we come to understand that different people have profoundly different visions of reality and that there is no "objective" way of sorting out which of these visions is correct. As a result we are beginning to understand the full implications of John Maynard Keynes' statement that "Practical men are all slaves of some defunct scribbler."

None of us can cope with *all* the realities of the world: they would overwhelm us. Each of us must develop organizing principles (or theories) which permit us to make sense of our own world. The need for change is being felt today because more and more of us sense that the ways of organizing reality we were taught by the culture do not work effectively for us.

Where do our management concepts come from? I think many of us will be surprised to discover that they are directly descended from the idea that God created the world, understood where it was going and that the things which happened in it were therefore desired and wished by him. Authority and power were therefore vested in a person who was inherently beyond our understanding and it followed that we should be content with whatever happened. Not so incidentally we should remember that this belief of man's control by God was, in its extreme form, always heretical: the central religious struggle has always been to understand the interplay between an autonomous individual with "free will" and the "will of God." The feeling that we must struggle with "fate" has never perhaps been better expressed than in the lines of poet Dylan Thomas:

Do not go gentle into that good night,
Old age should burn and rave at close of day,
Rage, rage against the dying of the night.

The belief in an all-knowing God served as a practical support for

---

Robert Theobald likes to describe himself as a generalist. His latest book is We're Not Ready for That, Yet! *He makes his home in Wickenburg, Arizona, and Dingwall, Scotland.*

authoritarian decision-making by the Popes. They claimed (and indeed claim to be) the direct line to God and they therefore have the right in certain circumstances to speak *ex cathedra* as the direct representative of God. Thus Popes were seen as inherently superior to Kings who also gained their authority from God but not directly. Popes therefore wielded enormous authority because of this situation.

However, as both piety and superstition declined, it became both possible and desirable for Kings to deny that the Pope had a better line to God than they did. King Henry VIII gained increased authority by successfully challenging the power of the Pope. He continued to maintain his own legitimacy, however, by stating that he still had his direct line to God—if by a different route.

The societal credibility of this claim continued to decline over the centuries but the belief that individuals who held positions of power were inherently better able to make good decisions continued to exist. Until quite recently, we have invested Prime Ministers and Presidents of countries with a quasi-mystical aura, believing that the office carried with it some assurance of almost super-human wisdom.

Our belief in the extraordinary potential of those with power was centrally linked with our understanding of the operation of the world as mechanical. We learned to accept the idea of a Newtonian clock-work universe which had been wound-up by God and which operated the way it should. If, by chance, something went wrong the person at the top of the system was then believed to be in the best position to find out what had gone wrong and to mobilize the resources required to mend it. This assumption was essentially logical, given the pattern of assumptions, because the power to learn what was going on and the power to act could "obviously" be mobilized by the person at the top of the society.

This model of power and authority was seen as valid throughout the society until recently. Legitimacy was assumed for people at the top of all organizations, whether they got there through voting, or promotion through the ranks of a business or a church, etc.

It was only possible to maintain the "legitimacy" of this model of power and authority by stressing the machine-like nature of the society. The person holding structural authority was assumed to be confronted by relatively few problems needing decisions—"the government is best that governs least." It was usually assumed that the proper way to handle problems was to return to the status quo ante: to put the system back into its previous situation.

It is possible to track simply—but inevitably superficially—the process by which breakdown in the belief in this clockwork system model developed. Toward the end of the nineteenth century, the levels of social injustice and economic malfunction were so great that measures to change the system were demanded and passed. Each malfunction, however, was treated as a separate problem and a cure which it was hoped would be appropriate to each was created.

In the mid 1930s, there was a catastrophic collapse in the total system. At this point most people and the government that represented them agreed that fundamental change was needed. The right of the government to alter the socioeconomic system was conceded and a number of measures—such as Social Security—were introduced: these had far greater impacts than their originators had expected.

It was in this climate that John Maynard Keynes introduced his "revolutionary" idea that governments could effectively control "trade cycles." This thinking was seen as naive and irresponsible originally, but its post-World-War-II successes were so dramatic that his ideas were rapidly adopted. Administrations began to present themselves as active changers of the Newtonian mechanism, which was seen to deliver unsatisfactory results.

The high point of this interventionist model came in the Kennedy and Johnson years. The people that Kennedy recruited held a passionate, if simplistic, belief that the society could be changed to be more just and more humane. Legislation was proposed to deal with many of the traditional evils of the society. Heavy resistance was encountered from Congress and the country: they were far from certain that they wanted to adopt the highly interventionist model being pushed by Kennedy. It is a highly fascinating "what if," to wonder what would have happened if Kennedy had not been assassinated.

In reality, of course, the death of Kennedy opened up a flood of legislation. It was felt that we "owed" Kennedy what he would have wanted. A great many badly conceived laws were passed and the breakdown of many of them was inevitable from the start.

As policy failures proliferated, politicians wanted more and more information in a form which they could use. They were unwilling to tolerate presentations from a large variety of different viewpoints and they therefore tried to obtain an overall picture which would set out the type of policies which needed to be followed. The word *interdisciplinary* came into vogue both within university structures and outside them: more and more groups became involved in problem-solving.

An extraordinary number of new structures developed; they were often called Institutes. Some of them were general in nature; prepared to take on practically any task, they claimed wide competence. Others were concentrated in areas such as poverty or housing or rural development or health. However, reports from these structures were nearly always based on the assumption that there was a single right way to look at the issue being studied. It was also rather generally assumed that it was possible to develop a single, unambiguous set of policy recommendations to deal with the realities which had been described.

The failures of the sixties and seventies made us wary of this belief. We have discovered that the war on poverty didn't work. The effort to improve the educational system has largely failed. The sickness system has been consolidated rather than altered to encourage the promotion of health. There is more crime than ever before.

We are therefore being led to new understandings. We are being forced to recognize that societies operate on organic rather than mechanical principles. We are learning that we cannot substantially change one element in a culture without changing all the culture. It is this recognition which has forced a growing number of people to give up on the extrapolist assumptions: the belief that we can continue in essentially the same directions as in the past.

It is increasingly obvious that we have a fundamentally malfunctioning system and we are trying to deal with various failures through partial measures which cause further breakdowns elsewhere. This, in turn, creates additional immediate problems for those who are in decision-making systems: they then have even less time to think about how to achieve the fundamental changes which are required. It is not difficult to write a scenario based on current trends which would end in a profound breakdown in all of our systems.

The danger of this direction is greatly increased because we now "know" as a society that we cannot permit people to make decisions *just* because they hold power. The process of development of this feeling through many stages, including Nuremberg, Vietnam and the Saturday night massacre, is too lengthy to track here. The reality, however, is that we are trying to run a complex interrelated society on the basis of a set of assumptions which not only are known to be invalid intellectually but which the general public no longer believes.

The Romantic Viewpoint

There have been many attempts during the industrial era to build more human and humane institutions. These attempts started from a desire to honor the dignity of the individual. Unfortunately, most planners of institutions which aimed toward a more human future failed to understand the constraints of the society or the forces which could undermine their hopes.

This pattern has been seen in a large number of cases throughout the nineteenth century. The Owenites, the Shakers, etc., shared a belief that they should reform the society by setting a better example. In almost all cases, the institution died out or was changed so radically by outside pressures that it failed to fulfill the dreams of its founders.

Much the same pattern developed with the communes in the sixties: a large number of people hoped to set up alternative human patterns of living. Typically, these communes lasted a shorter time than the intentional communities of the nineteenth century. There would appear to have been two predominant reasons for this less permanent pattern: first, a great many of the people who entered the commune movement really did not have too much idea of the type of society they wanted to create. Second, the degree of impermanence and lack of norms in the society affected the people in the commune movement as well as the rest of the society.

The Romantics start from the correct assumption that institutions cannot be effective unless they are composed of decent people. Tragically, however, they often do not perceive that while this is a necessary condition it is not a sufficient one. Decent people have all too often made a mess of deciding on the perceptions and norms which will enable them to create good societies. The continued wreckage of the high hopes with which alternative institutions start shows that the skills required for effective functioning are all too often not known or applied.

The typical pattern in the sixties and seventies seems to have been to try to minimize rules. The problem has been that a large number of specific problems then necessarily emerge which are all treated on an *ad hoc* basis. The consequent jumble of rules are then continued into conditions for which they were not designed and where they may not be at all appropriate.

The Communications Era

Those who still accept the extrapolist Newtonian model assume that we do live in a clockwork universe: the trends in the society are then considered to be stronger than the effects of either individual or group action. Those who accept romantic models argue that if one changes one's life style and that of one's group, there will be an alteration not only in one's own community but in the way of life of the overall society.

People who are trying to create the communications era are aware that the world is formed on the basis of self-fulfilling and self-denying prophecies. They know that people help to bring into existence the "realities" toward which they choose to strive and help prevent the emergence of those "realities" against which they exert effort. There is no certain future: people determine what they obtain within broad limits. An old saying for children is "Be very careful what you want, you may get it." This is even truer for total societies. It is in this context, also, that Churchill's statement "We build our buildings and then our buildings build us" makes sense.

This truth was well known to Joseph Schumpeter. He stated that there are very few things that are worth accomplishing that would be undertaken by a "rational" man. He was arguing that the truly worthwhile effort is one which changes the future toward a more desirable direction.

It follows that individual, group and societal directions can only be changed if new concepts are understood. It is our collective inability to break out of our present way of seeing and organizing the world which is the real factor which prevents us from inventing the new society which we so urgently need. The "objective" studies we presently carry through do us great harm, for they reinforce our belief that today's perceptions are accurate.

If an individual, group or institution is to survive present traditional problems, three processes must be developed:

First, we must envisage our future in ways which excite us and allow us to break out of our present understandings. We must learn to look for and see relationships which are not obvious—or even visible—within the present type of world order.

Second, we must look back at our past and reexamine our personal, group and societal histories. We now recognize that history is always written by the winners but we have still not dealt with the awkward reality that the winners may not inevitably have been right. The revisionist historians of the civil war, for example, have

46

raised some very awkward questions about the relative morality of slave-ownership in the South and the patterns of job-holding in the North.

Third, we must learn communication skills so that we can examine both past and future in the context of today and thus decide how the transformation is going to be effectively managed. We have been unable up to the present time to discover the ways in which we can help people to see how they can change their present ways of living and working without intolerably damaging their self-interest.

If we began to look at past, present and future in these ways, what would we begin to see? We would discover that the concept of the universe as a clock has indeed been disproved by the work of such scientists as Einstein, Bohr and Heisenberg. They have shown that everything does affect everything else, that realities are probabilistic and that uncertainty always exists in all situations. We are now confronted with the task of adapting these understandings to the social sciences and to management theory.

How can we do this? There is a danger that a recognition that everything affects everything else in probabilistic ways would paralyze us. We need to understand the world in which we live in order to be able to act and we certainly cannot hope to understand everything in the world. We are therefore driven to accept that we shall always act on the basis of inadequate and incomplete knowledge and that the good decision-maker will be the person who develops skills to cope with this reality. More and more studies are now being published which show the importance of "intuition" in management.

It is possible, however, to begin to develop ways of structuring knowledge which start from the reality that there is no certain objective truth rather than from the Newtonian models which create a determination for each individual to state his or her own understanding and then to fight for it as though it is the *only* truth. We need to look at each issue, to determine those factors which are most crucial and to sort our the possible and likely patterns of interconnections. We also need to recognize that the complexity of views is so great and the levels of uncertainty so high, particularly at this time, that we must prepare ourselves to meet an uncertain future rather than plan for a particular, clear-cut future.

Our present styles of high-powered competition—even deliberate conflict—add to the uncertainties that beset us. Because we must have a viable model of the world in which we live in order to make "reasonable" decisions, we cannot afford to make deliberate efforts to distort the truth in order to achieve narrow partisan advantage. It is my conviction that cooperation is therefore becoming a societal necessity. One reason that we do not accept this conclusion is that we assume that a cooperative universe would be a soft and flaccid one. On the contrary, trust relationships between people permit them to challenge each other's perceptions and beliefs in ways which are not feasible when people work together without knowing each others' concerns and passions.

One final, general theoretical point needs to be raised here. The evaluation of "failure" and "success" needs to be far more careful and complete than in the Newtonian universe. In a Newtonian universe, the meaning of success is relatively unambiguous. In a post-Newtonian era, we must recognize that each person and institution will define success differently and that evaluation of that individual or institution is not feasible until the defined success criteria are known.

This is not the only difficulty in defining success and failure effectively. In many circumstances, it will be possible to come up with a fan of possibilities:

Route A leads to a small gain and has an 80% chance of success.

Route B leads to a medium gain and has a 50% chance of success.

Route C leads to a large gain and has a 20% chance of success.

If Route C is deliberately chosen, one cannot reasonably say that the choice was wrong because the route fails, for it was believed that the large chance of gain overpowered the fact that the odds were only 20%. It is also important to recognize that different temperaments will tend to choose different routes with different degrees of risk attached to them.

What then can we say about management in general terms:

1. Given the reality of diversity some people will be better in management roles than others. Similarly, some people will be better in high-risk situations than others. (We need to remember that these differences result from both genetic and specific educational/socialization processes. It is long past time that we laid to rest the question of whether nature or nurture controls.)

A good management team is one where peoples' temperaments fit the tasks they do and where an overall sense of purpose is created. However, despite talk of 9/9 management approaches which are meant to stress both task accomplishment and personal satisfaction, we are still remarkably ineffective in permitting people to use their skills. For example, successful salesmen and teachers and engineers are often promoted to be administrators. Individuals accept the promotions in order to get more money even though task competence and work satisfaction may be decreased. It is this situation which leads to the reality and the pervasiveness of the Peter Principle.

2. It is obvious that the more closely a person observes a particular area, the more knowledgeable the person will become about it. Thus, bright salesclerks will have more knowledge about evolving sales trends in their own area than the executive who is responsible for their work. This factor has led to situations in which executives go out and work in the field so as to get an understanding of current realities: this trend is carried to its extreme in China. It has also caused an understanding of the need for more effective information transmission throughout companies.

The basic problem in promoting effective communication is the lack of trust—and even of a common language—between levels of a company. Messages do not necessarily reach the receiver in the form that is intended: this is particularly true when the sender is trying to get the receiver to pay attention to new trends. Changing the perceptions of people is difficult at the best of times: problems in this area are still further increased when information may well be threatening to the sender or the receiver or even both. It is important to recognize that there may be a threat from new information regardless of whether the information is moving up or down the company.

It is for this reason that "management by exception" remains more of a theory than a reality. It is relatively easy for subordinates to pass on information about problems which have already been defined as being of importance to the management of the company. It is extraordinarily difficult for subordinates to find ways to inform their superiors of new trends: difficulties are compounded when a subordinate may only sense a shift in direction without being able to articulate it clearly.

Unfortunately, however, in today's world it is those things that we don't know that are likely to hurt us most seriously. Thus, the potential for an energy crisis was obvious to those who had analyzed the situation, but it was not taken into serious account even by most futurists (see Kahn's study on Japan), by most institutional decision-makers and certainly not by the general public.

It seems clear to me that there are still many problems and possibilities which are relatively close in terms of the time when they could happen which we have not yet begun to integrate into our social planning:

- the fact that the energy shortage is only the leading edge of a raw materials crunch.

- concentration on the relatively controllable dangers of communist/capitalist strife rather than on North/South or rich/poor breakdown.

- exclusion of the dangers of chemical/biological warfare from discussion, with all the stress on the danger of nuclear conflict.

- failure to perceive the impact of communication technologies over the next decade.

(These examples taken at random could be enlarged several times.)

The harsh fact is that we have not yet even developed, let alone adopted, communications and management techniques which would enable people to perceive and grasp the new realities which surround us. I believe that there are two primary reasons for this. First, our underlying models assume that fundamental change does not and should not take place: this concept results from the Newtonian paradigm on which our social structures are based. Second, we are not yet aware of the extraordinary difficulty of getting people to accept new ways of looking at the world. We therefore continue to assume that the receiver obtains the message intended by the sender: it is only today that we are really coming to understand the extraordinary degree of distortion that can intervene between a sent and a received message.

The underlying implication of this argument is that we must change our understanding of patterns of authority. As we have seen, we have inherited a belief that position ensures wisdom and that the person holding a position of power has the information that he requires to behave wisely. We are now learning that this model is inadequate and that power can, in fact, distort information flows.

Lord Acton was aware of this when he stated that "Power tends to corrupt and absolute power corrupts absolutely." This statement has usually been treated as an aphorism. However, it becomes a sober factual reality when it is rephrased as follows: "Power tends to corrupt information and absolute power corrupts information absolutely." The statement then refers to the undeniable fact that people who are afraid of others will tend to give them inaccurate information and the greater the degree of power, the worse the information flows will tend to be.

What elements need to be taken into account as we try to manage the overall world socioeconomic system at the present time? The following material is brief and tentative and will be enlarged as feedback comes in:

1. The trend in recent years and decades has been toward increased centralization of decision-making and therefore increased power. This power therefore has led to increased distortion of information in an effort to ensure/force the most attractive decision for various groups: the pressure of different views on public and private decision-making is increasingly unmanageable. During a recent visit to Washington, however, I was informed that a counter-trend may be beginning to develop where people with well-prepared information are getting more of a hearing.

As I see it, our only present hope of gaining clarity is to bring together people to look at single problem/possibilities (issues) through widely divergent windows. They should then be challenged to define as clearly as they can the status of the general discussion of the subject. This information should then be made widely available to those who can benefit from it. This process of creating new knowledge is ideally carried through on a networking basis using people working in different interest areas.

2. The other challenge we face as a society is to carry through efficiently the tasks which *we have decided* are necessary rather than discussing what needs to be done. This requires well-organized systems which can act with maximum efficiency and minimum waste.

This type of action requires an organizational hierarchy, for the person at the top of the system should have the clearest overall perception of the nature of the task. Each person operating within the institution should then have the clearest possible perception of the task they are meant to perform and should be able to perceive if his/her way of performing his/her required activities is getting in the way of other necessary work. To do this, each individual must have a sense of the overall vision of the system—this sense will be far more clear at the top, if the system is to work well, than at the bottom. However, in many types of activity, particularly service activities, the image of the institution will be made or broken in the lower ranks of the organization.

This set of statements leads to a different view of the nature of today's socioeconomic/political crisis than is usually advanced. In effect, one way of stating our current problem is that more and more issues are kept "permanently" open and there is therefore no clear-cut, definable task before many institutions. For example, we are not prepared—once we have decided on the building of a power plant—to trust the utility company to build it to the best of its ability: there is therefore widespread, continuing interference from many groups.

The essential reasons for this situation are clear. First, there are, as we have seen, *real* questions about appropriate directions and people try to stop the development or continuation of a certain policy because they genuinely fear its consequences. Second, we have less and less faith in the honesty of systems, often including our own, and feel that somebody must look over everybody's shoulder to prevent bad behavior.

However, while the reasons for this situation are understandable, the consequences are disastrous. The waste of time and resources ensured by continuous changes in plan are increasingly intolerable in today's conditions. Effective societal management will require:

● Agreed statements of the realities of our situation to be achieved by cross-system networking. This must be coupled with an understanding that Utopias are not going to be achieved and that individuals, institutions and societies will inevitably make mistakes.

● Institutions with agreed missions must then act effectively to carry them out. While it is inevitable that mission statements will alter over time, we shall have to accept the reality that doing things is one primary way in which we learn, that having learned we could do what we have just done better but we cannot continuously revise our planning and preserve an acceptable degree of effectiveness.

Action and activity plans must be frozen at some point. If they are frozen too soon, they will incorporate too little of the available knowledge. If they are frozen too late or left permanently unfrozen, efficiency levels drop dramatically. To put it in a different way, action is necessary but if we do not know enough at the time the action is taken then many of the components of the activity may turn out to be unduly costly over the long haul.

We need to find ways to define the world in which we actually live and gain a general acceptance of this definition. We then need to act to meet the real needs of the situation. Both of these tasks will require levels of management which are far higher than those we are able to create at the present time.

Identifying the Planetary Coalition for a Just New World Order

by

Hazel Henderson

In general terms, we are quite aware of the basic principles on which the New World Order must be built. Fundamentally these principles are:
- the value of all human beings.
- the right to satisfaction of basic human needs (physical, psychological and metaphysical) of all human beings.
- equality of opportunity for self-development for all human beings.
- recognition that these principles and goals must be achieved within ecological tolerances of lands, seas, air, forests and the total carrying capacity of the biosphere.
- recognition that all these principles apply, with equal emphasis, to future generations of humans and their biospheric life-support systems, and thus include the respect for all other life forms, and the earth itself.

This three-dimensional view of justice and equity is not contradictory, but complimentary. For if access to resources, power and wealth is broadly shared within and between nations today, this in itself reduces the dangers of concentrated power and wealth, which lead to over-exploitation of resources, human oppression and the depletion and destruction of future options. Only social systems that learn to use today's resources frugally and fairly can create perpetually renewable resource-based systems of production managed for long-term sustainability. Solar Age societies will be based on scientific understanding that living in harmony with each other and nature is not merely a moral imperative—it is now the only pragmatic course of action.

Historically, human development can be viewed as many local experiments at creating social orders of many varieties, but usually based on partial concepts; i.e., these social orders worked for *some* people at the expense of *other* people, and were based on the exploitation

---

Hazel Henderson, who describes herself as an independent futurist, is the author of Creating Alternative Futures *(G.P. Putnam, 1978). Her paper is drawn from the manuscript of her forthcoming book* The Politics of Reconceptualization *(Anchor, Doubleday, 1980).* © *Hazel Henderson*

of nature. Furthermore, they worked in the *short*-term, but appear to have failed in the *long*-term. Today, all these experiments of local and partial human development, when seen in a planetary perspective, have been failures in one way or another, based on some form of short-term exploitation (destabilization), or the underlying ideas of human domination of nature, the maximizing of sub-systems at the expenses of whole systems, and the recent rapid development of reductionist science and manipulative technologies. Today, we know that such societies are impossible to maintain and that the destabilizations on which they have built themselves are now affecting their internal governmental stability, and the global stability of the planet. Interestingly, these instabilities can all be stated in scientific terms:

1. In classical equilibrium thermodynamics, in terms of the First and Second Laws: the Law of Conservation and the Entropy Law, that all human societies (and all living systems) take negentropy (available forms of energy and concentrated materials) and transform them into entropic waste at various rates, and that we can measure these ordering activities and the disorder they create elsewhere. An understanding of this process leads to the realizations that, properly-speaking, the U.S. (or any other) Department of Energy should be termed the Department of Entropy. Another example of the workings of the laws of thermodynamics in human societies is the ratio of order/disorder we see within and between societies, e.g., the structuring of European countries in their colonial periods at the price of the concomitant disordering of their colonies, culturally and in terms of indigenous resources.

2. In terms of biology and the evolutionary principle, "Nothing Fails Like Success," i.e., the trade-offs between short-term and long-term stability and structure; between adaptation and adaptability.

3. In terms of general systems theory, the phenomenon of suboptimization, i.e., optimizing some systems at the expense of their enfolding systems.

4. In terms of ecology, as violations of the general principle of interconnectedness of ecosystems and the total biosphere; i.e., the continual cycling of all resources, elements, materials, energy and structures. This interconnectedness of all sub-systems on planet Earth is much more fundamental than the interdependence of people, nations, cultures, technologies, etc.

Thus, the aspirations for a new World Order are not only based on ethical and moral principles, important as these emerging planetary values will be for our species' survival. The need for a new World Order can now be *scientifically* demonstrated. We see the *principle of interconnectedness* emerging out of reductionist science itself, as a basis, and the concomitant ecological reality that redistribution is also a basic principle of nature. Since all ecosystems periodically redistribute energy, materials, structures through biochemical and geophysical processes and cycles, therefore all human species' social systems must also conform to *principles of redistribution* of these same resources that they use and transform, whether primary energy and materials or derived "wealth" (capital, money, structures, means of production and "power") as well as continually changing institutions.

The new scientific understanding of interconnectedness and the fundamental processes of redistribution are accompanied by the emerging paradigms of *indeterminacy, complementarity* and *change* as basic descriptions of nature. These five principles operate not only at the phenomenological level of our everyday surface realities and in our observance of nature (in the "middle-range" realm of classical physics) but also at the subatomic level of phenomena of quantum mechanics. The frontier of quantum mechanics is building on the last question raised by Einstein, set forth in his paper in 1935 with Podolsky and Rosen, *Can Quantum Mechanical Description of Physical Reality Be Considered Complete?* The issue concerned the fact that quantum mechanics built on the assumption that causality was *local* (the idea that events happened in certain space/time locations, discretely, and that events and phenomena could not affect each other at a distance, without an intervening medium or means of connectedness). Most physics continues in this assumption, in search of behavior and interaction of ever smaller, more numerous particles, waves, quarks and improbable phenomena, properties, tendencies, and the like. Yet, as Gary Zukav describes so enthrallingly in *The Dancing Wu Li Masters,* in 1964, J.S. Bell, a physicist at the CERN laboratories in Switzerland, devised a theorem demonstrating the limits of the mathematics used in quantum mechanics, and presented physicists with a very fruitful paradox; calling into question this local causality and discreteness on which all physics is founded, thus leading to the new hypothesis that subatomic events and phenomena are also fundamentally interconnected. Similarly, we have seen how the principles of indeterminacy, complementarity and change apply, not only to quantum-levels, but to biological, ecological and social processes and phenomena, as well. Thus these five principles emerging in Westernized science itself imply behavioral human adaptation and learning and social principles:

- INTERCONNECTEDNESS (planetary cooperation of human societies)
- REDISTRIBUTION (justice, equality, balance, reciprocity)
- CHANGE (re-design of: institutions, perfecting means of production, changing paradigms and values)
- COMPLIMENTARITY (unity *and* diversity, from either/or to both/and logics)
- INDETERMINACY (many models, viewpoints, compromise, humility, openness, evolution, "learning societies")

Thus the new World Order can be founded both on scientific *and* ethical principles. We are *discovering* the new World Order in science and *remembering* that we know it already, since these same five principles are found in all religious, spiritual traditions. Ethical principles have become the frontiers of scientific enquiry. Morality, at last, has become pragmatic, while so-called idealism has become realistic.

But it is equally clear that the needed global transformation will either occur amid increasing human resistance and social rigidity, or that it will be accommodated and encouraged by more enlightened and flexible social policies and shifts in human values and behavior. Thus the global politics of reconceptualization involves the emergence of pragmatic strategies, new coalitions and what might be termed "a new proletariat": not only workers, as Marx preached, but *all people* who have been tyrannized by arbitrary symbol-systems and social designations of their roles, for example, all the world's people whose work has not been monetized, and therefore not valued: rural, subsistence farmers, India's Harijans and other so-called lower-caste workers, ethnic peoples in all nation states who have been ghettoized in some way, such as the Native American Nations, the Aborigine of Australia, the Ainu in Japan, who have been driven off their ancestral lands into reservations, and all people undervalued by discrimination because of color, sex, race or religion. In the same way, countries and regions have been subordinated to the tyranny of the global monetized economy and their contribution to the world's development and human culture thereby devalued. We now see in the emerging paradigms in science, that *all these issues flow from erroneous, abstract drawing of boundaries where none exist in nature.* Yet the conscientizing of human societies of these errors is a *political* task, *requiring* that these issues and existing power centers be confronted.

This planetary consciousness-raising activity must be militant, reasoned and non-violent; for example, the important new struggle over the world's finite electromagnetic spectrum. It is now clear that a blatantly unfair monopoly by industrialized nations of this vital global resource exists over the medium of communications from radio, TV, telephone to air and marine navigation, microwave relay, radar, satellites and other strategic systems. Here the division between nations of this planetary resource is such that, for example, 90% of the radio spectrum is monopolized by 10% of the world's population. The battleground for the electromagnetic spectrum is the World Administrative Radio Conference, and its implications for the development of a more balanced, planetary information sharing are crucial. The lengthy set of issues involved in a new, equitable distribution of the planet's information and communication systems will be another vital arena for the politics of reconceptualization, since only when all cultures have the means to enter the world's dialogue on an equitable footing can we hope for a large enough forum for conflict-resolution, and the creation of new cultural alternatives. Such information-sharing can also re-balance the current tyrannies of *some* cultures' paradigms, symbol-systems and values over *other* cultures. Appropriately, UNESCO has become an ongoing forum for dialogue on these issues.

Another key issue that is helping clarify our vision of new planetary realities is arising out of the distillation of the major ideological views of "development" that have operated since the industrial revolution, particularly in communism, socialism and capitalism and their various expressions: the growing concern for the needs of *real human beings,* and the general issues of *injustice* and *inequality*. These concepts are illustrated in three recent, major views of social progress:

1. The Cocoyoc Declaration's definition of "development," i.e., the development of human beings, not the development of countries, the production of things, their distribution within social systems or the transformation of social structures, thus entailing redefinition of the whole purpose of "development," which has confused means with ends.

2. The socialist view, based on Karl Marx's legacy, concerning the issues of oppression of groups in societies by other groups, and Marx's historical documentation of the oppression of working classes by capitalists and property-owners, as a prime example of this arbitrary oppression.

3. The liberal legacy of the Enlightenment; of political democracy (often stated in still-arbitrary languaging as one-man, one-vote) which has, however, led inevitably in the U.S.A. to Jimmy Carter's focus on "human rights" as a major policy.

Thus, lip service, at least, is now generally paid to this focus on the rights of the human being, and in our communications-rich world, few nations can ignore the public opinion sanctions against blatant violations of these human rights. Today's leaders have also experienced the double-edged sword of this human rights issue, which exposes paradoxes of injustice and oppression of minorities within their own borders, and leads to such examples as the pressing of such domestic grievances of Native Americans and blacks in the U.S.A. into the world forum of the United Nations and public opinion. Thus the general issue of all forms of arbitrary oppression is coming to the fore, as we have seen vividly in Iran, where both American and Soviet interference have been equally protested, and in the new protests from many non-aligned nations at the Soviet troop movement into Afghanistan.

Today, therefore, a new type of planetary coalition must emerge to undergird politically the aspirations for the new World Order: a winning coalition, not only of workers, as in the earlier concepts of the International Workers of the World, since workers in industrial countries are now in the anomalous position in many cases, enjoying better conditions at the expense of more oppressed groups, such as blacks in the U.S.A. or Pakistanis in Britain, and unwittingly, through their corporate employers' exploitation of cheaper labor in many countries of the Southern Hemisphere. Similarly, the world's women (the latest "developing nation") have been overlooked and their basic roles in production, maintenance, and agriculture uncounted in the economic definitions of capitalist, socialist, and virtually all economic data of their monetized sectors. Revealingly, even the inspired definition of development in the Cocoyoc Declaration grew out of concepts such as expressed by the Tanzanian Minister of Development, M. Chagula: "Our first concern is to redefine the whole purpose of development. This should not be to develop things but to develop *man*" (emphasis added).

Similar statements that *man* has not been able to control *his* technology, and concerning *man*'s alienation from nature are precisely correct. The winning planetary coalition must now include woman, if it is to be large enough to form a politically-viable majority. It is also clear that our chaotic societies now need "mothering" as well as "fathering," in a more balanced sharing of leadership responsibilities. Thus, the meta-issues of human needs, human rights and all arbitrary oppression, resting on secure scientific knowledge now emerging, provide the action formula to operationalize the ethics of the Solar Age and actualize its social expressions in a balanced, harmonious, ecologically-aligned, new World Order.

Preparing Tomorrow's Corporate Cosmopolitans:
Implications for Twenty-First Century Managers and Consultants

by
Philip R. Harris

Global Transformations

With the landing of man on the moon, the traditional images of the human species were ended. For millions of years, human beings thought they were earthbound. Now that such "perceptual blinders" have been torn asunder, we are challenged to look at our collective selves and our world in another way. What are the upper limits of human potential? Is our real home as a race on this planet, or out there in the unexplored universe? Our conception of reality also alters as we create *new images* of our species, its place and purpose in existence. The revision of this collective self-concept will probably be the greatest force for change in the century ahead. As people project these new images of themselves, their roles, their organizations, and their world, they powerfully influence their own behavior and accomplishments. Furthermore, they affect the responses of others to these different images. For example, when we conjure up the conception of "Spaceship Earth," or envision our society in terms of "Global Village," we act differently toward our environment and toward our distant neighbors. When we think in terms of the whole Human Family, then differences in that family are considered natural, unique, and precious. So too, as we develop a sense of "World Culture," we grow beyond particular cultures, while cherishing and respecting our origins.

To grow beyond cultural limitations means to become truly "cosmopolitan." The dictionary provides this interesting definition of that word: "belonging to the world; not limited to just one part of the political, social, commercial, or intellectual sphere; free from local, provincial,

Philip R. Harris is a management and organizational psychologist who serves as president of his own consulting firm, Harris International, Ltd., La Jolla, California. He is the author of Managing Cultural Differences *(1979),* Effective Management of Change *(1977), and other books. Most recently he co-edited* Innovations in Global Consultation *(1980).*

or national ideas, prejudices, or attachments." Literally, a cosmopolitan is one who is effective *anywhere* on this planet and beyond. For a successful transition to the twenty-first century, the point of this presentation is that organizational leaders and consultants must move toward becoming more *cosmopolitan* human beings!

To grasp the significance of this observation, consider the *history of human development* in terms of four principal stages. Try to visualize this conceptual model in the form of a straight line that is divided in this manner:

	Agricultural Revolution	Industrial Revolution	Cybercultural Revolution
Hunting Stage	Farming Stage	Industrial Stage	Post or Super Industrial Stage
Millions of Years	Thousands of years	Hundreds of years	Decades
EPOCH "A"		⟶	EPOCH "B"

Notice that in the first stage of human existence, we were hunters, operating at the survival level of human needs—besides eating and sleeping, much time was devoted to the work of hunting and there was little time for creative leisure. This situation lasted for millions of years, over half of the species' collective lifeline.

Gradually, a major turning point occurred that transformed human life and society: the Agricultural Revolution. The main body of mankind then devoted themselves to domesticating animals, planting seed, and harvesting food that could be stored up for tomorrow. Thus, mankind moved up to the next level on the hierarchy of human needs. Although farming took many hours in the day, it did allow enough free time for building villages, cities, and eventually civilization; for some education; and for the expansion of cultural activities. Later, another critical juncture occurred: the Industrial Revolution. Again the human mainstream shifted—from the country to the city, from the farm to the factory. In this industrial stage of the last few hundred years, society was again transformed as people worked less time in new occupations, played more and dramatically raised the level of their education and consciousness. Marvelous breakthroughs occurred in science and technology, communication and transportation—a staggering number of changes which produced more advances in a chain reaction up to the end of World War II.

About midway in the twentieth century, mankind has begun to experience yet another profound transition: the Cybercultural Revolution. In *Survival of the Wisest*, Jonas Salk has aptly described the first three periods of human development as Epoch "A," and the post or superindustrial stage of the present as Epoch "B." As we look back over mankind's history, note that it is marked by ever-accelerating change in each stage—millions, thousands, and hundreds of years contrast to what is happening now in just decades!

With the onset of this new epoch, humans work less time each day and can go anywhere on this planet and beyond with lightning-like speed compared to previous generations. Leisure time has suddenly increased and we are given the choice of wasting it, or using it to achieve new peaks in the development of human potential. Perhaps we can better comprehend what is happening to the human race if we think in terms of average lifespan: Primitive Man lived about 18 years, Agricultural Man lived approximately 35 years, while Industrial Man typically lives in the 70-year age range; but it is projected for the next century that Cybercultural Person may live on the average well over 100 years! As knowledge or technical workers, benefitting from automation and cybernation, the current generations and those to come have unparalleled opportunities and traumas compared to our ancestors.

Such a rapid alteration of our life and society means that we are the people of change and transition, caught in a pivotal position, challenged to create a new "cyberculture" to replace our comfortable past. The late physicist Norbert Wiener coined the word "cybernetics" to describe the self-regulating systems that dominate the emerging information society. Thus, he used the term "cyberculture" to signify the new age of automation. As our traditional ways of life give way under the impact of this accelerating change, we humans need to expand our consciousness: our way of perceiving, thinking, and acting. In the homogenization of the race now taking place, the cosmopolitan will contribute to the creation of a new world order. Lewis Mumford reminded us in his work, *The Transformation of Man*, that we must form "new pictures" of human nature and the cosmos itself. The revolution underway in social roles and institutions, cultural premises, and dominant values, attitudes and lifestyles will foster further profound changes in the very image of ourselves! Willis Harman observed in his book, *An Incomplete Guide to the Future*, that the industrial-era paradigm is no longer viable to our ideology or world view. That term "paradigm" refers to our particular vision or perception of reality. Today's leaders can contribute to the development of these new conceptions by creating more relevant organizational models and practicing more appropriate management skills. Consultants to human systems have a major responsibility to delimit "organization shock" so that corporations and other agencies can make the transition to the next century. They need to help people develop coping skills for what Alvin Toffler has aptly described as "The Third Wave."

Because of the occurrence outlined above, the social, economic, travel, national, ethnic, religious, and cultural barriers that tend to separate human beings continue to crumble. People, especially our employees or members, need to learn the skills of dealing with the differences in individuals and groups who are more diverse and less similar than those with whom we have been raised. Cross-cultural education and training becomes more essential today, especially for those in management positions, if culture or future shock is to be managed. This preparation involves the study of the factors that influence the analysis of what an individual outside that group should understand and do in order to facilitate communication with these "others." It requires that they become ultracultural, capable of operating effectively in pluralistic societies that are emerging.

Changing Managers

All of us need to manage ourselves and our own life space more effectively, but this is especially true for those who have a leadership responsibility in the supervision of others.

The art and science of management is relatively modern and it already is in the midst of intense "revolution." As Peter Drucker observed, all of the assumptions upon which management practice has been based for the past fifty years are obsolete. In line with the new realities of this superindustrial age, managers are challenged to reconsider their *image of their role*, so as to alter their organizational culture and their individual leadership style. The author of *The Step to Man*, John Platt, underscored a number of special crises that endanger our society, our world, and ourselves. One of them is an administrative crisis in all forms of management—schools, business, government—which seemingly lacks the flexibility, speed, and knowledge to meet the changes which we must face before the end of this century. The cosmopolitan leader now and in the future must direct personal energy toward learning new ideas, gaining new insights, experimenting with new approaches to people.

In reevaluating our roles as contemporary managers or consultants, there are eight key concepts to be considered among many. The human resource development programs that are futuristic will include:

1. The Concept of the Cosmopolitan—learning to become a sensitive, innovative and participative leader, capable of operating comfortably in a global or pluralistic environment. The cosmopolitan manager is open and flexible in approaching others, can cope with situations and people quite different from one's background, and is willing to alter personal attitudes and perceptions.

2. The Concept of Intercultural Communication—learning to become more aware of what is involved in one's image of self and role; of personal needs, values, standards, expectations; all of which are culturally conditioned. Such a person understands the impact of such factors on behavioral communication, and is willing to revise and expand such images as part of the growth process. As a manager, this individual would seek to get into the "world" of the receiver, and improve cross-cultural communication skills, both verbal and non-verbal. Not only does such a leader seek to learn appropriate foreign languages, but is cognizant that even when people speak the same language, cultural differences can alter communication symbols and meanings.

3. The Concept of Cultural Sensitivity—learning to integrate the characteristics of culture in general, with experiences in specific organizational, minority, or foreign cultures. Such a leader acquires knowledge about cultural influences on behavior; cultural patterns, themes, or universals; diversity of macrocultures and microcultures. As a cosmopolitan manager, this individual can translate such cultural awareness into effective relationships with those who are culturally different.

4. The Concept of Acculturation—learning to adjust and adapt to a specific culture, whether that be a subculture within one's own country or abroad. Such a person comprehends what is involved in self and group identity, and is alert to the impact of culture shock or differences upon one's sense of identity. Therefore, when operating in a strange culture or dealing with employees from different cultural backgrounds, this manager develops skills for adjusting and avoiding ethnocentrism.

5. The Concept of Cultural Management Synergy—learning to appreciate the influences of cultural conditioning on the management of material and human resources. The cosmopolitan manager is aware that what is acceptable for leaders to do in one's own culture may be unacceptable and cause strife in another culture. Such an individual tries to adapt modern principles of administration to the indigenous circumstances, or educate the local populace to contemporary management practice and expectations. A synergy is thus created between the managerial styles of host and home culture.

6. The Concept of Effective Intercultural Performance—learning to apply cultural theory and insight to specific cross-cultural situations that affect people's performance on the job. The multinational manager must understand the peculiarities of a people that influence productivity at work. Such a leader makes provisions for foreign deployment, overseas adjustment and culture shock, reentry of expatriates, international report reading, changing organizational environment, and overcoming cultural handicaps and limitations.

7. The Concept of Changing International Business—learning to appreciate the interdependence of business practice throughout the world, as well as the subculture of the managerial group in all nations of similar ideology (e.g., capitalistic or communist nations). The cosmopolitan manager appreciates the effect of cultural differences on standard business practice, especially in terms of profits, organizational loyalty, and such common activities as reward/punishment of employees. The multinational or world corporation manager is also aware of acceptable, universal business principles and procedures.

8. The Concept of Emerging World Cultures—learning to keep up with trends that break through traditional barriers between peoples of different cultures, to take care of human needs on a transnational basis, to develop new markets and services that contribute to a more polycultural society. Such a manager is alert to developments in the creation of an international culture, common to inhabitants of earth. The furtherance of world trade and commerce, the sharing of rich nations with less affluent countries, the cultural and commercial exchanges of the world's peoples—all foster human prosperity and development throughout the globe, and prepare us to function more effectively in the universe beyond this planet.

Such pregnant concepts are key ingredients in the competencies of the cosmopolitan. They also should be part of any program of cross-cultural education, training, and development.

Global Leadership

In examining here the new role of cosmopolitan management, we should remind ourselves that institutions and organizations are changing in the manner and way they operate both domestically and internationally. It is more than a major shift from the traditional bureaucracy of the industrial age to the emerging ad-hocracy. It is more than mere expansion into worldwide markets, or even creation of multinational organizations. It involves a fundamental change in business perspective toward a view of the world without borders, and to the eventual creation of world corporations. Such trends demand that today's leader have a high degree of cultural knowledge, skill, and sensitivity.

Obviously, we need more cross-cultural competencies, but we also need to create a new mental-set—a world consciousness that grasps the human situation in global terms, while appreciating the *interdependence* of all life on our breathtakingly beautiful planet. As the late consultant Milton Feldman urged, we must be aware that in a world of ever growing interdependency and complexity, the contributions of all people are needed to sustain the delicate web of life. Since peoples and cultures can no longer exist independent of one another, we must facilitate meaningful intercultural interaction among the earth's inhabitants.

The reality faced by cosmopolitan managers is that the world is a single marketplace in which national boundaries serve as convenient demarcations of cultural, linguistic, and ethnic entities, and do not define business requirements or consumer trends.

Cross-Cultural Studies

Managers need training in understanding culture, particularly from the perspective of cultural anthropology. Cultural knowledge provides insight into the learned behaviors of groups related to their traditions and customs, values and beliefs, attitudes and concepts, hierarchies and roles, time and space relations, communication both verbal and nonverbal, and a whole host of other aspects that make a people distinctive. Intercultural skills enable managers to cope more effectively, reduce stress, and resolve conflict within the arena of international business relations. Transcultural awareness cushions the shock of living and doing business in an alien context. Presently, cultural awareness training, as well as future studies, seem to be the missing ingredient in most management or professional development.

In *The Secret of Culture*, Thompson reminded us that culture is fundamentally a group problem-solving "tool" for daily coping in a particular situation. He maintained that it is group self-actualization which impacts on human evolution, and enables us to create our world and control our destiny. Mankind alone among creatures seems to have this sense of culture, so as to mould our environment for our assistance. Furthermore, we can, it appears, pass along the techniques for doing this from one generation to another by cultural rather than genetic means. Through this dimension of culture, *Homo sapiens* has occupied and utilized a far wider range of environment than any other creature on this planet.

Education in cross-cultural factors and influences supplements a cosmopolitan manager's learning in foreign languages, international economics, and future studies. It not only helps one to meet the competition for world markets, but may cut costs and waste in foreign deployment. For example, two multinational corporations working in the Middle East reported respectively a 50% and an 85% premature return rate of Americans sent to that country. The estimated return cost for such employees and their families ranges from $55,000 per family to one-third of a manager's annual salary. This does not include the replacement cost for substitute personnel abroad. The price of establishing a program of cultural awareness training for overseas employees, or better still a foreign deployment system, is a miniscule investment in comparison to the waste and damage caused by disgruntled and disenchanted personnel who must be brought home from international assignments ahead of schedule. Furthermore, research indicates the biggest payoff may be obtained when organizations study the performance abroad of their high-achieving employees.

But the cosmopolitan leader can benefit by transcultural studies in these ways as well: (1) facilitates adjustment and well-being when serving abroad; (2) fosters international goodwill and client relations; (3) improves understanding of international business and financial reports, especially when written by "foreigners"; (4) provides insight relative to the impact of organizational culture upon employee behavior; (5) offers understanding of markets and customers who make up domestic subcultures; (6) increases human relations skills with minorities and ethnic groups in one's home country; (7) assists re-entry into one's native culture and organization upon return from abroad; (8) sensitizes management to the needs of foreign nationals on assignment here. International relations, in general, are bound to be better when management, sales, and technical personnel who work in the world marketplace can manage cultural differences. Such understanding will delimit false assumptions and stereotyping of people from other cultures, as well as contribute to the more effective utilization of human resources.

The emerging theory of "cultural ecology" maintains that all humans in different groups and societies develop unique forms of production, tools, and knowledge to use and enhance a particular environment. Human social and technological advances are the legacy of all mankind, and various cultures should borrow from one another to promote a new level of human development, a new cultural synergy.

This, then, is the rationale for cross-cultural learning, especially on the part of those with leadership responsibility. Finally, such human resource development has implications for *organizational culture*. It can enable leaders to overcome the negative image that research confirms workers have of senior managers. Studies indicate that line employees view top management as remote, impersonal, and less significant to job satisfaction than are their immediate supervisors. The cosmopolitan executive is attuned to the need for active changing of management

64

styles and organizational environment. If innovations are to be rapidly transformed into profitable products and services, executives of the future will need cultural sensitivity, change skills, and results orientation. These global managers will blend technical business with socio-political expertise, as well as interpersonal competence!

Freedom and the Future
of Local Action

by

Joseph P. Martino

The Tragedy of the Commons

Garrett Hardin's fable, "The Tragedy of the Commons," neatly captures the attitudes of many futurists toward the environment, and the actions which are appropriate for protecting it from people.

In this fable, there is a village with a "commons," on which the villagers pasture their cows. At first, there is plenty of room, and each villager can add more cows as he is able to afford them. Eventually, however, the size of the herd reaches the carrying capacity of the commons. At this point, adding one more cow will reduce the productivity (meat and milk) of all the other cows, since the additional cow will reduce the grass available to the others. Consider an individual villager deciding whether to add one more cow to his herd. The additional cow will reduce the productivity of all other cows, including those he already pastures on the commons. However, he gains *all* the increase in productivity from the additional cow, while the costs are distributed equally across all the cows already there. So long as the increment in productivity from an additional cow (his marginal gain) exceeds the loss on his own cows (his marginal cost) he will add one more cow. Thus even though the total loss in productivity for all villagers may exceed his gain, this is of no concern to him. He is concerned only with his own gain and loss.

This creates a vicious trap. To each villager, it appears that he gains all the benefits from an additional cow, while his fellow villagers suffer most of the losses. But if each villager adds one more cow, on the average each gains the benefits of an additional cow and also suffers the entire losses from an additional cow. Thus each villager is worse off than before the cows were added. But now the trap springs shut.

Although each villager receives both the benefits and losses of one additional cow, losses which exceed the benefits, he *cannot improve*

Joseph P. Martino is Senior Research Scientist, University of Dayton (Ohio) Research Institute. He is Technological Forecasting Editor for THE FUTURIST *and author of* Technological Forecasting in Perspective.

his condition by removing one cow. If he removes one cow, he loses the benefits he gained from that cow, but continues to suffer the losses from the excess cows of all the other villagers. Removing his extra cow merely makes him worse off while benefitting his neighbors slightly. Even though it would be to the advantage of all the villagers for each to remove one cow, no one will do so unless he can be sure all will do so, since any "cheaters" will benefit at the expense of the rest of the village.

From this fable, Hardin concludes that freedom in a commons leads to tragedy. Each person, seeking his own self-interest, is led to injure his neighbors and himself. Moreover, he cannot escape the trap, since even if he has a "conscience" and refrains from action which hurts his neighbors, he will suffer from their actions. Hardin concludes that the only solution is a system of "mutual coercion mutually agreed upon by the majority of the people affected." Thomas Schelling remarks that there ought to be a softer word than "coercion," but Hardin refuses to shrink from the implications of his own term; he "prefer[s] the greater candor of the word coercion."

Coercion Is Needed for Survival

Garrett Hardin is not the only futurist who believes that coercion, established by majority rule and centrally controlled, is required for survival. Many futurists have made very strong statements to this effect.

Daniel Bell, in his book *The Cultural Contradictions of Capitalism,* made the following statement: "Ours is a world that will require more authority and more regulation."

Robert Heilbroner made a similar assertion: "The passage through the gauntlet ahead may be possible only under governments capable of rallying obedience far more effectively than would be possible in a democratic setting."

Lester Brown, Patricia McGrath and Bruce Stokes, writing in *THE FUTURIST,* gave a similar argument:

As more and more people require space and resources on this planet, more and more rules and regulations are required to supervise individual use of the earth's resources for the common good . . . The need for more extensive political control is painfully illustrated by the tragedies born of the unregulated use of common resources like air and water. A finite world pressed by the needs of increasing numbers can no longer afford such uncontrolled self-seeking. One possible result of the re-emergence of scarcity may be the resurrection in modern form of the pre-industrial polity–a polity in which the few govern the many and in which government is no longer of or by the people.

These futurists at least believed that the necessary coercions could be applied by national governments. Not all futurists accept that view. Some argue for replacement of national governments by world government.

Harrison Brown, for instance, had the following to say in his book

The Challenge of Man's Future:

In the first place, it is amply clear that population stabilization and a world composed of completely independent sovereign states are incompatible. Populations cannot be stabilized by agreement any more than levels of armament can be stabilized by agreement. And, as in the latter case, a world authority is needed which has the power of making, interpreting, and enforcing, within specified spheres, laws which are directly applicable to the individual. Indeed, population stabilization is one of the two major problems with which a world authority must necessarily concern itself.

Luther Evans, speaking to a meeting of the World Future Society, also expressed the need for world government:

The world can no longer afford the luxury of separate countries around the globe, no more than each country can any longer afford the luxury of nineteenth-century individualism in its midst.

Frank Snowden Hopkins, of the World Future Society, sees further restrictions on individual rights as being needed. Writing in *THE FUTURIST,* he had this to say:

Materialism seems to be an integral part of what Max Weber once described as the Protestant Ethic and the Spirit of Capitalism. John Locke, whose philosophic thought was a major influence on the American Constitution, saw freedom largely in terms of a man's right to enjoy property which he had accumulated by strenuous personal effort. It is encouraging to think that we may now be developing a far more humane system of ethical principles and be well on our way toward de-emphasizing property rights and taking a much broader view of how men can best live together in peace and happiness.

Nor are the futurists who see the need for centralized coercion at all bashful about denying the need for human rights, or even the legitimacy of those rights.

But if these futurists are right, then what is the future of "local action"? In a world of centralized strong governments, or especially a strong world government, there would be no scope at all for local action.

This is the critical issue. If survival of humanity does demand coercion, constraint and centralization, then local action is a myth. Those who propose it might just as well fold up their tents and go home. Therefore it is worth examining whether these futurists are correct. Do we really need coercion and constraint? Do we really need strong national government or a world government?

The Nature of the Problem

Let us look at the tragedy of the commons as it actually occurs in the world today, rather than in the abstract form of a fable about a village with a common pasture. There are many real-life illustrations of the tragedy which results when people are free to pursue their own interests in a commons. These include overfishing the oceans, polluting the air with factory smoke and the rivers and lakes with sewage and other wastes, and the deforestation of developing countries by people seeking firewood. Thus Hardin's fable has real-life counterparts. It is not just a cautionary tale. The world is full of examples to show that freedom in a commons does lead to tragedy.

As a practical example in the U.S., consider air pollution emitted by a factory. When the factory can simply dump its pollutants into the air, production costs are lower. The costs of pollution are simply passed on to the victims downwind. If the factory owner were to install pollution control equipment, the people downwind would be spared the costs of pollution. But manufacturing costs would be higher, and the factory owner would be unable to sell his products in competition with other factory owners who did not make the investment in pollution control equipment. It thus appears that Hardin's "mutual coercion" is required. None of the factory owners can afford to install pollution control equipment unless all are forced to do so. Then when all have to make the investment in pollution control, none has an economic advantage over the rest, and all are back to an equal basis in the market.

While the "mutual coercions" do seem to work, they limit freedom. And as is well known in economics, any limitation on freedom always causes a loss of efficiency. Consider the restrictions on automobile emissions. These restrictions have "killed" the big car. Each auto maker was forced to achieve a so-called Corporate Average Fuel Economy (CAFE) standard. Each auto maker tracked the sales of various sized cars, to determine whether it was achieving the standard or not. All the major auto makers deliberately manufactured fewer "big cars" during 1977 and 1978 than the public was willing to buy. There was much demagoguery to the effect that the CAFE standards would force the auto makers to be "socially responsible," and to quit making "gas-guzzlers." But the real victims were the car buyers. The makers didn't lose any sales. They simply sold a different mix from what the public really wanted.

Of course, there were many commentators, including some futurists, who asserted that the public really "shouldn't" want big cars, since they wasted fuel and caused pollution. But this is simply one more instance of those who think they know what's good for the rest of us imposing their values on us by government coercion.

Consider someone who feels he has adequate reason for wanting a big car. Suppose he is willing to make a tradeoff. He is willing to cut down on other polluting activities enough to offset the extra pollution from a big car. For instance, he might voluntarily use less electricity generated by his local coal-burning utility. If he were allowed to make this tradeoff, he would be better off (by his own values) and the rest of the people would be no worse off. To prevent him from making that tradeoff is to impose other people's values on him. To assert that he doesn't "need" a big car and therefore he shouldn't even want to make the tradeoff is sheer arrogance. And yet, this is precisely what happens to him under any system of "mutual coercions."

This program of inflexibility in "mutual coercions" is not the fault of stupid bureaucrats or power-hungry administrators. While these may make a bad situation even worse, the inflexibility is inherent in a system of rules. It is administratively impossible to set a pollution limit for each individual, and allow him to allocate that limit among his various activities, so as to produce his greatest degree of satisfaction. Instead of allowing the individual to budget his own pollution, the rules must budget it for him, allowing no more than specified amounts for each of his activities. It is necessary, from an administrative standpoint, to force everyone into the same mold, regardless of their individual needs and preferences.

Placing the rule-making process under democratic rather than bureaucratic control provides no solution either. Democratic voting to clean up, with the minority bound by majority vote, may simply let the majority pass some of its costs on to the unfortunate minority. This is likely to be accompanied by some demagoguery about why the minority "should" bear those costs. Democratic voting may result in an even worse situation. Legislators attempt to put together packages of issues which will attract a coalition amounting to at least a majority. Such a package often consists of programs each of which benefits a small minority at the expense of all the rest. The total cost to all may exceed the sum of the benefits to those who do benefit. There may not be even one individual who gains more out of the package than it costs him. But each party to the coalition sees that it receives something to offset part of the costs. If it fails to join the coalition, it receives no benefits at all but still bears its share of the costs. Thus a coalition is likely to be successful in implementing some unfortunate and inefficient package of pollution controls.

We can see then that mutual coercions don't really solve the problem either. They may impose excessive costs for the worth of the pollution reductions achieved. They may allow majorities to pass their costs on to unfortunate but outvoted minorities. And they provide no scope for local action and individual tradeoffs. Clearly, what is needed is a system which is self-enforcing, which provides incentives to reduce pollution by making the polluter pay, which makes the amount of payment equal to the damage done as perceived by the victim, and which channels payments directly to the victim.

Before trying to devise an environmental protection system which meets these criteria, let's look at the reason for the problem. The tragedy of the commons is indeed a prototype of the environmental problems we have today. Freedom in a commons does lead to tragedy. Thus it appears necessary to limit freedom by mutual coercion, imposed by a majority.

The proposed solution, however, really results from looking at the problem backwards. Those favoring mutual coercion argue that people's freedom to exploit the environment must be restricted. But what is the source of this alleged right to exploit the environment? To argue the existence of such a right is to deny any rights to the victims of that exploitation.

Let us look at an alternative to coercion in the commons. Let us consider again our villagers and their commons. Suppose the commons is divided up into individual pastures, and each pasture deeded to one villager. Each villager may then graze as many cows as he wishes on his own pasture. If he overgrazes his own pasture, he suffers but no one else does. If he finds that he has added too many cows and has driven his pasture beyond the point of diminishing returns, he is no longer caught in a social trap, since he receives all the gains and losses from his own actions. He can remove cows and gain the full benefits of his conservationist action.

Moreover, each villager will have an incentive to add cows only until the gain from an additional cow is equal to the losses from all cows on his pasture. At this point, he is receiving maximum production from his pasture. Since this will be true for all villagers, the total number of cows on the entire (former) commons will be precisely that number which maximizes production from the entire area. No coercion, mutual or otherwise, is needed to achieve this optimum condition. Self-interest alone is sufficient. Thus once again we see the advantages of freedom combined with individual rights, in this case the right to private property; when each individual seeks his own best interests, the well-being of society is also maximized, where that well-being is measured in terms of the values of the people making up the society.

This solution to the tragedy of the commons is not just a theory. In a region in northern Africa the Sahara Desert is growing southward. A combination of drought and overgrazing has completely killed all vegetation throughout most of the region. Most of the land was "unowned," and used by nomads for grazing. It was thus a commons. To make matters worse, foreign aid money was used to drill wells which were also "unowned," and free to all comers. This amplified the "commons" nature of the situation. The result was just what should have been expected: a tragedy of the commons, leading to complete destruction of the area and starvation for the people. However, there are some plots within the region which are privately held. Within these plots, grazing has been kept to a tolerable level, and the vegetation is not dying. Carl Sagan and others, writing in *Science*, note that "A simple wire fence is enough to keep out the desert."

Here is a perfect "textbook" case of how the right to private property can eliminate the tragedy of the commons, and allow the owners to use the land at a sustainable rate. The proper response is to learn from this textbook case, and expand the concept of private property. Then human freedom can be expanded in areas where it would otherwise lead to another tragedy of the commons.

Well, all right, it may be objected, you can divide up a commons into individual plots. You can put up fences and keep trespassers from grazing their cows on your pasture. But you can't fence in the air, nor the lakes and rivers. Air pollution is a collective problem, which must be solved on a collective basis. There can be no market solution to pollution of air because there is no market in which you can buy clean air regardless of what your neighbors do. Either everyone has clean air or no one does.

But the argument amounts to looking at the problem through the wrong end of the telescope. The problem is not that there is no market in which you can buy clean air. The problem is that there is no market in which you can sell the right to pollute your air. That sounds absurd, doesn't it? Who would want to sell the right to pollute the air he breathes? But wouldn't that be better than the present system, in which the right to pollute your air is taken without compensation?

Suppose we recognize each individual as having property rights in clean air. That is, we quit treating the atmosphere as a commons. Each individual would then be able to sell the right to pollute his air, but his air only, not anyone else's. Similarly, a would-be polluter could buy the right to pollute by compensating the victims, but he would have to compensate each victim.

Consider the owner of a factory who wishes to operate in such a manner that he pollutes the air over a residential tract. He would have to buy pollution rights from each and every owner of a plot of land in the tract. He would have to pay each owner an amount which the owner felt was fair and equitable recompense for putting up with the pollution. Such a system is self-enforcing, in the sense that an offended party could bring suit for the damages to him, without regard to whether he was more offended than others. The would-be polluter has an incentive to reduce the amount of pollution, until the costs of further reduction exceed the costs of payments to victims. The price of polluting is set just like the price of everything else in a free economy: by supply and demand. In this case, by the supply of pollutable air and the demand to pollute it. Thus payments are automatically equal to the value of the damage done, as perceived by the victim. Finally, the payments go directly to the victim, not to a bureaucracy.

Thus contrary to the suggestion of Frank Hopkins, quoted earlier, we need to protect the concept of private property rather than reduce or abolish it. To avoid the tragedy of the commons, we need to extend the concept of private property. We need to recognize each of us as having property rights in our environment, especially the air and water around us. We must demand that any would-be polluter pay us for the use of these rights, just as any other user of our property must pay us. We must treat pollution as trespass, just as we treat any other transgression of property rights as trespass.

It has to be asked, how did it come about that we now don't have property rights in our environment? Largely because no one recognized the scarcity of environmental "sinks," into which waste could be dumped for natural recycling or permanent storage. Historically, the pollution dumped into the rivers, oceans, and the air required only a small fraction of their capacity to recycle the wastes. These sinks were considered a "free good," a good so abundant in nature that it cannot command a price. No one needs to give up anything in order to get all he wants of it. The economists' classic example of a free good was the air itself. It was only when these sinks became overloaded that people recognized they were scarce. Like other scarce natural resources, people want more of them than the total available.

Since these sinks are no longer free goods, they should be treated like any other natural resource with economic value. A user of these sinks should pay for their use. But that is not all. The sinks should be used for those purposes which society values most.

But directing resources to the most highly valued use is just what a price system does. Would-be polluters will bid up the prices of the sinks, in response to the prices set for their products by supply and demand. Thus the sinks will be utilized for those purposes which consumers value most highly. Lower-valued uses will be unable to meet the costs of the sinks. The owners of the sinks will determine what it is worth to them to have their resources used, just as do the owners of other resources such as mines or favorably situated plots of land. That is, they economize on those resources which society values most, and make greater use of those resources which society values less. Moreover, the costs of pollution will be paid by the final consumers of the products. Since consumer demand is the reason the products were manufactured, it is proper that the consumers pay all costs of production, including clean-up costs.

The solution of vesting individuals with property rights in clear air and water, rights which are both transferable and enforceable just as are other property rights, is superior on all counts to coercion as a means of avoiding the tragedy of the commons. The "property rights" approach may be more difficult for the polluter to cope with than other schemes are, but we are not necessarily interested in making things easier for the polluter. We are interested in making things predictable for him, so he can make rational calculations about how much it is going to cost him to operate at the most efficient mix of cleaning up part of the pollution and buying rights to emit the rest. We are interested in making things as easy as possible for the victim of pollution, and the property rights solution puts him in direct control of his fate. It is the ultimate in "local action" approaches.

The tragedy of the commons is all too prevalent today. But it is an unnecessary tragedy. It can be avoided by admitting private property rights in the environment. These rights must include the right to have the air over one's property, and the water adjacent to it, free of any pollution not voluntarily accepted. These rights must also extend to the ownership of all kinds of resources, including those now owned by "everyone." When these resources become the private property of individuals who gain all the benefits and suffer all the losses associated with them, they will be properly cared for and no longer overexploited.

In the meantime, the fable of the tragedy of the commons serves an important purpose. It serves as a useful litmus test to distinguish between those who would abolish freedom to preserve the commons, and those who would abolish the commons to preserve and extend the freedom of every individual.

Editor's Note: This article by Joseph P. Martino proposes a solution to the problem dramatized in the famous essay by Garrett Hardin,

"The Tragedy of the Commons." The editors of the present volume leave to individual readers the task of forming their own judgments on the practicality of Martino's proposals, but since one of the editors, Frank Snowden Hopkins, is mentioned twice in the argument, he has requested that we append some comments embodying his personal reactions, as follows:

Comments on Martino's Proposal
by Frank Snowden Hopkins

Mr. Martino has written an interesting and stimulating article. I am not disturbed that he has taken issue with some comments of mine in *THE FUTURIST* some years back, but I do feel I should point out some respects in which I think the practicality of his approach is questionable. The essence of his idea seems to be that the way to avoid over-exploitation of publicly-owned entities like pure water, pure air, public grazing lands, and so on is not to coerce private industries into sound conservation practices by government action, but rather to expand the concept of private property in such a way that large public properties are divided into millions of privately-owned shares or rights. Then the would-be polluters or exploiters of public lands, lakes, rivers, estuaries, and bodies of air would purchase from private owners the rights to pollute or exploit. The injured parties would be compensated directly by those deriving benefit and causing damage, and government coercion would be eliminated or minimized.

I see some merit in Mr. Martino's proposals, and I think there are cases where they might work out in practice. Certainly private owners do have, as he points out, more incentive to conserve and protect property values than do individuals who are competing against each other to maximize each their own benefit from a "commons" which every one is free to exploit. And certainly there are problems when government bureaucracies try to work out equitable rules and regulations and to enforce them against private industries with resulting inequities both to the industries themselves and to the general public.

What worries me most is how to divide huge areas of common public property in any equitable manner among individuals, and then how to insure that millions of busy individuals, each owning a tiny share of something, could bargain effectively and throw any effective weight into the scales against important corporations or wealthy property owners. If millions of individuals owned Lake Erie, for example, how could they each bargain effectively with a Detroit or Cleveland industry dumping waste into that lake, making sure by the price they charged that the industry would find it worthwhile to invest its money in reducing pollution levels? If millions more individuals living in the Chicago area owned rights to the atmosphere over Chicago, how could they bargain effectively to get the smoke from smokestacks made less noxious? And if members of either group of owners of pure water or pure air claimed legal compensation for damage done them, how could they individually collect financial damages in the courts? Would not government agencies become just as involved in trying to defend the rights of small owners

74

of pure water or pure air as if they enforced coercive rules governing industrial processes from the beginning?

Moreover, how far would damage to individuals extend? Might not people living hundreds of miles away suffer pollution injuries—as for example, from acid rains in polluted air falling on their crops and pasture fields? And what about pesticides, of which DDT has been the most dramatic example, flowing into rivers and lakes and estuaries and even into the great ocean itself, destroying bird life and fish life and making food fish—such as the salmon in Lake Michigan—unsafe to eat? How can the people who suffer from such injuries properly bargain with the farmers and graziers who use noxious pesticides? Government regulation of pesticides and herbicides appears inevitable in the general welfare, even though it unquestionably takes some freedoms away from farmers and from manufacturers of chemicals.

And finally, I am concerned about situations in which enormous damage has already been done and can only be restored by vigorously coercive government action. I grew up many years ago in the Virginia-Maryland Chesapeake Bay country, and all my life I have followed the fortunes of commercial fishing and oystering in this largest of all American saltwater estuaries. The great Chesapeake Bay shad industry, which in my youth produced millions of pounds of shad annually, has dwindled to a tiny trickle, just a few thousand shad harvested each year. And the oyster grounds which once covered the bottoms of the bay and its tributaries for thousands of square miles were depleted and destroyed by the enterprise of thousands of oyster tongers, prating of their "God-given rights" to whatever the bay produced. The Maryland oysters, parts of the "commons" in that state, have almost entirely gone; some Virginia oysters were preserved longer by a practice of renting barren bottoms to commercial planters and denying them to ordinary tongers. But now chemical pollution in the James River seed beds has also hurt the private oyster planters, and the entire bay is suffering from oil spills, much of it caused by foreign tankers which wash out their storage tanks as they depart down the bay. And sewage pollution from municipalities and from tens of thousands of waterfront homes is a problem everywhere. Who will protect Chesapeake Bay unless government agencies have coercive power and exercise it? The "tragedy of the commons" has come to a sad climax in the Chesapeake, and only a long period of closing the "commons" to everyone, large and small, will make possible restoration of what was once our country's greatest single seafood storehouse.

Response to Hopkins's Comments
by Joseph P. Martino

The "private property" solution to problems of the environment is so radical in concept that many people reject it out of hand. Mr. Hopkins has not rejected it, but instead has raised some thoughtful questions. I am glad to have the opportunity to respond to them.

First, how do we go about dividing up property rights to lakes, etc., in an equitable fashion? Let's take the easy problems first. Each of us either owns or rents some property, on which we live. Let's start by recognizing that each of us has the right not to have the air over our property polluted. That is, let's start treating pollution as trespass on the land we now own or rent. The problems involved here are comparatively simple. Once we iron them out, we will be in a better position to decide what to do about the tougher problems.

Second, what should be the limits on allowable trespass from pollution? If I live 100 miles from a factory, and can detect its emissions only with the most sensitive of laboratory instruments, should I have the right to sue? There can be no answer which is *a priori* correct. But "we the people," acting through our legislatures, can settle the issue. We are all both polluters and victims. The lower the limits of detectability and liability, the better for us as victims, but the worse for us as polluters. Establishing the balance is a political problem, and should be settled through the political process. After all, that is how the present balance was reached, in which we have no rights as victims and full freedom as polluters. The same process can change the balance if we wish.

Third, the question of how a large number of individuals can bargain with the polluters has the question backwards. There is no need for the victims to bargain "collectively." Each victim is free to demand as much as he can get from the would-be polluter, or take the polluter to court. The proper question is, how can a would-be polluter bargain with each of several hundred or several thousand victims who own the property rights he wants to buy? Especially when each property owner wants to be the last "hold-out" and thereby gain as much as possible? My response is, that's the polluter's problem. In principle, it is no worse than the problem of the real estate developer who has to buy up many individual plots of land in order to assemble the area he needs for a new housing development or shopping mall. It is a tough but solvable problem. The private property solution places the problem in the lap of the polluter, not of the victim.

Fourth, Mr. Hopkins's example of Chesapeake Bay is a perfect illustration of the problem. At present, the Bay is a "commons." Each oyster tonger is free to take as many as he can. But suppose, instead, the states of Maryland and Virginia sold rights to specific plots of Bay bottom. The technology to survey and mark off plots of Bay bottom is already available. A tonger could be assured, under law, that the oysters on his plot were his and his alone to take. Trespass by others would be punishable just as it is on dry land. Each "owner" would then have the incentive to increase the growth of oysters on his plot by feeding them, by protecting them against disease, etc. Moreover, he would have the right to sue the polluters who are degrading the waters of the Bay, since they would be depriving him of rights he had purchased. Far from presenting insuperable problems, private property *is* the solution to the problems of the Chesapeake Bay.

The transition to a private property solution will present us with some new problems. However, the present system also presents us with problems, and we seem to have to resort to government coercion to cure them. Thus the problems of a private property solution are not an adequate reason for rejecting that solution. We should examine those problems to see whether they are easier or more difficult to solve than the problems we have in our present "commons." I think a fair comparison will show that we want to abandon the commons and adopt a private property solution.

Motivating People to Build a Better World

by

Thomas E. Jones

The Missing Ingredient

The energy crisis of 1973-74, rising prices of fossil fuels and raw materials, pollution problems, and regional food shortages have dramatized the perils inherent in unrestricted industrial and population growth on our small planet. Such growth has inadvertently spawned a world macroproblem, the threatened consequences of which underline the need to make further growth ecologically and societally sustainable by modifying its dangerous characteristics. Recent reforms, typified by increased energy conservation, have raised hopes of redirecting established growth policy so that it no longer mortgages the future to the present. Nevertheless, today's wasteful "linear economies" (Figure 1) and autonomous nation-states continue to assign top priority to the competitive short-term growth of income and power, thereby hastening encounters with limits to growth and exacerbating the inequitable distribution of the fruits of growth.

What poses the chief obstacle to national and international cooperation aimed at moving from relatively undifferentiated, excessively rapid economic growth to selective, sustainable growth in relatively "circular economies" that rely on recycling (Figure 1)? Several analysts have devised coherent descriptions of attractive sustainable societies aligned to human growth and to meeting basic human needs. Creation of such societies depends significantly on the adoption of fitting goals (e.g., circular economies), which in turn presupposes the revision of certain motivating cultural beliefs and values (e.g., the shift from maximizing GNP, and thereby assigning value to built-in obsolescence, to manufacturing long-lived quality goods). Specification of out-moded beliefs and values and of appropriate substitutes is a much easier task than detection of the means by which a revolutionary shift to the substitutes might be facilitated. Yet this shift is crucial for eliciting sufficient

Thomas E. Jones is an Adjunct Associate Professor at the Graduate School of Management, Polytechnic Institute of New York, Brooklyn, New York. A frequent writer on futurist topics, he holds doctorates in both philosophy and the social sciences.

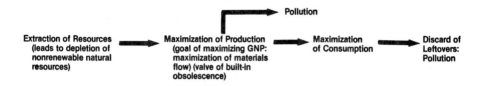

LINEAR ECONOMIES

Pollution

Extraction of Resources (leads to depletion of nonrenewable natural resources) → Maximization of Production (goal of maximizing GNP: maximization of materials flow) (valve of built-in obsolescence) → Maximization of Consumption → Discard of Leftovers: Pollution

CIRCULAR ECONOMIES

Pollution Minimized &Recycled If Feasible

Extraction of Resources (done efficiently to minimize loss) → Production of Quality Goods That Last and That Meet Basic Human Needs (efficient production to do "more with less" natural resources) (lower rate of the materials flow) → Consumption to Meet Basic Needs & Enhance the Quality of Life

Recycling of Leftovers, Providing Resources for New Production; Minimization of Pollution

FIGURE 1

motivation to negotiate the transition to sustainable societies. Hence no scenario could depict a feasible path to such societies without providing a plausible account of how the shift could be brought about. More generally, *the missing ingredient in today's recipes for sustainable societies is a detailed specification of efficacious, acceptable techniques for motivating individuals and institutions to cooperate intelligently in ways that would lead them to produce and accept the appropriate changes.*

Bridging the Motivational Chasm

How limited are the motivational resources for promoting the transition to sustainable societies? At present, such resources appear to be meager. Constraints on them have undermined the path to sustainable societies. However, these elastic human limits can be stretched, thereby expanding motivational resources in ways that are consistent with the other resources

79

and constraints that decision-makers face. The aim is to stretch them enough to span the motivational chasm that now prevents passage to sustainable societies.

Still, not all of the constraints on motivational resources should be removed. For instance, authoritarian attempts to manipulate people by coercive means are incompatible with the option-maximizing, pluralistic, humanistic character of the envisioned societies. Moreover, coercion is likely to be confronted by powerful rebellions, at least in the long run. Voluntary support can be buttressed by sanctions but not replaced by them.

Societal incentives and disincentives that now encourage harmful patterns of growth must be revised so that only beneficial patterns are rewarded and, where necessary, harmful patterns are penalized. However, this undertaking must not be allowed to drift into a program to implement B.F. Skinner's strategy for social reform, which is too oppressive to harmonize with values that structure the concept of a sustainable society. What about Garrett Hardin's suggestion that U.S. food assistance during famines be restricted to developing nations that have effective birth control programs? An attempt by a rich country to enact such Draconian measures would provoke outrage and would probably backfire.

Thus the objective is to motivate the transition to sustainable societies by means that are primarily non-coercive. What is needed to illuminate methods of securing voluntary support is a comparative examination of a variety of cases in which major shifts in collective motivation occurred rapidly. Though the kind of motivational change required to reach sustainable societies is unique in certain respects, an examination of cases that are somewhat similar can still prove to be instructive. Admittedly, even the representative cases appear to lack a single set of common elements. Yet examination of their imprecise "family resemblances" yields insight into the dynamics of large-scale shifts in motivation.

From my survey of a number of instances of major motivational changes, I have sought to detect those characteristics that might conjointly evoke sufficient motivation to pave the road to sustainable societies. Thus I have constructed a model of a general pattern of change that seems quite germane to the situation today. My interdisciplinary analysis focuses primarily on instances drawn from the past forty years, but also touches on several historical instances. It employs data and theories selected from various social sciences, though primarily from historical sociology (comparative structural-processual analysis of revolutionary societal and civilizational change), social psychology (attitude change), and psychology (motivation, cognition). The aim is to present a responsible analysis that will lay a foundation for thorough, comprehensive ongoing analyses. The conclusions are tentative but, I believe, plausible enough to stimulate further investigation and to suggest appropriate guidelines for decision-makers in various societal spheres.

A Crucial Type of Transformed Perception

In a Nutshell: My preliminary survey of instances of rapid motivational change has concentrated on situations in which individuals and groups pursuing diverse goals suddenly joined in common efforts to attain collective goals. The situations include: the Manhattan Project, Project Apollo, national unity in England during World War II, the European Economic Community (with special attention to the work of Jean Monnet in promoting a spirit of Western European cooperation), the Marshall Plan, Japan's recovery after World War II, Gandhi's success in securing the national independence of India, Martin Luther King's contribution to the civil rights movement, and the ecology movement in the U.S. during the late 1960s and early 1970s. The survey suggests that *one type of shared perceptual change tends to be most conducive to the rapid arousal of sufficient motivation to meet major group or societal challenges. The individuals and groups involved reinterpret the situation as having become one in which they can avoid or overcome mutual disaster and attain mutually beneficial goals only by intelligent cooperation.* Consequently, relatively uncoordinated actions aimed at satisfying the conflicting self-interests of many parties are typically replaced by collective actions oriented toward common goals. Thus the requisite motivation and appropriate changes in beliefs and values spring from the transformed future-oriented perception of the situation and of one's role.

Motivational Power of "Conditional Deliverance" Images: This sudden shift in perception and motivation usually springs from the occurrence of a threatening crisis and the graphic, believable depiction of two contrasting types of posssible future:

● Likely collective disaster if current patterns of divisive behavior persist.

● Deliverance from disaster and to a desirable future, but only if the participants in the situation cooperate to make an appropriate response to the crisis.

History and the social sciences testify to the effectiveness of presenting images of conditional deliverance, as well as to the failure of such "repent-or-perish" warnings when they go unheeded (as in Cassandra's case) or are unrealistic. In *The Image of the Future*, Frederick Polak supplies numerous examples of the impact that positive and negative images of the future have exerted on the development of Western societies. Wendell Bell and James A. Mau call attention to the importance of the future in the creation of new nation-states. Experiments conducted by such psychologists as Elliot Aronson furnish additional evidence that people tend to fulfill their expectations. Harold Lasswell has centered attention on the importance of "developmental constructs" that express expectations. And Elise Boulding, like her husband Kenneth, stresses the influence of accepted images of the future on the subsequent course of events.

The most effective motivation appears to be mediated by images of disaster and deliverance operating in tandem, with emphasis placed on the latter. Crises and the danger of disaster can arouse success-oriented people to act constructively, as in the successful "challenge-response" pattern analyzed by Arnold Toynbee. The major reason for mobilizing the Manhattan project was concern that Hitler alone might develop the atomic bomb. Similarly, the cooperative heroism of British citizens during World War II arose as a constructive response to Hitler's onslaughts.

Images of catastrophe, intended to become self-negating, can become self-fulfilling when unaccompanied by an image of an attainable attractive alternative to impending disaster. If the only thing provisional about the future is the degree of catastrophe, people may experience a loss of nerve and overlook opportunities for constructive responses. From the viewpoint of psychology, anxiety about undesirable outcomes produces "fear-of-failure" motivation, which can paralyze action or result in either obsession with escapist strategies or non-constructive anger. Conversely, positive expectations induce constructive, reward-oriented "need-achievement motivation," which is more likely to lead people to attain their goals than fear-of-failure motivation. An achievement-motivated person realistically aims at goals of intermediate difficulty and relies on a constant stream of feedback to improve performance. Conversely, a person who fears failure tends to attempt tasks that are too easy (so that failure is quite unlikely) or too difficult (so that failure can be rationalized).

To stress the importance of presenting a desirable alternative future, I have coined the term "conditional deliverance" to replace the more negative "provisional catastrophism." A realistic image of rewarding deliverance tends to possess "the power of an idea whose time has come."

The conditional deliverance mode of forecasting is prone to oversimplification, for often many possible futures lie between the two extremes of catastrophe and near-utopian deliverance. Moreover, the self-fulfilling propensity of action-oriented forecasts of deliverance encourages exaggerated estimates of likelihood, as does the self-negating propensity of disaster ("crying 'Wolf!' when there is no wolf"). If the prospect of deliverance looks attainable, it will tend to evoke policies directed toward actualizing it. Likewise, unless the danger appears real, it may be ignored. Believable exaggerations of both the likelihood and desirability of positive and negative futures are sometimes more suitable for mobilizing people to work together for drastic change than are accurate estimates. But action based on faulty information can easily generate counterproductive results. Fortunately, forecasts of conditional deliverance need not recognize only two extreme alternative futures or engage in exaggerations of likelihood and desirability in order to induce marked shifts toward cooperation to escape undesirable futures and achieve desirable ones. An example is the formation and growth of the European Economic Community.

The human species appears to be moving into a conditional deliverance type of global situation, though the alternative futures can by no means be reduced to the extremes of utopia or oblivion. Generally speaking, the need for cooperation to avoid distinctly undesirable outcomes and attain desirable ones seems to be increasing on both the global and regional levels. While oversimplified, excessively negative forecasts have recently provoked adverse responses, the opportunity exists for using credible conditional deliverance forecasts to promote changes in perception and motivation conducive to the creation of sustainable societies.

Reconceptualization of Self-Interest: As illustrated by the mottos "United we stand; divided we fall" and "We hang together or hang separately," conditional deliverance from disaster is perceived as dependent upon increased cooperation. The common interests that unite the participants in a disaster-prone situation need to be reinterpreted as more important than their narrow, short-term divisive interests. Thus self-interest can be broadened to embrace more people and lengthened to encompass the relevant future. Accordingly, individuals and groups become more willing to defer gratification and, where necessary, to sacrifice what they previously viewed as self-interest. To a considerable extent, actions motivated by such reconceptualized self-interest overlap cooperative actions inspired by a desire to promote human well-being.

Since the tendency to act from self-interest is so strong and frequently causes difficulties that give rise to a conditional-deliverance situation, the broadening and lengthening of self-interest provides an especially potent force for deliverance from such a situation. Taking into account the interrelations of the world system and of its subsystems, much of what individuals and groups still view as legitimate self-interest is misconstrued. This is particularly evident in the multifaceted "tragedy of the commons," which can be triggered by such diverse activities as pollution generation, farming, and natural resource extraction. A "commons" is a situation in which a group shares an environment from which benefits are extracted by its members, each of whom is allowed to keep all he extracts. For instance, when each herdsman in a publicly owned pastureland keeps adding animals to his own herd for his temporary benefit, the pasture eventually becomes overgrazed to the detriment of all. Garrett Hardin graphically depicts the structure of such situations as the tragedy of the commons, which arises from the irresponsible, unrestrained private use of a publicly owned resource. Even if such use—or rather, abuse—of the commons can be justified when production, consumption, and population density are low, it cannot be when they have become high.

More and more in our increasingly interpenetrating, interlinked, technologically changed, perceptually shrinking world, short-term self-interest appears to be intertwined with longer-term communal interest. This means that the beneficial consequences of increased cooperation would be substantial, perhaps even enormous. Instead of continuing to be dominated by the "zero sum game" mentality according to which some groups or nations must be losers when others are winners, leaders and other citizens could profitably explore the possibility of making synergistic exchange agreements as part of a "planetary bargain."

For instance, a number of influential voices in the industrialized world are calling for what amounts to a global fairness revolution. Among them are Harlan Cleveland of the Aspen Institute, Lester Brown of the Worldwatch Institute, Richard Falk of the Institute for World Order, and Willis Harman of SRI International, as well as Wassily Leontief, who conducted a project for the United Nations, and Jan Tinbergen, who coordinated one for the Club of Rome. These analysts stress the importance of meeting the basic human needs—food, clothing, shelter, medical care, and so on—of all people in abject poverty. A probable by-product of the successful implementation of this strategy would be major reductions in birth rates. Such reductions have already occurred in the People's Republic of China and other developing nations that have combined family planning with progress toward providing minimum living standards for all of their citizens. Other by-products would be the progressive elimination of a major cause of hostility between developing and developed countries and the creation of new markets to buy products from developed countries.

Intensification of Fellow-Feeling: People motivated merely by reconceptualized self-interest may be quite unwilling to sacrifice for future generations or for starving peasants in a populous, resource-poor developing country. Situations can be found in which such people could probably advance their perceived self-interest, even in the long run, by engaging in forms of exploitation that seem likely to go undetected or at least unpunished.

Fortunately, the transformed perception that characterizes conditional deliverance efforts also encourages "affiliation motivation." Instead of making calculated self-interest the criterion for all action, people motivated by fellow-feeling seek to enhance the well-being of others. Their feelings of affiliation often extend to destitute citizens of poor countries and to future generations. In short, they may identify their own well-being not only with that of their friends, but also with that of the entire ongoing human species. Hence affiliation motivation is an appropriate type of motivation for bringing about a more equitable distribution of the world's wealth and for accepting the sacrifices inherent in effective long-range planning aimed at creating sustainable societies.

Clearly, affiliation motivation is especially conducive to acceptance of deferred gratification and to altruism. Unlike calculated self-interest, love is not a mathematician. The question of whether such fellow-feeling is really a form of extended self-interest is largely semantic. Interestingly, the "self-actualized" people studied by Abraham Maslow transcend "deficiency motivation" and tend to be quite other-oriented. Self-actualization is generally enhanced by constructive commitment to the well-being of a collectivity.

People who are motivated to alleviate human suffering tend to experience the subjective reward of being integral parts of a meaningful whole, rather than being alienated from others by the competitive pursuit of self-interest. Such people experience corresponding changes in their self-images.

Furthermore, affiliation motivation may prompt acts of heroism. "Heroic motivation" differs from "need-achievement motivation." Instead of selecting goals of medium difficulty and being dependent on frequent rewards as indications of success, a person who is heroically motivated may even delight in difficult challenge-response situations that offer minimal objective rewards. Such motivation, coupled with the individual's ability to work for the benefit of groups and with the desire for national prestige, helps to explain the extremely high economic growth rates since World War II in Japan, a country lacking most of the factors typically associated with rapid growth. Likewise, the heroic motivation of the ancient Greeks issued in a tremendous outpouring of creative energy to produce something "immortal" in an ephemeral, imperfect world. The Renaissance was also powered by heroic motivation, as expressed by Michaelangelo's statue of David.

If the human species today would become aware of the internal payoffs of heroic motivation, a reinterpretation of the human place in the world could result. Then human beings might be able to summon the courage to pursue diligently the difficult but challenging goal of creating sustainable societies.

Affiliation motivation also encourages distinctly moral motivation. A person ought to do what is right because it is right, acting from proper motives and correct reasons that can be relied upon to lead him to do his duty. Such motives include empathy and compassion as well as reverence for the moral law. A moral person is willing to accept in advance impartial principles for resolving disputes in which his interests conflict with those of other people. Thus he is willing to do his duty even if it is unlikely to benefit him. By becoming responsible members of the ongoing global system, human beings can both become valuable "moral resources" and make their lives more meaningful.

People can make their lives more meaningful by choosing to be responsible members of the global system. As such, they are valuable "moral resources."

Despite the worth and importance of strictly moral motivation, one can hardly expect it to bridge the motivational chasm by itself. Hence it must be linked with various forms of "nonmoral," as distinguished from "immoral," motivation. For instance, even a person acting from reconceptualized self-interest will often perform his objective duty because doing so promotes his broadened self-interest. Both from the viewpoint of moral motivation and from that of reconceptualized self-interest, duty and genuine self-interest coincide more extensively than is generally acknowledged.

To summarize, affiliation motivation is extremely useful for coping with problems that call for cooperative remedial efforts. It also nourishes other sorts of useful motivation, including moral, heroic, need achievement, and power motivation.

Revision of Recognized Payoffs: Societal rewards and punishments play crucial roles in sustaining entrenched habits and in promoting the adoption of new ones. Despite recent commendable reforms, some types of growth that have far-reaching, long-range deleterious consequences are still excessively rewarded. Some of the more beneficial types tend to be inadequately reinforced by the rewards of income, power, and status. For instance, a well-intentioned businessman may be unable to avoid bankruptcy if he invests in expensive pollution-control technology that his competitors need not adopt.

Unless the objective payoffs were appropriately revised, many of the needed changes that would result from initial societal acceptance of a conditional deliverance outlook would not be sustained. Fortunately, the transformed perception would help promote corresponding changes in recognized societal incentives and punishments. To encourage goal-oriented behavior rather than fear-of-failure behavior, emphasis would be placed on rewarding desirable sorts of behavior. However, negative sanctions would still be necessary.

Strategy for Motivating Intelligent Cooperation: Just as neither re-conceptualized self-interest nor affiliation motivation by itself seems capable of supplying sufficient motivation to create sustainable societies, so revision of recognized payoffs appears inadequate when considered alone. The same is true of heroic motivation and moral motivation. However, their synergistic combination as an expression of the transformed perception of conditional deliverance movement might well bridge the motivational chasm.

The educational process and the mass media reinforced by group discussion would be employed to encourage widespread acceptance of the transformed perception. Their images of threatened disaster and conditional deliverance should rest on sound analysis and be projected responsibly. Appropriate perceptual change could be facilitated by the open, non-manipulative use of such techniques for attitude change as cognitive dissonance theory, which claims that attitudes can often be changed by exposing people to information that is inconsistent with their beliefs and then by encouraging them to act in accordance with their revised beliefs.

To secure voluntary support and implement reforms that prove to be rewarding for people generally, societies must encourage extensive public participation in making the transition to sustainable societies. Yet the importance of perceptive, respected leadership to encourage the change in perception and to implement appropriate reforms in ways that are both effective and not excessively traumatic can hardly be overestimated. Efforts should be made to provide every individual and group with a meaningful role in the transition. The perceptual transformation may begin with a small "carrier group" and then spread throughout society, or it may be experienced and disseminated by several societal leaders at the outset.

Indeed, the pioneering effort undertaken in this study needs to be subjected to the closest scrutiny. Some aspects of the present analysis might need to be revised. Yet today's decision-makers might well gain from it a better understanding of the motivating role that conditional deliverance images of the future could play in the transition to sustainable societies. Moreover, acquaintance with the various kinds of motivation that can be aroused to support cooperative efforts could prove quite useful to decision-makers.

Evidence supports the claim that only by working together could human beings avert unprecedented suffering and successfully make the transition to rewarding sustainable societies. This kind of cooperative orientation typically arises only *after* a crisis has come about. The subtle danger of problems generated by unrestricted growth is that they may not be perceived as constituting a crisis demanding unprecedented cooperation until after catastrophe could no longer be averted. Will human beings anticipate the consequences of unsustainable growth and the worth of sustainable societies vividly enough to mobilize effective programs *before* these problems become unmanageable? This is the crucial question that we must help to answer.

Inventorying
Our Resources

International Resources

by

B.B. Goldner

Economic resources are found in every nation in the world. How these resources are utilized and exploited often determines the economic development of each nation. The interactions of these resources truly make our world a global entity.

Here are some objectives for the development of international resources, together with examples of cases and situations that illustrate effective maximization of resource development.

1. Mutual Dependence and Benefits

The Peruvian anchovy *Engraulis ringins* offers a remarkable instance of worldwide benefits and non-benefits that can arise from a local situation. The anchovy is manufactured into a fish meal that is 60% protein by volume and enters international trade as relatively inexpensive feed supplement for cattle, hogs, and poultry. When anchovy meal is available, more expensive feed supplements—soybeans and other grains—do not have to be used in the production of meat and other animal products.

Our modern saga of *Engraulis ringins* starts about 1972, when it thrived with all its cousins along the Pacific coastline of Peru. Ironically, warm currents interfere with anchovy reproduction and these warm currents returned in 1972. As a result, the anchovy catch plummeted in 1972, and the following waves of events crashed upon many shores:

● Peru's entire fishing industry went bankrupt and was nationalized. It lost up to 40% of its foreign exchange credits.

● Some nations like Canada, Norway, and Sweden started to use food fish for fish meal, depleting herring schools and reducing availability of cheap fish protein for human consumption.

● World prices of soybeans and grains started to rise rapidly. In the United States, West Germany, and Holland, livestock producers had to buy these feed supplements in larger quantities, thereby forcing prices still higher for both grains and meat.

● Wheat prices soared because other grains were in short supply.

● Russia found itself paying higher grain prices as the world market churned.

B.B. Goldner is Professor of Management at La Salle College in Philadelphia.

Whether the anchovy industry becomes profitable again and how the world will benefit depends on *Engraulis ringins*. Further studies are recommended for case analysis in this area. Can recent scientific knowledge be shared so that similar shortages are predicted and prevented? Can more trash fish (not considered edible and too bony) be ground into fish meal and used as both animal and food supplements? Can more liberal credits be extended to nations like Peru to encourage the resurgence of the fishing industry? It is to our mutual benefit if we all share our resources.

2. Generate More Jobs

Our seminal case here can be entitled Netherlands Natural Gas or The Dutch Treat. It all started in 1959 with the discovery of seemingly unlimited reserves of natural gas in the Dutch province of Groningen and in the North Sea. These gas revenues mounted rapidly, and Holland amassed a huge surplus in its international balance of payments ledger. This helped the guilder become a very solid and respected currency on international money markets. The Dutch people enjoyed high incomes with advanced living standards. Roads were built, the nationalized rail system was extended and improved, schools and hospitals were given subsidies. These were the result of political decisions designed to grant the most generous social benefits in history to a deserving populace. So what is the problem? "The politicians mortgaged our future by using the gas money for the simplest, most popular social programs," says a prominent Dutch banker. "If only a bit more of the money had been given to private industry, we would have much fewer problems." The word "given" in a banker's jargon implies tax credits for investments in job-producing plant and equipment, some long-term loans or grants to key industries, and special concessions to encourage the growth of small businesses. The wise use of the natural resources, teamed with capital and entrepreneurship, would create jobs and economic growth. While the people have been enjoying life in the gas bubble, many professors, economists, and business people, as well as the bankers, fear it will explode as the unnoticed pressure builds. Another Dutch banker recently estimated that the government's use of the oil monies for social benefits has cost about 300,000 jobs since 1970. The money has been called a curse in disguise because the present affluence will generate long-run economic weaknesses. Already unemployment is rising and little capital investments are being made by large companies. Businessmen see fewer and fewer jobs being created, politicians are fearful for the stability of their government, and economists predict little or no growth for the near future. Fortunately, the gas and its revenues are expected to last into the twenty-first century. Perhaps it will be used more effectively to create more jobs and benefits.

Jobs are usually generated by investment. When management is poor or not competitive, jobs disappear as the enterprise goes out of business. As another example, let us look at Japanese investment in the United States which has produced good results. As of March 1978, Japanese direct investment in the United States aggregates close to $5 billion and in recent years has been concentrated more in the manufacturing areas. Our case is Quasar, formerly Motorola, now owned and managed by Matsushita of Japan whose well-known trade name in the United States is Panasonic. Here the teacher, the vaunted United States, is being taught by the student, Japan, and in the process, jobs are saved and more created.

In 1974, Motorola was failing for many reasons: top management was making wrong decisions resulting in no profits, excess water had to be squeezed out of too many layers of management, manufacturing productivity was low, quality control almost non-existent, equipment was old and obsolete, and public acceptance of the product was practically nil because of the poor quality and after-the-sale service.

Matsushita management carefully analyzed its new purchase. It sent over Japanese managers who recruited (probably pirated) effective American managers from the electronics industry, and fired many existing personnel. Matsushita invested heavily in new equipment and redesigned the television sets so they could be made on the more automatic equipment. The new management trained the workers to be more conscious of productivity and quality. The managers involved everyone in the decision-making process, and even introduced the Japanese custom of having each worker clean his own workplace.

Matsushita, and other Japanese companies like YKK, the largest zipper manufacturer in the world, have committed themselves to long-run investments in the United States and other countries. They also are willing to wait a reasonable time for returns on their investments. Each Japanese company has patiently tried to inculcate into its American workers the Japanese business values of strong company loyalty, close identification with the company's objectives, personal pride in quality work, and a desire to be more productive. In 1978, Matsushita has a larger share of the market than ever before, and its patience and painstaking care and persistence have paid off in profits.

Of course, some jobs were lost and others destroyed, but much more was created than destroyed. More jobs are being generated each day.

3. Teach and Share Knowledge

World organizations like the United Nations are working constantly with member nations in the areas of technical cooperation and sharing of knowledge. Perhaps it was best stated recently when it was emphasized that the exchange of technical skills should be *among* all nations and not merely a north (industrialized) to south (mostly agrarian and non-industrialized) flow of information and monies. The UN is encouraging member nations to provide financial mechanisms to develop resources of all types in the so-called underdeveloped countries. They are arranging for the transfer of technological expertise to these poorer nations and establishing a technological information network to "at least get everyone thinking about and implementing these ideas."

Since food production is a fundamental concern, it is significant that 114 nations in December 1977 established IFAD—the International Fund for Agricultural Development—with a budget of $1 billion dollars.

This Fund grew out of recommendations made at the World Food Conference in Rome in November 1974. Its primary purpose is to help the poorest nations produce more food in the next 3 years.

Here are some recent developments:

Mariculture or farming the sea has been done in the Orient for centuries. In fact, the Chinese introduced the highest form of ecological cooperation about 1,000 years ago when they placed six different species of carp in the same pond, with each feeding on different foods. Oysters have been raised with nutrients in the United States and Japan in sheltered areas and safe from predators, which resulted in a harvest of 6,400 tons of oysters per kilometer of float. Mussel farming can net an astounding 27,000 tons per kilometer of float. In the United States, salmon eggs are raised until migrating age, then released to the sea. They return 2 to 4 years later, having fed themselves, and are harvested. Mullet and milkfish are good food fish. When ponds are fertilized with sewage in Taiwan, the yield is an incredible 1,300 tons per square mile. It is estimated that needful-Asia has about 140,000 square miles suitable for fish farming. Using the Taiwanese technique, this could yield more than the total catch today from all the oceans of the world.

Aquaculture is farming in any water, not just the oceans. It is estimated that the world has about 1 billion acres of coastal wetlands now going to waste! For comparison, there are about 8 billion acres of land used for agriculture—about half for grazing only. If we could farm the 1 billion acres by introducing food fish with very little capital investment and minimum labor, it is possible to produce close to an unbelievable one billion tons of food, very cheap and high in protein. But it will require effort, teaching, and the ever-necessary *follow-up.*

Other areas for further investigation include: (1) drip irrigation techniques as practiced in Israel; (2) growing rice in salty and brackish water which is being started on the Gulf Coast of the United States; (3) growing the "green revolution" rice all over the world and learning from the Philippines experiences; (4) growing weeds in Africa which are high in cellulose that can be raw material for non-woven fabrics; (5) engaging in hydroponics all over the world, since it is now commercially feasible as proved by General Electric and General Mills; (6) planting trees in huge quantities to reclaim deserts as in Algeria and Israel; and finally (7) the ambitious project of creating a sea in the Sahara Desert.

With teaching and sharing knowledge, all this could happen by the end of this century.

We must create a *cooperatively competitive attitude* throughout the world. We have to interchange or even barter natural resources to help each other. We can use the automobile as our first example. A typical intermediate-size car contains (among others) the following materials (as of 1977).:

High-strength steel—125-130 pounds
Aluminum—97-100 pounds

Plastics—168-175 pounds
Rubber—150 pounds

Most of the high-grade iron ore from which steel is made has been depleted in the United States, which now imports most of its ore from Canada and Latin America. Aluminum is initially made from bauxite (ore) and the United States imports 90% from Jamaica and Guyana. Alumina is refined from the bauxite and we import alumina from Jamaica and Australia. Aluminum ingots are cast from the alumina and the United States is a net importer of ingots, getting 81% from Canada and 14% from Ghana. We can understand the need for cooperation as we note this cycle and situation and recognize that the United States may need increasing amounts of aluminum for its automobile industry, because car manufacturers are mandated to reduce weight and improve fuel consumption in all United States-made cars and imports by the early 1980s. At this point, General Motors and Ford are shifting to all-aluminum bumpers (instead of chrome, which is 100% imported) to reduce weight. And aluminum will be used in engines and other parts of the automobile.

If we turn now to plastics, we note they are made from petroleum and natural gas. It is clear that problems and complications will form in this area, and creatively seeking substitute sources will become imperative. Natural rubber is used very sparingly in tires and other rubber parts and we can secure all we need from Malaysia and Liberia (since rubber trees only grow in arboretums in the United States). Synthetic rubber is used where the tire hits the road, and it is also derived from petroleum and natural gas, compounding the problem areas. As an interesting addendum to this section, automobiles consumed 31% of all petroleum products in 1975 and the percentage is probably higher now.

An interesting phenomenon in this area, which has evolved from the dollar's decline, is that the United States has recently become a low-cost production area. The capital resource now becomes the overriding factor, and competition shifts thinking into another gear. European and Japanese manufacturers are now assembling cars (and various other items like television sets, zippers, and soy sauce) in the United States for the United States market. Workers, managers, stockholders in the domestic companies which supply these "invaders" will benefit. In the case of automobiles, like the Volkswagen Rabbit plant in Pennsylvania, this includes original equipment manufacturers.

Every nation and company is becoming more conscious of competition. In Communist Russia, its managers, who were almost always trained as engineers, are now being sent back to graduate school to learn Western management techniques, the Human Resources Model, and to be more responsive to the consumer, who is a customer even in Russia. Another Russian example which exemplifies cooperative competition and West-to-East technology transfer is the Kama River Truck plant, 600 miles east of Moscow in the Tatar Republic. It was planned in the 1960s, assembled its first truck in 1976, will reach full capacity of 150,000 trucks a year in 1982—and is already outdated by Western standards. It is a perfect example of cooperation and coordination of resources and political detente, and it showcases what can be done with $5.4 billion dollars, Western know-how, Russian muscle and goodwill, and generous credit.

In the United States, a giant is lately learning to be competitive: American Telephone and Telegraph, a form of legal monopoly, is being prodded by some court decisions, into learning and re-learning a basic functional area—marketing. AT&T now is hard-selling services and equipment, and has become much more competitively customer-conscious. It seem ironic that AT&T, the darling of conservative investors, and Mother Russia, seemingly adhering to Marxian ideology, should follow the same marketing mandate.

Lastly, *we must create really new ventures and products.* An excellent example is Exxon Enterprises. About 10 years ago, Exxon decided to reach far out and explore the peripheries of human knowledge for its future growth. It settled on three areas: energy, replacing basic materials, and information-processing. At a time when venture capital investments are avoided by most companies, Exxon has intensified its efforts into exploring the unknown. It has become the protector of the entrepreneur, who it sees as an endangered species. It has encouraged all its people, management and rank and file, to be creative and not fearful of being smothered in negatives and red tape. In short, it has become wholly supportive of imaginative roaming in search of a future profit. It had to enhance its economic well-being but avoid any anti-trust litigation, hence the thrust into non-energy fields. It is investing in high-risk start-up situations for the dollar of the future. Let's examine one of these Exxon enterprises.

Zilog is Exxon's microcomputer company. It not only makes micro-computers and chips and boards, but also offers software and educates customers. The author saw the first modern computer, ENIAC, at the Moore School of Electrical Engineering at the University of Pennsylvania in 1946. It was a monster even then: It took up the equivalent space of a good part of an air-conditioned football field with its 18,000 vacuum tubes; weighed about 30 tons; and the wiring was brain-shattering. This was the child of Eckert and Mauchly which launched the computer age and is now an authentic relic living out its existence at the Smithsonian. It cost $500,000 of 1946 dollars. It seems difficult to comprehend this, but Zilog's microcomputer uses a one-quarter inch silicon circuit wafer which is 20 times more powerful in its computations than ENIAC, and it costs a 1978 ten-dollar bill. Now what can Zilog's microcomputers do? We can just begin to challenge their capabilities with the following: controlling traffic in the air, on rails, and on the road; controlling auto-mobile carburetors to reduce fuel consumption; controlling hotel and airline reservations; controlling inventories; controlling microwave ovens; letting people enjoy TV games and electronic toys when they are fortunate enough to buy one. There may be 100 million microcomputers working in the world of 1985.

Forecasts for the Future

The nations of the world will have to engage in serious *Resource Recovery Programs*. Some countries will follow the lead of Holland and recover land from the sea. Since our earth is almost 10% desert, we will need to learn about the aggressive reclamation of desert land by Russia, Israel, and several African nations. We will pursue desalinization more relentlessly and economically derive precious fresh water from oceans. We will use solar energy for irrigation as practiced in the southwestern United States. A very promising area, reported recently by the U.S. Department of Commerce, is the production of fuel from refuse and garbage. The technology is proven and well established— we now can do it competitively and with economically viable programs. From formerly discarded refuse, sewage, and garbage, we are not only producing usable fuel and methane gas, but also valuable compost for farm and urban gardens and nutritious animal feed. In a similar direction, the sale of scrap waste materials amounted to $9.6 billion dollars in the United States in 1976. This included recovering 60% of the steel used and recycling that steel along with very large amounts of scarce tin, strategic aluminum, and ever-necessary glass.

We all have to become futurists in our thinking about resources. Each "mover and shaker" in the world must acquire certain habits of attitude and thinking. Every he and she must be positive, practical, and creative with a global concern for people. The following *"Characteristics of a Futurist"* complement the entrepreneurial and creative thinking spirits, as you note the golden thread of optimism running through all their thinking (this is an abbreviated version of a summary created by the World Future Society in its study "An Introduction to the Study of the Future" for the National Science Foundation):

a. Openness to Experience ... appear to be remarkably open to all types of ideas; in fact, they seem to be constantly searching for new information about the world and are never so happy as when they have found a genuinely exciting idea ...

b. Global Perspective ... They all seem to think in global rather than national terms ...

c. Long-Term Time-Perspective ...

d. Ecological Orientation ...

e. Broad Concern for Humanity ...

f. Rationality ... Though open to experience, futurists quickly reject notions that lack an adequate scientific or rational basis ...

g. Pragmatism ... As a group, the futurists seem to be primarily interested in what will "work" ... The test of effectiveness is not any ideology of left or right—but good data and methods, genuine concern about people, and realistic assessments ...

h. Reality of Choice ... deeply conscious of the freedom of individuals to make decisions that will have tremendous consequences for good or ill ...

i. Interest in Values ... The criteria by which one decides what to choose.

j. Optimism ... generally seem to believe that mankind will survive and perhaps prosper in the years ahead ...

k. Sense of Purpose ... They seem to feel that what they are doing is important and will help to create a better world.

Our final thought is a Prayer for the World with special emphasis on human resources:

WE BELIEVE IN TOMORROW. We believe that we have the power to make tomorrow different from today. We believe that poverty need not be permanent and that men need not learn war forever. We believe in man despite all that we know about him. We believe that there can yet be a time of peace, a time of justice, a time of brotherhood, and a time of tranquility for all who live on earth. We believe that we can have a share in bringing that day closer by the way in which we live all through the year. The world may smile at our dreams—but no matter, we still believe.

The above prayer can epitomize the world of the future if we bring all our resources together for the betterment of the world in which all mankind lives.

Looking at Resource Trends Through a Population Lens

by

Lester R. Brown

As of early 1980, there are some 4.3 billion people in the world. Our numbers are increasing by some 70 million per year or 192,000 per day. Although the rate of world population growth has begun to slow, the reported year-to-year additions continue to increase. On a finite globe, population growth cannot continue indefinitely. What is not agreed upon is the level at which population growth will finally stabilize.

The official U.N. medium-level population projections, which are widely used for planning purposes throughout the world, show population expanding to some 21 billion before eventually stabilizing a century or more hence. These population projections are the product of two sets of assumptions—one explicit and one implicit. The explicit assumptions are demographic in nature. They include country-by-country assumptions about future fertility levels, sex ratios, life expectancies, and numerous other demographic variables. If these explicit assumptions hold, then the projected increases in world population will materialize.

But population growth does not occur in a vacuum. Current projections of world population are based on the implicit assumption that the basic energy, food, and other natural resources required to support human life are going to be as available in the future as they have been in the past. They assume that the production of the major biological systems—fisheries, forests, grasslands, and croplands—that satisfy basic human needs for food, shelter, and clothing will continue to expand along with population.

Human population growth is also closely tied to the earth's energy resources. The great postwar growth in food production that sustained the massive increase in world population depended heavily on the abundance of cheap energy, particularly oil. Recent changes in oil production

Lester R. Brown is President of the Worldwatch Institute, Washington, D.C., and the author of such books as The Twenty-Ninth Day *and* Running on Empty, *a book about the future of the automobile in an oil-short world. This article was adapted from Worldwatch Paper 29,* Resource Trends and Population Policy: A Time for Reassessment.

and pricing policies in key producing countries are altering the oil supply situation. As the oil outlook changes, population projections must be reconsidered.

Assessing the impact of population on the earth's resources is complicated analytically because population growth and rising affluence both increase pressure on the earth's resources. Not only are the effects similar, but from 1950 through 1973 each accounted for roughly half of the 4 percent annual growth in the world demand for goods and services. Since then, however, global economic growth has fallen to only 3 percent per year, and the population component of the overall growth in global demand has become dominant.

An abundance of evidence indicates that pressures are mounting in a way that will influence future population trends. To be realistic, demographic models need to incorporate feedback mechanisms that reflect changing attitudes toward population size at both the national and the individual levels as the various ecological and economic stresses associated with continued population growth become evident. This in turn calls for an analysis of the relationship between population growth and both the earth's basic biological resources and its oil supplies.

Pressures on Biological Resources

The increase in human numbers thus far has depended heavily on the product of the earth's basic biological systems—fisheries, forests, grasslands, and croplands. These four systems supply not only all our food but, with the important exception of minerals and petrochemicals, all the raw materials for industry as well. With the exception of croplands, these are essentially natural systems that cannot always be improved by human management.

The carrying capacity of the three natural systems is essentially fixed by nature. A natural grassland can support a set number of cattle or a somewhat larger number of sheep. A fishery can supply the protein for a certain number of people and the forest surrounding a village can satisfy the firewood needs of a given population. If the trees removed from a forest exceed its rate of regrowth, then the forest will eventually disappear. If the catch from a fishery exceeds its regenerative capacity, stocks will dwindle, and it will eventually collapse. If herds grow too large, livestock will decimate grazing lands and the resulting erosion will turn the pastures into barren wastelands.

As world population has moved toward four billion and beyond, human needs have begun to outstrip the productive capacity of many local biological systems as currently managed. At the global level, these excessive pressures can be seen most clearly for oceanic fisheries. Throughout most of human existence, there were more fish in the oceans than humans could ever hope to catch or consume. As world population expanded following World War II, so did the fish catch and the investment in fishing fleets. The catch increased along with world population until the latter reached 3.6 billion in 1970. At this point, population continued to grow but the fish catch did not. Since 1970, investment in fishing fleets and fish farming has increased markedly, but the annual catch has remained around 70 million metric tons. With the catch leveling off since 1970, the fish supply per person has fallen by 13% (see Table 1).

The second global life-support system that is under mounting pressure is grasslands. Although data are not as complete as for fisheries, the signs of excessive stress are unmistakable. The pressures are evident in the deteriorating condition of grasslands in vast areas of the world and in the production trends of livestock products themselves.

Table 1: World Production Per Capita of Key Commodities of Biological Origin, 1960-78, With Peak Year Underlined

Year	Forests Wood	Fisheries Fish	Beef	Grasslands Mutton	Wool	Croplands Cereals
	(cubic meters)			(kilograms)		
1960	—	13.4	9.43	1.91	0.86	287
1961	0.65	14.3	9.67	1.91	0.85	278
1962	0.66	14.5	9.90	1.90	0.85	292
1963	0.66	14.7	10.25	1.89	0.83	286
1964	0.67	16.1	10.12	1.84	0.81	297
1965	0.67	16.2	10.09	1.82	0.79	288
1966	0.67	17.1	10.39	1.80	0.80	308
1967	0.67	17.7	10.59	1.92	0.79	308
1968	0.66	18.4	10.86	1.92	0.80	318
1969	0.66	17.7	10.90	1.88	0.79	316
1970	0.66	19.5	10.80	1.90	0.76	314
1971	0.66	19.2	10.57	1.91	0.74	335
1972	0.65	17.6	10.75	1.92	0.73	319
1973	0.66	17.5	10.63	1.83	0.67	337
1974	0.65	18.1	11.16	1.80	0.65	322
1975	0.62	17.6	11.49	1.80	0.67	321
1976	0.62	18.2	11.81	1.79	0.65	342
1977	0.62	17.4	11.53	1.78	0.63	333
1978*	0.61	16.6	11.21	1.77	0.64	340

*Preliminary estimates.
Source: Food and Agriculture Organization and U.S. Department of Agriculture.

The areas of the world used for grazing are almost without exception those areas that are too dry or too steeply sloping to sustain crop cultivation. Once the plow has run its course, the area remaining in grasslands around the world, roughly double that in crops, is essentially fixed by nature. Human intervention can sometimes raise the productivity of grasslands, and productivity can always be reduced through mismanagement, but the resource base itself cannot be significantly expanded. Indeed, as world population has expanded since mid-century, the area of grassland per person has diminished steadily.

The world's forests are also under mounting pressure. The demand for firewood, the principal fuel in countries with the fastest growing populations, is rapidly outstripping the sustainable yield of local forests. While the use of firewood declines as development proceeds, with modernization the use of forest products for newsprint, packaging, and other purposes soars. The need for new and replacement housing also levies an ever growing claim on the world's forests. While the demand for forest products is spiraling, the area in forests is shrinking by some 11 million hectares, an area the size of Cuba, each year. Deforestation as a result of excessive demand for wood is not an entirely new problem. What is new is the global scale. By the time world population passed the three billion mark in 1961, national populations were outstripping the sustainable yield of forests in most Third World countries. Worldwide, wood production per capita peaked in the mid-1960s at 0.67 cubic meters. Since then it has fallen by an estimated 9% (see Table 1).

In terms of human well-being and survival, the single most important product from a biological system is cereals—the grain crops that occupy some 70% of the world's cropland area. Together, wheat, rice, corn, and other cereals supply well over half our food energy supply when consumed directly and a sizable part of the remainder when consumed indirectly in the form of livestock products and alcoholic beverages. Between 1950 and 1971, world cereal production nearly doubled and production per capita climbed from 251 kilograms to 335 kilograms, an increase of over 30%. Since 1971, however, cereal production per person has leveled off (see Table 1).

This leveling off can be traced to a lack of new land to bring under the plow, rising energy prices, rigid agrarian structures, the conversion of cropland to nonfarm uses, soil erosion, and other forms of soil degradation. Expanding the area under irrigation is becoming much more difficult. Diminishing returns on the use of additional fertilizer in the agriculturally advanced countries are also slowing the growth in food production.

Even more discouraging than the leveling off in cereal output per person is the possibility that the same pressures will lead to a gradual decline in the years ahead. All of the principal forces that have led to the stagnation of per capita grain output during the 1970s will be at least as strong, if not stronger, during the 1980s and 1990s. Short of an abrupt slowdown in world population growth, the prospect of a decline in per capita food production between now and the end of the century must at least be considered. A more equitable distribution of food supplies could ameliorate the impact of this decline, but the rationing of scarce supplies through rising prices in the world market may leave some people unable to get enough food while others enjoy a surfeit.

Aside from reducing demand, there are two principal responses to the scarcities of basic biological resources—trying to improve the productivity of the system and substituting synthetic products. In an effort to cope with the scarcity of fuelwood and lumber, some countries are turning to tree farming, the systematic cultivation of specially adapted, fast-growing species. Farmers in the United Kingdom and New Zealand fertilize grasslands heavily in an attempt to raise the livestock carrying capacity of their holdings. Unfortunately, the share of the world's grasslands where there is enough rainfall to make this feasible is very small. While these human interventions to improve the productivity of natural systems are important, particularly at the local level, they have not been sufficient to reverse the unfavorable trends of recent years. The prospect for expanding these energy-intensive interventions will be influenced by future oil price and supply trends.

The scarcity of commodities of biological origin and of cropland has been partially offset by the extensive substitution of petroleum and petroleum products. Kerosene has been substituted for firewood and charcoal. Gasoline and diesel fuels used to power tractors and irrigation pumps have been substituted extensively for draft animals and for human muscle power. In their efforts to meet the continuously expanding demand for food, farmers have substituted fertilizer for the new land that is no longer available. Between 1950 and 1978, the world's farmers increased their use of energy-intensive chemical fertilizers more than sixfold, from 15 million tons to over 90 million tons. The use of pesticides, many of them produced from petrochemicals, has climbed even more rapidly.

The substitution of synthetic materials, produced by the petrochemical industry, for commodities of biological origin has also become widespread over the past four decades. Per capita production of wool, cotton, and other natural fibers leveled off or declined, and the use of synthetic fibers has climbed, partly because of relative prices and partly because of consumer preferences. Fully one-third of the clothing and textile demands of four billion consumers are now met by products of synthetic origin. With rubber, the substitution has progressed even further. Although world production of natural rubber has managed to keep pace with population growth since 1950, it has fallen far behind the rapid overall growth in demand for rubber, a demand spurred by rising affluence. By 1978, synthetic rubber produced by the petrochemical industry accounted for over two-thirds of the world's rubber supply. Plastics, another synthetic product dependent on petroleum, have similarly been widely substituted for such commodities of biological origin as paper, cardboard, wood, and leather.

This use of oil and of products derived from it has figured prominently in the economic evolution of the third quarter of this century. The substitution has eased the pressures on many biological systems, but whether it can continue depends on future petroleum supplies and prices. If this process is reversed, either because of changing price relationships or because of absolute shortages as petroleum supplies dwindle, it will intensify pressure on the earth's basic biological systems. In the absence of some revolutionary new technologies and energy sources, future population growth may thus be strongly influenced by the future supply and price of oil.

The Petroleum Constraint

Between 1950 and 1973 the world economy expanded at some 4%

per year. This unprecedented increase in the output of goods and services was closely tied to the 7% annual growth in world oil output during the period. Without such a rapidly expanding supply of cheap oil, it is difficult to imagine either the impressive economic growth or the enormous increase in world population.

The ways in which oil has boosted the earth's capacity to sustain a growing population are numerous. Not only is oil the principal fuel that powers the global economy, but it has numerous special uses for which there are no readily available substitutes. Any projections of future population growth must therefore take into account the changing petroleum supply.

The world of the foreseeable future promises to be one where petroleum or its equivalent is scarce and costly and where the supply is growing slowly, if at all. Such a situation will contrast sharply with the time when oil was cheap and when the supply was growing several percent per year. National population policies and individual childbearing decisions will be affected both directly and indirectly by the changing energy situation.

After growing at a phenomenal annual rate of about 7% between 1950 and 1973, and then slowing to about 1.6% after the OPEC oil embargo of 1973, world oil production may decline further over the next few decades. Several independent projections of world oil production made by petroleum companies and private consultants before the 1979 Iranian revolution indicated an annual rate of growth to 1990 of somewhere between 1.4 and 2.9%. However, considering the direct and indirect impacts on production of the Iranian revolution, changing oil policies in the rest of the Middle East, and the steady depletion of oil reserves around the world, increases in overall production between now and 1990 may not average more than 1% per year. Just as the 1973 OPEC price rise slowed the growth in world oil production from 7% to 1.6% per year, the 1979 price rises along with those in prospect are likely to slow further the growth in production in the long term.

If projected population growth materializes, a 1% growth rate in oil production would lead to a steady per capita decline. Between 1978 and 1990, overall production would increase by some 12% but production per person would fall from 5.23 barrels to 4.66 barrels. As oil reserves dwindle and as more countries try to stretch out their remaining reserves, total oil production is likely to turn downward around 1990, declining slowly from that point onward. As overall output declines, production per person falls rapidly, dropping from 4.66 barrels in 1990 to 3.55 barrels in 2000. Whether world oil production follows the exact path projected here is not of overriding importance. What is important is not only that the period of rapid growth in per capita oil output has ended but that the oil produced per person at the end of the century will be far less than it is today.

The projected decline in world oil production per person from now until the end of the century contrasts so sharply with the tripling of production per person that occurred between 1950 and 1973 that it is difficult to assess its impact on the global economic system. It was relatively easy to substitute oil-derived synthetic products for many commodities of biological origin when the oil supply per person was climbing rapidly, but as per capita output declines, this will be far more difficult. Likewise, the use of petroleum and petroleum products to offset the shrinkage in cropland per person will become more difficult. To the extent that the leveling off of oil production per person during the 1970s contributed to the simultaneous leveling off of food production per person, the prospective downturn in oil production per capita is a matter for concern.

The transition from an era of rapidly rising oil production per person to one of static oil output per person coincides with a pronounced change in the performance of the world economy. The 1950-73 period was one of unprecedented economic growth throughout the world. Since then there have been severe stresses on the international economic system. It is impossible to determine the extent to which the convulsions in the world economy since 1973 are due to the changing oil supply situation, but few would doubt that there is a relationship. If the transition in oil production per person from rapid growth to stagnation contributed to the economic stresses of recent years, what will a further transition to declining oil production per person lead to?

The Picture in Focus

As world population approached four billion, the global economy was staggering under the first double-digit inflation during peacetime. The decade in which population reached the four billion mark has brought the highest unemployment since the Great Depression and a marked slowdown in global economic growth. For the first time since the beginning of the Industrial Revolution, there are signs that continuously expanding human demands are overriding the capacity of new technology to offset the constraints inherent in the natural systems and resources on which humanity depends.

As world population moves toward five billion, there is widespread evidence of excessive demand. Overfishing is now the rule rather than the exception, forests are shrinking in most countries, overgrazing is commonplace on every continent, and at least one-fifth of the world's cropland is losing topsoil at a rate that is undermining its productivity. Demand pressures appear to be converging as output per person of key resources of biological origin declines and as production per person of oil threatens to turn downward. For much of the period since mid-century, the open-ended substitution of oil and oil products for cropland and for products of the major biological systems served as a safety valve. That safety valve may now be closing. Adequately supporting even six billion people will not be possible without greatly improved management of biological systems, widespread rationing, stringent energy conservation measures, recycling programs, and a more equitable distribution of vital resources such as food, land, and petroleum.

Bringing population growth to a halt is not in itself likely to solve all of humanity's pressing problems. In many cases, however, it is a necessary prerequisite. If the demographic brakes are not applied soon, overfishing, overgrazing, deforestation, overplowing, and their associated economic stresses are certain to worsen. The rapidly expanding demand for basic energy and food supplies is driving humanity up a rising cost curve. An immediate slowdown of world population growth will buy time to make needed adjustments and to develop new technologies and alternative energy sources. In any case, the resource scarcities and economic stresses cited earlier—energy shortages, land hunger, the deterioration of basic life-support systems, inflation, crowding, and rising unemployment—ultimately will spur governments and individual couples to act in a manner that will eventually stabilize world population size.

There is now considerable evidence that governmental policies can directly influence fertility, but most governments will not know how quickly they can check population growth until they have made a serious effort to do so. To date, only two countries—China and Singapore—have launched comprehensive programs to reduce birth rates. There are at least five areas in which governments can act to slow population growth: providing family planning services, improving social conditions (such as nutrition and literacy), reshaping economic and social policies (such as those governing the minimum age of marriage or the number of children for whom tax deductions can be claimed), improving the status of women, and encouraging population education to help people understand how population size affects the quality of life.

The population problem is simultaneously a global problem and a local and individual one. In an interdependent world, plagued with resource scarcity, continuing population growth anywhere can affect people everywhere. All national political leaders will have to deal with the consequences in one form or another.

Energy: Plentiful Through the 1980s and Beyond

by

Anton B. Schmalz

Oil Imports Can Be Virtually Eliminated by 1990

There is plenty of domestic energy available today! The equivalent of 8-to-12 million barrels of oil a day can be produced and conserved in the U.S. with resources and technologies available locally now.

Where the commitment to local energy alternatives has already been made, the price has been primarily in terms of individual and institutional innovations, adaptations, and cooperation. Even with the distortions of $15 billion a year of federal subsidies to conventional fossil and nuclear technologies, the economics of local alternatives are proving to be competitive with, and increasingly superior to, conventional energy options.

Many individuals, institutions, and communities are well on their way to maximizing their local self-reliance with locally appropriate approaches to energy goal-setting, issue mediation and resolution processes, conservation, and renewable resources.

We're fortunate to have energy options, because, while every bit of energy helps, we're not likely to have significant commercial quantities of energy from other sources—either synthetic fuels or the breeder reactor—in this century. There is a 10-to-15 year minimum leadtime to demonstrate the *first* commercial-scale versions of these new technologies. Commercial quantities of energy would come from successive plants in the years and decades following successful demonstrations of the first commercial-scale modules and, later, complete plants.

The process of evolving new technologies to commercial criteria and scale rarely lends to acceleration. No amount of money will substitute for the time required to progress from where the required technologies and supporting infrastructure are today up to the scale generally contemplated for commercial purposes.

Anton B. Schmalz has been an independent consultant to leaders of government and industry on energy and environmental goals and policies for 11 years. He was chairman of the World Future Society's special forum on energy in 1974 and principal consultant to the 1978 White House Domestic Policy Review of Solar Energy.

Commitment to a large number of plants is unlikely until the first ones have demonstrated acceptable reliability and economics. Miracles may be possible, but it hardly seems to serve any national or world interest to base energy policies and expectations on the supernatural.

Everyone now seems to agree on the ideal of independence from oil imports. The questions are: *What* are the resources and technologies available today to achieve this independence? and, *How* can we best achieve it?

Three Energy Options Are Available Now

One or a combination of three options appear to be available to contribute significant quantities of domestically-controlled energy in the U.S. for the rest of this decade and, very probably, for the rest of this century. The three options are:

- **Conservation**—improving the efficiencies with which we use *all* resources and technologies; recycling many materials and exploiting the many combustibles in the waste streams of our "throw-away" economy; substituting transportation modes such as car pools and public transportation—even bicycles—for many driver-only trips.
- **Renewable resources and appropriate-scale technologies**—including "active" systems such as solar heating and cooling, wind, industrial process and agricultural heat, biomass (wood, vegetation, and organic solid waste), small-scale hydroelectric dams and solar electric systems; and "passive" approaches such as insulation, weatherization, greenhouses, and basic architectural designs which maximize and cooperate with the free work of nature and minimize the disruption of natural systems.
- **Unconventional natural gas**—using established drilling and mining technologies, most of the methane in many local coal seams can be recovered in quantities and at pressures which are usually ample for local facility purposes, but are not sufficient for commercial utility or pipeline service.

Three Basic and Often Overlooked Considerations

The facts and uncertainties for achieving an energy future may be summarized by choice in the light of three considerations, namely:

1. *What exists?* What do we have to draw from, and to build up?
2. *Where do we want to be?* What conditions and relationships would we like to have prevailing by certain future points in time?
3. *How do we get there from here?* What decisions, assumptions of responsibility and adaptations are both needed and feasible to get from where we are to where we say we want to be by a specific future time?

1. What Exists? What Do We Have to Draw From and Build Upon?

We have an enormous resource base of facts and experience to draw upon and, thereby, to improve the probability of achieving future energy outcomes of choice rather than by reaction or default. Our resource base can help us minimize costly stresses and "surprises," and maximize the long-range stability, productivity, and continuity of our government and society.

Our Resource Base Is Rich
With Pertinent Knowledge and Experience

Our cumulative resource base contains much pertinent experience and knowledge which can help us influence the direction, the timing, the outcome, and the impact of the global resource transition in which we find ourselves. Our knowledge and experience resources include:

- *The capability to assess* the "unknowns" as well as the "knowns"—the successes and shortcomings—of prior conventional wisdom and approaches to energy goal-setting, expectations, and policy formulation.
- *Appropriate processes* for issue identification, mediation, and resolution of differing viewpoints from parties whose active and informed support is essential to a successful outcome.
- *Realistic understanding* of the availability, feasibility, and adaptations of the energy resources, technologies, and institutions available today.
- *The considerations for commercializing new energy technologies*—factors such as the leadtimes, players, plays, processes, and relationships required to bring new energy technologies to a level of credible, accepted, and routine functioning in the lifestream of our society.
- *The assumptions* underlying our energy goals, promises, assertions, and expectations as well as the rejection of new ideas and experience.

An Assessment of Conventional Wisdom
and Traditional Approaches

Energy has proven to be more of a social, political, and institutional issue than a question of supply or demand or technology.

Conventional wisdom and traditional approaches to energy issues have often been incomplete and unclear in their assumptions. These approaches have frequently been without specific goals, implementation strategies, and provisions for issue resolution and commitments for deliberate transition to maximum energy independence and self-reliance.

Today, after seven years, four congressionally-mandated energy organizations (possibly six by the time this is published), eight energy "czars," hundreds of billions of dollars, hundreds of thousands of studies, thousands of federal program plans and reorganizations, the U.S.—as a nation—does not have alternative energy resources, technologies, institutions, directions, or contingency plans to deal with the possibility of interruptions in the flow of imported oil or with the prospect of continuing price increases.

Different energy outcomes will require some different assumptions and different approaches—perhaps a goal-oriented approach.

Establishing an On-Going Issue Mediation and Resolution Process

Issue identification, mediation, resolution, and commitment to courses of action is the essential process present in successful local energy initiatives.

A successful process is basically a cooperative forum in which participants with diverse viewpoints can learn from each other as they identify areas of agreement and focus on areas of different perceptions and disagreements. The objectives of a cooperative forum process are:

- *To identify and deal with* the genuine gaps in knowledge.
- *To mediate and resolve differences* in a non-adversarial manner.
- *To ultimately implement* the consensus and commitments of the participants into the lifestream of their societal roles and responsibilities.

An exemplary cooperative forum process emerged in the National Coal Policy Project which emphasized reaching agreement, where possible, rather than seeking victories. To facilitate this effort, the participants adopted a set of negotiating principles known as "the Rule of Reason" which include the following:

- Data should not be withheld from the other side.
- Delaying tactics should not be used.
- Tactics should not be used to mislead.
- Motives should not be impugned lightly.
- Dogmatism should be avoided.
- Extremism should be countered forcefully—but not in kind.
- Integrity should be given first priority.

Achieving a general understanding and maintaining expectations within realistic bounds are other values of a cooperative forum process.

Energy Resources Available With Today's Technologies

Estimates of how much energy can be produced or conserved with different approaches and technologies also vary widely. Comparative economics of resource recovery and energy production by various methods are distorted by the billions of dollars in subsidies enjoyed each year by the industries based on fossil and nuclear fuel cycles.

Prices have historically been subsidized through federal tax policies, price controls, and unpaid environmental and national security costs. Conventional energy is, therefore, priced below the cost of replacing it.

Opportunities for Conservation

Substantial savings and self-reliance have been demonstrated through:

- *Achieving lower energy growth rates* which are neither easy or cheap, but are less costly than continuing our historically high rates of annual energy growth. Experience is continually showing that substantial reductions in energy requirements can be made without adopting measures which involve important changes in lifestyles.

- *Getting more from the energy we use* in our homes, businesses, industries, and transportation systems.

The U.S. uses 3 times as much energy as Japan and twice as much as Sweden—neither of which are living primitively. The U.S. economy can operate on 30-to-40% less energy through technical improvements which reduce the energy required per unit of output.

Similar, though perhaps less dramatic, improvements are possible in most industrialized and developing countries.

Opportunities for Renewable Resources and Conservation

CBS-TV News began the decade with a Special Report on January 5, 1980, showing how—by 1990—Americans can dispense with almost all of the 8.5 million barrels of oil which the nation imports daily, and do it with currently available technologies.

Dan Rather and Charles Collingwood interviewed mayors, technical people, business and citizen groups throughout the country who are already applying practical and proven ways to achieve energy efficiency in homes, factories, on highways, and in local communities.

The CBS-TV assessment of the energy which can be saved or contributed by 1990 in each sector of U.S. society tallies to an admittedly conservative equivalent of 8.2 million barrels of oil a day as shown in *Exhibit 1.*

Exhibit 1
Conservative Estimate by CBS-TV in 1980
of Potential Energy Savings by 1990

Millions of Barrels of Oil Equivalent (per day) by 1990	Sector of U.S. Society Contributing or Saving the Energy
2.0	From improving energy efficiencies in the homes we live in.
2.7	From improving energy efficiencies in the facilities and operations of businesses, industries, and governments at all levels.
2.5	From achieving the 1985 goal of 27½ miles per gallon fleet average mileage for U.S. produced cars.
1.0	From renewable resources (arbitrarily reduced 50% from the 1979 "Energy Future Report of the Harvard Energy Project")

8.2*

*An additional potential savings of 725 million barrels of oil a day is possible by 1985 from a maximum effort at co-generation—using a single heat source for multiple applications.

"Unconventional" Natural Gas May Be
Our Energy "Wild Card"

Fortunately, some forms of energy can be substituted for nearly all stationary uses, i.e., coal for oil, gas for liquids or solids. Unfortunately, the least flexible sector is the one on which the entire economic structure of industralized economies is based, namely, transportation.

"Unconventional" sources of natural gas are found in at least six previously unexploited geologic environments. These sources can serve as our domestic energy "wild card" to minimize the difficulties in a deliberate transition to alternative energy lifestyles, and also to minimize the trauma from any possible interruption of imported oil.

Estimates of the quantities which are available, and those which are recoverable, are shown in *Exhibit 2* for four of the six unconventional geologic sources. Estimates vary according to the assumptions regarding the extent of the deposits and the amount of research and development needed to improve the drilling and extracting process technologies.

Exhibit 2
Estimated Unconventional Gas Resources for the U.S.

Resource	Estimated Total Resource in Place (in trillions of cubic feet)		Recoverable Resource
	Gas Research Institute Digest (March 1979)	*National Geographic* (November 1978)	*Gas Research Institute Digest* (March 1979)
Methane from Coal Seams	72-860	850 (above 6,000 feet)	16-487
Western Gas Sands	50-600	800	25-313
Eastern Gas Shales	75-700	1,000	10-504
Geopressurized Methane	3,000-50,000	50,000	150-2,000

The substitutability of gas for oil in many applications can "free up" liquids for transportation needs and keep energy flowing to other consumptions sectors through channels which are well known and largely in place. The social, financial, environmental, and political costs will be far less than for any other fossil fuel or nuclear option in the foreseeable future.

Unconventional natural gas—particularly from coal seams—offers the cheapest, most readily available, and environmentally clean option of any fossil fuel for increasing domestic energy supply with current technology.

Sheikh Yamani, the Saudi Oil Minister, commenting on the conservation policies being adopted by oil producing countries, has made some dramatic observations about gas:

... the amount of natural gas being flared (by producing countries) is equivalent to 4 billion barrels a day of oil ... though unjustified by prevailing market prices ... the energy conserved as a result of the "master plan gas gathering system" (in Saudi Arabia) is no less than 10% of its total hydrocarbon reserves.

2. Where Do We Want to Be?

What conditions and relationships would we like to have prevailing by certain future points in time?

The willingness to adapt to alternatives is inherent in today's energy policy success stories. Unsuccessful energy policies have not had specific goals and realistic implementation strategies.

Successful policies have focused on the feasibility and appropriateness of alternative goals in terms of the scale, the form, and the quantity of energy needed *regardless* of the resource, technology, or institution(s) involved.

Active individuals and communities have accepted the responsibility of determining for themselves which energy resources, technologies, standards, and institutions are most appropriate for their particular needs—often in spite of the federal government and its general preference for research, development, studies, and demonstrations rather than the exploitation of technologies and ideas which have already proven themselves. A balance of both approaches would seem more appropriate than the traditional "either/or" polarizing approaches which have prevailed for seven years.

Additional motivation for many communities and institutions in a nationwide environment of "politics of the shrinking pie" is the experience of the cost to apply for, and administer, federal grants, which exceeds the value of the grants in far too many cases.

The Trend of Local Initiative
to Increase Local Self-Reliance

There are enough energy alternatives operating successfully in the U.S. today to regard local innovation and responsibility as a genuine trend. Routinely functioning examples of energy innovations and information "hot lines" abound in major cities, small communities, and neighborhoods. A few of these "hot lines" and sources of information for community energy projects include:

- President's Clearinghouse for Community Energy Efficiency: 800/424-9040
- Institute for Local Self-Reliance, 1717 18th Street, N.W., Washington, D.C. 20009 202/232-0235
- Neighborhood Information Sharing Exchange (NISE): 800/424-2852
- Center for Renewable Resources, 1001 Connecticut Ave., N.W., Washington, D.C. 20036 202/466-6880
- National Center for Resource Recovery, 1211 Connecticut Ave., N.W., Washington, D.C. 20036 202/347-9193
- National Center for Appropriate Technology, P.O. Box 3838, Butte, Montana 59701 406/494-4572

   Additional sources of energy information are:

- Alcohol Fuels Information: 800/523-2929
- National Solar Heating & Cooling Information Center: 800/523-2929
- Bio-Energy Council, Suite 204, 1337 Connecticut Ave., N.W., Washington, D.C. 20036 202/833-5656

The community and institutional achievements to date did not materialize overnight by either magic or mandate. The results being enjoyed—and continuously improved upon—evolved as a *process*, not an event.

The process is usually ongoing for years; and no matter how divergent initial viewpoints may be, the fact that the process is continuing seems to motivate people to "hang in there" and to either accommodate or transcend any inclination toward an adversarial approach. The process is tedious, with all the phenomena of families and other human relationship systems built-in—the joys, frustrations, satisfactions, etc., etc.

In the case of each of the following examples, the process was initiated out of a shared concern or preference—or both. It mediates the assertions of proponents, detractors, apologists, and other "experts" regarding what should be done, and focuses on achievable goals, realistic implementation strategies and schedules.

The process resolves what *can* be done with today's technology. There is also a genuine commitment to use the available energy more efficiently and exploit whatever local resources are at hand.

Examples of Innovative Communities and Public Utilities

Davis, California, is the most comprehensive example of an on-going community issue mediation/resolution process. Since 1973, ordinances, building codes, and regulations have been adopted, adapted, or removed to ensure local control for maximizing the use of renewable resources—solar and recyclable solid wastes—and alternative transportation modes. There are 27,000 bicycles compared to only 12,000 automobiles in this university town of 37,000.

Energy savings by 1979 included a 25% reduction in gasoline, an 18% reduction in electricity use, and a 33% reduction in the use of natural gas.

Greensboro, North Carolina, began the nation's first door-to-door energy audit program in 1977 as a collaboration between citizens, the city, and Duke Power Company. Firemen are used in teams of 3 to make about 500 calls each week. The energy cost savings are providing more income dollars for life's other choices.

Seattle, Washington, and Portland, Oregon, initiated the most extensive major city-wide programs of the 1970s as they faced the limits of hydro-electric power, the rising costs and other uncertainties of nuclear power and imported oil.

Public processes explored energy alternatives and their implications. The result was a thoughtful commitment to get future increments of energy from a combination of new zoning laws and building codes coupled with programs to encourage conservation—improving efficiencies and eliminating waste wherever possible, solar energy, low-cost parking for car pools, and recycling garbage. Cogeneration of heat and electricity has also been inaugurated to capitalize on heat which would otherwise be dissipated to the atmosphere.

Hartford, Connecticut, is dealing with high energy costs and high unemployment simultaneously. Food and other necessities are produced elsewhere and shipped in at considerable energy and financial cost. City-sponsored cooperatives, community gardens and canneries, and a growing number of local small farmers are participating in a self-help process which involves direct participation by residents in the production, distribution, and consumption of high quality, lower cost food. Unemployed youngsters are trained to help residents insulate and weatherize homes in depressed parts of the city.

Crystal City, Texas (population 8200), purchased and installed 1000 Korean War army stoves and created a continuously replenished 500-cord stockpile of mesquite wood for fuel. Solar water heaters and residential greenhouses are sprouting up all over town. Neighboring rural communities are emulating the example.

Fitchburg, Massachusetts, evolved the premise that every community already has most of the human and technological resources necessary to accomplish many energy-saving objectives.

All over town, everyone—senior and junior—is pitching in like an old-fashioned barn raising. Energy savings of at least 2 million gallons of heating oil alone are possible. The value of an increasing sense of community and self-reliance is inestimable.

Without help from the federal government, several utilities are expanding their own energy bases in innovative ways:

- **Wood Power for Burlington, Vermont,** came in 1977 through the addition of a wood-burning capability to a 10-megawatt (Mw) plant which could already use coal, oil, and natural gas. In 1978, Burlington voters were so impressed with the results that they approved bonds for a 50 Mw plant which will use 1500 tons of wood chips a day.

- **Refuse-Derived Fuel for Ames, Iowa,** comes from shredded garbage—84% of the total mass of municipal solid waste. The electric utility burns a mixture of 80% coal and 20% refuse-derived fuel from the nation's first full-scale solid waste recovery system. Fuel costs are currently on a par with costs for using coal only—and the life of the landfill has been extended for decades.

- **Wind Power for Southern California Edison** will provide electricity to about 1000 homes near Palm Springs from a 3 Mw wind machine beginning in 1980—and save about 10,000 barrels of oil each year.

With Department of Energy assistance, several utilities are installing early models of 200-megawatt wind turbine generators in Rhode Island, Puerto Rico, New Mexico and Hawaii.

Utility innovation and diversity with alternative energy resources and technologies are increasing each year.

3. How Do We Get There From Here?

What decisions, assumptions of responsibility and adaptations are needed and feasible to get from where we are to where we say we want to be by a specific future time?

Man is the only organism on the planet that has a sense of history and a sense of the future. We can wait and react to what comes, or we can make choices on the basis of the best experience and information available. There are always options, but options have a way of changing form, cost, and availability with time.

EXHIBIT 3

OVERALL CONCEPT OF A BASIC STRATEGIC POLICY
FORMULATION AND ANALYSIS PROCESS

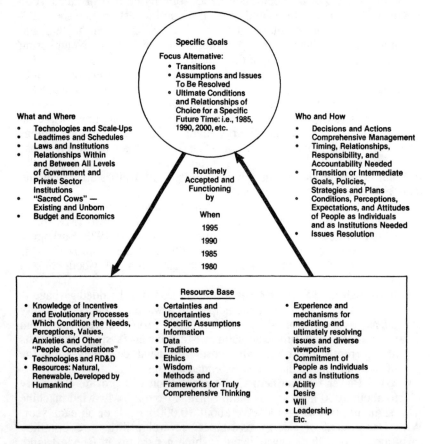

Specific Goals

Focus Alternative:
- Transitions
- Assumptions and Issues To Be Resolved
- Ultimate Conditions and Relationships of Choice for a Specific Future Time: i.e., 1985, 1990, 2000, etc.

What and Where
- Technologies and Scale-Ups
- Leadtimes and Schedules
- Laws and Institutions
- Relationships Within and Between All Levels of Government and Private Sector Institutions
- "Sacred Cows" — Existing and Unborn
- Budget and Economics

Routinely
Accepted and
Functioning
by

When

1995
1990
1985
1980

Who and How
- Decisions and Actions
- Comprehensive Management
- Timing, Relationships, Responsibility, and Accountability Needed
- Transition or Intermediate Goals, Policies, Strategies and Plans
- Conditions, Perceptions, Expectations, and Attitudes of People as Individuals and as Institutions Needed
- Issues Resolution

Resource Base

- Knowledge of Incentives and Evolutionary Processes Which Condition the Needs, Perceptions, Values, Anxieties and Other "People Considerations"
- Technologies and RD&D
- Resources: Natural, Renewable, Developed by Humankind

- Certainties and Uncertainties
- Specific Assumptions
- Information
- Data
- Traditions
- Ethics
- Wisdom
- Methods and Frameworks for Truly Comprehensive Thinking

- Experience and mechanisms for mediating and ultimately resolving issues and diverse viewpoints
- Commitment of People as Individuals and as Institutions
- Ability
- Desire
- Will
- Leadership
- Etc.

A Framework for Goal-Setting

A framework for goal-setting and strategic energy policy formulation is depicted in *Exhibit 3*. It provides a way to favor comprehensiveness and completeness in the delineation of factors. It also contributes to an appreciation of the interconnectedness of *all* the considerations which can be identified as affecting the acceptance, credibility, and routine

114

functioning of an energy choice in society today.

Once the feasible alternatives and preferences have been characterized for a specific future time, one can think backward to identify the *what*, *where*, and *when* of the items which would have to be accomplished and functioning by each preceding year in order for the goal to be achieved by the desired time.

The analysis can draw on a resource base which would include the diverse viewpoints of all the stakeholders. Working from the resource base, one can think *forward* through the years to determine *who* is most appropriately responsible for required actions by specific times, and *how* these actions can be best supported and accomplished—a strategy for implementation.

A Successfully Demonstrated Goal-Oriented Approach to Commercialization

The commercialization goal for any energy technology can be characterized by some quantity of energy production, for example 1 million BODE (Barrels of Oil per Day Equivalent), which is credible and accepted by the necessary constituencies and is *routinely functioning* in our society by a certain future time—as contrasted with the first commercial-scale module or integrated demonstration model of a technology.

The seven questions shown in *Exhibit 4* provide a comprehensive and credible framework for a goal-oriented approach to understanding and relating the considerations for commercializing new energy technologies. The seven-question framework was successfully demonstrated for the U.S. Congress in delineating the considerations for commercializing the breeder reactor and for commercializing synthetic fuel technologies.

The questions can be used in combination with the framework shown in *Exhibit 3* to identify the essential building blocks and interconnections for realistically assessing the considerations and prospects for *any* energy alternative. This comprehensive methodology helps improve credibility and minimize costly "surprises" by identifying and relating the technical, schedule, cost, and other uncertainties *before* performing cost/benefit analyses and making major commitments.

This methodology was mandated by the Congress to be used by its Office of Technology Assessment for its current assessment of alternative energy futures for the U.S.

Exhibit 5 characterizes the seven steps of the coal fuel cycle. When the questions and framework presented in Exhibits 3 and 4 are applied to each of the seven steps, then the realities and fantasies of synthetic fuel commercialization would be apparent to everyone.

Exhibit 4
Seven Questions Provide a Framework for Realistic Energy Commercialization Expectations and Strategies

Use of the seven questions ensures consideration of key issues which are identifiable today and which need RD&D or other clarification by certain future times in order to:

a. Develop and implement a realistic commercialization strategy and schedule.

b. Achieve the routine functioning and institutionalization of the technologies, institutions, and consumer acceptance essential to successful commercialization by specific times.

The seven questions are:

1. What will be the principal characteristics of a routinely functioning commercial solar/synthetic fuel/breeder reactor/etc. industry?

2. What natural resources, supporting facilities, and institutions would be required to bring the industry into being by specific future times and, thereafter, to maintain it?

3. What physical and financial capacity exists in domestic industry to initiate solar/synthetic fuel/breeder/etc. commercialization; and when will additional capacity be needed?

4. When is a demonstration needed of the required technologies on a scale sufficient to warrant the commitments of those individuals and institutions whose support is essential to solar/synthetic fuel/breeder/etc. commercialization?

5. What factors are likely to influence the timing and rate of solar/synthetic fuel/breeder/etc. introduction and proliferation?

6. Who is, will be, or should be responsible for the policies, decisions, and commitments which will ensure the timely and orderly availability of all the technologies and resources required?

7. What federal policies will be needed by specific times to ensure an equitable, competitive market entry, acceptance, and functioning for each solar/synthetic fuel/breeder/etc. technology?

Note: This methodology was developed by Anton B. Schmalz and demonstrated for the U.S. Congress in "Considerations for Commercializing the Liquid Metal Fast Breeder Reactor," for the U.S. General Accounting Office (1976), and "Considerations for Commercializing Synthetic Fuel Production from Coal & Oil Shale," for the Office of Technology Assessment (1977).

Exhibit 5
Seven Steps of the Coal Fuel Cycle

COAL FUEL CYCLE	Resource Assessment/ Availability	Extraction	Refining and Conversion	Transportation and Storage	Central Station Conversion Decentralized Conversion	Waste Management	Demand Category Sector
MAJOR COMPONENTS/ FUNCTIONS	Reserve Assessment Federal Leasing	Surface Underground	Cleaning Gasification Liquefaction	Rail/ Unit Train Barge Truck Slurry	Utility Direct Firing Direct Wet Alkali Scrubbing Regenerative Scrubbing Fluidized Bed SRC Liquid Firing Low Btu Gas Med. Btu Gas Coke/Steel	ASH Slurry INK Scrubber Sludge Acid Mine Drainage	Utility Industry Residential/ Commercial Import/ Export

Some of the larger and presently unanswered questions which may constrain scale-up and eventual commercialization include:

- **Some basic chemistry of coal and the catalysts required** in several of the plant processes.
- **The disposal and management of toxic and solid wastes**—i.e., one ton of oil shale solid waste is produced to make 25 gallons of liquid product.
- **Water requirements and waste water management**—up to 72 million gallons of water per day would be required by some plants currently contemplated.
- **Air and water pollution.**
- **Socio-economic and political considerations**—Who will pay? When? and How?

As the interactive goal-oriented process evolves, participants develop the experience and the will to:

- **Transcend traditional "either/or" polarizing approaches** such as supply *vs* demand, centralized *vs* decentralized, small *vs* large, coal *vs* nuclear, or solar *vs* all others.
- **Transcend expectations of simple solutions** or other forms of magic such as waiving accountability for management of hazardous wastes.
- **Explicate assumptions,** particularly as substitutes for hard data.
- **Thoroughly consider all feasible mixes** of energy resources, technologies, and institutions on a case-by-case basis—and, thereby, resist the temptation of macro approaches.
- **Identify factors requiring resolution** and commitment by specific future times.
- **Establish a continuing process** for issue identification, mediation, resolution, and commitment to implementation of agreements.

A goal-oriented approach can illuminate the exhortations of both proponents and detractors regarding "what should be done" with the pragmatic realities of "what can be done."

Today's Energy Choices Are Tomorrow's Opportunities or Crises

Conservation, renewable resources, and unconventional gas alternatives offer significant and early opportunities to reduce unemployment, inflation, and dependence on imported oil.

"Real world" experience is daily proving that the most difficult energy issues to be faced and resolved involve "humanology," not technology. Expectations, credibility, and support are enhanced if the "unknowns" as well as the "knowns" and operating assumptions are acknowledged and appropriately provided for as early as possible in the *process* of choice.

The benefits of any amount of energy independence and local self-reliance are significant. There are many things which every individual, community, institution, and government can do for themselves—with today's technologies.

Today's energy choices are truly tomorrow's opportunities or crises.

Renewable Resources:
Will They Be Scarce in the Future?

by

Larry W. Tombaugh and Robert N. Stone

Differing perspectives and assumptions about changes in technology or in social trends lead to widely divergent images of the future demand for—and supply of—renewable natural resources. Advances in electronics and information-processing capability are likely to create a very different set of demands for wood products. Radical changes in housing styles and methods of construction might greatly reduce the demand for lumber, but advances in natural product chemistry might bring the price of chemicals, fuels, and pharmaceuticals from cellulose into the competitive range of other materials. These differing images of the future create serious problems for the professional resource manager and for the public officials responsible for national public policy concerning our natural resource base. What should they do in the face of great and substantial differences in images of the future?

In order to reduce the question to manageable size, we will concentrate on the goods and services provided by one set of renewable resources—forests. Forests are selected for several reasons. First, they are a prominent feature of the landscape. In the United States, one-third of the land area is forested. Second, they are important economically. Thirty of the 500 largest industrial corporations in the United States are in the wood products business, producing such important commodities as lumber, paper, plywood, cardboard, and containers. Finally, and most importantly, production functions for wood extend over long periods of time. This is an extremely important biological reality. It takes a long time to grow a mature tree. This is why widely divergent views of the future are troublesome to the forest manager or the policy maker. A key assumption behind forest management is that a variety of wood products will be needed by society in the 30, 40, or 100 years that it takes trees planted now to mature.

Larry W. Tombaugh is Chairman, Department of Forestry, Michigan State University, East Lansing, Michigan.

Robert N. Stone is Forest Economist, U.S. Department of Agriculture Forest Products Laboratory, Madison, Wisconsin.

118

Forester's Image of the Future

Let's speculate on the image of the future that guides the forester and compare this image with that portrayed by others who seriously think about the future. The most stark observation is that, by and large, North American foresters have not given much thought at all to the future as a variable. Rather, the forestry profession, which is involved with a very long-range activity, appears to have been guided much more by the past or by deterministic views of the future. The concept of scientific forest management is less than a century old in North America. Forestry techniques are strongly rooted in the practices and the concepts of efficiency that developed in Europe—primarily in Germany—over the past several centuries. Furthermore, forestry in North America was stimulated by the obvious and extensive destruction of the forest resource that occurred as the United States and Canada were settled. Lumbering and the clearing of land for agriculture spread westward at prairie-fire speed, leaving destruction and waste behind. The fear developed that forests would disappear without some form of public policy and resource management. This image of future shortages has played a key role in forest policies and practices.

The business of the forester is to perpetuate stands of trees for use over long periods of time. Because of his training, he is very good at visualizing how a mature stand of Douglas fir timber will look one hundred years from the time that seedlings are planted. Biologically and ecologically, he knows what to expect. He is not accustomed to thinking about the social and economic milieu that will exist at the time that the timber is ready for harvest.

Recent governmental actions have begun to force a change in the way that foresters and other natural resource managers think about the future. Most prominent are the Forest and Rangeland Renewable Resources Planning Act of 1974 and the National Forest Management Act of 1976. Among other things, these laws require the Secretary of Agriculture to systematically and periodically prepare an analysis of present and anticipated uses, demand for, and supply of the renewable resources of forest, range, and other associated lands and a program for managing these resources that is compatible with the findings of the assessment. The assessment is to be done every tenth year. It has forced the forestry community to look ahead to future needs and supply of resources and to marry planning and programming.

In response to the legislation, the U.S. Forest Service initiated a major planning and programming process. Last year, it issued a review draft of the 1980 Program and Assessment. The assessment was based on a 50-year planning horizon.

As might be expected, the explicit and implicit assumptions about the future that undergird the resource assessment are highly constrained by the present and by historical trends. The draft document states that "barring major catastrophes, such as a world war, recent trends are likely to persist over a considerable period of time." From that starting point, projections are made about population, economic activity, and income. A narrow range of projections, based on marginal change in past trends, provides the basis for the assessment and related programs. Ignored are changes in the economic structure, in technology, in customs, in life styles, and in the geography of population centers. The image of the future portrayed by the forestry professionals is quite different from that envisaged by other thoughtful people approaching the future from different perspectives.

The Future of Forests

How important should these different perspectives be in terms of actually affecting resource management decisions? What should the forest resource manager, faced with widely different images of the future, do? We offer three thoughts.

First, in the absence of any clear pictures of the future, we probably are better off if we err in the direction of maintaining too many acres of forest lands than too few. Land can be cleared relatively easily if needed, but it takes years or decades to establish a good stand of trees. Forests represent a low investment and relatively low-risk land use. They can be produced on land areas not useful for other purposes.

Most importantly, forests provide an array of other benefits as joint products. These include outdoor recreational opportunities, protection of watersheds, habitat for wildlife, natural "scrubbers" of air pollution, and sources of atmospheric oxygen. Thus, even though the anticipated demands for wood products never materialize, forested lands produce many other goods and services for society.

It also makes sense to manage for the highest-value products that can be anticipated at any point in time. High-quality walnut veneer logs can be cut up into firewood if need be, but many wood products cannot be made from small, low-quality timber.

Second, an accelerated level of investment in research dealing with wood as a material is warranted. On the one hand, trees are a plentiful resource and, by applying technological advances in genetics and forest management, they could be much more plentiful. Trees currently cover a third of a billion acres in the United States. We currently harvest about a half a billion tons of wood each year and could easily harvest two to three times that much without jeopardizing the resource. On the other hand, trees are potentially an important source of chemicals, pharmaceuticals, and fuels. Unfortunately, the amount of research on natural products chemistry dropped off to practically nothing as low-cost petrochemicals became available. Yet many of the products currently produced from petrochemicals could just as well be produced from cellulosic materials. It is a matter of concern that the United States government has supported 16 university-based materials research laboratories, and not one of these has conducted research on renewable resources as materials.

Third, there should be more communication between persons involved with natural resource management and policy and people from other disciplines who are grappling with better ways of structuring thinking about the future. Both groups would gain. Even though forest management is, and probably should be, insensitive to widely divergent views of the future, forest planning still needs to consider potential "surprises," or non-marginal changes of such magnitude that they would definitely have an impact upon resource management. Futurists, as mentioned, could also gain by developing a clear understanding of some of the biological and economic realities of resource management that create significant momentum in the social system.

Vanishing Plants and Animals:
The Mega-Extinction of Species

by

Norman Myers

Of earth's five million species, we could well lose at least one million by the end of the century. Within the foreseeable future of the next 3-5 decades, i.e., until growth of human numbers levels out and until growth of human appetites for raw materials stabilizes, we could say good-bye to probably one-quarter, possibly one-third, and conceivably one-half of the planetary spectrum of species. It is far from unrealistic to reckon that we are already losing one species per day, and that by the end of the 1980s we could be losing one species per hour.

Extinction of species constitutes an irreversible loss of unique natural resources, now and forever. Earth is currently afflicted with many other forms of environmental degradation; but from the standpoint of permanent despoliation of the planet, no other form is anywhere so significant as the fallout of species. When a species disappears, it is gone for good. Often enough, that will be for bad. Of the small number of species already investigated for their economic value, many have made significant contributions to industry, agriculture and medicine.

Industry's Use of Species

Industry utilizes many species. Plants already serve the needs of the textile manufacturer, the toilet-goods producer and the ice-cream maker—likewise the butcher, the baker and the candlestick-maker. As technology advances, in a world growing short of just about everything except shortages, industry's need for new raw materials will grow ever more rapidly.

Examples of industrial materials from plants include latex products (e.g., rubber), pectins, resins and cleoresins, gums and other exudates, essential oils for flavors and related juices, vegetable dyes and tannins, vegetable fats and waxes, insecticides, and growth regulators and other biodynamic compounds. In like manner, animals supply furs, leather goods, fibres, glues and many other substances for industrial processes.

One category of products is exceptionally important—lubricants. Be-

Norman Myers is a Consultant in Environment and Development, Nairobi, Kenya. This article is adapted from his book The Sinking Ark *(Pergamon Press, Oxford, 1979).*

cause of the increasing cost of petroleum-based lubricants, there is a premium on finding substitute materials. Of 6,400 plant species recently screened by the U.S. Department of Agriculture for new oils and waxes, among other products, promising leads were revealed by 460. Principal candidates include a number of plants with oil-rich seeds, including the buffalo gourd and the jojoba shrub of the deserts of northern Mexico and southwestern United States.

As a measure of commercial prospects awaiting development of jojoba's potential, its oil now sells to Japan for $3,000 per barrel, as compared with an OPEC price for fossil petroleum of around $25. To meet projected world demand for jojoba oil and wax, plantations covering 40,000 acres and yielding one ton of nuts per acre are required, laying the foundation for a $250-million industry.

Species As Sources of Energy

Certain plant species can serve as sources of energy by virtue of their capacity to produce hydrocarbons like oil instead of carbohydrates like sugar. These hydrocarbons can be of various kinds, one of which we have long used—rubber from *Hevea brasiliensis* of the Euphorbia family, exactly the same hydrocarbons as produced by the guayule shrub of Arizona. Various other Euphorbias produce significant amounts of milk-like sap, latex, that is actually an emulsion of hydrocarbons in water—though these hydrocarbons are superior to those of crude oils, since they are practically free of sulfur and contaminants found in fossil petroleum.

All in all, some 30,000 species of plants produce latex. But the genus Euphorbia seems to be especially suitable for "growing gasoline," notably 12 Euphorbia species identified in Brazil that contain about 10% dry weight of hydrocarbon-like materials. Not only do they yield valuable products, but they can be grown in areas that are too dry for other conventional purposes, or on land that is otherwise useless, such as strip-mined areas—thus opening up the prospect that a piece of land, having been devastated through extraction of fossil hydrocarbons from below the surface, can then be rehabilitated through growing of natural hydrocarbons above the surface.

Small-scale experiments in California, Israel and South Africa indicate that one acre of Euphorbia trees can produce between 10 and 50 barrels of oil per year, at annual production costs that average around $30 per barrel, to be compared with current OPEC prices of around $25. Geneticists have no doubt that production could be doubled through seed selection in the first year, while agronomists believe they could achieve similar increases in yield within a few years. After all, the rubber tree in 1945 was producing a mere 200 pounds of rubber per acre, an amount which scientists pushed upwards 10 times within the space of 20 years, and even bred a few trees that yielded 40 times as much. Commercial plantations have been established on Okinawa by two large Japanese corporations, Nippon Oil and Sekisui Plastics.

Species and Medicine

As for medicine, there is one chance in two that, when we take a medical prescription to a pharmacy, the drug we receive is derived from a wild species. Of 250,000 plant species on earth, some 3,000 have been found to possess potential anti-cancer properties. The World Health Organization, seeking ways to manufacture a safer and more effective contraceptive pill, believes that its best prospect lies with plant species of tropical rain forests.

In light of experience to date, it seems a statistical certainty that earth's stock of species offers many utilitarian benefits to society. Indeed, species could rate among our most valuable raw materials with which to meet unknown challenges of the future. Yet the earth's stock of species is being depleted more rapidly than many of the earth's most precious mineral deposits.

Main Cause of Species Extinction: Loss of Habitat

The main process by which species are driven extinct is loss of habitat. Loss of habitat occurs mainly through economic exploitation of natural environments; and natural environments are exploited mainly to satisfy consumer demands for numerous products. By consequence, species are eliminated through the activities of many millions of people, who are unaware of the "spillover" impact of their consumerist life-styles.

Increasingly, this impact extends to lands around the back of the earth. Rich-world communities of the temperate zones, containing one-fifth of earth's population, account for four-fifths of raw materials traded through international markets. Many of these materials derive from the tropical zone, which harbors between two-thirds and three-quarters of all species on earth. Yet extraction of these materials generally causes disruption of natural environments. Thus affluent sectors of the global community are responsible—unknowingly for sure, but effectively nonetheless—for destruction of myriad species' habitats in lands far distant from their own.

A Special Case: Tropical Moist Forests

By way of illustration, let us take a brief look at the case of tropical moist forests. These forests cover only 7% of earth's land surface, yet they contain at least 40% of all species. Were these forests to be grossly disrupted if not destroyed outright, as seems entirely likely during the next 3-5 decades, the process would drive extinct many potential sources of new foods. It would wipe out startpoint materials for whole pharmacopeias of new drugs, thus setting back the campaign against cancer, heart disease and a dozen other major scourges.

Elimination of these forests stems in part from market demand on the part of affluent nations for hardwoods and other specialist timbers from the forests. Moreover, the disruptive harvesting of tropical timber is often conducted by multinational corporations that supply the capital, technology and skills without which developing countries could not exploit their forest stocks at unsustainable rates. In addition, many tropical forests, notably in Latin America, are being cleared to make way for artificial pasturelands, with the aim of producing more beef—but the extra meat, instead of going into stomachs of local citizens, makes its way to North America, Western Europe and Japan, where it supplies the hamburger trade and other fast-food businesses. This foreign beef, being cheaper than similar-grade beef produced from tropical-zone grass-lands, is considered to make a marked contribution to the developed nations' campaign against inflation—and the fat-cat citizen, looking for a hamburger of best quality at "reasonable" price, is not aware of the spillover impact of his actions. So whose hand is on the chain saw?

Looked at this way, the problem of declining tropical forests in particular, as the problem of disappearing species in general, can be seen to be intimately related to other major issues of an interdependent global community: food, population, energy, plus various other problems that confront society at large. In fact, it is not going too far to say that the challenge of conservation of species is a microcosm of broader problems that arise from integrated living in the global village.

The World Community's Response to the Challenge

What can the world community do to respond to this challenge? Various possibilities arise.

1. Primarily, there is need to acknowledge the size and scope of the problem—that we are impoverishing earth's endowment in species without taking the ultimate consequences into systematic account. The marketplace does not recognize ultimate values such as those represented by species, nor does it take account of future needs and opportunities extending into the indefinite future.

2. After recognizing the nature of the beast that we must tackle, we can come to grips with it by accepting that we are all part of the problem. Although the great majority of earth's species exist in the tropics, destruction of their habitat lies, in major measure, with consumerist life-styles of developed nations. Just as we are all contributing to the problem, and just as we shall either all lose together or all win together, so we should all share in the costs of a comprehensive conservation campaign to safeguard species.

3. Corporations and other organizations can actively support conservation campaigns. It seems curious that leading pharmaceutical enterprises, for example, do not seek to protect their future sources of raw materials by supporting efforts on the part of tropical nations to set aside protected areas in, e.g., tropical forests. These areas need not all be parks and other areas that are "off limits" to exploitation of whatever kind; they could include areas that are designated as "natural resource ecosystems," where selective extraction of high-value materials such as phyto-chemicals could be conducted with little disruptive impact on the original forest.

The need for the world community to cast an eye over the conservation scene can be illustrated by evaluating the contribution of genetic materials—germplasm, etc.—to industry, agriculture and medicine. The United States' economy, for example, depends on genetic materials to an extent of at least $10 billion per year, possibly a great deal more. The bulk of these genetic materials derive from the tropics, i.e., from developing countries—with all that implies for the North-South confrontation. It is probably not going too far to say that this dependency of the American economy on foreign supplies of genetic resources amounts to a kind of "strategic interest."

Breakout into Space

Gerard K. O'Neill and William T. Bryant

Beneath the surface turmoil of humanity during the 1970s, futurists of many disciplines quietly made substantial progress toward a practical understanding of the exciting new era now so rapidly nearing reality—including humanity's impending breakout into space.

Entering the 1980s, the great interdisciplinary task of futurists must be to assert vigorously, in terms understandable to the citizens of all nations, the urgent need to re-examine Earth's problems—and opportunities—in the better light made possible by the knowledge and technology developed in recent years.

The immediate challenge is to set in motion an ambitious program for translating our global concepts into realistic local action. The time has come to share with the people, generously, the lessons we have been learning about the future. What is now the insight of a few must become the common knowledge of the many.

To accomplish this vital educational mission, we should of course begin by seeking a stronger cohesion among ourselves, a better synthesis of the results of the work we have variously been doing, a greater harmony of our diverse interests. If we mean to offer a workable alternative to the dangerous future-scenario now dominating the headlines, we need to become more familiar with the reportable progress of our colleagues in many fields of study, in order to form a better picture of the whole.

The purpose of this presentation is to contribute to a better appreciation of the potential role of space technology in the 1980s and beyond, as a vital component of the general uplifting of the human condition in the near future.

A comprehensive overview of the progress of space research and development would require far more time than this occasion permits. Space may have kept a much lower profile in the 1970s, but the decade in fact produced a thorough rethinking of humanity's near-term prospects

Gerard K. O'Neill is Professor of Physics at Princeton University, Princeton, New Jersey, Founder and President of the Space Studies Institute, and author of The High Frontier: Human Colonies in Space *(Bantam, 1978).*

William T. Bryant, a former journalist, is a consultant to the Space Studies Institute, Princeton, New Jersey.

in space, with increasingly dramatic results. The powerful thrust of the emerging High Frontier concept is radically changing the future-perception of many people in many nations, just as predictably as Neil Armstrong's first step on the moon proved to be such a powerful single event in our history.

Space development, as preliminary and as primitive as it has been so far, has nonetheless irrevocably changed the world in which we live. Now, in ways virtually unimaginable even as recently as the Apollo missions, we are ready for the next great leap, which depends upon the satisfactory answering of three very fundamental questions:

1. How plentiful are the resources available in space?
2. How obtainable are those resources?
3. How costly will the breakout be?

If these questions can indeed be answered satisfactorily—not only in technical jargon, but also in nontechnical language more understandable to the general public—then our common hopes for the future should stand a much better chance of realization.

How Plentiful Are the Resources Available in Space?

It is true that Earth is finite, that its resources are limited, and that humanity's horizons must inevitably be limited, too—if our future is confined to Earth.

It is equally true that space offers us a potentially incredible expansion of resources. Contrary to the popular notion of space as an empty place, it is, in fact, a rich and habitable economic region, continually bathed in the sun's mostly wasted energy and liberally sprinkled with the totally unused raw materials of the moon and asteroids—resources many thousands of times greater than what is available on Earth, resources capable of satisfying humanity's evolving needs for many thousands of years.

The limits to growth may soon be shattered, permanently, and humanity's horizons may eventually extend to the furthest reaches of space and time, through the historically logical development of the space option.

Consider the sun. While we on Earth prepare to do battle over our remaining fossil fuels, there streams by in space, every second, more than 30% more watts per square meter than falls on the most favorable desert area of Earth at high noon on a clear day. This intensity of 1,400 watts per square meter means that a solar cell in space would give a total amount of energy eight times greater than the total annual output from an identical cell located on Earth.

The surface of Earth happens to be the worst place imaginable to try to harness the energy of the sun. Space is ideal, because sunlight is available in space all of the time. If it can be intercepted there, it can be converted to continuous electric power with no problems of storage, whatever the weather may happen to be. The technical challenge, of course, is to get it from there to here.

America's Apollo missions to the lunar highlands and seas collected 836 pounds of rock and soil. Extensive analysis has shown that the lunar material consists of 40% oxygen, 20% silicon, and as much as 30% metals, mainly iron, aluminum, titanium, and magnesium. As a result of three billion years of meteorite impacts, the moon is a prospector's paradise. Additional mapping of the lunar surface may well reveal the presence, at the poles, of yet another essential element of human activity—water.

Beyond the moon are the asteroids. Not all would be suitable for retrieval and mining, but many would be excellent candidates. More are discovered every year, and the total number is estimated at more than 100,000.

Making Earth-based telescopic observations, astronomers have classified the chemical composition of these asteroids by means of spectral analysis, comparing their data with the results of laboratory studies of the optical properties of meteorites found on Earth. Results indicate that the asteroids may contain not only all of the elements found on the moon, but also hydrogen, carbon, nitrogen, and water. Just one relatively small asteroid of 10 million tons would make available approximately 4.5 million tons of usable raw materials.

Moreover, recent research supported by the Space Studies Institute has opened the door to what could be a most attractive storehouse of raw materials. Following a suggestion by Nobel laureate Hannes Alfvén, a Princeton University graduate student named Scott Dunbar has written his doctoral thesis on a difficult problem in gravitational theory. Dunbar has shown that small asteroids could be trapped along Earth's orbit. If so—and an inexpensive telescopic probe could find them if they do exist—those nuggets would be retrievable at almost no cost in energy.

Lunar and asteroidal material represents, therefore, an effective answer to one of humanity's most pressing questions regarding the future. The sun represents another. The potential is there, if we can and will utilize it.

How Obtainable Are Those Resources?

We can begin to utilize the raw materials and solar energy of space within this decade—within existing technology—if we apply ourselves to the opportunity. No new breakthroughs are required. The pace at which we proceed will be determined not by technical ability, but by national and popular willpower.

Already, we are developing the knowledge and the hardware to implant a mining and manufacturing capability in space, to obtain and then chemically process lunar and asteroidal material into the pure elements needed for the building of large structures in space, and for other industrial purposes on Earth and in space.

We now depend on chemical-fueled rockets to lift men and their machines and supplies from Earth, and to propel ships in open space. In the future, using the resources of space to build objects in space, we will need not only a device for launching materials from the surface of the moon to processing and manufacturing facilities in open space, but also a more efficient propulsion system for carrying freight from low-Earth orbit to higher orbits and beyond, and eventually for retrieving asteroids.

Potentially answering both of these needs is a unique new machine called the mass-driver, an electromagnetic propulsion system already being developed jointly at Princeton University and at the Massachusetts Institute of Technology. Essentially, the mass-driver is a device for accelerating materials to very high speeds, very quickly and very efficiently.

Research has produced several scenarios for taking advantage of non-terrestrial resources, beginning with the establishment of a lunar mining facility, together with a processing and manufacturing facility either on the moon or, more likely, in open space. For example, by the end of a decade, a fully operational mass-driver on the moon could be launching 600,000 tons of raw materials annually toward a mass-catcher and companion industrial facilities about 40,000 miles away.

Once we have gotten our hands on these materials, of course, we need to be able to use them. The breakout into space thus ultimately depends on our learning how to separate lunar and asteroidal materials into their component elements. Considerable progress already has been made in that direction, and the Space Studies Institute has put its highest priority on raising funds to build and test a working pilot plant, to extract pure elements from soils identical to those of the moon.

How do we "obtain" the energy of the sun? Efforts at ground-based solar collection have made great strides in recent years, but there are inherent limits to such efforts. In 1979, a committee of the American Institute of Physics concluded that ground-based solar power would be most unlikely ever to supply more than 5% of U.S. needs for electricity, because above that level we have yet to solve the problem of how to store the electricity cheaply.

In 1968, Peter Glaser introduced the concept of supplying Earth's electric power system with energy transmitted from satellites located in permanent sunlight. Because of the world's worsening energy crisis, the Solar Power Satellite idea has steadily been receiving more serious attention.

Basically, an SPS would collect sunlight, convert it into microwaves (or possibly laser beams), and send the power down to receiving antennas on Earth, where it would be reconverted to electricity and fed into the power grids. One such 100,000-ton SPS would be 10 miles long, a couple of miles wide, and several hundred feet thick. It would be capable of delivering to Earth 10,000 megawatts of baseload (round-the-clock) power, enough for metropolitan Washington and Baltimore combined, or the equivalent of 10 nuclear- or coal-fired power plants. (It is worth noting that just one relatively small asteroid could provide enough raw material for the construction of 10 to 40 Solar Power Satellites.)

The effects of microwave power transmission are the subject of governmental research under sponsorship of the U.S. Department of Energy. The first two years of research have found no unacceptable environmental effects. If studies continue to produce positive results, SPS may offer a workable and less expensive alternative to nuclear and fossil-fuel power. The first SPS could enter service during the 1990s and dozens could be in orbit within 20 years, greatly easing Earth's energy crisis.

How Costly Will the Breakout Be?

As with any great human enterprise, the likely cost of making the breakout into space must be weighed against the likely benefit, and both must be measured in societal and environmental as well as energy and economic terms.

Obviously, a vast amount of research remains to be done in the social and natural sciences, ongoing research to see us through the challenging period ahead. So far, however, studies firmly indicate that space industrialization (with or without SPS) will be acutely "profitable" not only for the people of Earth, but also for a growing population in space. Enormous human benefits may be expected to flow from an orderly development of space resources.

In this time of high inflation and tight budgets—at the same time we need to be proceeding with the breakout—the Space Studies Institute has been supporting workshops to find the quickest, lowest-cost method of reaching high economic productivity in space. This research into scaling (the examination of each component in a productive system to determine the minimum scale on which it can be built to operate with high efficiency) and bootstrapping (the rapid expansion of industry in space through replication of some of its own components) has produced some exciting results.

The workshops have found that an investment of $6-8 billion—no more than the cost of some wholly private ventures like the Alaska Pipeline—would be enough to establish a partially automated industry in space with the capability to produce 100,000 tons of products annually, with a value of more than $10 billion.

This scaling and bootstrapping approach would permit the cost-effective short-term use of nonterrestrial materials while leaving open all long-term options.

The availability of nonterrestrial resources makes the whole space industrialization and humanization picture much brighter. Construction in space, using space resources, will permit the more efficient and less costly expansion of many existing space-based systems, such as communications, remote-sensing, and scientific satellites—as well as the building of Solar Power Satellites, large-scale factories and agricultural stations, and permanent communities comfortably and safely supporting large populations.

Previously, our thoughts about building large structures in space centered on making the components on Earth and developing new heavy-lift launch vehicles for lifting the components to orbital assembly points. But recent studies increasingly show that the financial and environmental costs would be far less by using nonterrestrial materials for construction in space itself.

An SPS built in space, with more than 90% of its components made from nonterrestrial resources, could actually cost less than a nuclear or coal-fired power plant built on Earth. According to economist Peter Vajk, what this means, among other things, is that we could save more than half a trillion dollars in the next 50 years just by replacing worn-out generating facilities on Earth with SPS units. Further, the saving in energy costs is a conclusive reason to use nonterrestrial resources—they are available for space manufacturing at about 1/20 of the energy costs of lifting finished components up from Earth's strong gravitational field. (And keep in mind that if asteroidal material is indeed trapped along Earth's orbit, it would be retrievable at almost no energy cost.)

We need more energy, and more raw materials, if we are to sustain the momentum and broaden the horizons of our civilization. Space offers us what we need, in abundance.

How costly will the breakout be? Perhaps, we should rephrase the question: How costly would it be if we fail to break out into space?

Since the launch of Sputnik, humanity has made good progress in the development of our space capabilities. From unmanned to manned activity, from suborbital to orbital flight, from standard orbital missions to spectacular lunar landings, we have been steadily learning how well human beings can function in this new environment.

Once the exclusive province of the United States and the Soviet Union, space development is becoming a vigorous international enterprise. No fewer than 146 nations are now engaged in space-related activities, and more than 100 regularly receive, transmit, and process data through space-based information systems. Eight nations and several multinational groups have made approximately 2,500 launches into Earth orbit or deep space. Fifteen nations have already demonstrated suborbital flight capabilities, and 24 maintain launch facilities.

Worldwide, the trend (especially among the developing nations) is toward greater involvement in space—and cooperation, of which Intelsat, now linking 102 nations, is a prime example. It is actually easier these days for a nation to get into space than to develop nuclear weaponry. Many nations are doing it, or are planning to do it fairly soon.

Already, there is ample evidence that our preliminary investment in space is generating huge benefits for humanity, that spinoffs from space technology are routinely revolutionizing large sectors of our life. Projections for the 1980s and 1990s point to an ever greater impact, particularly in communications, education, transportation, food production, public safety, industry, and commerce.

Aside from often subtle ways in which space technology is reaching the public marketplace, increasingly sophisticated satellite systems are making more obvious contributions. Communications satellites now represent not only instant TV, but also the tools for teaching people anywhere and everywhere, for providing long-distance medical diagnosis, emergency rescue, and disaster-relief services. Remote-sensing satellites are proving their worth in everything from land-use planning to estimating crop yields, inventorying mineral and forest resources, tracing coastline changes, and measuring industrial pollution.

Cheaper space transportation systems (the American Space Shuttle and comparable vehicles of other nations), combined with the logical utilization of nonterrestrial resources, will make possible in the near future larger communications and remote-sensing systems. At the same time, rapid advances in microelectronic circuitry will be making more efficient, less expensive ground stations more widely available.

More so among the developing than among the developed nations, because the impact is proportionally much greater, space activity is acutely relevant and should be strongly encouraged. An SPS that added only 2% to America's generating capacity could add 40% to India's. A communications satellite system of limited value within continental Europe could prove indispensable among the thousands of islands of Indonesia. Our hope of achieving a better economic and educational balance among the nations may well largely depend upon space technology.

If some of use seem especially anxious to move ahead with the breakout into space, it is because we are sensitive to the dangers and adverse human effects of every day's delay. There is an urgent need to prevent the breakup of active research groups and preserve momentum, to broaden and deepen our research.

There are other sources of anxiety, of course: concern that confrontational trends might race too far ahead of our growing ability to counteract them, that we might blow ourselves up on the basis of outdated information. Concern that economic and social conditions might deteriorate to a point where we would be incapable of taking advantage of the knowledge we possess. Concern that we might make the tragic mistake of underestimating ourselves, our resources, and our options, thereby delaying space humanization (and its benefits) and/or permitting space to be unfairly exploited and used for the extension of nationalistic military confrontation.

We can pay strict attention to humanity's needs on Earth while at the same time accomplishing the breakout into space. Indeed, the two efforts seem logically to go hand in hand. Space technology may not be the solution to all of our problems, or even the whole answer to any one of them, but it can and should be viewed as an integral part of whatever solution eventually emerges.

The vastness of space and the abundance of its resources mean that the opportunity for extending and expanding human civilization, within this solar system and beyond, may be considered virtually limitless. Materially, we should now be moving from an economics of scarcity to an economics of plenty, from competition for decreasing resources to cooperation for increasing resources. The challenge is to create a new capability for incorporating this dramatic new reality.

It should be made an assumption of human society that the breakout into space is inevitable and imminent, and our planning for the future should be adjusted accordingly.

We may now view space itself as our goal, not merely as an avenue to the discovery of habitable planets. And we may view the goal as reachable in the reasonably near future, not in some remotely distant time.

The astronauts and cosmonauts have been preparing the way for the mass of humanity to be able to enjoy the benefits and to take advantage of the opportunities of space. The humanization process obviously extends far beyond highly technical or purely industrial activity to a time when large numbers of men, women, and children are living and working in space—when the relationship between Earth and the communities of space will be as natural as the relationship between Earth's Old and New Worlds.

By the end of this century, thousands of people could be working in space, and the first permanent communities could be ready for occupancy, giving humanity the capability of rapidly expanding its presence in space.

Within the next one or two centuries, our civilization, at home throughout our solar system, may well include pioneers beginning the journey to other stars.

This view of the future, however, depends on the decisions we make and the actions we take in the months and years immediately ahead. In the final analysis, ours is the historic responsibility of unlocking the door to an open future for humanity.

The Oceans As the Common Heritage of Mankind

by

Arvid Pardo and Elisabeth Mann Borgese

On November 1, 1967, the Delegation of Malta introduced the concept of the Common Heritage of Mankind in the First Committee of the General Assembly of the United Nations. "We are strongly of the opinion," the Maltese statement read, "that the following, among other, principles should be incorporated in the proposed Treaty:

1. The seabed and the ocean floor, underlying the seas beyond the limits of national jurisdiction as defined in the Treaty, are not subject to national appropriation in any manner whatsoever.

2. The seabed and the ocean floor beyond the limits of national jurisdiction shall be reserved exclusively for peaceful purposes.

3. Scientific research with regard to the deep seas and ocean floor, not directly connected with defense, shall be freely permissible and its results available to all.

4. The resources of the seabed and ocean floor, beyond the limits of national jurisdiction, shall be exploited primarily in the interest of mankind, with particular regard to the needs of poor countries.

5. The exploration and exploitation of the seabed and ocean floor beyond the limits of national jurisdiction shall be conducted in a manner consistent with the principles and purposes of the United Nations Charter and in a manner not causing unnecessary obstruction of the high seas or serious impairment of the marine environment.

This, as the same delegation pointed out in a later statement (October 29, 1968) was "a new legal principle which we wish to introduce into international law." The concept of the common heritage "implies the notion of peaceful uses, since it is clear that military use of the ocean floor might impair or endanger the common property. The common heritage concept implies freedom of access and use on the part of those having part in the heritage, but also regulation of use for the

Arvid Pardo has long represented Malta in the United Nations and has played a leading role in international discussions on the Law of the Sea.

Elisabeth Mann Borgese is a member of the Delegation of Austria to the Law of the Sea Conference and Professor of Political Science, Dalhousie University, Halifax, Nova Scotia, Canada.

purpose of conserving the heritage and avoiding the infringement of the rights of others; inherent in the regulation of use is, of course, responsibility for misuse. The concept finally implies the equitable distribution of benefits from exploitation of the heritage. It is possible to go further: the notion of property that cannot be divided without the consent of all and which should be administered in the interest and for the benefit of all is a logical extension of the common heritage concept."

The Delegation of Malta explained that it preferred the term "common heritage" to the term "common property." "We did not think it advisable to use the word "property" ... Property is a form of power. Property as we have it from the ancient Romans implies the *jus utendi et abutendi* (right to use and misuse). Property implies and gives excessive emphasis to just one aspect: resource exploitation and benefits derived therefrom." The content of the common heritage ought to be "determined pragmatically in relation to felt international needs." It is not limited by a complex of real or potential resources. "World resources should not be conceived in a static sense. New resources are being constantly created by technology." The Common Heritage of Mankind, however, also includes *values*. "It includes also scientific research." Thus if there were a set of ethical and legal rules to be derived from the principle of the common heritage, these would have to be applicable to science policy as well.

In a 1970 statement, Malta suggested three characteristics of the Common Heritage of Mankind. First of all, "the absence of property." The common heritage engenders the right to *use* certain property, but not to *own* it. "It implies the management of property and the obligation of the international community to transmit this common heritage, including resources and values, in historical terms. Common Heritage implies management. Management not only in the sense of management of resources, but management of all uses." Thirdly, common heritage implies sharing of benefits. "Resources are very important; benefits are very important. But this is only a part of the total concept."

In international law, the concept of the Common Heritage of Mankind is certainly a revolutionary innovation. It has the potential of changing the relationship between rich and poor nations by substituting the principle of sharing and common management as central for development planning, for the postcolonial and humiliating concept of foreign aid.

New Theory of Economics

A whole new theory of economics can indeed be built on this distinction between the right to *ownership*, which is rejected, and the right to *utilize* and *manage*, which is upheld. The building of such a new system has been attempted by Orio Giarini in his 1979 Report to the Club of Rome, *Producing Value for Wealth and Welfare—The Role of Capital and Capital Needs*. The source of wealth, in that report, is called the "patrimony" and it comprises all the natural, biological, man-made and monetarized assets from which we derive our means of livelihood. It is a "stock" of an accumulation of assets which have "utilization" value.

This notion of a value is thus related to a "stock" and not, as in the conventional economic process, to a "flow" (where the notion of value is linked with the transformation process of products and services). A "flow" can in fact have also *negative* effects (deducted values) rather than added values in terms of real wealth and welfare. The real value of products and services cannot be measured by their cost/exchange value at a given moment, but by their utilization value over a period of time.

Such a theory of value would be most applicable to a common heritage regime–or a common heritage system would be the logical outcome of applying such a theory of value. For what cannot be owned can have no cost/exchange value; what can be utilized and managed must have a utilization value.

An economic theory based on the principle of common heritage and its utilization value is more in harmony with the present phase of the industrial revolution and its economic and ecological implications than a theory based on the concept of ownership, whether private or State.

United Nations Declaration

The principle of the common heritage of mankind, as proposed by Malta in 1967, was incorporated in a UN General Assembly resolution in 1970, "Declaration of Principles Governing the Seabed and the Ocean Floor, and the Subsoil Thereof, Beyond the Limits of National Jurisdiction." The essence of the principle is contained in the first six paragraphs of the Resolution:

1. The seabed and ocean floor, and the subsoil thereof, beyond the limits of national jurisdiction (hereinafter referred to as the area), as well as the resources of the area, are the common heritage of mankind.

2. The area shall not be subject to appropriation by any means by States or persons, natural or juridical, and no State shall claim or exercise sovereignty or sovereign rights over any part thereof.

3. No State or person, natural or juridical, shall claim, exercise or acquire rights with respect to the area or its resources incompatible with the international regime to be established and the principles of this Declaration.

4. All activities regarding the exploration and exploitation of the resources of the area and other related activities shall be governed by the international regime to be established.

5. The area shall be open to use exclusively for peaceful purposes by all States, whether coastal or land-locked, without discrimination, in accordance with the international regime to be established.

6. States shall act in the area in accordance with the applicable principles and rules of international law, including the Charter of the United Nations and the Declaration on Principles of International Law concerning Friendly Relations and Co-operation among States in accordance with the Charter of the United Nations, adopted by the General Assembly on 24 October 1970, in the interests of maintaining international peace and security and promoting international

cooperation and mutual understanding.

Subsequent versions of the Negotiating Text elaborated at the Third UN Conference on the Law of the Sea have somewhat weakened these principles—partly through interpretation, partly by dispersing them in the text. The conference has never attempted to define the term "common heritage of mankind" or to give it a precise legal and economic content. This may seem strange, considering the fundamental importance of the principle and the often repeated claim that it should be the basis not only of the new Law of the Sea but of the entire New International Economic Order.

If one combines fragments, now dispersed in four different articles, one could arrive at a concise definition of the common heritage, in two articles:

First Article

The area and its resources are a Common Heritage of Mankind.

Second Article

For the purpose of this Convention, "Common Heritage of Mankind" shall mean that:

1. No State shall claim or exercise sovereignty or sovereign rights over any part of the area or its resources, nor shall any State or person, natural or juridical, appropriate any part thereof. No such claim or exercise of sovereignty or sovereign rights, nor such appropriation, shall be recognized.

2. The area and its resources shall be managed for the benefit of mankind as a whole, irrespective of the geographic location of States, whether coastal or landlocked, and taking into particular consideration the interests and needs of the developing countries as specifically provided for in this part of the Convention.

3. The area shall be open to use exclusively for peaceful purposes by all states, whether coastal or landlocked, without discrimination and without prejudice to the other provisions of this part of the present Convention.

4. Necessary measures shall be taken in order to ensure effective protection of the marine environment from harmful effects which may arise from activities in the area, in accordance with Part XII of the present Convention.

The Articles express the legal and economic attributes of the Common Heritage concept. Quite succinctly these attributes are:

- non-appropriability
- shared management
- benefit-sharing by mankind as a whole
- use for peaceful purposes only
- conservation for future generations.

The concept of the common heritage of mankind—a new principle in international law—is indeed complex, with legal, economic, and institutional implications that will require interpretation and adjustment to the ever-changing realities of the international system for years to come. It should also be clear that it is an explosive and expansive principle. Once enshrined as a norm of international law, it will find applications far wider than the oceans.

The International Context

The Future of International Governance

by

Harlan Cleveland

The Background

Earlier prescriptions for world governance, from Alexander and Rome down to *Deutschland über Alles* and the global ambitions of Stalinist Communism, projected vertical structures of power so fashioned that a comparatively few (chosen for their birth or race or class or wealth or military capacity but always chosen by themselves) would make the rules of international politics for the many. It was a quite natural assumption. The highest form of order had been the single state (whether city-state, empire, or modern nation-state), which had assembled the power to govern by exercising the leadership of a few on behalf of, or at the expense of, everyone else. Wouldn't government at the world level have to be the same? The extrapolation of history said yes.

The League of Nations Covenant and the United Nations Charter still required a club of the like-minded to keep the peace and make the rules for change. With their emphasis on self-determination of peoples and human rights for individuals, they began a breakaway from the heirarchical patterns of earlier centuries. But the prime actors they recognized were sovereign nation-states, leaving little room for leadership other than by governments and no recourse if the initially like-minded governments fell apart.

Meanwhile, the expectations and ambitions of real-life men and women have in this century proved too various and too vigorous for the static "structures of peace" their transient leaders established to contain them. The urgent rush of science and technology, the rivalries of great powers, the success of the anti-colonial movement, the mass migrations of people, the awakening of submerged races and classes, and the importunities of plain people who came to consider their universal rights and needs more important than universal order and organized to struggle for the blessings

Harlan Cleveland has been Director of the Aspen Institute's Program in International Affairs, Princeton, New Jersey, since 1974. On August 1, 1980, he becomes the first Director of the Hubert H. Humphrey School of Public Affairs at the University of Minnesota. He served as U.S. Ambassador to NATO during the 1960s and later was President of the University of Hawaii. His article is excerpted from a prospectus for a three-year project on the evolution of international institutions.

they felt were due them kept creating problems of global scale that made the structures of international governance at best irrelevant and at worst dysfunctional. And to make things worse the nation-state, still and for the foreseeable future the most important building-block of world order, itself grew to be arthritic and crotchety, progressively less able to cope with an environment of accelerating change.

Traditional approaches to the study of international organization are deficient in several respects. Work on international affairs is usually focussed on specialized fields—on monetary policy, on arms control, on human rights, on foreign aid and development, on trade and investment, on science and technology, on educational and cultural interchange—without asking the questions that link them together. Moreover, much "foreign policy" analysis assumes a much clearer distinction between "domestic" and "international" affairs than is now discernible in the real world. In addition, there is the temptation to assume that international institutions are destined sooner or later to take on governmental powers analogous to those of nation-states.

We start, then, with the assumption that the evolution of international institutions will not follow the double helix of the nation-state, and that the way to think creatively about the future of the international system is not to replicate at the global level the formulas that are failing to cope with complexity at the national level. In a world in which no nation or alliance or class or racial group will be in charge, the institutions for the resolution of conflict, the protection of people's rights and the fulfillment of their needs, and the management of resources, production, consumption, employment, money, and information will be expressions of a mandatory pluralism. With this as our hypothesis, our inquiry will explore what this state of affairs will mean, and should mean, in practical terms for the future of international governance during the 1980s and 1990s.

The term *governance* is used to make clear that our inquiry will consider not only the prospect for intergovernmental organizations and relationships, but also the evidently expanding role in world affairs of nongovernmental institutions—national and international, "public" and "private," business and nonprofit.

The Inquiry

A fresh look at the international system must begin with an effort to summarize, in a comprehensible framework, a myriad of trends that constitute "the transition we are in." The purpose of our whole inquiry will then be to *consider the implications for international institution-building and institution-adapting of the already observable and inherently probable changes* in (a) *the content* of relations among nations and among societies, and (b) *the processes* by which individuals and groups and whole societies deal with each other. From these it should be possible to derive a sketch of the functions the "international system" of the future must somehow get organized to perform.

The "transition we are in" is a variety of changes in beliefs, loyalties, fears, aspirations, doctrines, and assumptions about personal and national futures. They involve, in effect, widespread changes in the meaning of, and the relative priority given to, three basic motivations in social and political behavior:

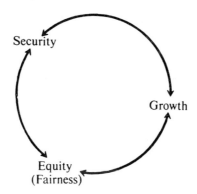

1. Security

From:

Military defense

National security
Balance of power, based on
  reciprocal certainties
Nuclear superiority
Conventional and nuclear arms
  build-up
Imperial rule
Nuclear oligopoly
Big-power domination

Emphasis on geographic regions

To:

Wider concepts of defense (e.g.,
  energy, balance of payments,
  environmental risk, religious
  and cultural tradition)
International security
Mutual deterrence, based on
  reciprocal uncertainties
Nuclear parity
Arms control and disarmament

Decolonization
Nuclear proliferation
Diffusion of initiative;
  pluralistic leadership
Emergence of "functional regions"
  (such as OPEC and OECD)

2. Values

From:

Exclusive national sovereignty
  over people's livelihood

Exclusive national sovereignty
  over security of the person
Population as a "domestic"
  concern
Cultural domination, homogeniza-
  tion of cultures
Immobility of people
Rural center of gravity
"Demand-pull" migration
Man's world

To:

International economic/social
  entitlements ("basic human
  needs")
International political/civil rights

Population as an international
  concern
Stress on cultural identity ("roots"),
  both national and subnational
Mobility of people
Urban center of gravity
"Supply-push" migration
Equality of the sexes

143

Racial discrimination	Racial equality and nondiscrimination
Family-centered societies	Atomization of individuals; large-scale social mobilization
Rugged individualism	Social responsibility
Education for elites	Universal education
Traditional, institutional education	Informal, nonformal, life-long education
Specialized education and research	Integrative education and research; "policy analysis"
Curative approaches to health	Preventive approaches to health
Social security, unemployment insurance, housing entitlements, the "welfare state"	Emphasis on productivity, full employment, earnings rather than entitlements

3. Resources

From:	*To:*
Focus on nonrenewable resources and energy	Focus on recycling the nonrenewables
	Focus on renewable (biological) resources and energy
	Focus on information as a resource
Limits to growth	Limits to governance
Fossil fuels and nuclear energy	More emphasis on "soft energy paths"
Centralized systems	More emphasis on decentralized systems
Urban investment	More emphasis on rural reconstruction
Waste disposal	Waste as a raw material
Focus on short-term advantages/ profits	Focus on wider (ecological) consequences of today's actions
Exploitation; "slash and burn"	Focus on interest of future generations

4. Growth

From:	*To:*
"Growth" measured and symbolized by GNP	Selective, purposeful growth ("Growth for what?")
Growth with trickle-down	Growth with equity ("Growth for whom?")
Unlimited growth	Ecodevelopment
Cyclical (erratic) growth	Sustainable growth
"Stages of growth" (singular path)	Alternative paths to development
Modernization with Western cultural trappings	Melding of modernization with local traditions
Modernization with Western political forms	Modernization with varying political forms
"Capitalism"	Mixed economy, in which control has become more important than ownership
"Socialism"	Mixed economy in which aspects of ownership (e.g., incen-

tives to farmers and managers)
are combined with "planning"

5. The World Economy

From:

Independence for some, dependence for others
Economic hegemony
Markets managed by early arrivals

Freedom of trade, investment, communications

Dollar as "key currency"

"Effective demand"
Focus on *exchange* (of things)
Proprietary information

To:

Interdependence as a two-way street

Self-reliance
Markets organized by political bargaining
Negotiated trade agreements, codes of conduct, allocation of frequency spectrum
Monetary pluralism; IMF as source of "world money"
Human needs
Focus on sharing (of information)
Concepts of "free flow" of information; international science; claims of entitlement to access to technology

6. The Global Commons

From:

"Freedom" of the seas, of outer space, of the airwaves ("freedom for the technologically strong")

National air space

Local and national weather forecasting and modification

Local environmental awareness

Local, national, and regional technologies

National academies of science; national science policies

To:

"The common heritage of mankind;" proposals for revenue sharing from off-shore oil and for a seabed mining enterprise; outer space legal regime
Cooperation on navigation, air traffic
World Weather Watch; Environmental Modification Convention; principle that "Weather belongs to nobody"
Awareness of global environmental risks (CO_2, ozone, ocean pollution)
Awareness of threats from "national overspill" (air and water pollution, acid rain)
Awareness of global threats to biosphere's resource base (overcropping, overgrazing, overcutting, overfishing, desertification)
Inherently global technologies
• Missiles, arms control, verification
• Satellites for weather forecasting, telecommunication, environmental monitoring, resource sensing
International community of scientists

7. Planning and Management

From:	*To:*
Concepts of automatic self-regulating systems ("invisible hand" of the market; "inner logic" of science and technology)	Concepts of social determination to serve human needs and purposes
Traditional economics	New, broader analytical system ("internalizing the externalities"); technology assessment; social indicators
Equilibrium systems	Sustainable dynamic flow systems
Division of functions	Interdependence of functions
Prestige of specialization	Growing requirement for integrative thinking
Premium on specialized excellence	Premium on "getting it all together"
Government as problem-solver	Shared public-private responsibility for outcomes
International politics	Planetary politics
Vertical systems ("Pyramids;" "recommendations-up-orders-down;" executives "driving")	Horizontal systems ("Flat organizations"; "Collegial relationships"; "consensus"; "collective leadership"; committee work; executives "steering")

"Functions of the Future"

Once we have a reasonably clear idea of "the transition we are in," it becomes possible to project the international "functions of the future." These are those activities of consensus-building, policy-making, conflict resolution, legitimation, planning, regulation, financing, and executive action that in the foreseeable future will have to be handled through international arrangements and institutions because national governments will not be able to cope with them by national action alone.

Following is a typology of these functional futures. This is not, of course, a fully thought-out forecast of the future evolution of international agreements, arrangements, and institutions. But it may be enough to suggest some of the implications for international institution-building of the six substantive categories just used to sketch "the transition we are in."

1. Security

The Goal: **To increase international security, to reduce the risk of war, and to facilitate peaceful change.**

The Tasks:
1. To prevent nuclear war.
2. To reduce and reverse the nuclear arms race.
3. To reduce the conventional arms race to levels consistent with legitimate self-defense.
4. To promote, at the bilateral, regional, and international levels, confidence-building measures through negotiations and unilateral national actions, to reduce the risk of war.

146

5. To promote greater resort by states to the different institutions and methods for the peaceful settlement of conflicts and disputes.
6. To facilitate peaceful change and to minimize the need to resort to violent means to bring about changes.
7. To explore the changing dimensions of security.
8. To enhance the U.N.'s and other international peace-keeping capacity.

2. Values

The Goal: **To translate into reality the international norms, principles, and standards of human rights.**

The Tasks:
1. To develop a system for establishing and reviewing international standards for individual entitlement to food, health, education, employment, and any other agreed components of basic human needs.
2. To keep under review the international migration of people, in all its aspects, as a basis for international action to minimize human suffering and international conflict.
3. To develop an effective international system for reviewing the individual enjoyment of civil and political rights.
4. To ensure freedom of movement and expression for people in pursuit of educational and cultural objectives.
5. To spread internationally the products of national research into coping with the physical and human dimensions of urban living.
6. To monitor the problems of and help sustain minority and tribal cultures.

3. Resources

The Goal: **To regulate the use and prevent abuse of our shared resources.**

The Tasks:
1. To develop a system that promotes exploration for, and keeps a world inventory of, nonrenewable resources that may be needed by people outside the nations where the resources are to be found.
2. To develop a system that monitors world production of food and fibres and provides for the exchange of timely information on national harvests and food requirements.
3. To push agricultural productivity in the developing nations, and meanwhile to make sure there is enough food for all through a world food reserve.
4. To hold, finance, and manage buffer stocks of selected world commodities, in order to assure continuity of supply and stability of prices for producers and consumers in relation to long-term market forces.
5. To promote cooperation between oil producers and consumers, to help reduce energy waste in the indus-

trial nations, to encourage international research and
development of alternative energy sources, and to
assist developing countries in devising sound energy
strategies as a crucial part of their development planning.

6. To seek international agreement to limit overcropping,
overgrazing, overcutting, overfishing, and overcon-
sumption.

7. To examine the implications for international relations
of the emerging concept of "information as a resource."

8. To promote the fullest access to information in all
parts of the world.

9. To set international disposal standards and storage
control systems for nuclear and other toxic wastes.

4. Growth

The Goal: **To promote the better dissemination and utilization of
information and knowledge for human purposes, as a
critical tool for growth, development, and modernization.**

The Tasks:
1. To assist developing countries to gain access to relevant information (including science and technology),
and make appropriate and selective use of information
for development.

2. To develop a system for relating economic
cooperation, including aid, to progress towards the
fuller achievement of basic human needs.

3. To raise funds for development financing directly by
fees and taxes related to the use of international
"commons" and to marry the allocation of these to the
meeting of basic human needs.

4. To consider methods of utilizing for world development projects the technical and civilian skill resources
held within existing military structures.

5. To fund R & D into technologies utilizing the renewable resources, especially those disproportionately
available in developing countries (biomass, solar radi-
ation).

5. The World Economy

The Goal: **To manage the world economy so as to promote
purposeful growth and greater equity.**

The Tasks:
1. To assure access by developing countries to markets in
the industrial countries.

2. To help manage constructive shifts in industrial geography and help nations plan investment in their own
industries in the light of investment policies of other
nations.

3. To resolve differences among transnational enterprises, host countries, and home countries over such
issues as taxation, employment, competitive practices,

and contributions to meeting basic human needs.

4. To provide for effective international consultation on actions by international monetary and budgetary authorities that substantially affect the money supply, and create international money in a manner and at a rate that is compatible with economic growth at reasonable rates of inflation—the definition of what is reasonable being itself the product of an international process.

5. To manage shifts in currency exchange, with the aims of limiting unproductive speculation and enhancing predictability as an assist to international trade and investment.

6. The Global Commons

The Goal: **To protect and enhance the human environment, and manage for the common benefit the global commons.**

The Tasks:

1. To develop a system that negotiates and monitors standards of air and water quality and reviews national actions that pollute beyond national frontiers.

2. To develop a system that keeps under review the damage and potential damage from human processes and blows the whistle on those that may affect people beyond national frontiers.

3. To report on, to forecast and prudently modify the world's climate and weather.

4. To monitor and protect the ozone layer.

5. To regulate traffic through, and pollution of, the atmosphere and the oceans.

6. To regulate the exploitation and conservation of the living and non-living resources of the oceans.

7. To utilize, for the benefit of mankind, the developing technologies and resources associated with outer space, celestial bodies, and the earth's vacant spaces such as Antarctica.

The "Community" of the Future

by

Charlotte Waterlow

It is popular among intellectuals today to regard the individualism embodied in the concept of Human Rights as a "Western" cultural expression, which is distorting the development of other regions of the world. In this essay I will suggest that the free expression of the individual person is not so much "Western" as "modern"; that modernity represents the first stage in a worldwide transformation of planetary consciousness which happened to start a few decades ahead in the West; and that the goal of the transformation is the emergence of the "community spirit" throughout the world, expressing itself at every level, from tiny groups to planetary bodies. The brotherhood of mankind is struggling to be born.

My first hypothesis, which is shared by some modern mystical thinkers such as Teilhard de Chardin and in a sense by Marxists, is that biological evolution is an aspect of the evolution of consciousness. (This hypothesis involves, of course, following Whitehead and other philosophers in rejecting the "reductionist" philosophy of orthodox biology and psychology, called by Arthur Koestler "ratomorphism.") My second hypothesis is that in terms of historical development this evolution has three main phases. The first is that of the traditional civilizations (in the plural); the second is "modern civilization" (in the singular), whose foundation stones are the concept of Human Rights and the development of science; and the third, just dawning, is the era of world community.

What is "community"? I will answer this question by contrasting it with three other kinds of social groups: the organic group, the "organization" and the "herd."

An "organism" may be defined as a living body whose parts are related to the function of the whole. Generally speaking, with the important partial exceptions of those of Greece and Rome, traditional societies were organic. Medieval political thinkers were constantly using the analogy between the human body and the "body politic." In them the pattern of human relationships was regarded as reflecting the divine pattern of the spiritual cosmos. Their structure was therefore both hierarchic and static. The purpose of a person's life was to fulfill the divinely

Charlotte Waterlow is the author of Superpowers and Victims: The Outlook for World Community *and other books. She lives in Cambridge, Massachusetts.*

ordained function attached to his or her "station"—whether that of a peasant tilling the ground, or a craftsman making "masterpieces," or a warrior fighting for the group, or a priest intervening with God or the gods on its behalf, or as a wife and mother looking after the home and rearing children. This static concept of "station" or caste produced the rule of custom. Every aspect of a person's life—his housing, education, marriage, food, costume, pastimes, even forms of speech—was governed by customs relating to his function. If freedom of choice or idea were allowed to creep in, it would upset the whole structure of society and the religious beliefs on which that structure was based. In ancient Japan, for instance, where there were rules regulating every detail of life, according to one's caste, down to the material of the thongs of the sandals or the ornaments in a woman's hair, to behave in an "other-than-to-be-expected" way, that is, in an original, individualistic way, was punishable by death. In Malawi, in Africa, anyone with exceptional talent was thought to be bewitched. Gandhi's eldest sister, when aged about 90, "exploded with toothless anger and tears" when asked about her world-famous brother. His breach of all the caste rules had meant for her "a life-time of ostracism and humiliation by the people about whom she minded: the orthodox of her own sub-caste and neighborhood." Many of these societies developed culture of the highest order; but the leap into modern technology was never taken. Ninety per cent of the population remained peasants—crude, ignorant, superstitious, toiling at back-breaking labor from dawn to dusk, living in hovels in which a modern American would not house his animal, and with a range of consciousness extending barely beyond the village. Dynasties rose and fell, conquerors swept to and fro, but the basic customary way of life remained unchanged for millennia. Today, Afghan men are shooting each other because the modernizers want to break immemorial custom by allowing women to choose their own husbands and attend political meetings.

It is a fact of history that in the "modern" age, which dawned some 200 years ago in Western Europe, two utterly new historical developments have occurred. The first is the general urge for the individual *person*, man and woman, to express his or her self *as such*, to rise out of his station, to learn what he wants, to marry for love, to choose his work, to dress and live and travel and think and speak as he likes, to develop his unique creative potentialities. The second is the extraordinary development of theoretical and applied science; the latter is making it possible, for the first time, for the 90% at the bottom of the social pyramid to have the material conditions essential to the expression of human personality. In Europe these developments have necessitated the shattering of the traditional medieval organic society and the religious *Weltanschauung* which suffused it. *"Ecrasez l'infame"* ("crush the vile thing") was Voltaire's famous attitude toward the Church.

The underlying purpose of the Human Rights is therefore, I suggest, to provide the conditions which enable the individual, as such, to realize the inherent creativity of his or her personality. The civil rights establish the personal freedoms of speech, meeting, worship, travel, marriage,

151

and "due process of law." The political rights enable him to take part in the government of his society; and the social rights ensure him the material standard of living "indispensable for dignity and the free development of his personality." The philosophy of Human Rights is therefore explosive; it aims at liberating the energy locked up in the human psyche, as the splitting of the atom is liberating the energy locked up in physical matter. But if an individual is to express his unique creativity, he must first differentiate him- or herself as a person; he must break away from the organism in which he is, essentially, merely a functional cell. It is difficult not to believe that this process is as natural a transformation for all men and women everywhere as the transformation from childhood into adolescence. If this be so, then one of the most crucial questions for the modern world is: how are the differentiated individuals to unite? What form of social structures should replace the religion-dominated organic societies of the past?

In the 18th century the majority of the philosophers who formulated the concept of Human Rights in Western Europe and America believed that these rights stemmed from God—an attitude implanted into the European mind by Greek philosophy and embodied in medieval theology as "natural law." It is significant that in the vast development of the theory and practice of Human Rights in the 20th century God has been left out of the picture. For the first time in history there is a public ethical code which does not claim to derive from an accepted transcendental source. This may be just because it claims to be universal—its most important formulation is called the "United Nations' *Universal* Declaration of Human Rights"—while there is no generally accepted universal religion. Yet it is hard to believe that these momentous rights relate merely to "naked apes," superior rats, or bundles of atoms. The very concept of Human Rights seems to imply that man has a divine spark, what Plato called the "madness" of inspiration by the gods, which drives him forward to transform the world, or upward to seek the light of Heaven. The divine spark is not only the spark of creativity, but also the spark of love, the only force which can unite people in freedom. The more this spark in the individual psyche is fanned into the flame of self-development, the more the individual is thereby united to others in whom the flame also glows. At this level of consciousness, the greater the unity, the greater the diversity, and vice versa. This is the great paradox which lies at the heart of *community*, the union of free and differentiated persons in fraternity.

The individual who is liberated from the organic group may, however, choose to use his freedom in a destructive rather than in a creative way, to be aggressive and exploitative rather than fraternal. These urges have led Western man to fill the vacuum created by the collapse of the organic order with two kinds of groups of a negative nature, which I will call the "organization" and the "herd."

The "organization" is a group in which people are treated as "things," possessing a utilitarian, not an organic, function. The urge to "use" people to satisfy greed for material goods and personal power and profit is fostered by the tendency of the secular society, not geared to a vision of divine purpose, to regard selfishness as a kind of virtue. ("The business of America is business.") This tendency is abetted by the all-pervading scientific *Weltanschauung.* Science, by its nature, is concerned with analyzing and manipulating *objects*, with which the scientist establishes what Martin Buber has called an "I-It" relationship. This enhances the tendency to depersonalize people, to turn them into human machines, to be trained in schools and colleges, worked in factories and offices, repaired in hospitals, and finally, in the bitter words of Gabriel Marcel, flung at death onto the scrap heap, as beings which *are* nothing, because they are no longer of any *use.*

The counterpart of the group organized by the rational intellect as a machine is the "herd." For in order to accept the fate of being reduced to a machine, the "organization man" must suppress his feelings, his imagination and his creativity. His "unconscious" psyche becomes a whirlpool of frustrated emotions. He finds release in the "herd," the group bound together by passion which seeks release at the instinctual level—the collective "projection" of emotion onto an enemy and/or an idol. In our times we have seen this herd instinct evoked by pop stars, religious cult leaders and dictators—supremely by the diabolic figure of Hitler. The Nazi regime was probably the most sinister combination of "organization" and "herd" which the world has hitherto known, illumined as it was by what Churchill called "the lights of perverted science." The ultimate "absurdity" produced by the schizophrenic split between thought and feeling which the organization/herd mentality fosters is to be found in the "war games" played by the decent men in the nuclear arms establishments of the superpowers.

The hallmark of both "organization" and "herd" is *uniformity.* The individual must suppress the development of his unique personality and conform to the norms of the group; otherwise he threatens its cohesion and must be disciplined or eliminated.

Let us glance very briefly at the situation in the three major kinds of society of the present time, those of the industrialized "free world," of the Communist countries, and of the "developing countries" in which traditional social structures still partially prevail.

The "free world" is pervaded by a paradox. The first society in history which is struggling to encourage all persons to express their individual creativity is at the same time being impelled to depersonalize them in an ever more sophisticated and systematic way. On every hand are the symptoms of "sick" societies of lonely and alienated people, who as machines or herd members lack the sense of worth and belonging which dignified the lives of many humble peasants in olden days. But on the other hand, this world is buzzing with every kind of group and relationship in which people come together as *persons*, regardless of job, status, sex, or age, to express their interests and exercise their abilities. If a person wants to engage in politics, to hike, play chess, race pigeons, meditate or do a thousand other things, he or she can join a group of like-minded persons. And the revolutionary implications of the fact that, in the "free world," for the first time in history, it is thought "right" that the central human relationship, that of marriage, should be based on *love between persons*, have not perhaps yet been fully appreciated. At the dawn of the modern age William Blake wrote:

Children of a future age,
Reading this indignant page,
Know that in a former time,
Love, sweet love, was thought a crime.

Blake was not writing idly. In February 1980 a man and a maid in the village of Gundikani in Turkey were executed by their families for the "crime" of loving each other.

To put love at the heart of human society—how difficult—but how marvelous!

This thick carpet of creative groups, sprouting like green shoots through the dreary structures of the "organization" and the fumes of "herd" emotion, are surely the seed-bed of the community consciousness. Nor are the symptoms of this consciousness confined to leisure-time groups. Many state education systems are struggling to provide education according to "age, aptitude and ability," as the British Education Act of 1944 puts it. In work, the idea of "worker-participation in management" is growing, particularly in Western Europe. In Western Europe democratically elected parliaments have created "welfare states" in which the rich pay taxes to provide social services for the poor, thus implementing the social rights—surely an expression of fraternity. The question of public or private ownership, hitherto a matter of dogma, is beginning to become secondary to the "participatory planning" of national assets. In the "European Community" some of these ideas and practices are being developed at the supranational level.

The "individualism" which pervades the "free world," and which is embodied in the theory and practice of Human Rights, is thus producing a confused pattern in which the characteristics of organization, herd, and incipient community are mixed up together. In this century, the herd/organization mentality, erupting as the fruit of the freedoms derived from the Human Rights philosophy, has fueled two terrible world wars and today suggests menacing symptoms of moral and psychological breakdown throughout Western society. And since this secularized society has cut God out of the picture, and tends to see man in "ratomorphic" terms, and to evade the spiritual implications of the Human Rights philosophy, it is not surprising that the free world is pervaded by cynicism, alienation and despair. Its peoples are at present more anxious to be "free" than to be "fraternal." They do not understand that freedom and fraternity are two sides of the same coin; and so they are stumbling unwittingly into community, rather than reaching out to it as a conscious goal.

The Communist world, in contrast, is based on a dogmatic secular theology which sets out a vision of a Utopian society in which men will freely and fraternally share the fruits of their labor, in order that the creativity of each may find full expression; the state, as an organization of rules and enforcement systems to deal with human greed, will "wither away"; and men will rule themselves in an atmosphere of brotherly love. This is the goal, according to Marx, towards which history is

154

inevitably moving; and its achievement involves the moral transformation of man, for greed and rage have no place in the classless community which he foresees. But Marx also claimed to be a "scientific" thinker, offering an objective socio-economic analysis of historical facts as the basis for his essentially religious vision. While this analysis is regarded by many intellectuals all over the world as a useful conceptual tool, his vision "speaks to the condition" of many modern people who have an idealistic longing to escape from the herd-organization societies in which they feel trapped. But the critique and the vision are incompatible marriage partners. The idea that when the enraged proletariat has smashed up the capitalist system the community of free and loving individuals will spontaneously emerge is a fantasy. In fact, the point has just about been reached when, in the minds and hearts of many Marxists, the marriage is breaking up. In the Communist states, grounded on Marxist theory, the characteristics of "herd" and "organization" are far more strongly and crudely entrenched than in the "free world." (In all Communist states, the only non-official, non-Communist groups whose existence is legally permitted are the churches, and these are closely supervised.) In order to inspire millions of simple peasants to work hard and to make huge sacrifices to "build communism," they have been impelled to foster the "herd" mentality—hero worship of the leader, hatred of the enemy; and in order to achieve the material goals of modernization as quickly as possible they have created "organizations" as impersonal as those in capitalist countries, unconstrained by constitutional and legal systems which safeguard personal civil and political rights. The groundwork for a true community is being laid by redistributing wealth, and educating and providing comprehensive social services for all. As a result, there is now, in the USSR and Eastern Europe, for the first time in history, a large, educated, bourgeois, technocratic class, capable of forming opinions on all matters, a class on which the regime's functioning depends. To deny civil and political rights to this class, and to treat its members as a "herd" and an "organization," is to create in their psyches a more dangerous schizophrenia than the tension between heart and mind which prevails in the "free world": the schizophrenia produced by asking them to believe, as a matter of dogmatic faith, that the *actual* herd-organization society *is* the fraternal community prophesied by Marx in the making. Brutal dictatorship is a necessity in order to ensure that the citizens continue to act out this fantasy, whatever they may be thinking and feeling. The "free world" has no coherent goal; the Communist world has a distorted vision of a marvelous goal; in both the missing factor is the general provision for the transformation of man himself, so that the community spirit can spontaneously blossom.

The developing countries, where three quarters of the world's population live, confront the challenge to develop the community consciousness in a particularly stark form. In the next 20 years the world's population will have increased from 4 billion to 6 billion. Ninety percent of this increase will be in the developing countries, where one billion people are malnourished, and one billion jobs will have to be created to provide work for all—unemployment at present averages at least 30%. In the shantytown suburbs of the huge Third World cities, exploding with the migrants from rural unemployment, the herd phenomenon is already manifest in the irrational and desperate violence of "militant" youth; and in many countries ever more repressive governmental "organizations," practicing what the Latin American bishops have dubbed "institutionalized violence," are being created to repress these "herds." Communist China has embarked on a great experiment. It has ruthlessly suppressed the traditional institutions and beliefs and then sought to integrate "herd" energies into an authoritarian system which is suffused with a sufficient amount of the community spirit—a major concern for social rights, a minor concern for constitutional legitimacy and personal self-expression—to give the masses a sense of positive purpose in participating in the development process. But the dilemma which stares the USSR in the face is already beginning to arise in China. When education is widespread and basic human needs are satisfied, individualism rears its head. In February 1980 the Chinese authorities announced a ban on wall posters in which a few daring spirits were demanding "democracy"!

A number of Islamic countries, and the Buddhist countries of Sri Lanka and Burma, have embarked on another kind of experiment: to modernize within the organic structure of the traditional religion. But their experience is already indicating that science and technology and the education needed to foster them are inherently related to individualism. Iranian President Bani-Sadr's attempt to integrate the computer and the Koran, and the Theravada Buddhists' attempt to promote "Buddhist Socialism" are likely to result in victory for the secular component. It would seem that any religion must first modernize itself, re-emphasizing its perennial assertion of the divine spark in man and of the transcendental nature of the cosmos, but rejecting doctrines, rules and structures which were relevant in the far off days when it emerged into history, if it is to inspire the development of "community." Significantly, a religion which rises to this challenge will universalize itself, shedding exclusive claims; and this will turn it into a religious background for the Human Rights, providing that great universal concept with its missing ingredient—a philosophy about what man's creative potential is, whence it originates and how he can develop it. There are two major religious movements in the Third World which seem to have taken this great step: Gandhiism in India and radical Christianity in Latin America. The aim of both movements was/is to stimulate the peasant masses to awaken out of the apathy of centuries and to act *themselves* to secure *all* the Human Rights; to act in a spirit of *Ahimsa* or "benevolence" (Gandhi) or "charity" (Christianity), confronting the "institutionalized violence" of the Establishment by *Satyagrana* or "soul force" (Gandhi). Both Gandhi and the Roman Catholic "theologians of liberation" have affirmed that man cannot change society without also changing himself, that the Marxist idea that the transformation of material systems and conditions will automatically produce the "new man" is a half-truth—as Communist experience has shown. Gandhi asserted that a bad means—violence—cannot achieve a good end—the brotherhood of man—but that a good means—to confront oppression with "soul force" and love—will of itself promote a good end. Gandhi sacrificed his life for the principle of fraternal association of different cults in a secular society; he believed that society should be infused, not by *a* religion, but shall we say by spirituality, expressing itself in different modes. The Catholic bishops of Latin America formulated the same idea when they met at Medellin in Columbia in 1968: "We are on the threshold of a new epoch in the history of our continent," they announced. "It appears to be a time full of zeal for full emancipation, of liberation from every form of servitude, of personal maturity and of collective integration. In these signs we perceive the first indications of the painful birth of a new civilization. And we cannot fail to see in this gigantic effort towards a rapid transformation and development an obvious sign of the Spirit who leads the history of man and of peoples towards their vocation. We cannot but discover in this force, daily more insistent and impatient for transformation, vestiges of the image of God in man as a powerful incentive. Progressively this dynamism leads us to an ever greater control of nature, *a more profound personalization and fraternal union* (my italics) and also towards Him who ratifies and deepens those values attained through human efforts."

It would seem that the world stands today at the hinge of history. If the human race does not blow up, it will grow up, moving painfully but inevitably towards its inherent potential—the development of "community."

The Tyranny of the Righteous

by

Howard F. Didsbury, Jr.

There are two universal processes of transformation at work on the planet today. One involves the modernization of undeveloped traditional societies, the other involves the advent of post-industrial (technological) civilization in highly developed societies. They both portend a great many good things for mankind. Undeveloped societies seek to modernize and gain the benefits of modernization as quickly as possible. Developed nations welcome the advent of post-industrial society. What is frequently overlooked, however, is that each of these processes, modernization and post-industrial society, at this juncture in world history, creates conditions which encourage the rise and growth of extremist movements; in particular, a rebirth of religious fanaticism. This disturbing prognosis envisions an "enthusiasm" for intolerance and hatred wedded to a creed of absolute surrender. It is a reaction to the process of modernization in the undeveloped traditional society, it is a reaction to the creation of a technological society. In both of these cases all sorts of forces are in turmoil, values and attitudes are in flux. Large segments of the population feel bewildered, insecure, "lost" and insignificant. Out of such contemporary matrices, future extremist movements, either Left or Right, secular or religious, may take shape and grow. Religious fanaticism seems an especially frightening aspect of the general dynamics of present-day extremism.

The Impact of Modernization on Undeveloped Traditional Society

No rational person would challenge the many desirable features and genuine benefits resulting from the rise in the general standard of living and quality of life associated with modernization. There is, however, a potential danger in the process of modernization in the contemporary age which seems to create a peculiar receptivity to political and religious extremisms.

Almost simultaneously an emerging society undergoes the wrenching

Howard F. Didsbury, Jr., is Professor of History and Executive Director, Program for the Study of the Future, Kean College of New Jersey, Union, New Jersey. He is also Director of the World Future Society's Special Studies Division.

experiences of modernization: disruption of the familiar way of life, disintegration of the traditional structure of family and community, individual and group tensions and stresses, bewilderment at the rapidity of change, confusion and uncertainty attendant upon current contradictory cultural values, the loss of traditionally guaranteed status, a new sharpened awareness of social, economic and political incongruities, and a growing sense of "isolation" in an "atomistic" society. In addition, the demands and dictates of modernization with its emphasis upon the prestige of science and technology serve to unravel the ancient fabric of faith.

The process of industrialization and modernization in the late twentieth century is taking place in a global context, one very different from that which existed in the late eighteenth and nineteenth centuries when Europe and the United States industrialized. Modernization in the late twentieth century is not a single revolutionary event. It encompasses a whole complex of revolutions. An immense series of radical changes in economics, politics and society in general are being compressed into such a very short period of time that those involved are hard pressed in adjusting to the shock waves. Peoples engaged in modernization are affected by industrialization and its social, political and economic ramifications; "the revolution of rising expectations"; the advent of the nuclear age; population increase; energy and natural resource challenges; and the increasing and compelling impact of telecommunications.

In past examples of industrialization and modernization, when the societies ultimately achieved the status of developed nations, the cornucopia of goods and services which such status made possible together with the passage of time ameliorated the harsh condition of the transition period. In time, an adjustment and accommodation to the new order of life took place.

Also, in the earlier age of industrialization there was no global system of telecommunications which now serves as the nerve cells of humanity. Today the pressure and complexity of events, a superabundance of information, and continuous examples of rapid change are conveyed vividly and immediately. Feelings of disquiet and unease can readily be exacerbated! Some years ago, Alexander H. Leighton, writing in *Human Relations in a Changing World*, summed up one aspect of the problem of change succinctly: "As part of the accelerated changes and contradictory cross-currents in society, values today are probably more confused for more people than they have ever been in the history of the world. Consistency and stability can only be found in a few remote and simple cultures, and even these are disappearing year by year under the impact of increasing communications and greater and greater interdependency of all parts of the world."

The Emergence of Post-Industrial Society

Among a host of writers who have described the characteristics of post-industrial society, one may cite Daniel Bell, *The Coming of Post-Industrial Society* and *The Cultural Contradictions of Capitalism*; Martin Pawley, *The Private Future*; and Robert L. Heilbroner, *Business Civilization in Decline*. The cultural ethos of such a society is one

159

which places great emphasis upon the self, personal freedom and personal rights, instant gratification, "self actualization," permissiveness, and "consumerism."

In post-industrial society there are dramatic indications of a drift from the conception of the person as a citizen with obligations and responsibilities to family, friends, community and nation to a conception of the person as a self-centered "consumer" seeking easy and quick satisfaction. His appetites are whetted by artificial, ingeniously contrived stimulation by means of advertising. Trivialities are glamorized. The self, comfort, and convenience are proselytized electronically. Such a cultural milieu may produce a comfortable life but it may also produce a life barren of genuine meaning. Such a society, in the words of Oscar Wilde, "knows the price of everything and the value of nothing." Decades ago the late Erich Fromm observed: "Freedom has a twofold meaning for modern man: that he has been freed from traditional authorities and has become an 'individual', but that at the same time has become isolated, powerless, and an instrument of purposes outside of himself, alienated from himself and others; furthermore, that this state undermines his self, weakens and frightens him, and makes him ready for submission to new kinds of bondage."

In a society which inordinately stresses human freedom, individuality and opportunity, how does one account for those who fail? If all are free and have many opportunities to succeed, the answer is clear and simple: It is the individual himself who is at fault for failure! In such a situation the result may be disgust with one's self and resentment toward others. This can be one among many of the factors in the likely growth of extremism and religious fanaticism in post-industrial societies. Trapped in a vortex of change, dwarfed by technological giantism and organizational impersonality, many people are lost and frustrated. The more uncertain and threatening the future the greater the appeal of "absolute" simple answers, be they cults, creeds or ideologies. Cults "serve to fill a need which science and technology have created by cutting away the power of the old established religions." For individuals confronted with the kaleidoscopic change of post-industrial society there is "the tendency to give up the independence of one's own individual self and to fuse one's self with somebody or something outside of oneself in order to acquire the strength which the individual self is lacking."

The Rise of Fanaticism

In the process of modernization of an undeveloped traditional society, forces are unleashed which make the emergence of extremism, especially religious fanaticism, likely. In a traditional society undergoing the trauma of modernization, there is an ambivalent attitude toward the whole process of modernization. While seeking the obvious benefits accompanying modernization, there is a fear and hatred of its unsettling effects upon the society and its values. All kinds of attempts are made to reap the benefits yet avoid the socially destructive concomitant aspects. Such attempts prove futile and increase the level of hatred and reaction.

In the older, highly industrialized or post-industrial society, the rampant

160

spirit of permissiveness, egotism, cynicism, relativism and hedonism likewise encourage the advent of intolerance. Though these two cultural matrices are different, the extremist reaction tends to be similar.

Total commitment to a creed or ideology brings relief from the anxiety of making individual decisions with respect to values and meaning in life. By following a leader, a creed or an ideology, the anxious, confused individual finds completeness and fulfillment. The cost is simply the abdication of one's personal judgement and responsibility. As Fromm notes, so much of the life "of the individual in modern society has increased the helplessness and insecurity of the average individual. Thus, he is ready to submit to new authorities which offer him security and relief from doubt."

Another way of finding meaning in the confusing environment of modernization or in the fluid world of post-industrial society is to try to "recapture" the past. This usually takes the form of an affirmation of loyalty to a prior "Golden Age" of patriotism or of faith. Notwithstanding the fact that such a vision of a golden age is largely a product of an unreflective nostalgic distortion of the past, its appeal is strong, particularly in an age of change and uncertainties. With the reaffirmation of the old-time faith, secular or religious, the individual finds a safe harbor from the troubled sea of "convulsive change."

The quest for meaning and the need for total commitment is one means of coping with an epoch of unsettling complexity. The affirmation of the "simple faith" and the relief gained by total, willful commitment fires the exuberance of the fanatic. All too easily the personal ecstasy of the "true believer" can become a virulent hatred for "non-believers" or, even worse, backsliders. The communal bond of likeminded haters should never be underestimated. An intense common hatred for sinners passes all too quickly into an unconscious hatred for humanity.

As has been noted, the act of total commitment solves the problems created by a gnawing sense of doubt or insecurity. The absolute surrender to the faith, secular or religious, provides an enviable "simplification" of life for the follower. For such a person, a sharp line is drawn. It separates the good people from the wicked ones; the saints from the sinners. Filled with a firm conviction and a sense of mission, the "Righteous" go forth to set the world aright. All too often, the Reign of the Righteous ends in a Reign of Terror for all, as the "incorruptibles" and virtuous seek to redeem their fallen fellow man. One recalls with justified fear the enthusiasm with which the Cromwells and Robespierres embarked on the pursuit of such worthy ends.

Extremists need some group to despise, chastise or reform. In this endeavor the adherents, unconsciously, have ample opportunities to vent their deep-seated frustrations, resentment and envy and, at the same time, relish a conviction of superiority. All of this is done in a genuine spirit of righteousness. The distinguished theologian C. S. Lewis describes this spirit well in *God in the Dock*:

> Of all tyrannies a tyranny exercised for the good of its victims may be the most oppressive. It may be better to live under robber barons than under omnipotent moral busybodies. The robber baron's

cruelty may sometimes sleep, his cupidity may at some point be satiated; but those who torment us for our own good will torment us without end for they do so with the approval of their own conscience. They may be more likely to go to Heaven yet at the same time likelier to make a Hell on earth.

Indeed, political extremists may not pose so great a peril to the future well-being of people; they are concerned with more worldly ends. Conceivably, the extremist authoritarian may weaken or mellow and, given time, he may even grow to see the wisdom and profit of restraint or compromise. One is less sanguine with the religious fanatic whose character has about it the brittleness of the authoritarian but also the delusion of divine sanction for his mission.

The alarming prospect for the future is that the process of modernization in some parts of the world and of post-industrial civilization in others may be contributing to the rebirth of this disquieting phenomenon. Stunted in their own inability to enjoy the richness of personal development, self-appointed moral censors convince themselves that they are peculiarly conversant with divine wishes for human conduct. In God's name they can inflict great suffering and even destruction. Devoid of any regret or remorse, they can wreak havoc!

Toleration achieved in the course of centuries of dedication and sacrifice is jeopardized by the rebirth of such movements of religious fanaticism. The fanatic regards tolerance not as a positive good but a necessary evil. The Righteous, were he in power, would espouse intolerance. In former times, behind the unctuous utterances of concern for the wayward, the Righteous had the dungeon, the rack and the block to ensure compliance!

The unfortunate fact of human existence may be that many people are incapable of knowing how to enjoy life. Human contentment, notwithstanding all the philosophers, may be the result of good judgement and good luck—both of which may be in extremely short supply among man. Fanaticism, either religious or ideological, may serve as a sublimation of unhappiness and frustration. For many, the perilous uncertain times now and ahead of us may make submission to an absolute authority increasingly attractive, if not necessary.

The Future of North America

by

Victor Ferkiss

North America exists as a geographical expression. Does it have any reality in human terms as a cultural, economic, or political entity? Is it likely to become more than a geographical expression in the future?

Few people think of themselves as "North Americans." *Norteamericano* is a term which Latin Americans apply to English speakers from the north, in part in reaction to the somewhat chauvinistic usage of *American* as a term of self-identification by citizens of the United States. Occasionally Canadians will find uses for the term as in George Grant's essay "In Defense of North America," but few south of the U.S.-Canada border think of themselves as "North American." Virtually no "North American" institutions exist, the most noteworthy being, (NORAD) the North American Air Defense Command, designed to counter aggression from across the north polar regions.

Yet in the past few years the concept of North Americanness has come to the fore in an economic context. The idea of a North American Common Market has been bandied about by Governor Brown of California and taken up by former Governors Connally and Reagan in their campaigns for the American presidency. It is noteworthy that this concept as so formulated includes Mexico in North America and has originated in American not Mexican or Canadian circles. Is the sudden interest in "North America" simply a reflex of American resource scarcities and economic imperialism, or will the future see a greater degree of interaction or integration among the countries concerned, possibly radically altering present economic, cultural, and political structures?

There is no question but that basic economic and cultural patterns exist which could enable us to speak of the existence of "North America," and that present political boundaries both obscure and distort these patterns. As often in speculating about the future, it is worth first looking at the past.

If we recollect what the map of North America and adjacent areas looked like before the present political outline of the United States began to take shape, we find important clues to basic realities which

Victor Ferkiss is Professor of Government at Georgetown University, Washington, D.C. He is the author of The Future of Technological Civilization *and other books.*

subsequent politics have overlain. At one time there were a score of British-controlled colonies in North America and its environs, enjoying varying degrees of self-government. The colonies which formed the nucleus of the American republic were among a larger group which included Nova Scotia, Quebec, Bermuda, Jamaica and other entities. What is now the American midwest was the scene of cultural and economic penetration by Frenchmen from Quebec and Spaniards from Mexico. The present American southwest was part of the Spanish empire while Alaska and the Pacific northwest were areas of Russian and British exploration or settlement. In short, the establishment of the United States along the Atlantic seaboard from the southern boundaries of what are now the Maritimes to the northern boundaries of Spanish Florida, and its subsequent expansion almost due westward across the continent disrupted and superimposed a new political structure upon what had been and still are complex economic and cultural systems which run largely north and south rather than east and west.

Are there present trends which suggest that in the foreseeable future these older patterns—or similar north-south ones—will reassert themselves in some form? The general drift of modern society would suggest that the answer is a tentative and qualified yes. Students of international politics have increasingly argued for the growing importance of what they call "transnational" politics, that is, systems of economic, cultural, and political interaction which operate across national frontiers but are not the relations among sovereign states as such. Multinational corporations, international trade unions, international religious bodies and political parties, and similar institutions are engaged in transnational politics, but such relations can take place on a more aggregate, de-centalized, and individual basis as well.

What are some of the transnational forces working to penetrate the political boundaries which separate the United States, Canada, and Mexico, and which tend toward the creation of a more North American political process which could even conceivably eventuate in changes in the existing international political structures of North America?

As recent talk of a North American common market suggests, a primary force for continental integration is economics. The United States and Canada constitute major trading partners for each other, so much so that many Canadians look upon Canada as an American economic colony (though Canadian investment in the United States is also relatively considerable). The United States and Canada send each other large numbers of tourists as well. Similarly, the United States and Mexico are major trading partners, and the pattern of American companies with Canadian subsidiaries has its counterpart in Mexico, along with the special feature of Mexican "border industries" geared to production for American markets. American tourism in Mexico is a major force in the Mexican economy, though the reverse is not the case. The United States has drawn and still seeks to draw important raw materials from its neighbors. In the past it has imported oil from Canada and even though Canadian exports are being curtailed, the United States casts a covetous eye toward the Albertan tar and shale oil resources, even though such also exist south of the border. The United States seeks to import whatever oil and gas Mexico produces beyond its current domestic usage. Mexico is, of course, itself a sufferer from aridness, but elaborate plans have been long ago concocted for a North American water plan which would draw Canadian water resources southward. Economic integration of the United States and Canada is a long-standing dream of some Americans; back in the 1930s, the Technocratic movement spoke of creating a "Technate of North America."

Another important element tending toward economic integration among the three nations is agriculture. The United States and Canada have similar patterns of production of agricultural export crops and Canadian and American wheat combined could constitute a powerful North American "food weapon" to rival the oil power of OPEC. Mexican agriculture has increasingly taken up the role of producing out-of-season and/or stoop-labor fruits and vegetables for the American market and could increasingly serve Canada as well. While labor migration between Canada and the United States is of little importance, Mexican labor migration to the United States—legal and illegal—is vital to the health of the Mexican economy (and indeed political system as well) and of increasing importance in the American economy.

Along with these forces which make the economies of the United States, Canada and Mexico increasingly interdependent and complementary (with, of course, the United States being the central pivot since direct Canadian-Mexican connections are minimal) there exist significant cultural and demi-political forces as well. A recent essay by Washington *Post* editor Joel Garreau outlined nine "cultural-political" regions of North America, most of which had an important North-South dimension. In his scheme, designed to replace inadequate conceptualizations of American political regionalism such as North-South, East-West or Sunbelt-Frostbelt, one finds the Maritimes joined with ethnically and economically similar New England, Ontario with the American industrial heartland, the Prairie provinces with their American counterparts, Alberta with an energy empire whose postulated capital is Denver, and British Columbia as part of an "Ecotopia" stretching down to the San Francisco bay area. Notable also in his scheme are three entities which do not mingle the United States and Canada: Quebec sui generis and alone, Mexamerica, centered in Los Angeles and largely (unnoted by Garreau) coinciding with what Mexican and Chicano irridentists sometimes call the American part of Aztlan, and the Miami area, which is recognized as being part of the Latin Caribbean both culturally, politically and economically. Though precise boundaries can be debated about, these regional divisions have much to recommend them as tools for understanding: Nova Scotians are closer to Maine culturally than to Saskatchewan, Albertans closer even to distant Texans than to denizens of Toronto, citizens of Vancouver more Californian than akin to inhabitants of Quebec, while much of Los Angeles is a cultural province of Mexico. The economic aspects of migration between Canada and the United States and Mexico and the United States have already been noted. But migration has cultural consequences as well.

Canadian-American intermigration has reinforced English-speaking cultural homogenization, though French Canadian penetration of New England presents a special case. But Mexican immigration into the United States is a different story, constituting something of a demographic-cultural rematch of the war of 1845, complicated by the fact that a substantial portion of immigrants from Mexico—especially illegals—come and go across the border, and may return home to settle after their northern experience.

Mention has been made of the special position of Miami, which constitutes an economic and communications center for much of Latin America, especially the Caribbean. What happens in Miami may increasingly concern Canada. Canada has long played an important economic and cultural role in the "Commonwealth Caribbean," the former British colonies in the area (a role complicated by the fact that some Canadian firms active in the region have American corporate ties). As the Caribbean becomes more politically volatile—a process not unrelated to increasing interaction between English-speaking nations and Latin ones, especially Cuba—and of increasing geopolitical concern to the United States, there will be increasing pressures for the United States and Canada to work together in the area to protect common interests, with perhaps some possibility of Canada acting as an intermediary between Washington and local governments.

But if all the factors discussed above push toward a greater integration of North America culturally and economically, other forces militate against such integration. It is no accident, as Marxists would say, that calls for a common market have usually come from the United States, not Mexico or Canada. Most Canadians and Mexicans alike do not wish their nations to become energy colonies of American industry or agricultural satellites of the United States, and most leaders of these countries would undoubtedly prefer if possible to build balanced economies on a national basis rather than allow their regions to become peripheries to American metropoles in a continentally balanced economy.

Cultural integration also faces obstacles. Canadians have long fought to preserve—or create—a special cultural identity, and while such might survive in a larger entity the way Southern—or even Western—regional culture has in the United States, most might prefer a political shell for what strength it might lend to cultural security. Mexicans already have a rich cultural heritage—however much many of their intellectuals might be ambivalent about its aspects—and would resist "Northamericanization." So, too, of course would Quebec cultural nationalists, who would be even worse off in a larger entity than at present. One culturally related but largely neglected aspect of greater integration would be the question of migration. Economic integration—even without political integration—would lead to freedom of migration throughout the continent. One usually unspoken consideration which might motivate Canadians to resist integration would be the possible movement northward of patterns of white-black ethnic conflict, especially in urban areas, which Canada has to date essentially avoided. Free migration among Canada, the United States and Mexico would also mean that the tides of Mexican migration—

166

indeed Latin American migration in general—which now flow virtually unhindered into the United States would reach Canada as well, with attendant possibilities of cultural conflict. While few Americans would have any objection to any unlikely increase of Canadian migration southward which might result from integration, many of course would find erasing the border with Mexico completely undesirable. Economic integration would result in an intensified export of Mexican poverty and labor surplus northward. Political integration would raise the problem of absorbing a political system noteworthy for its corruption and violence, one which makes New Orleans at its worst look like suburban Toronto. Would Mexicans welcome economic and political integration? Probably not. They are a proud people and their government's pressures on the United States to allow virtually unchecked immigration northward rests in part on lingering resentment of the war of 1845. For many south of the Rio Grande, Mexicans have a right to travel freely in "occupied territory" which really belongs to them. Occasionally Mexican voices are heard wishing that the United States could take Mexico over completely and reform it. But such utterances are the catharsis of despair, like the expressions of Indians who sometimes used to say the only hope for India was a Chinese conquest which would force India to shape up, and such opinions do not represent the depths of national feeling which exist in Mexico.

Given these conflicting trends, what is the future likely to hold? In all probability, we shall see maintenance of the status quo, with the degree of closeness of economic and especially political relations among the three countries depending largely on the ideological compatibility of their leaders at any given time, and the currents of world politics. Despite Richard Rohmer's fictional suggestions in *Ultimatum* and *Exxoneration*, the United States is not about to invade Canada for any reason, at least not short of the highly unlikely event of a Communist government in Ottawa. (Though what could happen short of invasion if a Castro-type government took over in Quebec City is worth speculating about.)

Mexico and the United States are now locked in a partial embrace probably as enduring as it may often be mutually repulsive. Not only is it unlikely to deliver economic or political ultimatums to Ottawa, the United States is not about to try to drive too hard a bargain with Mexico over oil and especially on immigration issues, for fear the possible consequent "destabilization" would result in a Cuba on the Rio Grande which would require a costly and possibly unworkable Afghanistan-type solution. Even in the unlikely event that separatist elements might arise in contiguous areas of Mexico which would welcome annexation, the dictatorial grip of the PRI over Mexico is too strong to be broken save by military coup or leftist revolution, either of which would be equally intolerant of any such separatism. Furthermore, nineteenth and even early twentieth-century American interest in annexing more of Mexico was predicated on an assumption of "Anglo-Saxon" ability to overwhelm Mexican cultural patterns which is no longer held. On the contrary, current American legal doctrine and ethnic political pressures have created a situation where all of the political and cultural problems of bilingualism which have riven Canada are beginning to arise in the United States, especially in the southwest, and additional accessions of Spanish-speaking areas would raise them to Canadian dimensions. Any American interference with Mexican territorial integrity is unthinkable.

But, of course, if the national political unity of Mexico seems secure both from internal and external pressures, that of Canada is far less so. Should Quebec become a sovereign state, the remainder of Canada would become essentially a geographically non-contiguous entity, the psychological division of which no complex of economic agreements could probably overcome. Such entities have a low survival rate in the modern world, as the fate of Pakistan illustrates. Even leaving the Quebec issue aside, economic differentials place great strain on Canadian unity even now, with the resource-rich west not anxious to carry the burdens of Maritime poverty. The independence of Quebec could trigger a breakup of Canadian federation which would render the option of joining the United States much more economically and politically attractive to the other provinces.

What would be the reaction of the United States to such a development? Geopolitical considerations would add to the economic logic of continental integration to make the joining of non-French Canada to the United States generally welcome, as a hedge against further political instability in an intimate neighbor. Especially with Quebec not part of the package, Canadian provinces would be welcome as cultural kinsmen. The welcome would be especially warm on the part of many Americans who would view the addition of millions more white citizens of English-speaking cultural background as a counterweight to increasing Latin American cultural, political, and demographic penetration into the American republic. Indeed, in the long run of cultural politics in North America, this is probably the most important single dynamic—the possibility of Anglo-American regrouping against the northward thrust of Latin culture.

Where would such an accession of the rest of Canada into what might be called the "United States of North America" leave Quebec? Obviously, the odd man out, viewed—despite the long history of the *Canadiens* on the continent—as a foreign presence and a bridgehead not only of continental European culture but possibly of European political influence as well, to be watched with suspicion and apprehension. The rise of another De Gaulle—of the left or the right—seeking influence in Quebec could only exacerbate the problem, especially if an increasingly larger and more powerful Mexico should move toward a combination of anti-Americanism and economic ties with France and/or other European powers. A movement toward the Marxist left in Quebec would, of course, be an even greater cause for alarm, especially if concurrent with similar drifts in Mexico, Central America, and the Caribbean. Indeed what might eventually come about would be a future for North America with many resemblances to the period before the war of 1812 when the United States was not unchallenged master of the continent but had on its borders potentially hostile territories with close ties to

168

extra-continental power configurations. The difference, of course, would be that among these a politically and economically declining Britain would not be included, and the remnants of British North America would have been forced for the sake of survival to rally to their southern cousins.

In this perspective, future developments relating to Quebec begin to take on their true significance. Often in history larger currents are set in motion by the fate of relatively minor entities. The first world war began over the fate of Serbia, and its expansion was due largely to the controversy over the fate of Belgium. Despite its small size—demographically though not of course geopolitically—the province of Quebec is the linchpin of the current North American system. Should Quebec become a sovereign state—even without immediately undermining the unity of the rest of Canada—it would be adding a new actor to the scene, making North American politics a radically different game, truly international for perhaps the first time in over a century. The unravelling of present geopolitical patterns could lead to consequences even the most prescient futurist would find difficult to predict.

Europe Facing Its Futures

by

Michel Godet

What Is the Prospective Approach and Why Is It Needed?

Why Carry Out Prospective Studies?

Our century is one of change, of uncertainty, and of action. The acceleration of change contributes towards the uncertainty of the future and so makes forecasting all the more necessary to guide our present actions.

But what is the use of anticipating future difficulties when we are already beset by the ills of the present? The answer is quite simply that today's problems are the result of the forecasting failures of yesterday.

During recent years we have been confronted with a series of crises—monetary, energy supplies, economic, and so on—and each time we have had to wait until the crisis has become a major one before we reacted to it. The steady acceleration of technological, social, political and economic change makes future disturbances increasingly probable and increasingly imminent. Our only alternative is to catalog the promising opportunities and to identify the problems before they become critical, so that appropriate actions can be taken in good time.

The Crisis in Forecasting

The monetary, economic and energy crisis has arrived—and no one (or almost no one) foresaw it. It will be recalled that in France in 1972, to take one example, decisions on energy were based on the assumption that the declining trend in oil prices would continue until 1980-1985. These forecasting errors led to the crisis in forecasting. The paradox of history is that forecasting developed at the precise moment when it was easiest—and least necessary. Economic models made it possible to demonstrate, with the aid of the computer, what everyone already knew: namely, that practically everything could be more or less correlated with the national product, and this was rising by 5% per year. Time, therefore, became the best of the "explanatory" variables.

Since 1973, however, the future no longer resembles the past. The

---

Michel Godet, an economist and scientist, is with the Commission of the European Community in Brussels. He is the author of The Crisis in Forecasting and the Emergence of the "Prospective" Approach *(Pergamon Press, 1979).*

horizon of the forecasting approach—that is to say the point where there are breaks in the continuity—becomes nearer. The models based on the data and relationships of the past are powerless to predict these discontinuities since they depend on new behavior patterns of the actors involved.

The Foundations of the Prospective Approach

What good is it to reflect on the future if it is already written in advance? In our opinion this is not a fair question since, apart from certain determinisms, the future remains largely free and open. This postulate of freedom conditions the greater part of our reading grid (actors, projects, wishes, problems, changes, etc.).

1. The Future Is Not Written: It Still Has to Be Constructed

The prospective approach was born of the realization that the future was, simultaneously, the field of operation of determinism and of freedom: what will be *experienced* in the future results from *past actions*; what is *wished* explains *present actions*. Furthermore, the future must not be seen as a unique and predetermined line forming a prolongation of the past: the future is both multiple and indeterminate. The plurality of the future and the degrees of freedom of human action find a mutual explanation: the future is not written—it still has to be constructed.

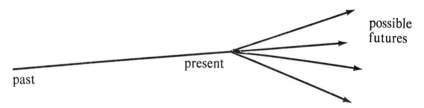

2. Multiple Futures and the Role of the Actors

In an essentially unequal and conflict-ridden world *the future is only the resultant of the confrontation of unequal human forces,* "corrected" by the "underlying" trends and the constraints. The future does not belong to all parties in the same way and to the same degree. Certain actors influence it more "heavily" than others. Thus several futures are possible, but that future which will effectively be produced will be born as much from the projects of the actors and of the force relationships as from the evolution of trends.

3. For the Actors the Future Is the Raison d'être of the Present

The image of the future is imprinted in the present. For example, the consumption of an individual at any given moment does not depend solely on his previous income (savings) but also on the future income which he anticipates (credit), as has been effectively demonstrated by Milton Friedman in his theory of permanent income.

It is necessary, therefore, to look to the future to illuminate the present, so that "the future is the raison d'être of the present."

171

The Logical Consequences

1. *The Necessity for a Global Vision*

Partial forecasting, retaining only a few generally economic and quantified explanatory variables, and not taking the evolution of force relationships and the appearance of new trends into account, misleads and is of no value. This failure to forecast realistic results stems from the fact that the economy is regarded as an autonomous sector, with economic forecasting being cut off from social and political forecasting and then finally divided up into forecasts concerned with the aspects of technology, population, etc. Furthermore, and as the rate of evolution accelerates, interdependence becomes reinforced, everything acts on everything else, all other things are by no means equal and so a global vision becomes essential.

On this point it is interesting to note that the French word *prospective,* as implying a global and normative vision of the possible futures, has no strict equivalent in English. The word *forecasting,* like its French counterpart *prévision,* remains imprinted with the desire for quantification and extrapolation.

2. *The Impossibility of Forecasting the Future Solely on the Basis of Data from the Past*

This principle explains the impotence of all the classical econometric models, which do not integrate qualitative and nonquantifiable parameters such as the projects and behavior of the actors. In passing, it should be pointed out that the *dangers of incorrect quantification*—since quantification always involves giving priority to what is quantifiable over that which is not—must not lead to the rejection of figures but only to great care in their use.

3. *The Absence of One Unique Model of Evolution*

Far from accepting deterministic interpretations of history, whether liberal or Marxist, which assume a unique model of evolution tending towards an ideal final phase, the prospective philosophy leaves room for a multiplicity of possible evolutions.

4. *The Plurality of Temporal Horizons*

To accept that there are multiple futures, and that there is no unique model of evolution, means also implicitly accepting the fact that the horizons of the prospective approach have to be seen in the plural.

In practice the concepts of short, medium and long term only have a real sense as a function of the problem being studied. The horizon of the prospective approach is that of the possible discontinuities, resistances and structural changes. The acceleration of change, coupled with the variety of systems being studied, leads to the acceptance of the plurality of temporal horizons.

5. *The Limits of the Prospective Approach*

The absence of neutrality in the prospective approach. Any approach

172

calls for choices to be made at the level of the basic hypotheses, and the result is impregnated by a values system, an ideology, both implicit and explicit, and is only valid to the extent that this system is itself acceptable.

Decisions are bets. The future is an emerging continent with unknown boundaries: the constraint is that, despite the unknowns, it is today necessary to take those decisions which commit the future. *Bets must be made, without mortgaging the future, since the future is increasingly changing and uncertain.*

6. Flexibility and Adaptability

The object of the prospective approach is to guide our present actions in such a way as to enlarge the field of what is realizable tomorrow, that is to say to seek the maximum *flexibility and adaptability in the face of the future.*

These are the characteristics which, in our opinion, distinguish the prospective approach, the development of which is now more than ever necessary if we are to meet the challenges of the future.

The Challenges of the Future

An Uncontrolled and Disturbed Backcloth

Over and beyond the multiple trends and constraints operating on Europe and its environment, one main characteristic of the coming decades seems now to be confirmed: *the increasing geopolitical, energy and technological uncertainties,* where no trend is certain and no discontinuities can be totally excluded. As a consequence, geopolitical, energy, industrial and food prospective studies are more than ever needed since the components of the world imbroglio are multiple, and it is difficult to see how they can be disentangled if we accept the view of Daniel Bell, according to whom "governments are becoming too large for the small problems and too small for the large problems."

The trend towards a relative American decline, while it may continue at the economic and political levels, and even at the military level when several Third World countries possess atomic weapons, will in no way resolve the existing disorder but will undoubtedly contribute towards reinforcing it. The bipolar world is no more, but the *multipolar world* will take some time to appear, and the absence of a regulator will be sorely felt. Japan is still too narrow a base to play this role, and the European Community is still too weak. It is undoubtedly necessary to envisage an affirmation of different poles of attraction for each major region of the world.

Faced with the monetary disorder institutionalized by floating exchange rates (the dollar now playing a role which is more disturbing than regulating), Europe has instituted a monetary zone of relative stability, giving rise to the European Monetary System (EMS) in 1979. The question still remains of knowing whether it can withstand the somersaults which wrecked the "snake."

Undoubtedly the EMS represents a step in the right direction, away from the vicious circle. If it succeeds, the EUA (European unit of account, based on a basket of European currencies) could, in tomorrow's world, play the role of a standard or at least share this role with the dollar, in the light of the fact that Europe, representing a third of all trading, is the leading commercial power in the world. However, the constraint which the EMS will exert will bear more heavily on those least able to support it. In fact, without a painful restructuring, the constraint of the reduced flexibility in exchange rates could lead certain countries into a situation of chronic deficits.

While waiting for this to happen there still remain, unfortunately, the various forecastable breaks such as wars and revolutions, and it is to be hoped that the chain reactions resulting from these will not involve a widespread conflict. At the same time, the domestic problems in the Eastern bloc countries, coupled with the formidable power of the USSR and the withdrawal of the United States, raise more acutely than ever the question of a real European defense.

An answer to this question becomes ever more urgent since the population of Europe does not account for more than 5% to 6% of the world total. The consequences of fluctuations in population structures and the aging of Europe are numerous: excess capacity of the educational apparatus, increasing needs for the elderly and aged, difficulties for pension funds, a questioning of the advisability of lowering the age of retirement, etc. In addition to these domestic consequences the aging of Europe faced with the vigorous population structure of the Third World could make the North-South dialogue more difficult, while the geopolitical equilibria become increasingly delicately balanced. It is difficult to see how aging Europe would be able to understand, adapt itself and find the necessary imagination to meet the challenges which the young nations of the Third World will continue to pose.

More particularly the contrast will be emphasized between a Europe with excess agricultural production and the hunger which will continue to exist in many Third World countries. Europe has a role to play in this respect; its domestic outlets remain limited, but how can it dispose of its production at prices two or three times those on world markets—and to insolvent populations? The answer may perhaps be found in a European Marshall Plan designed to convert interdependence into interdevelopment.

Energy: The Price of Abundance

1. *The Errors of the Past*

Oil accounts for nearly 20% of world trading and about the same percentage of France's imports. However, the energy bill (imports plus investments in replacements) for the nine countries of the European Community was, on average, 5% of their gross domestic product (GDP). Consequently the problem is less the size of the oil bill (the contribution of manufactured products to the GDP of the developing countries is very much higher) than its rapid rate of increase.

Energy is only too expensive because it was too cheap for too long.

We became accustomed to abundance at low prices, and all our socio-economic structures were predicated on a future seen as the image of the past. Retrospectively it may be regretted that oil had fallen back so far in the past. A progressive increase in prices during the sixties would undoubtedly have made it possible to avoid today's crises. Growth during the sixties might have been less frenetic, but certainly that in the seventies and eighties would have been much higher.

Following the same line of thought, it would perhaps have been better to have agreed to indexing raw materials as had been sought by the Third World countries after 1974, and to have extended this at the same time to oil. In this way we would have avoided sudden and uncontrolled price increases, since the price of oil would have kept step with our inflation.

Finally we dreamt of catching up with the United States, but this dream was not a reasonable one since an American consumes twice as much energy every year as a European. The world could no longer plan its future indefinitely on a model of hyperconsumption and wastage.

2. *Expensive Energy Is Abundant*

A countdown of reserves and the abundance of resources are two different propositions. The proven reserves represent those which are, with certainty, immediately producible from existing wells, under the existing economic and technological conditions. The total resources are the estimate of what actually exists, but of which only part can perhaps be worked under the present conditions of prices and technology.

Consequently the forecast evolution of economic and technological conditions implies a prospective consideration more concerned with resources than with reserves. In effect, the limit of the reserves, like the line of the horizon, retreats even further as we approach it. If the usable reserves are multiplied by three when the price rises from $10 to $25 per barrel then they will be extended even further when, as seems probable, the price of oil rises to $50 or $60 per barrel. The days of cheap energy are over for good and all. Yet expensive energy does not mean a shortage of energy—quite the contrary. *Energy will be abundant precisely because it is expensive.*

3. *The Price to Be Paid*

Saudi Arabian production, despite its importance today, is still not enough to ensure control of prices. The other OPEC countries, following the events in Iran, have discovered that the best way to get the highest return is to sell less at a higher price. Certainly, temporary falls in the price still occur as a result of fluctuations in the supply and demand situation, but the habit has now been formed, and the more the price of oil rises the less of it will the OPEC countries sell (why accumulate dollars when the best investment is to leave the oil in the ground!). Under these conditions, and with each increase in the demand, the price of oil will rise slightly—and will never fall. *In this way oil will move towards its true price*, namely the production cost of substitutes, at the present time estimated as at least $40 per barrel. Furthermore it must be pointed out that the cost of the substitutes (where they exist, which is not the case with all uses) is constantly being revised upwards. There are also limits to substitutions; for example, even if all the American maize harvest was fermented to produce alcohol it would still only supply one-eighth of the total demand for petrol. Finally, it would seem to be unreasonable in those countries suffering from malnutrition, as in the case of Brazil, to "cultivate" energy, that is to say to plant sugarcane for alcohol production at the expense of cereals.

4. What Crises Lie Ahead?

Despite the abundance of energy resources in the long term, particularly in the case of fossil fuels such as oil, natural gas and coal, it can be seen that:

- The physical abundance of fossil energy does not exclude the possibility of a temporary crisis of capacity resulting from the inadequacy of investment in research and exploration—as can be seen from the quasi-stagnation in proven resources since 1973, which is mainly explained by the fact that only 20% of all research drilling has been carried out outside North America.
- The inertia of the energy structures shows that it is necessary to develop the new forms of energy (solar, geothermal) immediately if they are required to play a significant role in the first decades of the 21st century. From this point of view *any price increase is a necessary stimulant*. The capacity crisis could serve as the detonator for *a double crisis in supplies, both political and economic*, as a result of a sudden price rise.

If the era of expensive energy is beginning, it is to be feared that the international disorder will be incapable of accepting and controlling progressive price increases. And the economic and political consequences will be all the greater as the rises become more brutal.

The necessary intensification of investment and research work in developing new forms of energy implies the mobilization of considerable financial resources at the time when other priorities are necessary (industrial reconversion). This *financial crisis* could double the problems of adjusting the energy structures to more decentralized forms.

5. The Route Towards a More Sober Growth

Finally, therefore, the era of high-cost energy has begun. Is it necessary to pull the emergency cord? Higher prices are not, of themselves, a bad thing (we are paying the consequences today for oil which had been too cheap for too long); it is necessary that the rise in prices should be *sufficiently rapid* to encourage economies and replacements, and *sufficiently progressive* for the economies of the industrialized countries to adapt themselves to them.

Resources exist, and are even abundant, but the price must be paid. This does not mean that supplies are safe, since they are subject to political factors (such as a revolution in Saudi Arabia?) and the desire to establish a dialog between the countries of the North and of the South.

Even if the era of high-cost energy does not announce the last days of labor-saving technologies (which replace human labor with energy), it does at least herald the dawn of energy-saving technologies. It is necessary to accept the fact that, up until now, all taxation and social systems have encouraged companies to replace human labor by mechanical energy. Legislative measures of an appropriate kind are therefore needed *if taxes are to kill off energy rather than human labor.*

Growth will, therefore be sober—or there will be no growth. Energy economies involve decentralized and autonomous modes of production and consumption, and consequently assume a complete reversal of our life-styles and of socio-economic organization.

Europe and Its Constraints

A rate of growth double that of today, three or four times less unemployment, inflation of a few percent—such is the image of the "paradise of the sixties" which the nine countries of the Community, like other Western countries, have abandoned and which they no longer can hope to recover.

At the same time that it is necessary to pay an increasingly large bill for essential imports of energy and raw materials Europe must face up to new industrial and technological challenges; the stakes are quite explicit—it is a question of not being surpassed by both the United States and Japan and of having the countries of the South catch up.

By turning towards those industries which are most advanced technologically, and which are in general capital-intensive, the developed countries run the risk of aggravating structural unemployment. The problem becomes the more critical since it is hardly possible to count on the existing tertiary sector to create jobs; the coming remote data processing revolution is more likely to reduce the number of jobs in the banking, insurance and similar sectors.

The fall in the European birth rate will not make its effects felt until after 1990 as far as the active population is concerned; meanwhile, and particularly between now and 1985, this population will be considerably increased. A rise in unemployment becomes even more probable.

The organization of the redeployment of the industrialized countries becomes even more urgent as the more advanced developing countries start their own reconversion and so present the new North-South threat which is emerging among the countries of the South. After the iron and steel and textile industries, the new threatened sectors could be automobiles, petrochemicals, and aluminum. Will the developed countries know how to adapt themselves to this new situation? The answer seems to be in the affirmative for some of them—Germany, Japan, the United States, and France. It remains uncertain for most of the other countries. Within the developing countries it is now conventional to distinguish the Fourth World from the more advanced countries; in default of having been able to organize redeployment in good time, should not such a distinction now be introduced between the various European countries? Will it not have, as a consequence, a general return to protectionism, this weapon of weakness which will take away from Europe its role as the leading commercial power in the world, and which would be the negation of the Treaty of Rome?

The increasing divergences (economic, monetary, energy, industrial, social and regional) present a problem insofar as it is the weakest countries and regions which need to become aligned and to make the maximum effort, but those are precisely the ones least able to do so. It is to be feared that for certain of them the price of convergence will be too high at the economic and social levels (unemployment). Under these conditions, and without having recourse to an active European solidarity, these divergences may become accentuated and so lead to a breakdown of the Community.

Parallel to this the permanent recourse to the Welfare State, in order to meet the aspirations (for health, education and security) and to control the contradictions (unemployment, inequalities) of society, at the very moment when the financial resources of society are being reduced, can be seen in the increasing preponderance of public expenditure in the national income, and by the increasing charges imposed on the populations. The weight of the State increases, but its efficiency is reduced. States have become rudderless; the wheel no longer responds.

Finally, European societies are confronted with the difficult choice between opening up their economies, and so increasing their sensitivity to external influences, or of limiting their trading and so restricting their prospects of growth. While competition from the developing countries poses problems for certain industries, it opens up prospects for others—the more the developing countries export the more they are able to import. In this way the *overall impact of competition from the developing countries on the industrialized countries is neutral or even positive*. This at least is what emerges from most of the studies so far carried out. Furthermore, and in the long term, *raw materials* present a problem which is quite as important as that of energy. Despite the abundant resources there is a fear of *inadequate supplies.*

Meeting the Challenges: Technology and Its Promises

How can Europe face up, at the same time, to these increasing divergences and to the changes in its geopolitical, energy, socioeconomic, industrial and technological systems?

Technology, the most abundant raw material in Europe, is one of the main levers which could be used to relieve the challenges of the future by facilitating the necessary evolution in our life styles and our socioeconomic organization. Mastery of technological development will be a determinant comparative advantage which Europe must possess if it does not want to trail behind the United States and Japan, particularly in the fields of electronics and the life sciences.

In the aerospace field the European Space Agency has demonstrated the way of fruitful cooperation with the technological and, before long, commercial success of the *Ariane* rocket. Although aerospace technology represents an enormous reservoir of potential innovations for the future we will deliberately restrict our survey to two fields: the technology of data processing and the life sciences, where Europe must also make its efforts towards cooperation.

The Microelectronics Revolution

The new data-processing technologies use means which have been strongly influenced, or have been made possible, by the technologies of data transmission and, to a large extent, by electronics (electronic data processing, automatic text processing, control and measurement technologies, etc.) and by progress in the field of semi-conductors (miniaturization, integrated circuits). The impact of these new technologies has been such that it is not unreasonable to talk of a process of the formation of the information society.

According to the theories of Colin Clark and Jean Fourastié, the development of economies should follow an inevitable trajectory towards the post-industrial society described by Daniel Bell: employment first moving from agriculture to industry, and then developing in the service sector. In other words, the growth of public and private services of low productivity and for which the social demand increases steadily (health, education, leisure activities) will compensate for the loss of jobs due to gains in productivity in industry and agriculture. But a report published by the French government on the development of the information society has swept away this illusion: "*Remote data processing* will result in considerable gains in productivity; initially this will *aggravate unemployment*, particularly in the service sector." (NORA-MINC report published by Documentation française)

The American professor Edwin Parker has suggested dividing up the various categories of workers into four sectors instead of three, separating off those engaged in the acquisition, processing or distribution of information (in the broadest sense of statistics, general knowledge, relations to events, thought, etc.). In this way we would have the four sectors of information, industry, agriculture, and services. As has been emphasized by A. Danzin, starting in 1980 "the number of active workers in information activities will be greater than the total of those in work of an exclusively agricultural, industrial or service nature."

The microprocessor revolution has the remarkable characteristic of resulting in gains in productivity not only in terms of labor but also in terms of capital because of the steady and impressive reduction in the cost of components—a reduction by a factor of 1000 since 1960. It is because of this past reduction, which can also be forecast for the future, that the spread of the microprocessor revolution must be rapid not only in the service sector and in households but also in industry. In this way the replacement of labor by capital in most industrial branches must accelerate: the almost complete automation of production processes is no longer fiction but is now reality, since several production lines of this type are already operating in the automobile industry.

As a consequence, microelectronics will introduce a new factor in the distribution of comparative advantages, since low wages have far less influence when a production process is completely automated; for this reason the return of certain activities such as textiles to the place where they were born can no longer be excluded.

It is also possible to put one's finger on one of the major problems associated with the microprocessor revolution: the attempt to hold it back in the name of its negative consequences on jobs and skills runs the risk of being more damaging than useless:

- Competitiveness would be affected.
- The exodus of certain activities towards the United States and Japan would be inevitable.
- Europe would not profit from the creation of jobs resulting from the growth of microelectronics, but would end up by suffering massive losses of jobs in industry and in the service sector.

This is a real threat from the U.S. and Japan which Europe must face. Under these conditions, Europe must reply, and reply quickly. It was to illustrate this that the Commission presented a report to the Council of Europe in Dublin, showing that European industry covered only an unequal share of the market (30% of the world market for telecommunications, 16% for data processing and 10% for components).

In conclusion, therefore, the importance of microprocessors and of the "new data processing" in general depends on:

- their positive and negative multiplying effects (jobs, skills) over all the industrial sectors, the service sector, and the international division of labor
- their influence on the behavior of consumers
- their potential for decentralizing economic processes and services
- their interrelations with "social innovations," with socio-political developments and trends.

The Biological Revolution

One can see, or at least catch glimpses of, many possible applications for the fundamental knowledge acquired in biology, so that biology could have as much influence on industry in the 21st century—and hence also on societies—as physics and chemistry had on the industry of the 20th century. To show this, it is only necessary to list some of the possible applications:

- energy: methane-producing bacteria; anaerobic production of methane by the *in situ* fermentation of algae; other fermentation processes
- animal feedstuffs: proteins obtained from the fermentation of algae or by the action of yeasts on hydrocarbons
- agriculture: bacteria capable of fixing nitrogen and converting it into ammonia, so making nitrogenous fertilizers unnecessary; non-polluting biological pesticides and insecticides
- chemistry and metallurgy: biological catalysts; bacteria capable of concentrating metals
- pharmaceuticals: bacteria producing pure pharmaceutical substances such as insulin
- genetic engineering: the possibility of creating animal or vegetable cells with preselected characteristics (e.g., silk).

Here again Japan and the United States are in an advanced position. According to certain estimates the utilization of microorganisms already

180

accounts for about 5% of the Japanese GNP. The major American companies, particularly the oil companies, have invested in biotechnologies such as bioreactors, pesticides and veterinary products.

In Europe, the activity of European companies in these biotechnologies generally remains at a lower level, as is shown by the percentage of patents applied for by companies in Europe, the United States, and Japan.

	Europe	*United States*	*Japan*
Enzyme technologies (1969-1975)	20	50	30
Stabilization of enzymes	10	21	69
Chemical products obtained by fermentation	15	18	67

And so, as a recent French government report (*Sciences de la vie et societe*) suggests, "If there is one field which demands the closest cooperation between the European nations it is that of research into the life sciences."

Mastering the Possible Futures

Technology plays a central role in making it possible to meet the economic, energy, and industrial challenges which confront Europe. Mastery of technological development will be a determinant comparative advantage which Europe must possess if it is not to trail along behind the United States and Japan. Consequently the European countries must, as they have already done in the aerospace field, work together and reinforce their efforts in scientific and technological development and cooperation, particularly in the fields of electronics and the life sciences.

The many promises of technology must not, however, make us forget those threats posed by biology for various species (including man) and by data processing for autonomy and freedom. To misunderstand these potential dangers would be damaging and could result in a backlash against biology and data processing—as already exists in the case of nuclear energy—so running the risk of holding back a development which, taken overall, could only be a healthy one. It is necessary, therefore, to separate the wheat from the chaff.

In this way teleprocessing, that is to say the marriage between electronics and telecommunications, opens up new lines of consumption (telecopiers, instantaneous data banks, video-texts, etc.) which are full of hope—but also of uncertainties and questions. In practice only quantifiable information can be effectively processed by computers; qualitative information totally escapes it. Clearly, major decisions and the search for a consensus cannot be formalized and, in any case, should not be formalized. The growing size of files is also a disadvantage. As their size increases, the risk of errors becomes very considerable, while detection of the origin of the error becomes almost impossible. But the most disturbing feature of all is the reductionist character of data processing, which simplifies what is not simple.

Furthermore, we must not ignore the fact that the new era of increasing yields from technology, which will result in fabulous increases in productivity in industry and the service sectors, will also initially have repercussions on *employment*. While it is true that the massive increases in productivity in the period of high economic growth of the sixties were accompanied by almost full employment, it is nevertheless true that, despite the fall in productivity in the seventies, unemployment increased because of an even greater fall in the rate of economic growth. Consequently, and in the absence of recourse to shortening the working week, to adopt the hypothesis that the rate of growth of productivity will be higher than that of economic growth is to admit that unemployment will continue to increase and that it is unfortunately not improbable that it will be doubled (from 6 million to 12 million) during the eighties.

Because of its destructive effects on the individual, such an increase in unemployment is intolerable. Paradoxically, however, necessity has its own laws and unemployment could be creative since the fight against underemployment will involve new life-styles and a new distribution of work. There can be no other result since *recourse to technology is a necessity which will aggravate unemployment, but which will do so far less than if we resign ourselves to a halt in innovation.*

In conclusion, therefore, the risk which Europe runs is less that of being caught by the countries of the South than of being outdistanced by the United States and Japan. It is the latter that will alone be able to benefit from the promises of technology if Europe decides to renounce the advantages in the name of real or potential threats. Since Europe will in the long run have to suffer from these, it would consequently be better to meet them here and now.

Only the accelerated development of technological innovations, and also of social innovations, will provide the essential flexibility and adaptability which our societies need to face the uncertainties of the future, and this is the price which Europe will have to pay if it is to master its possible futures.

Trend Is Not Destiny

by

Andre van Dam

In a big, busy society, the modern Paul Revere is not even heard in the hubbub of voices. When he sounds the alarm, no one answers. Then some day an incident occurs that confirms his warnings. The citizen who had refused to heed them now rushes to the window, puts his head out, nightcap and all, and cries: why doesn't somebody tell me these things?

−John Gardner in his book *Self-Renewal*

Incidents are plentiful. To name but a few: Afghanistan, California's Proposition 13, Iran, Three Mile Island, OPEC, the gold rush. Unfortunately, these warnings tend to fall upon deaf ears. They remind us of the messengers in the classical Chinese opera who, when bringing ill tidings to their Emperor, were beheaded because they were held responsible for the bad news. However, more often than not the Emperor preferred not to listen, thus saving the messengers' heads.

This messenger sounds the alarm about the utterly skewed development of the world economy; about the "benign" neglect of a good part of the Third World in global economic growth. In so doing he reminds all "Emperors" of an early warning by the late U.S. statesman Adlai Stevenson:

We travel together, passengers on a little spaceship, dependent on its vulnerable reserves of air and soil; all committed for our safety to its security and peace; preserved from annihilation only by the care, the work and the love we give our fragile craft. We cannot maintain it half fortunate, half miserable; half confident, half despairing; half slave of the ancient enemies of man, half free in a liberation of resources undreamed of until this day. No craft, no crew can safely travel with such vast contradictions.

What Can Be Done?

In his commencement address at Harvard University, General George C. Marshall introduced his plan to rescue Europe with these words: "Our policy is directed not against any country or doctrine, but against poverty, hunger, desperation and chaos." His strategy was backed up

---

Andre van Dam is Director of Planning, Corn Products Latin America, Buenos Aires, Argentina.

by an investment equivalent to $44 billion in today's U.S. currency. The Marshall plan brought Europe prosperity and unity; it meant growth and leadership to the United States; it brought world peace.

In 1980, the combined economies of North America, Western Europe and Japan produce $44 billion worth of goods and services in just two days! (This is one-tenth of what the world will spend on armaments in 1980.) If these assets were invested in the Third World in the same spirit and for the same general purposes as the Marshall plan, the investment might prove infinitely more rewarding and stimulating to all concerned than its utilization in the arms race or other wastes of modern society. And it would partially return to its donors in the form of fresh orders for capital goods, technology, and services.

One might even envision that a dynamically developing Third World, if only because it is the home of 77% of the world's citizens, eventually might become the engine of growth of the world economy. The crux of the matter is: what type and direction of development will the Third World require in the 1980s to fulfill such a function for mutual (north and south) benefit?

Hitherto, the opinion prevailed that sustained economic growth would automatically trickle down to the burgeoning needy masses. In that view, in the early stage of development, during the build-up of capital, infrastructure and the productive capacity of the core economy, the poor would have to keep on tightening their belts until the fruits of savings, investment and innovation could be reaped—but sooner or later modern, organized, large-scale industry would provide adequate income for all. The benefits of economic growth would widely spread through market forces, raising demand for labor, productivity and wages. And where such forces failed, governments would extend the benefits of growth by policies such as progressive taxation, social services and transfer payments.

In those countries where the population explosion is brought under control, foreign trade opportunities abound, government and private firms work hand in hand, social mobility exists, and the people are ready for take-off, the above strategy of economic growth does materialize, in some cases spectacularly. However, in too many countries dynamic economic expansion increases dualism: the growth of a modern, urban, large-scale manufacturing sector alongside stagnation of the rural sector. The ensuing massive exodus of landless peasants to the cities—originally viewed as the hard core of progress—creates slums, unemployment and discontent. This is due to the fact that the cities cannot absorb so many people, and modern industry is better equipped to raise productivity and efficiency than to create jobs for the unskilled.

Develop the Countryside

For most of the two billion underprivileged of the Third World, however, the hardship is not unemployment. Their problem is that they toil long hours and do hard work at unremunerative, unproductive forms of activity. Not only labor, but also capital is under-utilized. Sustained economic growth, which should incorporate the poor into the economy, more often than not reinforces and entrenches existing inequalities in income, assets and power. In order to remedy this huge obstacle to modernization and the fulfillment of the most basic human needs, it is essential to develop the countryside, where people are born and can make a living in a dignified, productive manner.

The task demands that the industrialized countries of the north and the developing nations of the south acknowledge their interdependence. Not the interdependency of horse and rider, but rather that of oarsmen rowing a skiff in the rapids. Awareness of interdependency is heightened now that a good number of Third World nations own some critical resources (petroleum, gas, minerals and metals, forests) which are direly lacking in Western Europe and Japan, and are either scarce or expensive to develop in North America.

The ultimate prosperity of the global economy may well hinge upon a more judicious husbanding of the world's four biological systems: croplands, grasslands, forests and fisheries. They supply not only all the food but also many critical raw materials for industry. The law of diminishing return favors those countries where the supply of such resources is largest, and the demand least.

The above four biological systems are presently the stepchild of research and development. Of the estimated $200 billion which the world will invest in R&D in 1980, only 3% is allotted to agriculture as compared to 24% for military purposes—and only 5% is done within the Third World itself. Presently agricuture is considered more as an inexhaustible reservoir of land for urbanization, industry and source of energy than as a supply of foodstuffs. The Third World has three powerful reasons to aim at reversing this trend:

Reversal of Trend

First, food production is the Third World's foremost priority, not only in order to feed its teeming masses but also to seek export revenues with which to pay for critical imports. Second, the Third World must distribute the available farmland more evenly so as to ensure that a billion landless peasants, sharecroppers and marginal farmers secure access to a modest plot of fertile land, enough to satisfy their most basic human needs. Lastly, the Third World must see to it that its factors of production—capital, energy, land, labor and raw materials—are blended in proportion to their cost and availability, and the last three factors are most plentiful.

In the same vein, petroleum-scarce Third World countries can still avoid the fossil fuel dead-end street. Most of the Third World is endowed with sunlight; its populations are fairly dispersed; biomass is mostly plentiful. By seeking *sui generis* solutions to the energy crisis—such as China's 5 million small biogas plants—the Third World may cautiously and modestly mechanize plowing, planting and harvesting—sufficiently so as to free human energy for multiple cropping.

Conclusion

In the light of the above appraisal, agriculture (including animal husbandry, forestry and fisheries) is perceived as the weakest link in the Third World's development chain. In order to remedy this weakness, rural infrastructures should become adequate, appropriate technology made available, family planning propagated, land reforms accelerated and, last but certainly not least, the terms of trade vastly improved. North America, Western Europe and Japan should be urged to reverse the present situation in which they import raw materials like raw cotton and cocoa beans all but free of duties, but impose stiff tariffs on manufactures like cotton garments and chocolate. A reversal of this trend would improve the Third World's balance of payments and raise its stock of technology, as well as its employment and income levels.

In short, I perceive the development of the rural sector in general and agriculture in particular as the main avenue to the Third World's modernization, the satisfaction of basic human needs—and thus as an engine of growth of the world economy. This assumes a reversal of current north-south relationships. But then, trend is not destiny.

Managing Growth Through
Epochal Change

by

Robert D. Hamrin

The intensity of the growth debate in the 1970s and its rapidly changing focus should be viewed as a history of attempts to comprehend first, the fact that the U.S. is in the midst of a time of epochal change and second, the nature of the transformation. The "fact" has been described variously by a number of leading historians and social critics as: "a great transition in the state of the human race"; "a time between civilizations"; "one of the great discontinuities in human history"; "comparable in the history of Western civilization to the Renaissance and Reformation."

An important element in this broad transition is the changing nature of the traditional sources of growth which made such positive contributions in the 1950s and 1960s. These have now departed onto new paths which are no longer so supportive of growth. In the area of natural resources, for example, the U.S. has moved from a "cowboy economy" to a position of serious resource constraints manifested in periodic energy crises. A part of the constraints is the no longer free use of the environment. Regarding human resources, there will be a sharp slowdown in labor force growth, particularly in the latter half of the 1980s. Thus, the labor force will grow by 12% in the 1980s compared to a 21% growth in the 1970s. Labor productivity, averaging 0.7% per annum in the 1970, has grown at less than one-third the 2.3% annual rate of increase during the 1960s. The productivity of capital has also experienced a long-run decline. From 1947-66, the output/capital ratio increased at an average rate of 0.5% per year while from 1967-74 it decreased an average 1.3% per year. The falling ratio is a key contributor to the general expectation that capital expenditures in the 1980s will likely be insufficient to generate enough capacity to meet the demands of

Robert D. Hamrin is Senior Policy Economist, U.S. Environmental Protection Agency, Washington, D.C. This article is extracted from a paper presented at the 1979 Woodlands Conference on Growth Policy held at the Woodlands, Texas. Full-length treatment is provided in Managing Growth in the 1980s: Toward a New Economics *(Praeger, 1980).*

the economy, with resulting bottlenecks and sporadic shortages. Research and development (R&D) spending for basic and exploratory research, measured in price-adjusted dollars, has been on a plateau for ten years. Moreover, it has been argued that a state of "technological maturity" characterizes much of corporate America—that much of the innovative thrust of corporations seems to have dissipated as several vital postwar industries have reached a mature stage.

Thus, it may be concluded just from changes in traditional sources of growth that the days of wide and handsome economic growth will not be seen in the 1980s. Since many of these same trends are being experienced by other OECD nations, they too will witness slower growth. The OECD recently concluded that even under favorable assumptions, growth rates of output would not return to those witnessed in the 1960s, while unemployment levels and inflation rates would remain on average higher than in that period.

As important as these changes are, however, the U.S. is experiencing three much more fundamental, long-run trends which constitute the heart of the transformation: (1) the structural transformation from an economy based in manufacturing and industry to one based in information, knowledge and communications; (2) the significant change in people's values, attitudes and priorities regarding growth and material progress, the environment, and work; and (3) the complete revamping of the international economy in which new actors on the world stage, wielding considerable power and largely "uncontrollable," have caused a significant diminution in the effectiveness of purely domestic policies to control U.S. economic activity.

The Information Economy

Electronics has been one of the most rapidly expanding sectors throughout the industrialized world in the last decade. Its tremendous future importance was emphasized in a 1979 draft report by the *Interfutures* Project (Organization for Economic and Cultural Development) on the long-run future of OECD's member countries:

> Through its links with data processing and telecommunications, the introduction of automation throughout industry, the changes which electronic office equipment is producing in service activities, and the actual services which it creates, the electronics complex will during the next quarter of a century be the main pole around which the productive structures of the advanced industrial societies will be reorganized.

Because of such tremendous growth and the central role anticipated for electronics and information activity in general, the information revolution could bring about a socio-economic transformation as far reaching in its ultimate effects as the industrial revolution, one which would certainly alter profoundly the pattern of growth. The two revolutions, however, are quite different. Whereas the industrial revolution made available and employed vast amounts of mechanical energy, the information-electronics revolution is extremely sparing of energy and materials. Much of the industrial technology was crude, with only a modest scientific or theoretical base. The information revolution, however, as the product of the most advanced science, technology and management, represents one of the greatest intellectual achievements of mankind.

The impact of the shift to an information economy will be pervasive—it will be seen in how and what we produce, how we transact business, how we pay, how news is gathered and spread, where we work and what kind of work we do, and how we communicate. Not restricted to just the computer or communications industries, the information revolution at minimum embraces banking, insurance, transportation, health, education, communications, entertaining and manufacturing.

Developing Nations Take Over Manufacturing

It is likely, as Daniel Bell argues, that in the 1980s traditional, routinized manufacturing, such as the textile, shipbuilding, steel, shoe and small consumer appliances industries will be "drawn out" of the advanced industrial countries and become centered in the new tier of rapidly developing countries, including Brazil, Mexico, South Korea, Taiwan, Singapore, Algeria and Nigeria. The response of the advanced industrial countries, as Bell sees its, "will be either protectionism and the disruption of the world economy or the development of a 'comparative advantage' in essentially the electronic and advanced technological and science-based industries that are the feature of a post-industrial society."

The U.S. government has not engaged in such systematic, long-range thinking and planning even though the U.S. is currently out front in terms of the technical sophistication and manufacturing distribution base of its telecommunications industries and the stakes are high. It has been estimated that $1.6 trillion will be invested in telecommunications outside the U.S. by the year 2000 to establish a global information network in which all information will be passed and stored electronically. In addition to this investment potential, a thorough examination of the shift underway to an information economy would reveal an increasingly anti-inflationary, more energy/resource-conserving economy which carries exciting potential for major productivity gains.

There is a great opportunity for the U.S. to exert a significant leadership role in the information field. To do so, the government must abandon its adversarial relationship with industry in the telecommunications field. The government should begin to consider positive initiatives which would help American industry retain both its technological leadership and its commanding share of the export market in the information-electronics field.

The potential is more than economic. The magnificently productive U.S. industrial machine has brought material goods not only to Americans but to many of the world's people in undreamed-of abundance. Tomorrow's challenge is even greater. Information and related technology could be directed to helping people achieve their full human potential once material needs have been satisfied, a goal more nebulous and complex than supplying material goods but likely more exciting and rewarding.

New Values and Priorities

The transformation is so profound because it consists of more than change in the underlying economic structure, fundamental as that may be. Equally important, perhaps more so, is the fact that the values, attitudes and priorities of the American people are undergoing substantial change. Much of this change became widely known through President Carter's' mid-July televised speech in which he spoke of a "crisis of confidence" and a "fundamental malaise." Daniel Yankelovich in his paper for this conference succinctly summarizes the source of this malaise; he has found that recent survey data and opinion polls show Americans

> ... midway between an older post-World War II attitude of expanding horizons, a growing psychology of entitlement, unfettered optimism, and unqualified confidence in technology and economic growth, and a present state of mind of lowering expectations, apprehensions about the future, mistrust in institutions, and a growing psychology of limits.

In short, the American people are extremely confused right now. The old "givens" are crumbling and there is nothing to take their place. America in the past had as a central goal the pursuit of growth through hard work and the application of new technologies. Now, growth is no longer an adequate goal, fulfilling work is being sought, and new technologies are being increasingly questioned, controlled and sometimes rejected. Such a state of confusion ultimately demands a resolution.

The god of growth has not brought full contentment. The vast majority of Americans have acquired an abundance of material things yet remain vexed, not only by the immediate non-economic problems in their individual personal lives, but by larger issues that extend outward to embrace their whole society and forward into the future. When an increasing number now think of the quality of life, it is not simply a vision of an overflowing cornucopia of personal material luxuries, but something less tangible and yet more important—job satisfaction, good schools, responsive government, fulfilling leisure activities. Most Americans have "enough," but many are beginning to think that this kind of enough is still not adequate.

Gardiner Ackley has offered one of the most intriguing statements on the relationship between affluence, value change and economic growth:

> I doubt that externally imposed limits to growth will require a new ethic and life style: rather, I suspect, an ever-increasing abundance will generate an ethic or life style which will cause economic growth to slow and ultimately to cease. And as that happens, we may not even recognize it because the question of growth will have become so uninteresting.

The Global Context

The international economy at the close of the 1970s is entirely different in character from that of 1970 and would have been undreamed of in 1960. All nations have become highly interdependent but this has affected the U.S. in the 1970s more than most because of its relative isolation from the world economy throughout most of its history. Ameri-

190

cans became vividly aware of their new interdependence in 1972 when bad weather in the Ukraine led to higher bread prices at home and in 1973 and 1974 when the actions of a group of small countries contributed to a quadrupling of oil prices in a period of a few months.

Trade historically has been a very small proportion of the GNP, as the U.S. was among the world's most self-sufficient countries. This is changing rapidly and radically. In 1971, the value of exports plus imports was less than $90 billion in an economy just over $1 trillion. By 1977, the value of exports and imports had tripled to $270 billion while the GNP had fallen short of doubling ($1.9 trillion). By the late 1970s, leading U.S. firms had so greatly increased their stake in overseas production that the output of their foreign subsidiaries and branches had grown to over one-quarter of the firms' U.S. production. Thus, with upwards of $350 billion of assets held by Americans in foreign countries and around $275 billion held by foreigners in the U.S., there can be no doubt that the U.S. is irretrievably linked to the world economy.

The nature of this interdependency goes well beyond such trade or financial figures. It is best understood through examination of five new factors with considerable power and influence on the world stage in the 1970s: the OPEC oil cartel; the Third World's demand for a New International Economic Order; multinationals; floating exchange rates; and the Eurodollar market. Each of these characters is largely "uncontrollable"—that is, no single national economic institution or policy can substantially alter their actions or effects. The result is a significant diminution in the effectiveness of purely domestic policies on economic activity; this amounts to a reduction in a nation's sovereignty over its economy.

Towards Qualitative Growth

A major challenge of the 1980s will be to encourage the shift underway in the national consciousness from an allegiance to quantitative economic growth to advocacy of qualitative growth and development of practical measures to achieve such growth in the future. Specifically, the U.S. should move toward an economic growth incorporating sound environmental, physical, and moral principles which will ensure that growth is both sustainable and productive of desirable human ends.

The pursuit of qualitative growth would follow two main guiding principles: (1) developing a Conserver Society which would require the use of the minimum amount of physical resources to carry out an activity or produce a product (including growth) without resulting in undesirable side effects and (2) pursuing total employment of human resources, wherein everyone desiring a job would have an excellent opportunity of obtaining one that satisfies his or her personal desires. Such new goals will require a thorough rethinking of economics and economic policies as well as substantial change in the attitudes, policies, and behavior of consumers, corporations, and government.

Economics must be completely rethought as a discipline because current theory and resulting policies are inadequate to deal with the new economic realities and do not complement well the goal of qualitative growth. The discipline's primary deficiencies are its short-run focus, the fact that it is not firmly grounded in institutional-power realities, its virtual neglect of such physical realities as energy, natural resources and the environment and its almost slavish adherence to analyzing only that which is quantifiable. To counter these deficiencies, economics must become more holistic—encompassing non-economic principles, facts, and trends, developing a long-run analysis capability and explicitly incorporating the workings of the global economy and subnational economies into its domestic, national-level considerations.

Such an approach is necessary for achieving a more comprehensive understanding of the problems plaguing us and would open up the way to potential solutions that the current narrow perspective cannot begin to suggest. For example, such an approach can begin to deal with inflation by exploring how to increase the growth rate of productivity. By concentrating on the rapid development and widespread diffusion of information technologies, industrializing services and providing a more flexible labor market, the foundation of all other "inflation-fighting" policies can be laid.

Market forces and corporate practices currently in effect will help significantly to foster qualitative growth in the 1980s. As information activity continues to generate an increasing share of the GNP at the expense of energy-intensive basic industries, we will move toward a more energy-conserving economic base and hence one that will also be more environmentally benign. Corporations, through a considerable variety of activities already taken, have recognized that resource conservation practices and pollution control can actually contribute positively to their bottom line on profits or lead to energy savings.

There is, however, considerably more potential particularly in the areas of recycling, energy conservation and process change for pollution control purposes. Actions taken by corporations to provide a more flexible labor market, such as quality of worklife experiments, flexitime, the reduced work week and sabbaticals, will, if expanded, also facilitate the goal of qualitative growth.

The natural workings of market forces and the restructuring of economics could both be enhanced by the development of a new government policy framework. The hard fact is that the really critical issues before the country are not the immediate and isolated ones, but the interrelated and long-range ones. Yet the current government policy framework is set up to handle only the crisis. If governmental policies are going to effectively govern the long-run forces influencing growth, rather than be governed by them, some form of national growth policy will have to be established. The level of success of such a policy would be determined by its comprehensiveness in harmonizing frequently conflicting aims within our broader social and environmental, as well as purely economic, objectives.

There are a number of actions the government could take to promote qualitative growth. To promote more recycling, it must ensure that price reflects scarcity and should consider subsidies, low-interest loans, price guarantees, research and development grants and preference for recycled materials in government procurement. It could also explore a number of steps to encourage the recycling of urban solid wastes and to promote greater durability and re-use of product. Though corporations would have primary responsibility for promoting total employment, the government could encourage a more flexible labor market and career pattern. All of these potential new policy initiatives call for a leadership with real vision regarding the challenge of a qualitative growth future.

We have just come through a unique period in U.S. history. The economy, drawing on a confluence of positive and often unique factors, was able to generate material wealth for most Americans which those living just 100 years ago could hardly have dreamed of. Yet in a fundamental sense, the U.S. has been too preoccupied with the material side of the great socioeconomic revolution brought about by its scientific and technological accomplishments. We have long given lip service to the fact that man does not live by bread alone but have rarely believed it. Only recently has the general feeling arisen that affluence does not buy contentment or a sense of community.

The Public Debate on Growth: Toward Resolution

by

Daniel Yankelovich and Bernard Lefkowitz

Over the course of the past three decades, surveys by a number of professional polling organizations, such as Harris, Gallup, the University of Michigan Survey Research Center, and Yankelovich, Skelly, and White, have all documented a growing ambivalence and uncertainty on the part of many Americans as they try individually and collectively to confront the issue of growth. A certain amount of anxiety may be inevitable as people attempt to puzzle out their response to a problem as complex, poorly understood and all-encompassing as growth. As sociologist Amitai Etzioni points out, a sense of divided and uncertain purpose in the economic domain creates stress in almost every sphere of life.

But Etzioni goes on to argue that "from an economic and social-psychic viewpoint, the present fairly high level of ambivalence and lack of clear priority needs to give way over the next few years to either a decade of rededication to the industrial, mass-consumption society, or a clearer commitment to a slow-growth, quality-of-life society. *In the long run, high ambivalence is too stressful for societies to endure.*" (Our emphasis.)

Yet the probabilities are that a high level of ambivalence is likely to persist for a long period before the public begins to order its national priorities. Given the present instability—the new economic pessimism, mistrust of business, anger against government incompetence and wastefulness, confusion about the sources of economic distress, the conflict between the cultural emphasis on entitlements and the limitations imposed by current economic conditions—it is possible that the feelings of disillusionment, frustration and betrayal will harden, that the divisions between the public and the economic and political leadership groups will widen and that the perception of inequity in the allocation of scarce

Daniel Yankelovich is President of Yankelovich, Skelly and White, a public opinion analysis and market research firm in New York City. Bernard Lefkowitz is a free-lance writer and a consultant on social issues to the Ford Foundation.

resources and unfairness in bearing the burden of inflation will destroy all sense of a common social and economic purpose.

A look back at the last six years forces the observer to raise grave questions about the future. Before America felt the impact of scarcities and before it was shaken by recession, its first priority was expansion of the economic product. During and immediately after these dislocations, the public seemed ready to accept a reduction in consumption and tried to apply certain conserving principles to everyday life. But the urgency of uniting to defeat a common enemy diminished as the memory of hard times receded. The pattern today alternates between breathless consumption, the buy-before-the-price-goes-up syndrome, and an awareness of limits to scarce resources and to the pleasures of materialism.

The temptation is to go along with the currently fashionable pessimism which foresees sharper conflicts and deeper divisions in the next two decades. We don't believe that is the only or inevitable course open to Western industrial countries. On the contrary, the public appears to be moving, slowly and unevenly to be sure, toward accepting a hard bargain—a trade-off of high consumption in exchange for a period of relative economic stability and the preservation of the material gains they have achieved in recent years—if this is possible. While the evidence is not conclusive, there are indications that the public may reduce the consumption of certain nonessential goods and services and practice moderate restraint in the acquisition and use of scarce materials.

The Preconditions for Resolution

We believe that there are three overall preconditions for forming a new consensus. Together, they provide the basis for reaching agreement on very different national priorities.

The first and perhaps most important is that the country has to *feel* the necessity for making hard choices. These choices cannot be abstract or theoretical. People must believe that their decisions will have a direct, immediate and significant effect on their lives. Practically and emotionally, the public has to recognize that it cannot postpone or deflect these choices. The continuing experience of scarcities and particularly the effects of inflation have brought the public almost to the point where it is prepared to choose between conflicting themes in American society.

The second precondition is effective leadership to guide the public toward resolution. The way leaders manage events and conditions often shapes the public response. It is incumbent on the national leadership to explain in compelling terms why the choices are necessary, and to chart the new directions.

The last precondition is that the public be given the opportunity to confront and think through the real choices. In the current climate of mistrust, people often sense that they have lost control over their lives. But some decisions are so important, so central to the security and stability of the average citizen, that the public must be given the time to challenge and probe and question the proposal that is being advanced. The question of growth is so complex, technical and all-inclusive that leadership will be tempted to parcel out different aspects of the problem to technicians, experts and special-interest groups. The temptation should be resisted. If the public feels it is being excluded from the decision-making process, it will grow ever more frustrated, angry, mistrustful and cynical. Under these conditions, the opportunity for compromise, civility and positive politics will disappear and rather than achieving resolution the country will remain mired in confusion and disorder.

We believe that resolution is possible if average Americans feel they are part of the decision-making continuum, if they feel that their point of view is heard and responded to, if they feel that their fundamental values are respected. A unilateral decision by leadership is not going to stick. If they are being asked to play, citizens must have a chance to make the rules. They will not accept someone else's judgment that they, the public, have to sacrifice. They have to reach this conclusion for themselves.

Alternative Models

Assuming that the preconditions for change are present, in what direction is the public likely to go? Because the public has just begun to conceptualize the choices, it would be premature to say that the direction is certain. But at this early stage various ideological forms can be dimly discerned. It is beyond the purview of this report to describe them in depth, but they can be summarized as follows:

● *A period of austerity and sacrifice during which the country committed its material resources to the rebuilding of the economic infrastructure.* For many reasons, it seems doubtful that the public is prepared to undergo an extended period of self-denial to reconstruct the high-consumption, heavily materialistic environment of the 1950s.

● *An emphasis on government intervention and social supports.* The public will not eliminate programs that it feels entitled to, such as social security, unemployment insurance, veterans' benefits and medicare. At the same time, people are in a "take back" mood, as exemplified by the Proposition 13 movement. Public support for foreign aid and assistance to the poor, which has never been high, has dropped even more sharply in recent years. There are other publicly supported programs in education, assistance for the elderly, job training and health, about which the public is uncertain. These programs will probably not be eliminated, but the level of support for them may not increase substantially. The liberal activist consensus, which provided the basis for government intervention through the 1960s, has splintered. It is unlikely then that the public would back a wider role for government in social welfare.

● *A society built around the principles of "voluntary simplicity."* There is a small group of Americans who have been influenced by some of the countercultural innovations of the 1960s. While they tend to resist conventional political labels, many are active in consumerism and the environmental movement. They are deeply committed to a simplified life-style which rejects materialistic values and seeks to limit possessions to a bare minimum. While some aspects of their philosophy appeal to the general public, such as their concern for physical well-being, it is unlikely that the majority of the public will voluntarily embrace an outlook which rejects many of the conveniences and comforts offered by the most technologically advanced country in the world.

• *A more conserving society with a greater balance than now exists between consumption and nonmaterialistic values.* The movement toward a more conserving society is accelerated by three significant psychosocial developments: the heightened emphasis on economic security, lowered economic expectations, and new values. All three may be converging to create a new fusion of the search for economic stability with the increasingly powerful impulse to claim control over one's own destiny. Most survey data indicates growing support for this form of resolution, although a firm pattern of consensus has not yet developed.

The New Values

Starting in the late 1960s and gathering momentum in the 1970s, Americans began to change their philosophy of life—their sense of what is important and what isn't.

The essence of the change is that in the past people were motivated mainly by earning more money, adding to possessions, gaining economic security, and providing material comforts for the family. Increasingly throughout the 1970s, new self-fulfillment motives have gained in importance. Moreover, the traditional material incentives and the new self-fulfillment ones have moved in somewhat separate directions. People still want material rewards but they no longer feel that it is necessary to give so much of themselves to achieve them. Also, they often see their self-fulfillment as something different from material success, and of equal or greater value. So they want self-fulfillment in *addition* to financial security. To oversimplify a little, people want more, but also are willing to give less for it. They desire more personal freedom, more time off, more self-expression, more flexibility, more of a say of how things are done, more variety, more opportunity. What they want is more of everything. In essence, they want to assert ever-greater control over how they live their lives. Money and status still count, but they are not as powerful or universal as they used to be. Increasingly, Americans want something different out of life than in the past.

Many of the new values have their roots in the social movements that began in the 1960s, such as the student movement and the women's movement. Most of the student-generated ideas of the 1960s, centering on political radicalism, the drug culture and the counterculture, have been rejected by the public. But at least three ideas have been carried over to the present and have been appropriated by a majority of Americans.

Briefly these are:

First, the growing conviction that what is regarded as a "nose-to-the-grindstone" way of life, with its hard work, its unquestioning loyalty to empoyers and its suppression of desires that conflict with obligations to others, is too high a price to pay for material success. Besides, many people have come to believe that it may not be necessary to make such sacrifices.

Second, the feeling that we have devoted too much of our time and attention in this country to the task of how to make a living and not enough to the question of how to live; hence, the current preoccupation with finding a "life-style" that precisely expresses each person's unique individuality.

Last, the belief that what counts most in life is that "I keep growing" as an individual, "that I have the opportunity to fulfill my potentials," and that "I have a moral obligation to myself to do so." This is a startling new conception of moral obligation.

These attitudes and values represent a large shift in the traditional American ethos and philosophy of life. Most people appear unsure of these new beliefs and are torn between the old philosophy and the new one. But despite their uneasiness and anxiousness, the public psychology continues to change.

The new values are now merging with the fear of economic instability. A new synthesis is forming, one that meshes three elements: the pursuit of economic stability (even at the cost of reduced consumption) with more modest material expectations and with the drive to establish maximum control over one's own life and destiny. The combination of these three elements creates a novel American outlook.

The core fantasy today is not the pot at the end of the rainbow or the dream of sudden wealth; if the price of a lifetime of shoving, struggling, and competing—even if it results in your becoming the most powerful man in the sales division or the wealthiest man in the neighborhood—is a nervous breakdown at 35 or a heart attack at 40, it's not worth it. The drive to reach the top has been replaced by the need to keep one's life on a relatively even keel. Success is defined in relative terms: achieving a relative degree of commitment to work and career.

The wealth-at-any-cost fever has given way to the more palliative "stay well and be happy." In other words, have a *nice* day. This theme of a relatively decent, happy, nice existence is the new connection between social and economic classes. When the shared goal is a life that has diversity and excitement but which does not careen wildly between failure and success, between sudden catastrophe and brief spurts of fulfillment, then the different groups in the middle socio-economic range seem to have much in common.

They all want job security; they all want an income whose real dollar value increases, however modestly; they want to preserve those material gains they have worked for and which represent an improvement over what their parents and grandparents had; and they want to keep those social supports which they have come to regard as entitlements. (At the same time they are reluctant to keep paying for the support of groups who do not share their values; e.g., they don't want to reward anybody for *not* working.) They are choosing security, stability and control over risk, adventure and expansiveness.

These themes—living on a human scale, devoting time to interpersonal relationships, improving existing facilities rather than breaking new ground—are repeated on many levels of the growth debate. They underlie much of the current discussion about the role of government and business in the lives of individual citizens, the emphasis on community and family, the desire to restore close personal relationships that may have been threatened by a preoccupation with career and social mobility, and the interest in living more simply.

As a practical matter, we do not believe that America is about to enter into a grand debate on the significance of materialism, the application of the new values, or the desirable rate of growth in the last decades of the twentieth century. What is more likely is a continuing discussion of many different proposals, programs and strategies presented at all levels of government and business, from town hall to Congress, from the executive boardroom to the company cafeteria. Whether these hundreds or perhaps thousands of proposals will collectively express the kind of dynamic consensus America enjoyed in the post-war period will depend on how consonant they are with the public's emerging value priorities and with the public's ability to confront painful choices—and make them.

Opinion survey data show that at the present time the public remains somewhat unrealistic about all that it wants. But the data also suggest that at a deeper level of consciousness Americans have begun to reconcile themselves to the need to accept greater—and diffferent—limits than in the past. The stage is set, therefore, for the next phases of working through as the nation moves toward some resolution of what it has to give up and what it insists upon retaining.

By way of conclusion, therefore, we summarize a brief profile of the priorities of the American public:

1. The public wants to retain the gains it won in the affluent years. It seems unwilling to sacrifice these in an effort to regenerate the economic machine or to expand vastly the existing system of social supports.

2. The public has little taste for self-denial and austerity for the purpose of adding new consumer products to the market or increasing efficiency. What sacrifices it is prepared to make will be directed toward maintaining economic stability and a reliable and fair supply of essentials (e.g., gasoline), even if the amount is reduced.

3. Americans want to strike a new balance between hard work and leisure. They are prepared to slow down their pursuit of luxuries if that gives them the freedom to explore the possibilities of self-fulfillment and allows them a measure of economic stability.

4. Americans appear to want to halt the expansion of certain government services if this will reduce their taxes and protect their privacy. They do want, however, to retain those services that they consider entitlements, such as social security and pension benefits. And they would like to be protected against the high costs of catastrophic illness.

5. The public has clear-cut priorities about what forms of con-

sumption it is prepared to give up and what it considers essential to its well-being and freedom. People don't want to give up their family cars, their central heating, their own homes, their washing machines. They are prepared, however, to make modest cutbacks in the use of energy, to keep their old model cars longer, to waste less, to reduce consumption of meat and clothing, and to reduce their use of items that can't be recycled if these involve waste.

6. A new antiwaste morality is gaining momentum. The public is unlikely to support any government program that it regards as potentially wasteful, and there is support for regulations that curb wasteful practices by the public itself. This attitude extends to the consumption of products that are in relatively short supply. So the public would go along with such measures as closing gas stations on Sunday to limit consumption and restricting the use of credit cards. It should be pointed out that in the public's mind the rising rate of inflation is fused with wastefulness. The public would support higher taxes on foreign-made "luxury" goods, such as color television sets, in the hope that it would reduce inflation and discourage the purchase of non-essential products.

There is no guarantee that these kinds of trade-offs—the bargain the public is willing to make—will bring people what they want. Americans are understandably reluctant to give up some things that they regard as essential to a comfortable life. They are just beginning to suspect that such choices may lie in the offing, which is an unnerving prospect. The result is a profound ambivalence and conflict. No one can state for certain how this conflict will be resolved, but we believe that Americans will not wish to turn the clock back to the great period of dynamic growth in the two decades following World War II. For all of its attractions and accomplishments—it was in many ways a golden age for America—there is a deep-seated conviction in the public that we overdid the materialist thrust of a consumer society. America now yearns for a more balanced life-style in which the needs of the spirit (including the demand for morally meaningful sacrifice) will be in better balance with materialist aspirations. Whatever the future may be, for social, psychological as well as practical economic reasons, it will not recapture the past.

Economics: Getting
Down to Business

The Economic Future

by

Herman Kahn and John B. Phelps

In this very brief paper we present an overview of the long-term future of the global economy and summarize some prospects for the 1980-2000 period. We offer a generally optimistic view of the economic future, but with caution and qualifications. We believe that—barring serious bad luck or bad management—the prospects for achieving eventually a high level of broadly worldwide economic affluence and beneficent technology are bright, that this is a good and logical goal for mankind, and that our images of the economic future may substantially determine our progress toward that goal. For 1980-2000, we expect reasonably good overall economic development in the world, particularly in the rapidly rising middle-income countries. In the relatively affluent countries, both capitalist and socialist, we anticipate a sense of continuing uncertainty and malaise, with somewhat slower growth than occurred in the 1950s and 1960s.

Our view of what is entirely possible and indeed highly desirable for our global future runs contrary to some relatively pessimistic, widely articulated intellectual fashions of the '70s, represented by aphorisms such as "limits to growth" and "small is beautiful." Many of the problems of much current concern—shortages (of which energy is getting the most attention), pollution, crowding, and various examples of national and international mismanagement—we describe as "growing pains of the superindustrial economy (or society)." These problems are basically solvable—there is, for instance, no physical shortage of energy in the world. We do not normally think of any of the above as being likely apocalyptic threats to mankind's future, but as new challenges to technology, management, political leadership, and our collective morale and wisdom.

The Long-Term Future: The Great Transition

Chart 1 provides a long time perspective of our economic past and

Herman Kahn is Director and Chairman of the Hudson Institute, Croton-on-Hudson, New York.

John B. Phelps, a futurist and physicist and a consultant to the Hudson Institute, resides at 4710 Bethesda Avenue, Bethesda, Maryland.

This essay is adapted, with additions, from a much longer article, "The Economic Present and Future," by the same authors in THE FUTURIST, June 1979. Readers are also referred to World Economic Development: 1979 and Beyond *by Herman Kahn (Westview Press, Boulder, Colorado, 1979).*

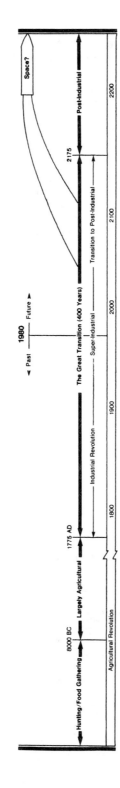

CHART 1
THE ECONOMIC PAST AND FUTURE IN TIME PERSPECTIVE

future. We identify two watersheds in man's economic history: the Agricultural Revolution that occurred gradually some 10,000 years ago and the Great Transition in which we are living today. (With respect to this description, much of Alvin Toffler's book *The Third Wave* refers to changes occurring in the latter part of our second watershed, namely the shift to a post-industrial economy and society as we move through the Great Transition.) There may be another watershed to come: mankind's movement into space, with settlements on other celestial bodies and/or in man-made space colonies. This watershed, which we think is likely, will lead to the development of new kinds of space economies that will differ radically from our terrestrial experiences. In this paper, we merely indicate this "space option" in the upper righthand corner of *Chart 1.*

In *Chart 1* we show the Great Transition as comprising three phases: the industrial revolution, the super-industrial economy, and the transition to a post-industrial economy. These three phases overlap and complement each other in time and in different parts of the world, but the overall economic evolution is clear. As noted above, many of the practical problems ("crises") that concern us now in the United States, and to a lesser extent

CHART 2

THE GREAT TRANSITION

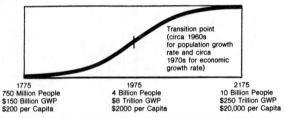

Transition point
(circa 1960s
for population growth
rate and circa
1970s for economic
growth rate)

1775	1975	2175
750 Million People	4 Billion People	10 Billion People
$150 Billion GWP	$8 Trillion GWP	$250 Trillion GWP
$200 per Capita	$2000 per Capita	$20,000 per Capita

Notes: Plot is semi-logarithmic, GWP-Gross World Product, Sums are in fixed approximately 1980 dollars

PRE 1775	All societies are pre-industrial. Income Ratio (ratio of richest 10% to poorest 10%) about 5 to 1
1775-1875	100 years for initial industrialization of Northwestern Europe, Japan, and North America. Income Ratio goes to about 20 to 1
1875-1950	Emergence of mass consumption societies in Europe, Japan, and North America and start of worldwide industrialization
1950-1975	Most rapid economic and population growth in history; initial emergence of super-industrial economies,* technological crises, and many historic transitions, e.g., inflection points in world population and perhaps gross product curves (also first steps into space)
1975-2000	Continued rapid growth in middle-income countries but less so for the rich countries; reduction in gap between rich and middle-income countries
2000-2025	Emergence of post-industrial economies* in most Western cultures, Japan, and perhaps USSR. Full development of super-industrial cultures* and societies* in advanced countries. First signs of a worldwide maturing economy. (First serious moves to colonize space.) Income Ratio of 100 to 1
2025-2175	Worldwide slowing down in population and economic growth rates (not only in percent but also in absolute numbers). As a result it takes almost 150 years for emergence of post-industrial economies almost everywhere. (Perhaps also the establishment of an independent solar system society.) Income Ratios (on earth) 40 to 1 or less—perhaps much less
POST 2175	Post-industrial society stabilizes or ossifies; or, the next development in mankind emerges

*We distinguish between economy, institutions, culture, and society as follows:

Economy:	economic and technological activity
Institutions:	laws and organizations
Culture:	style, values, national character, and attitudes
Society:	the whole

Super-Industrial Economy refers to the large size and scale of modern enterprise and its impact on the external social and physical environment.
Post-Industrial Economy refers to a future very affluent economy which meets its industrial and material needs with a small part of its work force and economic effort.
Presumably first the economy emerges, then the institutions, the culture, and finally one has a harmonious society.

204

worldwide, are associated with the emergence of a super-industrial economy.

Chart 2 shows the Great Transition, which may be summarized as follows: "Two hundred years ago, almost everywhere human beings were comparatively few, poor, and at the mercy of the forces of nature; two centuries hence, barring some combination of very bad luck and/or bad management, they should be numerous, rich, and in control of the forces of nature." We do not argue that this scenario is inevitable, but only that it is likely and plausible, given the data and trends that are known today.

Our model of past and future history is embodied in the "S"-shaped or logistic curve in *Chart 2*. After having been almost dormant for many millennia, growth rates for world population and gross world product (GWP) began to increase appreciably in the eighteenth century, and recently attained a rate which, if continued for a century or so, might indeed lead to overwhelming problems. But UN data indicate that the growth rate for world population peaked at just under 2% per year in the

CHART 3
SOME NEW EMPHASES

	New Emphases	It Is Both Natural and Inevitable That Increasing Affluence and the Increasing Capabilities of Advanced Technology Make It Easier to:	But the New Emphases Can Cause Creeping Stagnation and Other Problems, When They Go Too Far:
NEW REGULATION ISSUES	1. Selective Risk Avoidance	Reduce overall risk and choose more freely and flexibly which risks will be run. (It will still be necessary, however, to run some risks.)	Innovators, entrepreneurs, businessmen, and "do-ers" are forced to bear all the risks and the burden of proof as if only they, and not society as a whole, benefited from their profits and efforts.
	2. Localism	Put more emphasis on protecting the stability of local neighborhoods and communities. However, there can still be disturbances and annoyances as a result of many normal developments or high-priority projects (whether locally or externally generated).	Virtually all disturbances of local interests are blocked despite the larger needs of society; local policies clearly favor the "ins" over the "outs" (e.g., local vested interests over new or outside interests).
	3. Protection of Environment and Ecology	Repair some of the past damage and be able to afford both protection and improvement of existing environment and ecology. In addition, the magnitude and complexity of a modern economy raise many justifiable concerns about the possibility of irrevocable damage or major catastrophes. Many more remote and implausible concerns can also be taken more seriously (e.g. ozone layer or climate change).	Pursuit of environmental and ecological protection without regard to economic cost, or to other social goals; emotional, politically motivated, and demagogic discussions of risks from new and old projects. Attempts to create a risk-free world or to replace Faustian man and Western religious concepts with passive man and oriental spirituality.
NEW CONCEPTS ABOUT ACCEPTABLE BEHAVIOR AND ACTIVITIES	4. Comfort, Safety, Leisure, and Health Regulations	Satisfy basic survival needs rather easily. Indeed, since these can almost (but never completely) be taken for granted, there is then greater interest in (and ability to afford) more emphasis on the next level of need; these desiderata are on that next level.	Given excessive priorities and/or mandated by government in rigid and unrealistic regulations—approaching "health and safety authoritarianism."
	5. Happiness and Hedonism	Emphasize personal enjoyment and less inhibited gratification of various desires. De-emphasize success, achievement, self-discipline, conscience, rigid puritanical standards, etc., as the basis for a satisfactory life-style.	Become the major explicit goals in life, to be sought directly rather than indirectly (i.e., as a by-product of other goals).
	6. Public Welfare and Social Justice	Be more concerned about equity—in particular, the goal that individuals, groups, and regions should not be "unduly" harmed or left out of society's prosperity. Welfare for the deserving poor and many of the handicapped becomes a right rather than a privilege.	Life must be made "fair." Equality of result, not equality of opportunity. Justice should not be blind. Historical inequities should be compensated for, as well as rectified. Welfare for all who need it (or even want it) as a right rather than a privilege.
	7. Growing Pluralism and Freedom in the Larger and Higher Societal Objectives	Provide increased education, physical well-being, and security for all, and reduce overriding external imperatives; nor need there be so many pressures toward a conforming society. All this also allows for, or even encourages, growth of interest and social groups with a wide variety of objectives and images of the future, and more pluralism and freedom in the arts and literature.	A naive, emotional, and rigid over-rejection of past attitudes and values. This can lead to a loss of nerve, will, optimism, confidence, and morale regarding economic progress and technological advancement, and encourage excessive tendencies toward radical chic, "trendiness," and disastrous erosion of past social standards and structures, elitist attitudes, and indifference or hostility toward the aspirations and values of the silent majority. Finally, an emphasis on the adversary culture in the arts and literature.

(cont. on next page)

early 1960s and is now slowly declining. We expect a gradual leveling-off of population and GWP, with these stabilizing at high levels in the twenty-first century. This slowing down will occur as a social consequence of free choices brought about by urbanization, changing priorities and values, and the spread of better standards of health, safety, literacy, affluence, and other desirable factors throughout the world. In brief, under current or similar conditions, as the average person becomes better off, he tends first to show less interest in having a large family, and eventually also less interest in acquiring more material goods over his lifetime than his parents did. In our view, it is these *social* "limits to growth"—rather than the alleged physical limits that are the focus of so much current discussion and concern—that will be decisive in stabilizing our world in population and material wealth.

Chart 3, "Some New Emphases," is one exposition of these "social limits." We at the Hudson Institute see the emergence of a group of new values and attitudes that are playing an increasingly important role in the politics, culture, and daily life of all the affluent countries. Their impact is

Chart 3 *(continued)*

	New Emphases	It Is Both Natural and Inevitable That Increasing Affluence and the Increasing Capabilities of Advanced Technology Make It Easier to:	But the New Emphases Can Cause **Creeping Stagnation** and Other Problems, When They Go Too Far:
RE-EVALUATION OF BASIC SOCIETAL PRIORITIES	8. Progress Less Central	Reduce public interest in technology, economic progress, and big projects; also, an erosion of the work ethic and many other traditional middle-class attitudes and mores.	General anti-technology, anti-economic development, anti-middle-class attitudes (e.g., "small is better" and "limits to growth" movements). Also, enormous resources can be allocated or great economic costs accepted to promote emphases 1-7 above.
	9. Less Faith in Market Forces (Adam Smith's "Invisible Hand") and Utilitarian and Rational Ideologies	Place less emphasis on market forces, individual entrepreneurship, and "rugged individualism." A weakened belief that the results of these forces will be largely beneficial to the society as a whole, even when they are successful from the viewpoint of the individual.	Increasing interest in social control and overall planning of the economy (but mostly with "new class" values and attitudes and by "input-output" theorists). New emphasis on social responsibility and explicit representation of the "public interest" in running corporations.
	10. Growing Indifference to Business and Economic Motivation, Morale, and Efficiency	Show more concern for other social and cultural goals. After all, the richer and more technological the society, the greater is the likelihood that more riches and more technology will bring diminishing marginal returns.	Regulatory attitudes that are opposed to or just indifferent to the welfare of business. "Big business" becomes the arch-villain of many organized movements and much popular literature. The availability of acceptable jobs is assumed to be a right rather than a reward for effort and achievement. The productivity and profitability of business are taken for granted or considered irrelevant (or even reprehensible).
RE-EVALUATION OF PERSONAL AND FAMILY PRIORITIES	11. Modern Family and Social Values	De-emphasize many traditional values such as survival, orientation to one's job, and other "square" values, and place more emphasis on aesthetic, cultural, and personal ("human") values.	Emphasis by the educational system and family on happiness, adjustment, and self-fulfillment; almost total de-emphasis of objective achievement, responsible behavior, scholarship, good citizenship, patriotism, and job-oriented skills and attitudes.
	12. Concern with Self	Take continued well-being of society, community, and family largely for granted; opportunities for personal development and self-expression expand.	An almost anarchic and/or narcissistic self-indulgence. "Meism" is often accompanied by a cultist or fashionable emphasis on fulfilling oneself as an independent human being.
	13. New Rites, Ceremonies, and Celebrations—New Sources of Meaning, Purpose, and Prestige	Regard survival and economic development values as less important. New behavior emerges both against and instead of tradition. New values, institutions, and goals provide new standards of evaluation, comparison, and status. Culture and society evolve and change.	Protest as a way of life, as moral fulfillment, and as a mode of socializing and entertainment (particularly for the young adult). A revival of paganism, superstition, and gnostic rites and religions. "Negative success" status from impeding growth and progress; the dropout hero; manic "small is beautiful" and back-to-nature ideologies and fancies. "Rebel without a cause" even becomes a hero

NOTE: These "new" emphases are not, of course, completely new. However, they are becoming relatively pervasive in every developed country, but especially in the Atlantic Protestant culture area (i.e., Scandinavia, Holland, England, United States, Canada, and perhaps Australia and New Zealand). These new emphases are held with special intensity by the neo-liberal and humanist-left members of what is sometimes called the new class, which we often call the symbolist class—a class defined by the characteristic that it makes its living by understanding, interpreting, creating, and using symbols—i.e., by expertise in analytic, literary, artistic, educational, religious, and aesthetic activities.

not limited to a small elite; on the contrary, a majority in these countries is increasingly influenced by these emphases. During the past 10,000 years, many civilizations failed to take off economically, partly because of attitudes like these emphases. Indeed, anti-technology attitudes were sometimes even stronger in the past in that they were supported by religion. Furthermore, the authorities often confiscated or appropriated the wealth of the rising bourgeoisie. Such things are occurring again today—though perhaps in a somewhat different form.

The New Emphases include a disinclination to take risks, and a loss of nerve, will, and confidence—at least if the objective is economic development or technological advancement. Also prominent is an excessive preoccupation with protection of the environment, public welfare, social justice, and safety and health regulations, often enforced by regulatory authorities who are indifferent or even hostile to the welfare of business. Replacing the old "square" values are new emphases on hedonism and self-fulfillment and new attitudes toward the family and society. There is a growing development of anti-technology, anti-growth attitudes; opinion polls show that about 70% of Americans admit to being influenced by "small is better" and "limits to growth" arguments.

Some Prospects for 1980-2000

The period between now and 2000 is a particularly interesting and important time in human history. A foremost task is coping with and learning to manage the problems of a worldwide super-industrial economy. We anticipate that the controversy about these problems will continue unabated through the 1980s. But practical progress in controlling the problems should bring gradually a better overall perspective on them and a broadly shared sense of progress as we move toward a post-industrial economy. We see this as the central and exciting challenge of the next 20 years, particularly to those of us living in the advanced nations.

We believe that in the remarkably short space of two or three decades, the physical problems implied in what we call the current "problem-prone super-industrial" economy and society will have been largely alleviated in the affluent countries, and will have been prevented or largely alleviated in most of the developing countries. There are three main reasons for this:

1. The necessary advanced technologies are already under development.

2. These problems are receiving great attention in terms of resources and needed restrictions. (We believe that too much attention is now devoted to these issues in terms of cost/effectiveness in dealing with actual current dangers, but this is probably good education for the problems of the near future, and also research and planning should lead to prevention as well as cure.)

3. The affluent countries of the world have almost certainly already passed the all-important inflection point in their relative or percent growth rate curves. While economic growth will continue at a high rate, and may increase in absolute terms, the fact that it will decrease in percentage terms is already making many of these problems easier to deal with, and eventually should do this for almost all of them. We believe these problems

will peak in the 1980s. A confused understanding of and severe apprehension about this is one of the underpinnings of the present economic malaise.

We envision a complicated, complex, and probably somewhat dangerous transition period. On the whole (and always barring serious bad luck or bad management), this problem-prone, super-industrial period will be marked by rising living standards and less rather than more sacrifice. Eventually, almost all of the problems will be dealt with reasonably satisfactorily, so

CHART 4

A PLANET-WIDE ECONOMIC AND TECHNOLOGICAL ECUMENE

A.   A general understanding of the process and techniques for sustained economic development; a worldwide capability for modern industry and technology; and the development (incomplete but workable) of domestic and international institutions to sustain economic growth.

B.   A worldwide Green Revolution and enormous expansion of energy and mineral reserves. Around 2000, technological progress and huge investments (in the Arctic, oceans, and other currently unexploited areas) should produce a surplus (compared to today) of energy, other resources, and commodities—i.e., in the medium and long term these efforts are almost certain to swamp any diminishing returns.

C.   Despite much hostility, transnational corporations continue or expand as innovators and diffusers of economic activity and engines of rapid growth. However, American and European firms are joined and sometimes outpaced by others from Japan, Canada, South Korea, Taiwan, China, Brazil, etc.

D.   Indexed contracts and financial instruments flourish and a renewed role for gold in the international monetary system is possible (mainly as a store of value and perhaps as numeraire). Special Drawing Rights (SDR) are developed as a world currency, but fail to achieve full acceptance. Inflation and "poverty of affluence" become recognized as basic economic problems.

E.   "Futurology ideologies" and the concept of "progress" gain support as opposed to "limits to growth" and "gap" ideologies, but the latter also thrive—illusioned thinking and educated incapacity grow along with serious attacks on them.

F.   Sustained growth of international trade, communications, travel, and investment; high (5-15%) GNP growth in the "six dynamic areas" (Japan, "little neo-Confucian cultures," part of Latin America, Eastern Europe, emergent Mediterranean, most OPEC countries).

G.   Increasing unemployment in less-developed countries and labor shortages in developed countries; some partial solutions such as moving the labor to the work and the work to the labor; also two-way "brain-drains."

H.   The creation, ad hoc and perhaps consciously, of a dynamic Pacific Trading Investment Area (TIA)—perhaps a Western Europe-North Africa-Middle East-Central Africa TIA.

I.   Partial solution of many aspects of the kind of "technological crisis" associated with a superindustrial world—continued improvements in the quality of the environment in North America, Northwest Europe, and Japan—uneven progress elsewhere.

J.   But some serious possibilities for cool, cold, limited, and undeclared war—and for increasingly escalation-prone crises. Also increasing possibilities in the early eighties for a "Super Munich."

that at the end of the transition period, the true post-industrial society can emerge. Once the unintended impacts on the social and physical environment are controlled, the super-industrial society will no longer be problem-prone.

Chart 4 is a description of 1980-2000 that suggests profound effects, stemming collectively from economic and technological progress, that are new in human history, that tend to draw together the nations and peoples of the earth, and that help us to grasp some of the challenges of the next two decades.

For the next 20 years, we anticipate a continuing sense of "malaise" and economic growth rates of 3% or somewhat less in the rich countries of Western Europe, North America, Japan, Australia and New Zealand, and also in Communist Europe. Depending, of course, upon leadership, it now seems likely that Western Europe and Canada may be more afflicted by malaise in the next decades than the United States and Japan, partly because in the latter two countries the current malaise really began in the mid 1960s and countervailing forces are now operating. The middle-income nations of the developing world seem likely to have growth rates of 5 to 6%. Some nations now classified as poor but which have nevertheless a recent history of seriously coping with their economic problems—of which India is the largest example—may move into the middle-income range. And the very poorest nations, which have been economically stagnant, seem at least likely to begin to cope and make some limited progress.

Overall, we offer this broadly optimistic view of our economic future. We suggest that the prospects for worldwide economic and technological progress are far brighter than much of the discussion of the 1970s would have it. But to achieve progress and realize these prospects we need to develop long-range images and scenarios to replace essentially negative and pessimistic views based on such dubious concepts as physical limits to growth, the widening income gap between rich and poor nations, the unmanageability of modern society, and the eroding quality of life. We must have images of the future that are positive, realistic, and understood by most people. Now is a good time to think about these images, as we enter the last two decades of the twentieth century.

Technocracy As the Highest Stage of Capitalism

by

W. Warren Wagar

Whenever futurists assemble, certain general observations are mandatory. They are, indeed, the same observations that decorate the public meetings of politicians and churchmen. The times, one must say, are perilous. The future will test our courage and faith, but it also holds unprecedented opportunities. We stand at the crossroads of history, in an age of transition, on the brink of a glorious transformation; by our action here and now, we can surmount all obstacles and usher in the millennium.

This ritual alarm for the immediate future and ritual promise of bliss for the more distant future may also be rendered as a perception of crisis—in the original sense of the term. "Crisis" in Greek means "decision," from the word for "cut" or "separate." In a disease, the crisis is the turning point, the point of rupture, when all will soon be decided for better or worse. A crisis, properly, cannot last long. It is a point in time, not an aeon. But for futurists, as for politicians and churchmen, the crisis—the turning point of all history—is always now. Sampling the rhetoric of the Reformation, the French Revolution, or any political campaign of the twentieth century, one finds mankind bathed in an eternal sweat, always gravely ill, but always on the point of recovery. History assumes the character of a drama that consists only of climaxes.

Although the rhetoric of historical crisis was not unknown to prophetic voices in the Middle Ages or antiquity, its ceremonialization is an idiosyncrasy of modern Western history, reflecting the more rapid pace of social change characteristic of the modern era, and its time-obsessed world views. To a considerable degree, these world views in turn reflect the needs of the system of social relations of production operative in the modern age. Modern Western man's infatuation with the ideas of change, reform, revolution, utopia, and progress is congruent with his adoption of agricultural, commercial, and industrial capitalism as his

W. Warren Wagar, Professor of History at the State University of New York at Binghamton, is the author of such books as World Views: A Study in Comparative History *and* Building the City of Man: Outlines of a World Civilization.

way of producing and distributing wealth. In capitalism, time is money, and vice versa. Profit, growth, and progress are the goals of the system; yet as economists have realized for more than a hundred years, such progress can occur only dialectically, through periodic crises that interrupt growth and permit a shaking-down or flushing-out of the whole socioeconomic apparatus. Such progress also requires political revolution, in the form of a more or less sudden seizure of public power by the capitalist class; and in later periods progress requires the guarding of that power against threatened revolutionary seizures by the class of the underdog in capitalism, the wage-earning working class. One splendid way of guarding power already won is to invoke, time and again, the memory of the earlier bourgeois revolution, when feudal power crumbled, and to regain some of its creative energies by calling for "revolutionary" reform in the established capitalist system.

Thus, in more ways than one, it suits modern Western man to speak interminably of crisis, revolution, and transition to radically better times. It is the language of modern political economy, of bourgeois rise to power, and of workers' movements to overthrow bourgeois power. It is the language of all ideologies and all social sciences. Futurists, as captives of the belief-systems of their society, cannot help using it, too.

Nonetheless, the unending fuss about crisis, revolution, and transition does sometimes leave the historian a bit cold. He may even occasionally cry for a moratorium on the rhetorical overkill. Although times are indeed perilous, and great decisions do need taking, not every present instant is equally "critical." World-historical events, including authentic revolutionary transfers of power, do not succeed one another like so many firecrackers in a Chinese New Year celebration. There is a place for pauses, delays, and long stretches of quiet development in the economy of world history.

I share the sense of urgency of nearly all futurists, if only because the chances of a catastrophic world war remain unacceptably high in the kind of world political order that post-nuclear man inherited from nineteenth-century bourgeois nationalism. But if future studies are grounded in the social sciences, and have an empirical as well as normative component, respect must be shown for the empirically verifiable cycles and linear movements of world history. The sense that literally anything is possible is nonsense, or worse yet, a mask for the defense of the momentum of established power.

In this brief paper I will argue that the present-day world comprises a single economic system, that this system is capitalist, that capitalism is advancing to late maturity, and that the concentration and globalization of capital characteristic of this late maturity will lead in due course to a planetary technocratic order of formidable power and tenacity. In such a context, the 1980s are likely to be remembered as a period of economic recession, continuing the trends of the 1970s, and the 1990s may well signal a fresh upturn of economic growth, facilitating the long awaited capitalist integration of the world political order. Far from constituting a turning point, the year 1980 is very much a year of business as usual, in the capitalist business cycle. Well-meaning radical evangelists notwithstanding, we are doing little more than continuing a long forced march toward the total world mastery of capitalism. Only after such mastery is consummated, perhaps, will it be realistic to think seriously of a socialist reconstruction of society, and the wresting of power from the governing class of late capitalism, the technocracy. Shortcuts are always feasible; but the experience of most countries that have attempted to move directly from feudalism to socialism by means of a system of state capitalism casts doubt on the practicability of this particular shortcut. All of these countries have been woven, willy-nilly, into the fabric of the world capitalist economy, and the place of the bourgeoisie in their political systems has been taken by a new class of managers, bureaucrats, and technical experts who closely resemble the emergent governing class in the West.

The thesis of a single economic world-system characterized by the capitalist mode of production for profit has been well established in recent years by my colleague at the State University of New York at Binghamton, Immanuel Wallerstein, and several of his associates. For the general contours of that system, and for its historical evolution, see Wallerstein's books, *The Modern World-System* and *The Capitalist World-Economy*. Thanks to the globalization of capital, which recalls Lenin's vision of imperialism as the highest stage of capitalism, the rhythm of the business cycle is no longer a concern of Western countries only, but a worldwide phenomenon, affecting prices, wages, growth rates, and profits everywhere. It matters less and less what is the official system of social relations of production, or what constitutional order prevails, or what ideology dominates education and the media and state ministries of public enlightenment. Throughout the world, economic life waxes and wanes according to the demands of the international marketplace.

From the perspective of 1980, it grows increasingly clear that the capitalist world-economy ended a period of extraordinary growth about ten years ago, and is now in the midst of a downturn which—on the basis of past experience of the business cycle—should last for at least another decade. In short, we have arrived in the so-called "B period" of a Kondratieff long wave, whose "A period" began about 1940 and ended in 1970. Some features of the current recession are unusual, notably the absence of negative growth rates in most years, and the presence of a high worldwide rate of inflation. Throughout the 1970s, negative growth occurred only in 1970, in 1974-75, and again in 1979, and even then only in a few countries, such as the United States and Great Britain. Rates of inflation have tended to rise, rather than fall, during the same period. Unemployment has also been relatively low. All of these unusual characteristics of the downturn of the 1970s can be explained in large part by the influence of a policy of greatly increased public and private co-option of labor through costly payoffs that minimize mass unrest: payoffs in the form of welfare benefits, relatively easy credit, lavish endowment of education, continuation of the arms race at Cold War levels, and so forth. The plight of workers in the advanced countries has also been mitigated by the exploitation of Third World labor, which has furnished a steady flow of consumer goods at modest prices into the most advanced sectors of the world economy.

But inflation wipes out most of the benefits to workers of welfarism and world trade, just as the costs of co-option help to shave profit margins. Moreover, the classic purposes of economic depression are served in spite of the obvious idiosyncrasies of the system as it operates under contemporary conditions. If the world goes to the poorhouse in an automobile, paraphrasing Will Rogers, it goes to the poorhouse just the same. Specifically, the economic downturn of the 1970s and 1980s is having, and will continue to have, a chastening impact on capital and labor alike. For capital, it means business failures aplenty, coupled with an acceleration of the long-term trend, long ago foreseen by socialist political economists, toward the concentration of capital in fewer and fewer corporate structures. For labor, it means another kind of discipline: unemployment, or the fear of it; toleration of reduced purchasing power; the diminishment of pressure for social reform; and the acceptance of public strategies designed to extract fresh capital growth from the sacrifices of the people. All this is happening today in the nominally capitalist countries, and a version of it is happening as well in the nominally socialist countries.

At the same time, it is clear that the economic downturn will spur the search for a new technological fix geared to reviving the economy and postponing as long as possible the next downward swing of the pendulum. Here the futurist community can play a valuable role as handmaidens of established power, by creating a climate of public expectation for technological innovation and the glad acceptance of that innovation when it arrives, all shiny and glittering, in the 1990s. Improvements in the productivity of labor through technology have long aided market forces in reversing downward economic trends. It is possible to foresee, in the 1990s, a new boom in the world economy, fueled by breakthroughs in cheap energy production perfected in the 1980s, and by a whole range of other sophisticated technologies, including the biotechnical production of industrial raw materials and foodstuffs. Temporarily, all classes may experience an improvement in their living conditions. The net of the capitalist world-system will draw still tighter, as international trade and investment flourish.

The future of the world political order is much more problematic. At the present time there would appear to be a growing pluralism in that order, suggesting the pattern of international politics that obtained during much of the nineteenth century. But the system has always exhibited a powerful counter-tendency to polarize, as one and another "super-power" emerges to play a hegemonic role and stimulates the rise of a second super-power or coalition of powers working as one to block the ascendancy of the first. The political and trade rivalries of the super-powers furnish a stumulus to capitalist development, even or perhaps especially in time of war, but these rivalries are never absolutely under the control of the business community, and may easily get out of hand. Since 1945, the technologies of mass annihilation available to armed forces have become prohibitively dangerous, but the capitalist world-system has not succeeded in bringing the international order into line with its own long-term best interests.

Can the system avoid a global war? The answer is, probably yes: but there will be many harrowing moments along the way, and a fatal miscalculation is always possible. If success is achieved, it will most likely take the form of a stable Orwellian—meaning, Kissingeresque—system of carefully stage-managed rivalry between blocs of ostensibly sovereign super-powers containing their struggle within agreed bounds. Such a system will ensure that neither bloc grows strong enough to devour whole the nations of the Third World. These nations, in turn, will remain weak, divided, and easy prey to every kind of political and economic catastrophe, unable to rise above their current status as suppliers of primary products and cheap labor. Their apparent independence will cost them more dearly, perhaps, than would their outright assimilation into one of the blocs, but they will have little choice in the matter.

In time, there is good reason to assume that this new world order will take on some of the attributes of a true world government. One will not be amazed to find Soviet and American forces collaborating in the repression of political movements in the Third World that threaten to destabilize the international status quo. Such collaboration will be tentative at first, probably confined to tacit acceptance of interventionism by one power in the media of the other. In any event, each super-power will have an agreed upon sphere of hegemonic control.

Meanwhile, the further maturation of capitalism will bring with it the full empowerment of a new ruling class, a world mandarinate of economic managers, technical experts, and career bureaucrats whose only goal is collective self-perpetuation. The emergence of this new class, which I have labelled "the technocracy," was foreseen many years ago by H.G. Wells, James Burnham, and Milovan Djilas. It has been most exhaustively studied by political sociologists specializing in present-day Eastern Europe, but the phenomenon is much the same everywhere, no matter how well concealed by the glamorous trappings of super-power *Machtpolitik*.

The new class has arisen, to be sure, in response to the authentic needs of advanced industrial societies. As Evan Luard argues in *Socialism Without the State*, the shift of power in the modern state from politicians to administrators has been an inevitable result of the increasingly complex nature of government in an era of increasing centralization of authority. What is true of government is equally true of business life: with the progressive agglomeration of capital under the control of a shrinking number of giant multinational corporations, and the growing importance of technical and managerial expertise in manipulating such enormous entities, the role of the "tycoon" diminishes to the vanishing point. Only those who fully understand the dynamics of complex big-scale organization have any chance of controlling it. Growing complexity has also meant the growing interpenetration of governmental and business structures, to the point where their formal separation (under "capitalism") and their formal integration (under "socialism") no longer makes any difference.

214

The most likely scenario for the future involves, therefore, the welding of the governments and business communities of the major industrial powers into a single, more or less monolithic, more or less coordinated system of control that will manage the capitalist world-economy in the twenty-first century. The executives of the chief multinationals, the department heads of government ministries, and their counterparts in the nominally socialist countries will work together easily and pleasantly, speaking the same language and pursuing the same goals. International councils and commissions, informal networks of technocrats of all kinds, will gradually erode national and even corporate authority in their common dedication to a higher cause: the empowerment of the new class itself.

Thus, far from being a world whose face is glazed with the sweat of a great crisis, our world of the 1980s may simply find itself en route to a dull, stolid, but sophisticated new mode of class tyranny. The new mode is nothing more or less than the highest stage of capitalism, viewed from the perspective of sociology. Just as in Marx's economic analysis, the highest stage of capitalism is monopoly, and in Lenin's political analysis, it is imperialism, so in sociological terms the highest stage of capitalism is technocracy, the inheritance of supreme power from entrepreneurs and politicians by a new global mandarinate of managers, experts, and public administrators.

Alvin W. Gouldner, in his recent book, *The Future of Intellectuals and the Rise of the New Class*, revives the now venerable hypothesis (traceable *via* Veblen and Wells back to Saint-Simon, Comte, and ultimately the eighteenth-century vision of ministerial enlightened despotism) that the technocrats may somehow transform themselves into saviors, "a center . . . of human emancipation." Gouldner's hope has a human face. Perhaps defections from the ranks of this post-bourgeois bourgeoisie will indeed play a leading role in dissolving the new order from within. But all such events belong to a future beyond this generation, or the next. Meanwhile, any attempt to build a social movement capable of wresting power from its possessors for the sake of authentic emancipation must begin with a sober assessment of present realities and historic cycles and trends.

Capitalism has ruled over Western and world civilization for a relatively short time. It has not yet reached its foredestined dead end. It has not irrevocably alienated its working masses. Despite recurring petty crises, it has not reached the point of final implosion, but on the contrary retains its old power to inspire sacrifice, investment, and production. Even systems established in a bold attempt to replace it fall victim to its seductions, and are absorbed into it, in a manner reminiscent of the absorption of triumphantly invading barbarian cultures by the *force majeure* of old China. Capitalism is not immortal; neither is it senile. Leaders of radical movements, and futurists of all persuasions, would do well to keep both points firmly in mind as they confront the next decade, and the next century.

The Unimportance of Full Employment

Gunnar Adler-Karlsson

A child who is born in North Africa, from its first days surrounded by Moslem culture, naturally becomes a Mohammedan. A child who is born in Southern Europe in the same way becomes a Christian. A child who is born in the Soviet Union, from its first days surrounded by communist culture and propaganda, easily becomes a communist. And a child who is born in Northern Europe or America, from its first days surrounded by capitalist culture and advertisement, equally easily becomes a consumist.

In fact, Consumism has overtaken and replaced all earlier religions and ideologies as the dominant cultural trait in the richest nations of the world, commonly referred to as the West. Consumism is today the Western religion.

It can be shown that it is not only the capitalist enterprises with all their sales promotion that stimulates this consumist culture. The press, that normally earns much more income from the advertisers than from the readers and that often is owned by the same interest groups as the big companies, supports the same ideas. The political parties compete for voters by promises of even higher consumption levels if "our" party is voted into government. And the main object of the labor unions has become to raise the income levels of their members so that they can satisfy the demands that the advertisers have stimulated. The individual becomes a prisoner of this web of behavior of the major power interests of Western societies. Like a Pavlovian dog his consumist appetite is whetted from all sides. Culturally, he becomes a consumist.

It is in this context that a critique of the Western full employment policies should be understood—full employment at any average material standard of living. As things are now, full employment can only be had by economic growth. Growth is the lifeblood of the capitalist system. In this way the social-democratic parties in the Western nations have developed a common interest with the big companies. Full employment policy has been a major and wise goal for the labor parties for a long time. But now the situation has changed. Now it can even be

Gunnar Adler-Karlsson, a Swedish specialist in international economic and political relations, is a professor at Roskilde University Center in Roskilde, Denmark. Among his books is Thoughts on Full Employment, *published in Swedish in 1977 by Prisma in Stockholm.*
© 1979 Gunnar Adler-Karlsson

said that full employment has been perverted into a major instrument of the capitalist enterprises for furthering the Consumist culture also, with the help of social-democratic parties and labor unions. That is, at least, what I have tried to show in a small book that has stimulated some debate in Scandinavia. In Sweden it is called "Thoughts on Full Employment." In Denmark it has the more honest title "No Full Employment." Some of the essence of that booklet is summarized.

In recent years the OECD area—the developed nations belonging to the Organization for Economic and Cultural Development—has been shaken by some 17 or 18 million unemployed. The earlier Keynesian conviction that unemployment was a thing of the past has showed itself to be an illusion. In the absence of great redistributive reforms the West simply cannot maintain full employment any more. This is a common argument. But the whole political discussion following from it has concentrated upon how full employment can be recreated.

What is new in my argument is that I am not only stating that the West cannot, but also that it should not even try to continue the full employment policies.

The West cannot recreate full employment for three major reasons. It cannot control the capital intensity of modern technology, which tends to make man as useful to the economy as horses were to agriculture when tractors were introduced. For political reasons huge internal redistributive reforms which might create sufficient demand cannot be undertaken. And if we are going to show any solidarity in practice with the poorer nations, where one billion new jobs will be demanded within the next 25 years (according to the International Labor Office), we cannot egoistically maintain all jobs for ourselves in the West. Through import of goods, immigration of foreign workers, or export of capital, the development of the South will partly affect the employment situation in the West.

To these normal fears I add, however, that even if we could, we should not create full employment, as it leads to some results which are more or less undesirable or even absurd.

Full Employment Excess

This argument against full employment is not based upon the alienation debate. The so-called "instrumental attitude to work," tending to look upon it as a necessary evil to earn the money to buy the goods that really give a meaning to life, is no doubt widespread. But it can still be forcefully maintained that a certain amount of work is the best and richest way not only to earn one's living but also to fill one's existential vacuum with valuable content. That is the moral premise underlying the present thoughts. Employment is certainly not unimportant; quite to the contrary. But full employment at an already high luxury standard is an unimportant and unwise political goal for the rich nations, as it leads to consumist excesses.

Before illustrating these excesses it should, however, be observed that full employment originally was thought of as an instrument and not as a goal in itself. In the crisis of the 1930s with the emergence of

217

the Keynesian policies in societies where unemployment often meant starvation and outright material misery, the early full employment policies were thought of as instruments for giving what we today may call basic needs satisfaction for everybody. The elimination of hunger and misery was the goal, employment the means. But this instrument has gained such an importance that it now can be characterized as the super-ideology of many Western nations. This ideological change is what has led to the full employment excesses.

Here are a few of the excesses:

1. Some time ago, when OECD appointed a group of so-called wise men to find out what could be done in the West to counter the present unemployment, it was emphatically demonstrated that according to conventional economic thinking the only known way to recreate full employment is through increased economic growth.

Full employment policies thus lead to a harmony of interests between the companies—who want high profitable demand—and the labor parties—who want full employment. As already stated, this situation can be characterized as one in which the socialist parties in the West by necessity become major supporters of the capitalist interests in furthering the consumist culture. If full employment is an even better instrument than advertising for raising the Western level of demand for commodities that from the poor nations' point of view must be seen as luxury goods, it also has a number of indirect effects.

2. A widening of the gap between North and South in absolute terms is the first negative consequence. A 3% growth in the Swedish or U.S. economy—which may be too low to give full employment—means an average yearly *addition* to the present GNP of about $270, which is more than the yearly average income of the 500 million people who today suffer from absolute poverty. In other words, in order to maintain a high degree of employment in the richest nations it is absolutely necessary that we increase our standard of living year after year by more than the average yearly income of the poorest 500 million people. Full employment in the West necessitates a widening gap between rich and poor nations. This is the logic that can help to explain why all beautiful rhetoric on international solidarity remains nothing but just that.

3. If there is any realism in the fears about a future resource shortage, much debated since the oil crisis of 1973 and the first Club of Rome report on "Limits to Growth," then this necessity for growth in order to maintain full employment in the rich nations also implies that these nations by necessity will have to appropriate a disproportionately great share of the remaining resources. In this way the full employment policy in the West may be said to pre-empt the possibilities for the poorer nations ever to develop.

4. We now know that in the United States the taxation system in its totality is not redistributive. There are extremely good grounds to doubt that even the Swedish taxation system has any redistributive effects; the facts are not known and both the social-democratic and the conservative-liberal coalition governments have refused to investigate

218

this highly sensitive question.

If the absence of serious redistributive policies within the rich nations is assumed, the monetary support for full employment channeled into the general economy may be said to guarantee not only the income of those who are about to lose their jobs. Full employment policies then also guarantee them top incomes, and the ability to buy ever bigger Mercedes Benzes and ever more snobbish fur coats at the top of the income pyramid. Even more, this consumption becomes a necessity; take, for example, the one million Swedish leisure boats: a serious full employment policy necessitates the purchase of a $20,000 yacht by everybody in Sweden, preferably with the help of state subsidies, before the poorest half a billion individuals in the world even get access to clean drinking water.

5. The production of such luxury goods by those who do not themselves have very much increases the alienation of the latter. The instrumental attitude to work is bound to increase with the growth of this kind of wasteful production in a world of widespread misery.

6. The necessity to maintain full employment is today also regularly used as a legitimizing argument for almost any type of policy. It has long been used by various regional interests in the USA and elsewhere for maintaining the production and export of ever more refined armaments. It is used to explain why potentially very dangerous atomic energy simply "must" be developed. On the very day when this article was finally polished, the Swedish news media reported two typical cases. In one of the few remaining areas of beautiful nature in southern Sweden, Oesterlen, two big companies have demanded the right to investigate the mining possibilities. The local municipality, led by the summer-house owners, decided to turn down the application. But the social-democrats, with reference to the necessity to create more employment opportunities, wanted to permit also this destruction of nature. And sooner or later they are likely to be successful. On the same day, the conservative member of a Swedish government committee, appointed to suggest measures to press the South African government to give up apartheid, expressed herself against a legal ban on Swedish investments in South Africa "because it would have negative labor market consequences in Sweden."

All these invocations of the employment effects in order to justify a multitude of various policies usually do not say much about the specific relations between the issue at stake and the employment problems. But they say very much about the central ideological place that full employment has got in our societies. An invocation of it is believed to justify almost anything.

7. Another consequence of the full employment policies at any economic level has to do with the Western concept of freedom. It can be maintained that a continuation of the present trends is likely to lead the Western nations to a centralized power situation similar to that which exists in the Soviet Union and Eastern Europe.

In all business cycle downswings, when unemployment is on the rise, the Western governments demand a bigger share of total production in order to guarantee full employment. And what the governments once have got their hands on, they never give back. According to OECD statistics, the share of the public sector of total national income has in most member countries risen from less than ten per cent half a century ago to between one-third and one-half of GNP today. In some countries, especially those where full employment has been taken extra seriously, the expansion of the public sector has been accelerated. If present trends continue, several OECD governments will take over 90% of the total GNP before the schoolchildren of today have retired.

If these trends are permitted to realize themselves, the power situation in East and West will be similar. If it is state socialism in the East and state capitalism in the West, that will not matter much to the individual. He will be able to work only on what the state wants him to work on and decides to invest in; he will not be able to decide for himself to what he wants to devote his life and his working hours. Labor unions will be decorations and the situation may also occur that the state, as it is now doing in the East through criminal laws against loafers, will demand that the citizens work their eight hours per day for the good of the state, however rich the state may have become.

In fact, what I maintain is that the continuation of the full employment policies will destroy some of the central Western values, especially that of liberal freedom.

8. Finally, the importance of freedom is by no means only a capitalist idea. The main inspiration behind this criticism of a central Western policy concept is, indeed, Marx's idea of "the realm of freedom."

The step from the realm of material necessity to that of material freedom can never be taken in a consumist culture. Human beings will always be kept in bondage if their material needs are made to grow faster than production can satisfy them. As has been shown above, full employment policies demand such a bondage-creating economic growth. Full employment, while once having been an excellent instrument for liberating the poorest strata in the Western nations from hunger and misery, now is becoming an obstacle to the realization of the realm of material—and thus spiritual—freedom!

Towards a Synthesis of Capitalism and Socialism

If only a small part of the criticism of the present full employment policies in the West is considered justified, the conclusion must be that the Western nations must reconsider these policies. It is, however, much more easy to criticize and find faults than to suggest ways out of blind alleys. In order to stimulate thinking, it may, however, be worthwhile to try to concretize some directions into which future economic policies might be guided.

In groping for such a concrete proposal my starting point is that from a humane point of view the existing economic and political systems, both the capitalist and the socialist mixed economies, have failed. It is necessary to try to make a new synthesis, one in which the best sides of both systems are maintained and the worst sides avoided.

The best side of the existing socialist systems is that almost all of

220

them seem to guarantee a certain moderate material living standard to all of their law-abiding citizens. The worst side is the corresponding suppression of political human rights. The worst side of the existing capitalist systems is that they permit both very depressing pockets of material poverty and a ruthless exploitation of some men over others and over nature. The best side is that of the relatively high degree of political freedoms, at least for the lucky ones.

Would it be possible to come in the direction of this new and superior synthesis by changing the present economic goals of the state? I believe the answer is: Yes! If the Western states accept as their economic priority goal the creation of a guaranteed moderate level of living for all, combined with a just distribution of both the right and the duty to work for this real income, and if the governments then with a minimum of interference let the individuals choose to do what they want to do with their lives, we might start to approach the realm of material freedom.

To stress the employment aspect: the state should not try to guarantee full employment at any level of material standard. But it should guarantee that everybody gets the right, as well as the duty, to work enough to get the feeling that he himself has by his labor earned his income.

This, it might be added, is in contrast to the present situation where—besides the fact that some rich individuals can escape work altogether—we have some strong and deplorable tendencies to divide the labor market into an A and a B team, pushing out more and more "inefficient" people from work into a forced leisure, paid for by the state. This is destructive for the individuals afflicted as they feel ashamed of being secondary citizens, useless for society, when they are unemployed, on the dole, in forced retirement, or "only" a housewife. It is also bad for the development of society: A very serious author, on the basis of a study of the tendencies to do away with "surplus population" by Auschwitz methods (which he detects in all developed nations), suggests that:

> Bureaucrats in some countries might someday decree compulsory early retirement and, at the same time, grant the retirees 'la mercy death'. The social advantages are obvious. The most vigorous elements in society would constitute its work force and there would be no claim on society's resources by superannuated or economically redundant elements. [Richard Rubenstein, *The Cunning of History: Mass Death and the American Future*, Harper & Row, New York, 1975.]

But, to return from the possible horrors of the future to my suggested utopia, the new economic goal of the state could be realized through a conscious division of society into sectors: one in which people are occupied with satisfying the moderate human needs of consumption and labor; another in which people can work and consume at levels in excess of the moderate needs; and a third in which people are given freedom from material concerns, allowing them the chance to develop their innermost dreams in whichever way they wish, providing they do not thereby harm their fellows.

In the utopian society described here, there are actually four main sectors: the *necessity* sector, the *excess* sector, the *freedom* sector and the *power* sector.

The **necessity sector**, which must be state-controlled, should be responsible for supplying people's basic material needs. In this sector we should calculate the total material need which the state must guarantee to satisfy, as well as the total amount of labor needed at given levels of technological development in order to produce these material necessities. This volume of labor should be divided and apportioned out among all citizens, as a right as well as a responsibility. Payment for work done should be in the form of non-negotiable, non-transferrable and non-seizable purchase cards, which guarantee the individual his or her basic material security for life.

For individuals who want a higher economic standard than that allowed by the basic security of the first sector, there should be an economic **excess sector** in which people would have the greatest possible freedom—provided this brings no harm to others—to buy and sell, invest and produce, save and splurge, invest and lose. All the various forms of business ownership could exist here, with the exception of state-ownership. The state should be allowed to regulate this sector, but only with the most general of laws, and should otherwise be kept out. Privately-owned, co-operative or employee-owned companies should have complete freedom to compete in this excess economic sector.

For those individuals who are not primarily interested in working to earn a higher standard than that given them by the elementary needs sector, there should be a third alternative: this is the **freedom sector**—for culture, sports, being together with people, or whatever those individuals wish. Within this sector some people will need extra income to realize their dreams. This can be earned through temporary, extra work in the excess sector. People will thus be allowed the greatest possible freedom to attempt to realize, without material or psychological pressures, whatever dreams they may have.

The fourth sector, the **power sector**, should have approximately the same outline as it has in our present society. The representatives of the people should be chosen through open and free elections and they must, as in the present system, deal with the conflicts and differences which are a natural part of all social systems, including the one described here. A new constitution would, however, be required. The divisions between the three other sectors should insure their stability. For example, it should prevent the excess sector from expanding at the expense of the other two.

The power sector should own the means of production in the necessity sector. But those in positions of power should as a rule not be the same individuals who are the leaders of the government economy. This would insure the balance of power.

This combination should guarantee a moderate economic standard. It would also allow much greater freedom than exists today for people to have a many-faceted and harmonious life in a society that is less materially-oriented than the present one.

A crucial question is, of course, how much of one's life must be devoted to the necessity sector. This depends on what politicians decide to be the moderate economic standard that the state should guarantee. It can roughly be calculated that if the Swedes today decided that the present British standard (about half of the Swedish one and far above world average) was enough, and if all men and all women divided the necessary labor to produce this standard, between 15 and, at the most, 20 years of work would be enough to earn the guaranteed entrance ticket—"the realm of material freedom." Much could be said about this, but the important thing to realize is that as we today work an average 40 years per life, the potential leisure would increase by 20 to 25 years, or, if one would prefer to do some work all the life, a halftime job for 30 to 40 years would leave half the day for other activities. This, in turn, would require rather considerable changes elsewhere in society. The schools, for instance, should not as now only strive to produce humans who are good accessories to the machines, but should instead give young people a broad orientation in the art of enjoying active life, including life outside the relatively short working period.

Let us, however, now turn to a question that was not treated in my booklet. The above idea has been worked out on the assumption that Sweden was a closed economy. To realize it in practice, the OECD governments must of course jointly cooperate. But let us finish by asking if this idea potentially could have any importance for the North-South discussion. Could it possibly contribute to the breaking of the trend to a widening gap between rich and poor nations that in spite of all rhetoric has characterized both of the U.N. "Development Decades" and which, moreover, as was shown above, must continue as long as the West tries to maintain full employment by present methods?

The Necessity Sector and "Absolute Poverty"

In recent years, the problem of eliminating absolute poverty or of satisfying basic needs for the poorest people of the world has come increasingly into focus. It is likely that this central human problem may come to be the top priority goal for foreign aid and related North-South policies and possibly also for more general economic relations between richer and poorer nations. The specific question that can be asked in this context is if the moderate material needs, as here suggested for the richer nations, could in any way be connected to the policy of eliminating absolute poverty in the poor nations.

The instant this idea is posed, the elusiveness of the concept of "basic" or "moderate needs" clearly appears. I have assumed that no scientific norms, but only politically decided ones, can be established in order to define these material levels. In Scitovsky's book *The Joyless Economy* it is reported that legal "poverty norms" vary by a factor of 1 to 25 or even 1 to 30 between Egypt and Ceylon on the one hand and the USA and Switzerland on the other. These norms are heavily influenced by tradition and development levels and can, for practical purposes, only be operationally defined by appropriate political bodies.

What in this context could be done—for example, by the United

Nations—would be to establish an ideal norm for what might be considered the politically acceptable gap between truly "basic needs" in the poorest nations and the culturally determined, much higher moderate needs-levels in the richer nations. The permissible gap here could, in the most optimistic case for instance, be related to the suggestions by Jan Tinbergen and others in chapter 6 of the "RIO report," proposing that the present gap of about 1 to 13 be narrowed to about 1 to 3.

What then could be suggested is that the governments of the richer nations should, as top priority, establish a policy which guaranteed all the citizens of their country the moderate material level posed by the UN norms. When that goal had been reached, however, top priority might not, as now is the case, be to establish full employment at any luxury standard in a catch-up-competitive international environment. Instead, the richer nations, realizing their international responsibilities as well as present and future dependencies, might shift their top priorities in economic policies in the direction of eliminating absolute poverty for the poorest groups inside the poorest nations by suitable national and international policies.

Such a shift in policy priorities would correspond to much of present social thinking, e.g., John Rawls's contract theory of justice or Irma Adelman's and Cynthia Taft Morris's demonstration that present tendencies in the world economy are likely to increase absolute poverty. In other contexts I have tried to give a theoretical outline of what can be termed "inverted utilitarianism," i.e., an attempt to guide practical economic policies by the criterion of their ability to minimize human suffering, instead of maximizing happiness. Normal utilitarian thinking, unable to define happiness or even to agree upon the gross outlines of what it might be, easily turns into a maximization of the Gross National Product without regard to the distributive effects, thus neglecting the creation of more absolute poverty by the economic growth process. Combined with the intra-Western or East-West competitive catch-up game, this relegates the elimination of absolute poverty and of easily observable human misery and suffering to a position of low or zero priority, at the same time as the size of the gap, in absolute terms, between North and South is bound to grow to even more horrendous proportions than today. The impossibility to reach "happiness" in this process has also been well demonstrated by the late Fred Hirsch who, moreover, has warned us that the vain attempts to catch up may destroy the resources and the preconditions for a decent life for everybody. His analysis of "Social Limits to Growth" should be extended to cover also the international catch-up process.

The elimination of absolute poverty can logically be realized in only two ways. Either at least the head of the poorest families is provided with a job, by which he earns an income by which he can pay for the goods and services included in a basic needs standard. Or redistributive policies must one way or another be created by which the state takes part of the income of those who work and transfers it to the unemployed poor.

224

Theoretically any combination of these two extreme methods can be imagined, but one of them must be used if the other is not. In practice, however, there can be no doubt that the poor individuals in the poor nations have the same desire as the least rich ones in the rich nations of themselves working enough to earn their own bread. They are likely to feel equally depressed, alienated, shameful, and useless to their societies as those on the dole or in forced retirement tend to feel in the West.

As this is so, any basic needs strategy should concentrate upon creating enough of employment for everybody in the poor nations as well as in the rich. This is, of course, especially important in nations where the social security system is weak or nonexistent. Materially, one may say that the importance of full employment stands in inverse relation to the efficiency and comprehensiveness of the social security system. Psychologically, some productive employment may be equally important on all development levels. However that may be, a good case could be made for a social and economic policy in the poor nations that concentrated upon guaranteeing everybody both basic needs satisfaction and a possibility of work. This is, indeed, how some of the poorer socialist nations have tried to eliminate absolute poverty. In at least the cases of China and Cuba this policy seems to have been relatively successful, more so than in comparable non-socialist nations. But in these countries the above discussed excess and the freedom sectors, which at least Cuba should be able to afford, are non-existent.

Would it not be possible to envisage a new economic system also in the poor nations, similar to that above suggested for Sweden and the rich nations, whereby the elimination of absolute poverty was entrusted to a state sector while also here some room was reserved for an excess and a freedom sector, so as to avoid the historically observable abuses of state power in fully socialized nations? Of course, the proportions between the sectors would by necessity have to be quite different from what they would be in the rich nations, but the basic principles might be highly similar. And might not this be a practical and more realistic way to eliminate absolute poverty than the present inefficient growth policies? These questions should at least be put and serious efforts should be devoted to answering them. The proposed new system may be one way to avoid some rather ugly alternatives of mass starvation, internal and international conflicts, and the hardening of central powers into tyrannies.

If these suggestions for more internationally equitable internal policy goals in the richer nations are to have any realistic chances to become adopted, however, at least two preconditions have to be fulfilled.

The first one is that the East-West conflict is at least partially overcome. The present international economic catch-up competition is largely determined by the East-West conflict. The Soviet Union has time and again posed the *dognat i peregnat* ("catch up and surpass") of the leading capitalist nations in per capita production as their top economic priority, thereby legitimizing their new economic system. The West cannot let that happen, especially as economic power is easily transformable into military power, and it thus feels forced to continue its growth. When the GNP catch-up has failed, the so-called socialist nations have stressed their ability, and the West's inability, to maintain full employment. The East-West competition has thereby made this policy goal into a central ideological point of system competition, pressing the Western nations, as has been shown above, to increase already high absolute average income levels by hundreds of dollars per year in order to raise demand and thus maintain full employment. That the Soviet catch-up goal, if realized, by necessity will lead the Soviet society to the same material luxury levels before their rhetorical expressions of international solidarity can be transformed into practical action is a problem that the communist theoreticians seem to have refused to tackle. Anyway, a calming down of the East-West economic competition is a precondition for an increased willingness of either side to forgo employment opportunities or higher domestic income and production levels inside their own nations, in order to create higher employment and less misery in the poor ones.

The second precondition relates to the domestic policies inside the poor nations themselves. Most of them are now repeating the same class conflicts that have plagued the development of the now industrialized nations. The poor nations may even be worse off than the West ever was. On the one hand, e.g., their upper or ruling classes may want to catch up, in consumption or military levels, with an international elite many times higher up, thereby wasting much potentially employment-creating investment capital on vain luxury or armament imports. On the other hand, the poor countries today cannot, as did Western Europe, solve their surplus population problems by emigration and large-scale appropriation of continents and colonies. Both these, and some other differences, act to reinforce the "natural" class conflicts within poor nations arising in a process of economic change. This should be realized.

Nonetheless, it seems rather hopeless to ask the rich nations to shift their own economic policy priorities to the advantage of the poorer ones, if the concrete advantages of the new Western policies, behind the cloak of "sovereignty," are almost wholly appropriated by the already rich ruling classes in the poorer nations. Thus a precondition for a realization of the central ideas here presented is that the governments in the poorer, as well as in the richer nations are genuinely and concretely interested in creating employment possibilities also for the poorest strata of their own population, thus partly eliminating the worst poverty.

If these two preconditions, of a less intensive East-West conflict and less intensive class rule inside the South, were realized, then it might be conceivable that international priorities along the suggested sort could become a practical reality.

Getting Out in Front of Impending Issues

by

Graham T.T. Molitor

How can we tell where we are going?
What's in store for the '80s . . . for the year 2000 . . . for tomorrow?

Enormous Scope of Public Policy Change

Public policy change—more and more of it—is in store. The steady onslaught of public policy change, including new laws and regulations together with informal self-governing measures, probably does more to alter our world than any other single undertaking.

New laws steadily mount. The U.S. Congress enacts some 1,000 laws yearly. In addition, the ever-growing legions of federal regulators pour forth some 9,000 regulations and resolutions each year. Compound this by the 50 states; add inputs from some 78,218 provincial, county, municipal and myriad special jurisdictions; multiply it all by some 155 nations in the world. Totaled, the global sweep of government-imposed change can be overwhelming. We have come a very long way from the time when Moses received only Ten Commandments on Mount Sinai (c. 1500 B.C.), or the concise Code of Hammurabi (c. 2000 B.C.) was devised.

Why Public Policy Forecasting Has Become Urgent

No mistake about it—large organizations and undertakings stand in the growing pale of government regulation. Products can be banned from the marketplace by the stroke of the lawmaker's pen or a regulator's arbitrary edict. Government-imposed change can no longer be ignored.

Any organization whose products or services can be restricted or, worse, banned, by government action must be aware of signals of change. Wrenching dislocations may engulf the unwary, the unprepared.

Graham T.T. Molitor is President of Public Policy Forecasting, Inc., Potomac, Maryland. He was formerly Washington representative of General Mills, Inc., and served as Chairman of the World Future Society's Second General Assembly (1975). He served on the White House Advisory Committee on Social Indicators (1975-6), and formerly was Research Director, White House Conference on the Industrial World Ahead (1971-2).

In the same way that production know-how and marketing insights pace product offerings to the marketplace whims, so now must trained observers of government processes be equipped to provide management with foresight to help avoid fickle twists and turns that impair performance. Shortsighted planning is planning that limits itself to traditional change factors—economic, technologic, sociologic, demographic and ideologic. Government trends, domestic and international, must be given proper consideration as well. All too often, government impacts are "missing links" in otherwise well-informed management planning. Early warning systems for heading off problems are needed more than ever.

President Theodore Roosevelt put it this way: "Nine-tenths of wisdom is being wise in time."

The trick is to know what to do, how and when to do it.

Advantages Gained From Anticipating and Responding to Impending Consumer Issues

Anticipating emerging public policy issues gains precious lead time to:

1. Identify or corroborate new market prospects and problems.
2. Develop, redesign or reformulate products; devise new procedures; check redesign soundness; establish alternate supplies; carry out test marketing; reposition existing products.
3. Avoid, or at least minimize, the often costly impacts of government mandates which catch management by surprise (e.g., costly and embarrasing inventory recall and disposal problems following ban or restriction).
4. Prepare coordinated lobbying to champion, redirect or defeat impending change.
5. Develop public relations potentials (turn early responses to socially premised public policy objectives toward corporate image-building, avoid sullying corporate image).

Charting the "Issue Universe"

Analyzing a particular problem area begins with charting the issue universe.

First, the generic issue is designated—consumerism, for instance.

Second, groups of problems or issue sectors are delineated—product safety, advertising regulation, and food-drug safety, for example.

Third, to hone in on specifics, the disaggregated issues are further sub-categorized. One alleged food safety concern aimed at restricting sugar consumption included over 125 individual issues broken down into some 20 categories.

Cyclical Pattern of Substantive Issues

1. Consumerism

All seems to be quiet on the consumer front. Current anti-regulation and tax-cutting (Proposition 13) moods cast a temporary pall on costly government intervention. More basic, however, is the fact that historically, during economic readjustments and downturns, social interest programs—including consumer issues—are stifled and held in abeyance.

Relative inaction at this point can be deceiving. A growing backlog of consumer issues continues to build like the pressure in a knotted hose. Remove the constriction holding things back (current economic recession) and another wave of consumerism will be underway once again. Postponement does not mean abandonment.

Consumerism tends to move in spurts or bursts (see Exhibit 1). Among the techniques for investigating public policy change is this phenomenon of cyclical patterns—3 of them (each some 20 years in duration) since the turn of the century.

EXHIBIT 1

PATTERNS OF CHANGE

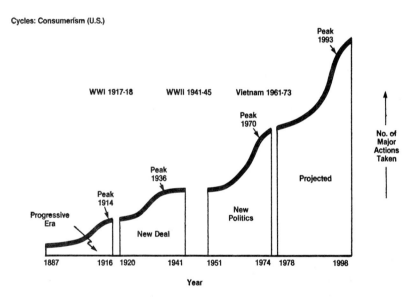

Cycles: Consumerism (U.S.)

The "issue universe" we currently monitor includes some 4,000 specific consumer issues that have *not* been enacted by the federal government. Compiling a comprehensive listing of specific substantive solutions for each of these issues would add enormously to this number—for example, there are as many as 125 for proposed sugar restrictions alone.

Food additives (direct and indirect), suspect for one reason or another, would add many hundreds, perhaps one thousand, additional issues.

No overall major reversal of the trend toward further government consumer regulation is in sight.

2. Advertising Regulation

The same cyclical phenomenon pertains to advertising regulation (see Exhibit 2).

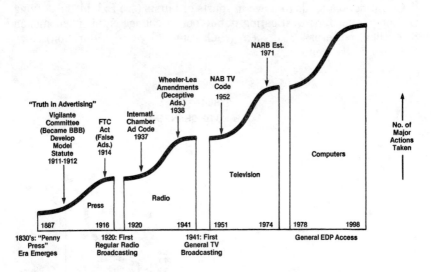

EXHIBIT 2
CYCLES: ADVERTISING REGULATION

© 1979, PUBLIC POLICY FORECASTING, INC.

New communications technologies were introduced and became the dominant information mode during each of the four consumer cycles depicted here:

—low cost/mass circulation "penny press" at the turn of the century;
—radio broadcast during the early 1900s;
—television in the mid-1900s;
—computers and electronic data processing systems at the end of the century.

In each case, over-zealous promotional or advertising practices in the new media introduced excesses or abuses. In each case, self-regulatory efforts eventually gave way to government-mandated standards.

TV content and advertising have been under siege in recent years by consumer critics. Over the last few years American advertisers have responded by undertaking self-regulation. The National Advertising Review Board, an industry supreme court of advertising review, was created. Better Business Bureau budgets and responsibilities were increased. The National Association of Broadcasters TV code was updated. Numerous business association and many private company codes of broadcasting ethics were revamped.

Despite these voluntary undertakings, efforts to impose government controls loom ominously. Such regulatory thrusts aimed at TV, the dominant media of these times, tend to lose sight of the *total flow* of consumer information.

Mandated government messages, language qualifications, warnings and educational stipulations for a 15-, 30-, or 60-second TV advertisement are an overkill. Ignored is the role that print media play in elaborating on details. Still more important are the ever-growing mandatory information disclosures on package labels and inserts providing the best means of conveying vital facts to actual users, the persons with the greatest need to know.

Massive new advertising restrictions and bans on alcohol and tobacco products currently are being imposed in an increasing number of European nations. Sweden's all-inclusive 20-year "negative marketing" program aimed at tobacco is a precursor of similar efforts likely to be aimed at other products. One novel approach requires constantly changing smoking health hazard warnings; the warnings are drawn from a pool or series of hazard warnings drawn from a repertoire of 16 different texts. Indeed, one abortive effort attempted to apply similar rotating labeling warning disclosures for food products high in sugar.

Total broadcast advertising bans are unlikely to be implemented in the United States. Products deleterious to consumers may be barred from advertising in certain media. Absolute bans prohibiting alcohol and tobacco ads have been imposed in some countries—notably the Scandinavian countries. Stricter government controls over specific products, services, claims and special audiences (e.g., children) *can* be anticipated. Pre-clearance of broadcasting ads in advance of publication may be imposed. Logical targets include products which already must meet regulation, licensing or label pre-clearance.

Other trends in advertising regulations are toward fixing legal responsibility and imposing strong penalties—fines and/or imprisonment—as deterrents. In Sweden, periodicals appearing 4 times a year or more must appoint a "responsible publisher." This designated person alone is answerable in courts for the contents of the publication and for Freedom of the Press Act (1949) violations.

Electronic data processing (EDP) technologies have all the promise of becoming tomorrow's dominant personal information media. In anticipation of what is to come, new privacy protection laws have been put on the books. These provisions cover: medical records, reporters' privilege, arrest record expungement, polygraph, consumer credit reporting, information systems regulation, criminal information systems regulation, and financial privacy.

Computer dialing/solicitation telephone ("junk") calls already have been prohibited in certain jurisdictions—Great Britain, for example. Computer trespass crimes have been written into penal codes. Royal Commissions, White House Blue Ribbon panels and investigatory commissions of all kinds have been addressing the emerging problems. The intellectual foundation for dealing with these embryonic problems is replete on the public record. Further congressional interest and action will come—eventually.

As computers become commonplace in the home, radical impacts will follow. The telecommunication-transportation trade-off, persons communicating—not commuting—to work, will heavily assault all transportation systems.

Enormous opportunities exist for central home computers to perform a wide variety of household tasks, such as optimizing energy use, regulating temperatures, lawn sprinklers, monitoring fire/smoke/burglar intrusion hazards—let your imagination take you where it will. Such things will come about over the next few decades.

3. Food-Drug Laws

Food and drug laws follow the same basic cyclical pattern (see Exhibit 3).

EXHIBIT 3
CYCLES: DRUG REGULATION

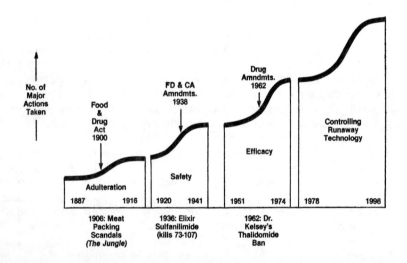

‹ 1979, PUBLIC POLICY FORECASTING, INC.

During each period, incremental increases in the stringency of safety standards were imposed:
- *adulteration* was the abuse first dealt with at the turn of the century;
- initial *safety* standards were imposed during the New Deal Era;
- still more stringent *efficacy* criteria were imposed during the 1950s.

Prior to the turn of the century the mortar and pestle of the familiar local apothecary began to face competition. Drugs, mass-produced in distant locations by persons unknown to (and beyond the control of) local patrons, began to appear in profusion. Unscrupulous snake-oil salesmen and worthless quack remedies abounded. The Progressive Era saw passage of the first pure food and drug law aimed at curbing *adulteration*.

America was not the first country to enact a modern pure Food

232

and Drug Law. England had enacted a Food and Drug Act in 1860—some 46 years ahead of the U.S.

The food industry currently has two primary food issues with which to contend:

- Micro-nutrient standards (Recommended Dietary Allowances —RDA's).
- Macro-nutrient guidelines (National Nutrition Goals).

Implicit in these standards are changes in the kinds and amounts of foods consumed.

Macro-nutrient goals suggest optimum percentages of fat/protein/carbohydrate and certain other dietary components.

So far, some 6 nations have put forward such policy statements: Sweden, 1971; Netherlands, 1973; Norway, 1975; Canada, 1976; United States, 1977; Great Britain, 1978. A 1977 FAO/WHO Report is likely to result in some 20-30 additional countries following suit within the next few years. Diet goals are in vogue.

Protein consumption, the most expensive diet component, may be overconsumed by a factor of two. Moderation—and shifts as to source—are likely.

Implications for foods high in fat—especially saturated fat—cholesterol, salt, sugar and alcohol are ominous. Declining consumption of foods high in fat and cholesterol (implicated with circulatory disorders) already is proceeding. The so-called "junk food" controversy is with us and must be dealt with.

Micro-nutrient standards are still rapidly evolving as new evidence and proofs are recognized (see Exhibit 4). Most of us tend to think of the essential 8 vitamins and minerals. Yet, Germany has established standards (Recommended Dietary Allowances) for some 26 vitamins and minerals. Beyond this are over 60 vitamins and minerals which are recognized as essential to human health and well-being. Even so, the end is not in sight. Over 200 nutrients and their components have been identified.

Micro-nutrient standards also vary enormously. RDA standards for Vitamin C range from a low of 30 mg in England to a high of 75 mg in Western Germany. Therapeutic levels of 50,000 mg and even higher have been noted.

Clearly, government efforts have just begun. Government action regarding micro-nutrient standards is still open-ended.

Perhaps one of the biggest "sleeper" issues in the field of nutrition involves nutrient deterioration.

The hundreds of assaults and insults from genetic selection of seed to ultimate individual biological assimilation are just beginning to be considered.

In many cases some nutrients do not survive at all, while proper handling and preparation (particularly for frozen foods) can make a decisive difference. Main selling points and educational/informational activities involving nutrient degradation/enhancement are likely to play an important role in new marketing strategies.

New thresholds of understanding emerge based on scientific capabilities

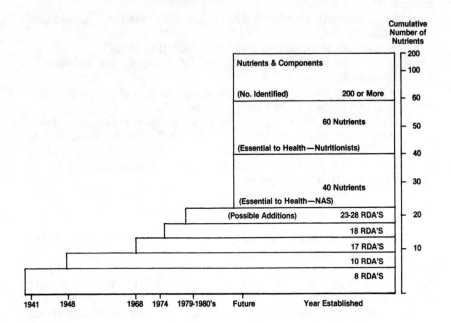

EXHIBIT 4

MICRO-NUTRIENT STANDARDS
—Recommended Dietary Allowances (RDA'S)

Cumulative Number of Nutrients

Nutrients & Components

(No. Identified)   200 or More

60 Nutrients

(Essential to Health—Nutritionists)

40 Nutrients

(Essential to Health—NAS)

(Possible Additions)   23-28 RDA'S

18 RDA'S

17 RDA'S

10 RDA'S

8 RDA'S

200 — 100 — 60 — 50 — 40 — 30 — 20 — 10

1941   1948   1968   1974   1979-1980's   Future   Year Established

for measuring down to parts per trillion. At these rates, almost any product can be indicted as posing a risk.

Measured in these terms, coffee contains an astounding 2,000 (estimated) individual chemical compounds. Diesel exhaust contains up to 30,000 different compounds. Such runaway technological capabilities of measurement underscore the folly of zero-tolerance prohibitions (such as America's Delaney Clause).

The meaning of micro-measurements is suggested by this table:
- 1 part per million: Not too hard to grasp: equivalent to 1 drop of vermouth per 80 "fifths" of gin.
- 1 part per billion: Tougher to comprehend: 1 drop of vermouth per 500 barrels of gin.
- 1 part per trillion: Boggles the mind: 1 drop of vermouth in 520 30,000-gallon tank cars of gin.

Decisions increasingly will be premised on such micro-data. Chemical reactions right down to the individual basic atomic elements are the new frontiers. Scientific knowledge will play an increasingly important role in food regulation.

Longer Life Expectancy

Persons born just prior to the birth of Christ (B.C. 1) had an estimated life expectancy of only 18 years. Americans born during 1976 had

234

a life expectancy of 72.8 years. Stated another way, persons born in recent times enjoy a "fourth lease on life."

But this isn't sufficient for concerned persons. There is room for still further improvement. Many countries other than the U.S. enjoy considerably longer life expectancies.

Swedes have the longest life expectancy of any population—75 years (see Exhibit 5). Furthermore, the longest living human being whose age has been authenticated lived 113 years. Obviously, there is plenty of room for improvement by most countries.

EXHIBIT 5

SOCIAL INDICATORS: LIFE EXPECTANCY AT BIRTH (1976)

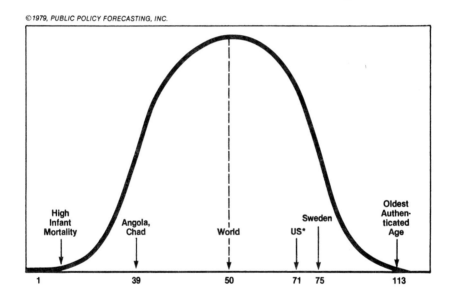

*28 countries enjoy average life expectancy longer than (or equal to) the U.S.

Based on "1976 World Data Sheet" by Population Reference Bureau

One strong imperative for new lawmaking is based on the rationale of an anticipated increase in life expectancy. Many new or impending government programs, although usually not thought of in this way, are intended to reduce specific mortality rates:
- occupational safety
- environmental protection
- automobile safety
- consumer product safety
- drug safety
- food additive amendments

- preventative medical health measures
- diet-health
- physical fitness and exercise
- alcohol control
- tobacco restrictions
- psycho-social work environment (Europeans perceive industrial demo-cratization, worker participation in management planning and job enrichment efforts as life expanding, if not life improving, under-takings.)

Western European government officials are steadfastly convinced that mortality/morbidity rates can be and are being reduced by stricter government controls. More life-extending government controls on this aspect of consumerism are coming.

Forecasting public policy change is a new art. One-hundred percent certainties are not realistic. The legislative and regulatory outcome of most issues, however, can be foreseen with surprising accuracy. Adoption of new laws and regulations up to 10 years ahead of time can be accomplished using a variety of quantitative techniques. Some of these methods have been described or alluded to in this paper. Institutions affected by regulatory onslaught can ill afford to ignore the benefits such anticipatory analysis affords.

Free the Fortune 500!

by
William E. Halal

This conference may be taking place at an especially crucial time because I have an instinctive feeling that we could be at a critical turning point in the social transformation that many of us have been working and hoping for. So the most useful thing that I could do in this short paper is to assess the progress that we futurists have made so far and to outline what I think our agenda should be for the decade ahead, particularly for major corporations.

I don't think it is possible to understand the events now surrounding us without first appreciating the revolutionary origins of this post-industrial era that first appeared during the transition to a service economy following World War II.[1] Far greater affluence was brought about by the maturing of industrialization, more permissive authority relationships were encouraged among the young, and powerful information systems like television and digital computers provided access to unprecedented levels of knowledge. These forces produced a dramatically different world which led to such ideological shifts that they constituted a social earthquake.

As a result, a more sophisticated social culture has been slowly absorbed into the American Dream. It is now common to find a widespread interest in personal development and self-fulfillment, a healthy acceptance of sexuality, disdain for violence, a critical attitude toward authority and large institutions, much greater tolerance for individual differences, a wholesome respect for the environment, reverence for the spiritual dimension of life, and other such vital new ideas that would have been considered bizarre just a decade or two ago.[2] Along with this cultural revolution, the technological progress that drives such changes has continued to advance at a rapid rate. It seems likely that we will create huge organizational networks and information systems by the turn of the century which will comprise an intricate central nervous system for the planet that should revolutionize the way we work, interact, and think.

These two developments—the evolution of a more sophisticated culture and the development of more complex technologies—represent an awesome advance in civilization that is rapidly becoming a reality. Sometimes it is easy to lose sight of what has been accomplished, but the fact is that within the short span of a decade or two the world has entered a vastly more powerful stage of evolution. This is truly a miraculous

William E. Halal is Associate Professor of Management, School of Government and Business Administration, George Washington University, Washington, D.C.

event, in my opinion, and I feel privileged to witness it in my lifetime.

Although prospects for the improvement of the human condition have never looked brighter in these respects, they have never looked worse in many other respects. The energy crisis remains out of control with no relief in sight, the economies of developed nations continue to suffer from chronic inflation and low growth, the crisis of major institutions that began with the Watergate scandals goes unabated, the slumbering giant of the Third World is being awakened by the revolution in Iran, and most recently the fragile detente between the two superpowers has been shattered, posing a serious threat of nuclear war. The prosperous new technological society that Hermann Kahn and other optimists envision may lie waiting at the end of the rainbow, but there is a serious question in many minds as to whether we will survive to reach it.

In view of these conflicting prospects for the future, it is not surprising that people feel confused and insecure. The world has changed so much that it doesn't make sense any longer. The old ideas don't work now, and there is no new vision to take their place. There is a pervasive fear that events are out of control, that we are lost.

This lack of direction is painful, of course, but it may be necessary because the void itself creates fertile ground for the seeds of new ideas to take root and grow. From my perspective, the events of the '70s are rather clear in their significance. The Watergate scandal, revelations of corporate malfeasance, the energy crisis, Proposition 13, the stagnation of the economy, the collapse of detente, the revolution in Iran, and other such crises of the past decade are unmistakable signs that the social order of industrialization is dying rapidly. Because industrial society is the only way of life that we know of, it is hard to accept this brutal reality, although we may realize it deep within. It is somewhat like seeing a loved one wither away from a terminal illness; we allow ourselves to be fooled into ignoring the steadily worsening symptoms until it is no longer possible to avoid the death that is imminent.

But, of course, society is unlike an individual in the sense that the passing of one stage permits the evolution of a new stage of civilization. For in the midst of the rubble and chaos that is left of the industrial order, a new social order is slowly forming about the more sophisticated culture and the soft technologies that are the hallmark of the future. All that remains until it blossoms forth is the emergence of new institutional forms that may harness these forces into constructive change.

Furthermore, I think it is possible to identify the embryo of this new social order and to encourage its growth. There have only been two generic types of social order in the long evolution of civilization and each focused on a primary institution that acted as the organizing force about which the rest of society revolved. In agricultural society the principal institution was the feudal estate that served to mobilize peasants and slaves to cultivate large holdings of land. In industrial society, the profit-making corporation served as the keystone in the capitalist system to create capital for building factories, roads, and other aspects of the economic infrastructure. So, too, in post-industrial society there now exists an empty ecological niche[4] for a central social institution which must be occupied before we can restore a sense of coherency and order to our world. I must admit I have only a vague understanding of what this institution should be like, but I do know that it must serve certain well-defined economic needs and that it should behave rather differently.

The best way I can describe this institution is to outline the conditions it must fulfill, somewhat like a product specification. First, it must address the needs of a mature society that faces subtle problems of a higher order of complexity than the simple tasks of creating and distributing consumer goods.[5] Now the demand is to provide efficient non-polluting transportation systems, to manage energy use rationally, to develop systems for recycling materials, to manage the environment with prudence, to assist individuals in maintaining their health in a holistic fashion, to handle data and knowledge more conveniently, to assure peace and order, and a variety of other such urgent concerns. In short, this institution must concentrate on the use of soft technologies to solve social, political, and intellectual problems that focus on improving the *quality* of life rather than material consumption.

Secondly, because these are highly personal and complex challenges, this institution must use a collaborative type of problem-solving that engages the cooperative talents of its various constituencies, and it must be sufficiently responsive to retain their legitimacy and support. Most institutions today are actually governed as benevolent dictatorships, which is a major reason why they have suffered a decline in confidence. Democratic institutions are notoriously difficult to manage because of their penchant for disorder and time-consuming debate, but there seems to be no feasible alternative. As Churchill put it, democracy is a terrible form of governance—but everything else is worse.

Finally, this must be primarily a private institution rather than a governmental one. There has occurred a decided shift of sentiment away from cumbersome government regulation and ineffective public programs, so it seems clear that the solution to the problem of restoring social order must emanate from decentralized, privately controlled organizations that retain the flexibility to act efficiently and to respond to the widely differing conditions that are emerging. And because this will be a democratic institution that is intended to serve the interests of its constituencies, it will have the unique status of operating within the free enterprise system with the avowed goal of maximizing social welfare rather than profit.

In other words, we are faced with the challenge of creating a pivotal institution that will act as a social machine for gobbling up disorder, waste, illness, misused resources, unemployed people, and other societal refuse in order to convert these lowly materials into social wealth. An institution that is explicitly designed to reverse the flow of entropy!

If the institution I have been describing sounds a bit familiar, it should because it represents a more sophisticated, benign version of the large, publicly-owned business corporation and its constituent groups, or what are often called stakeholders. I hope you didn't mind my playing a little trick here, but I thought it might be helpful to start looking at the future of the corporation from the future end rather than from the present. You see, one thing I have learned very painfully over the past 15 years or so as a management scientist is that most people resist tinkering with their institutions with the ferocity that a mother bear defends her cubs. The feeling seems to be that our institutions may not work very well, but they're ours, by God.

The profit motive itself seems to be the most revered of these institutional symbols, rather like a sacred cow. Criticize the concept of profit to a group of people and you will get some awfully strong reactions. The word is so loaded with emotional significance that it can mean almost anything: efficiency, self-interest, greed, reward, exploitation, free enterprise, love of country, apple pie, the flag, motherhood, and so on. In fact, the concept of profit means so much that it doesn't seem to really mean anything; I have come to conclude that it simply provides a rationale to do as we wish. If there is one single obstacle to the emergence of a new and more effective social order, it is the faithful allegiance to the rather archaic symbol of profit that forms the dominant principle by which we continue to operate a complex economy.

This is not the place for me to go into detail on why the profit motive can produce poor outcomes. But, if I put it in broad perspective, perhaps you will get the idea. In an agricultural society, those who owned land were accorded the power to govern because land was the principal, limiting factor of production. In an industrial society, holders of capital governed the social order for the same reason: capital was the critical commodity needed to build a modern economy, so profit was the supreme criterion of the public good. That's why we still measure "progress" in terms of GNP—a gross measure of profit—and that's why business executives continue to insist on "educating" the public on the important role that profit plays in keeping the economy thriving. That's also why our lives are suffused by the imperatives of making money, as in the commercials that constantly beseech us to buy, the "bottom line" we are measured by on our jobs, and the extravagant wealth of the "successful" who have made it to the top.

I do not wish to deny that financial realities are fundamentally important considerations. That is obvious. But the underlying crisis of our time can be most effectively understood as a deeply rooted contradiction between the operating goal of profit-making upon which our present society is built versus the demands of a new era. The problem with guiding a complex post-industrial society solely upon principles of financial profitability is very fundamental: it is that the very concept of profit inherently alienates the interest of the profit-maker from the interests of others from whom profit is made. Businesspersons, therefore, are unavoidably placed in an adversarial relationship with the rest of society, and they are thereby perceived as enemies of the public welfare. So it is little wonder that our dominant institution—the large business corporation—is not working effectively. The singleminded pursuit of profit by large firms discourages badly needed collaboration, fosters the relentless exploitation of scarce resources, glorifies consumption, exacerbates social costs, and obscures the more subtle concerns that

240

are increasingly important to a mature society: personal welfare, individual freedom and dignity, the creation of a sense of community, social justice and democracy, and other principles that once founded this nation.

Whereas the truth of the matter is that there is no good reason why the corporation cannot expand its present role so as to take upon itself the responsibilities for governing the ecological niche that I have described above, and there are many reasons why it should do so. In fact, this is slowly happening, although I do not believe that many people understand the significance of these developments. Major corporations are now of necessity adhering to a new ideal of social responsibility and finding it highly successful. They are developing a rigorous discipline of social reporting to measure and plan for these new involvements. They are also starting to work cooperatively with their various stakeholders. And in case they fail to move quickly enough, the stakeholders themselves are forming powerful coalitions like Big Business Day[6] which may take over the control of this institutional niche if they are slow to do so themselves. The Europeans and the Japanese are moving much further along in these developments than we are, which largely accounts for their greater success in adjusting to the new realities of a post-industrial era.

If these trends hold, I believe we may soon witness the evolution of modern corporations into a modified organizational form in which all of the corporate constituencies—stockholders, employees, customers, suppliers and distributors, and government—become roughly equal partners in a new and more democratic form of free enterprise that is specifically intended to maximize the social welfare. This may not be necessary for all firms in all industries, of course, and it may not be as tidy as I have outlined here. It would certainly not be appropriate in small firms. But I believe that there exists the possibility of establishing a new form of free enterprise for large corporations that will be vastly more powerful and more effective.

This "soft corporation" of the future merely represents the modern equivalent of today's limited form of corporate behavior. By explicitly incorporating the social dimension of business activity that comprises the growing frontier of modern economies, rather than considering these social effects as "externalities," corporations could become organic islands of productive cooperation floating in a turbulent sea of diversity and self-interest. The net effect would be to outgrow the profit-centered model of business that is associated with the negative aspects of capitalism, and to create a new human-centered model of business that I think of as Democratic Free Enterprise. The new pope captured the imperative of our age simply but most effectively, I thought, when he said that people should not work for the system; the system should work for people.

If this more powerful conception of free enterprise can be developed, I think we will see that many of our seemingly intractable dilemmas may be greatly ameliorated by resolving the conflict that is inherent in an outmoded industrial system. Take the most critical problem now facing us, for example: the energy crisis. It seems pretty clear by now that new breakthroughs in energy technology are not likely to occur for a few decades, if ever, and the immediate need is to simply manage the diverse energy sources we now have more effectively. But the corrosive conflict between the country and the oil companies has resulted in such a hemorrhage of public confidence and legitimacy that it is politically impossible to allow free-market mechanisms to manage energy development and distribution—in spite of the fact that most people well understand that government control over energy merely aggravates the problem further. Even the most rational and reasonable policies for decontrol of energy markets being advocated by many politicians are not acceptable because the public simply will not trust the oil companies.

The solution lies in restoring this trust by creating a diversified form of control over these quasi-public institutions through representation on the boards of directors by consumer groups, labor leaders, public officials and possibly other key constituencies. The energy industry could then be permitted to operate in a free market, although supervised by those parties who are affected along with business executives. This would thereby create a coalition of interests to foster the welfare of all concerned.

Inflation is another good example. The problem is now expected to get worse in the years ahead, possibly reaching 20 percent inflation rates. As a result, Draconian measures are being considered, such as even higher discount rates by the Federal Reserve, drastic slashes in public programs, and wage and price controls. It seems clear to the most casual citizen that this is a bankrupt holding action, a policy of desperation that cannot reach the roots of the issue—which are buried in the eroding productivity of the nation that is out of balance with escalating consumption. Inflation is akin to a fever in the body politic—it is the economy's way of telling us that the nation is seriously ill because we cannot work together effectively. The programs advocated above attack the symptoms rather than the causes, and leave the patient without effective care, suffering alone and growing worse.

Inflation persists by virtue of a tacit conspiracy among the various constituencies of business activity. Unions demand excessive wage increases that exceed the productivity gains provided by labor. Management passes the buck by raising prices to recoup profit levels and by delaying investment in capital improvements and innovation. Consumers indulge in spending orgies to beat the higher prices that are anticipated, which raises demand and dries up investment capital. Government attempts to "squeeze out" inflation by encouraging a recession, but this merely aggravates the problem even further. And so on.

The resolution of this dilemma requires a restructuring of the economy at the microeconomic level through the creation of more organic, comprehensive forms of decision-making among the constituent elements of major firms—which collectively form the economy. If major corporations could develop a workable coalition among their stockholders, employees, customers, the government, and suppliers and distributors, we could unleash powerful new levels of productivity and recreate the sense of community needed to enforce reasonable demands upon these

242

groups. By virtue of creating such "corporate communities," we may in effect produce a decentralized form of self-regulation by all affected parties. This would permit deregulation of the economy at the federal level, thereby unleashing the freedom and productivity that has been suppressed by the growth of government control. Such actions could provide the "disciplined self-interest" that is necessary to balance productivity with consumption and thereby break the spiral of inflation.

One more simple example may illustrate the promise this new role of business suggests at the international level. The world seems polarized by the conflict between two major ideologies. Capitalism is a highly productive system that retains freedom, but it produces wasteful consumption and social inequities. Socialism provides a good degree of social welfare, but it is inefficient and dictatorial. The two systems are polar opposites of one another, and this is responsible for the conflict that is now escalating between the two halves of the world devoted to each ideology.

If the Western powers could create a form of free enterprise that embodies democratic principles and fosters the social welfare, such an economic system would represent an effective synthesis of the best features of both capitalism and socialism that may defuse the explosive conflicts now threatening the world. Multinational corporations of the United States, which are usually seen as exploitative, could thereby take the lead in world affairs as the innovators of a new economic order, as the promotors of human welfare, and as champions of democracy. Rather than engage the Russians in a game of global chicken by escalating the arms race, we could cut the ground out from under totalitarian societies by appealing to the hopes of the Third World, which is now being driven into the hands of communist leaders.

If we could regard the corporation from this fresh perspective, we would observe that the structure of economic behavior is generically composed of the intersecting interests of five key constituencies that must be managed in a holistic fashion by corporate executives. And the ultimate goal of free enterprise is not simply to make money. To believe so is to invert means with ends. The true goal of free enterprise is to serve the interests of all these stakeholders—which comprise the welfare of society. In our frantic self-interest, we have lost sight of the true nature of the firm from which the legitimacy and the productive power of free enterprise ultimately emanates. The corporation is in reality constructed in the image of five constituencies centering about management. It can be thought of as comprising a star-shaped social system. What better symbol could America choose to represent its ideals than a star—the star of democratic free enterprise!

Now *that* is a mission for corporate executives that is worthy of their considerable talents and their million-dollar salaries. Rather than being perceived as mendacious Machiavellians who must remain hidden from public view for fear of confrontation with their constituents, they could become the guys with the white hats—the heros of society who solve our difficult new problems with their unique skills as entrepreneurs. They should be out front creating political coalitions among their constituencies through the skillful use of their talents as politicians, diplomats, and visionary statesmen. Because if they do not take on this role, they will find themselves fending off coalitions of consumers, labor leaders, government officials, and other interest groups who will assume this responsibility instead.

But if this is such a great opportunity for business executives, then why haven't they taken on this challenge? Of course, some of them are incompetents or misanthropes as the public imagines, but most are bright, hardworking, and dedicated professionals. They have families and religious ideals like the rest of us. I believe the problem is that business people are themselves the prisoners of the system they have created. There are many great executives, of course, who have always advocated the ideas described here, which simply represent applications of enlightened management and sound free enterprise. But most managers have accepted the gospel of the bottom line at face value, and as a result they have willingly imprisoned themselves in the roles that society has offered. That is the tragic flaw in capitalism. Good men and women, when obligated or even permitted to pursue profits alone, will do terrible things—not because they are bad, but because the system fosters a serious suboptimization of the public welfare.

So I have come to the interesting conclusion that business executives may be the last group of individuals in our society in need of liberation. Blacks, students, women, gays and everyone else have been freed from the confining bounds of their old industrial roles, so now it may be time for us to help tycoons gain their freedom as well. If we could urge and cajole them into shedding their masks as "Captains of Industry" to simply appear with us as ordinary human beings, I think we would find that the stereotypes we now hold of cold-blooded business executives would quickly vanish and we could all engage one another in more productive ways. In what I hope may become the ultimate liberation movement, therefore, I propose the following revolutionary motto—

FREE THE FORTUNE 500!

This short essay has obviously been an inadequate forum to treat the many complex issues that are involved in the concepts I am proposing here. I hope the interested reader will understand the limitations of this paper and will look elsewhere for a fuller treatment of the perplexing but fascinating possibilities that are being considered by many persons as we grope for ways to create a new paradigm of post-industrial economies[7]. The inability to acknowledge these realities for what they truly are is today's equivalent of the stubborn refusal of our ancestors to accept the knowledge that the earth was round, that it revolved about the sun, that we evolved from primitive species, and other revolutionary ideas that were once disturbing but are now considered self-evident advances of human awareness.

I am convinced that there is a vast and far richer world that exists in the near future, lying just beyond the world of the profit motive that now obscures our vision with its razzle-dazzle. Ironically, this is a world of more bountiful resources, but most importantly, it is a world of collaborative social relationships that offers the sense of community we sadly lack today, and the dignity, meaning, and purpose we hunger for. As futurists, a central goal of the coming decade should be to explore these possibilities more fully than we have in the past decade because developing a post-industrial model of the corporation is the key to unlocking the future.

REFERENCES

1. Daniel Bell, *The Coming of Post-Industrial Society* (Basic Books/Harper, 1973)
2. Daniel Yankelovitch, *The New Morality* (McGraw-Hill, 1974)
3. Starr Roxanne Hiltz and Murray Turoff, *Network Nation* (Addison-Wesley, 1978)
4. Kenneth Boulding, *Ecodynamics: A New Theory of Societal Evolution* (Sage, 1978)
5. Fred C. Allvine and Fred A. Tarpley, *The New State of the Economy* (Winthrop, 1977)
6. Larry Kramer, "Coalition Plans to Fight 'Crime in the Suites,'" *Washington Post* (December 13, 1979)
7. For instance, see Frank J. Bonello and Thomas R. Swartz (eds.), *Alternative Directions in Economic Policy* (U. of Notre Dame, 1978); Dennis Meadows (ed.), *Alternatives to Growth I* (Ballinger, 1977); William E. Halal, "Beyond the Profit Motive: The Post-Industrial Corporation," *Technological Forecasting & Social Change* (June 1978).

The Changing Economics
of the Urban Promise

by

John P. Blair

Just as the West was the place of opportunity during the nineteenth century, the great industrial cities were the centers of opportunity throughout most of the twentieth century. As the westward migration was predicated upon abundant land, the development of urban America depended upon high rates of economic growth that in turn depended upon abundant energy resources. The size of the urban movement dwarfed the westward migration.

The latter twentieth century will be a period of slow aggregate economic growth or decline resulting from global resource scarcities. Slow national growth and resource scarcities will undermine one of the engines of urban development. Consequently, global economic decline will be experienced severely in industrial cities.

A growing economy generally has opportunities at all organization levels. The availability of jobs is perhaps the most important element in the concept of opportunity. In addition, the opportunity path in growing areas is likely to make promotions easier and wage increases more likely than in declining areas.

The Emerging Urban Economy

The industrial cities of the northern United States led the national economy during the spree of affluence that followed World War II. The same cities that led the earlier economic growth are in the forefront of the post-affluent transformation. As their growth path changes, so will the urban promise.

Central city economies are changing in response to their internal dynamics as well as to national and international trends. The major economic trends that will shape the future of cities are:

1. The national economic growth rate is slowing and shifting from goods-producing activities to services.

2. The manufacturing sector is losing its relative importance in

John P. Blair is Associate Professor of Urban Affairs and Real Estate, University of Wisconsin at Milwaukee, and Policy Analyst, Office of Evaluation, U.S. Department of Housing and Urban Development.

the American economy. The service sector is becoming relatively more important.

3. Non-metropolitan areas are growing more rapidly than metropolitan areas. This is true for almost every major economic sector.

4. Central cities are growing less rapidly than their suburbs (or declining more rapidly).

5. Not all central cities are experiencing employment declines. The larger cities and those in the urban/industrial North are experiencing the most economic distress. Many newer Sunbelt cities are experiencing economic growth, as are smaller cities.

6. In economically distressed cities the manufacturing sector is leading the decline.

The six trends will continue because they are manifestations of fundamental social changes. Both the aggregate slow growth and structural shifts reflect the emergence of post-industrial society. The regional shifts are partly attributable to increased energy prices that encourage location in warm areas and the deposits of fossil fuel in the South and West. Higher energy (as well as other raw materials) prices accelerate the shift from manufacturing. This in turn accelerates the decline of the manufacturing cities. The development of suburban and non-metropolitan areas reflects value preferences that have deep roots. A survey by the Commission on Population Growth and the American Future showed a significant preference on the part of Americans for rural and semi-rural living. The newer, less dense cities offer more of the amenities associated with rural living than do the older, "trolley car" cities.

Many older cities also have internal problems that will reinforce the economic decline. The fiscal problems of central cities are a cause as well as a result of declines in commercial and industrial importance. The high urban tax rates are likely to continue even as central city residents deplete urban infrastructure.

The Urban Promise

There will be sufficient variation among cities to insure that while urban economic opportunities will diminish, they will not disappear. The urban promise will shift to the smaller, warmer cities. The older industrial cities will face the severe problems of economic decline.

Career Expectations: The large metropolitan areas, including those cities that are declining, will continue to offer opportunity to those who aspire to the pinnacles of success. However, the declining opportunities in central cities coupled with slow growth in the national economy will cause many individuals to revise their career and life expectations. Recent surveys have shown that an increasing majority of families no longer believe they will be better off than their parents.

Since the oldest and least productive plants are located in the central city, they will be the first cut back when product demand is less than production capacity. They will also be the last brought on line when demand increases.

Expectations will infrequently be abruptly altered by a dramatic event that clearly denotes a crisis. The closing of major steel plants like the Campbell works in Youngstown, Ohio, will continue to be exceptional. The primary mechanism will be slow decreases as divisions within major firms are relocated or abandoned, as well as closing of small, jobber manufacturing plants, and temporary lay-offs.

The manufacturing sector will continue to lead the urban decline. However, wages will continue to rise in the highly unionized industries since they are usually fixed by national contracts. The unemployment caused by the sluggish manufacturing sector will exert downward wage pressure on the less unionized service sectors. Thus, among workers in the manufacturing sector, fears associated with plant closings, such as unemployment and viability of pensions, will be common.

The central city transition to services will not be smooth, because the skills needed for manufacturing are not similar to the skills in the service sector. The service sector jobs will be people- and paper-processing as opposed to materials-processing. Job retraining programs offer limited help in the adjustment. The size of the employment declines in some cities will be too great to be offset by service employment increases.

Developmental Functions: The city has been described as an incubator of ideas, products and production processes. A related role is that of providing support to groups with low skill levels—particularly cultural skills. It has been estimated that these intangible factors rather than capital accumulation account for most of the increase in real income. The incubator function will be less tied to cities than in the past because of the development of rapid communications and transportation.

The city's human development role will also change. Most urbanists have recognized that cities are places where immigrants have been given a berth on a complex opportunity path. Currently blacks and Hispanics are concentrated in major U.S. cities and will be the principal beneficiaries of the human development function. However, as jobs decline or as firms cease to expand, the most recent urban immigrants will have fewer economic opportunities.

The problem of a permanent urban underclass may be mitigated somewhat by the decline in urban migration, but it will not be eliminated. Reverse migratory flows may also alleviate the problem. But while central cities will be losing jobs, the entire economy will be growing very slowly and there will be a dearth of widely known alternatives. The sectoral shift will also affect the types of opportunities available to low-skilled individuals. Manufacturing jobs frequently require minimal language and social skills. Yet manufacturing is one of the higher-paying sectors in the economy. Consequently, manufacturing was an excellent entry point for first and second generation urban immigrants.

The post-industrial service economy will require a wider range of skills than the manufacturing sector. Managerial, technical, and professional jobs will be attracted to the city because of economies of face-to-face communication. Unfortunately, this sector offers few opportunities for the low-skilled, minority workers who need access to opportunity ladders. Some of the lower service jobs available to marginally-skilled urban residents are quite suitable as entry points into

248

the mainstream economy. However, most lower service jobs require skills that the urban underclass lacks.

Fiscal Retrenchment: The aggregate economic slowdown and the concentration of that decline in central cities will continue to adversely affect the fiscal position of many cities. Both federal and local fiscal cut-backs will be reinforced by emerging views that many government programs, particularly programs designed to help those who are dependent or seeking entrance into the mainstream of opportunity, are ineffective and wasteful. Population declines will contribute to fiscal problems. As population falls, city costs will not decline proportionately because infrastructure (including the bureaucratic infrastructure) is only weakly related to size. The dilemma will be compounded because the middle- and upper-income households are the most likely to leave the declining cities.

Urban-oriented programs have been assigned a low priority in federal policy and the prospects are that their priority will not increase. Federal retrenchment policy will emphasize targeting, leveraging, consistence and related ideas rather than new or innovative programs. Currently intergovernmental transfers account for about half of total revenues for cities of over one million. The real value of these revenues probably will fall throughout the 1980s. New programs are unlikely.

The most likely areas for urban public employment cutbacks are in social services. The decline or slow growth of these areas diminishes opportunities for minorities because services to needy groups will deteriorate. More importantly, public sector jobs have been entry points into the upper service economy. Minority professionals are concentrated in a narrow range of activities such as teaching, health, social service, and recreational workers. All these important professional tracks are closely associated with the most vulnerable public sectors.

Minority job opportunities have increased rapidly in recent years as blacks and Hispanics have gained majority status and become dominant political forces in many cities. The demographic ratios may continue to shift in favor of minority political influence, but the economic trends suggest that it will be more difficult to translate political influence into employment opportunity.

Impediments to Migration: Migration benefits those who choose to relocate, although the social, psychological and monetary costs are substantial. However, many of the most rapidly growing areas have instituted "no growth" or "unwelcoming" campaigns to discourage relocation. Migrants will diminish the advantage current residents may have in turning regional prosperity to personal advantage. Alberta, for example, a Canadian province of energy-based prosperity, has generally discouraged new residents.

The geographic lockout will be even more of a barrier within metropolitan areas. Growth controls such as exclusionary zoning will be the restrictive tools. Both service and manufacturing jobs are increasingly attracted to the suburbs relative to cities. Manufacturing establishments are attracted by cheaper land (horizontal production processes and parking requirements have increased the importance of land costs) and the proximity to the workforce. Market-oriented service establishments are attracted to the outer metropolis by household affluence and demographics. The growth controls will make it more difficult for central city residents to obtain suburban jobs. Not only will transportation costs be a factor but also it will be harder for central city residents to learn of suburban job openings.

The filtering process whereby lower-income families move into housing previously occupied by higher-income families will slow down or cease as metropolitan growth slows and zoning becomes more restrictive. The filtering process creates social contacts, albeit temporary and tense, that were part of the urban development function.

Local Response

The market will be the principal mechanism used to mitigate the adverse impact of urban decline. In the absence of political change, local policy responses will affect locational decisions at the margin because the size of the market is much larger than the resources available to cities. Three kinds of responses will become increasingly important to the location of economic activity: locational inducements, local self-sufficiency, and legislative requirements.

Locational Inducements: Two approaches have been mainstays of local business development: (1) the blue skies strategy and (2) the private business subsidy. The blue skies approach attempts to attract business by providing decision-makers with information/propaganda. The emphasis is on propaganda. The importance of amenities to urban development is recognized by the blue skies approach, although amenities-creating policy is rare. Concern with the substance rather than the illusion of amenities may help reestablish the link between some basic cultural (in the broadest sense) functions of cities and opportunities.

The business subsidy strategy provides indirect payments such as below-market land sales, low-interest loans, or low-cost infrastructure provision to encourage plant location. The variety of techniques that have developed for indirectly subsidizing business enterprise is astonishing and will continue to proliferate.

Unfortunately, the locational competition will result in few net benefits accruing to all cities taken together. There is a likelihood that a "beggar thy neighbor" reaction will develop. Cities will compete with one another in an expensive but unproductive war of subsidies to attract business. Firms are still learning how to exploit their bargaining position when deciding where to locate.

Self-sufficiency: The susceptibility of local economies to external economic factors will cause many residents to become increasingly interested in policies that will isolate and protect their local economy. At least one city has designed a program to allow low-income residents to work for the city for a short period in lieu of paying taxes. More ambitious endeavors along the same lines will increase.

Plants that are being closed might be purchased and reopened by employees, community-based corporations, or cooperatives. Departing employers may be willing to sell the productive facilities cheaply. They may even give them away. At the same time a plant closure is avoided, the community may be able to keep in place the level of related establishments and job skills needed to maintain agglomeration economies. Robert Goodman in *The Last Entrepreneurs* documented an increasing number of cases where distressed plants have been purchased by worker and/or community groups.

Local governments may also assume some of the investor-entrepreneurial functions. Advantages of direct public ownership include: (1) The fact that employment will make a genuine contribution to community development. (2) The jobs will be permanent and will not require continual subsidization as is the case with many government work programs. (3) If the city carefully selects projects that would not have been undertaken elsewhere in the country, then net jobs for the nation as a whole would result. (4) The type of production and the type of job skill requirements can be judged for their contribution to the city's social economy. (5) Jobs development can be linked to other important life quality objectives. Some residents may trade lower wages for better working relationships that may develop in a community or worker-owned plant.

There are potentially grave problems with direct local government ownership even if it remains small in scale. In particular, the community enterprises could be unable to support themselves, in which case they could become a permanent drain on the tax base. Most industrial relocations are necessitated because the private owners under the existing institutional arrangements cannot earn an adequate profit. Thus community ventures must be very selective; only a few of the projects considered will be viable.

Locational Mandates: Some jurisdictions will attempt to mandate industrial locations. Federal legislation was recently introduced to require that tax credits and other government benefits be withdrawn from plants that relocate without sufficient reason. Although several Western nations have provisions for locational mandates, such measures have little likelihood of success in the U.S. They are politically divisive, difficult to implement, and the areas that are most distressed lack sufficient political clout. After the reapportionment that will follow the 1980 census, the urban industrial North will have even less representation. Targeted federal procurement policy could have the effect of mandating location for some types of establishments. But again, the areas most in need of such protection lack the political might to effect such a program.

The Promise of Policy

Social tensions may increase as opportunities diminish. Traditional policy dilemmas will be brought into sharper focus since resources needed to finance programs will decrease. Efforts to support one group will be increasingly viewed as detrimental to others. Programs based upon fragmented coalitions of narrow interest groups will be more difficult to maintain in a period of declining resources. Local policymakers will need to do more than select appropriate trade-offs among major constituents. Policymakers could lend support to definitions of opportunity different from traditional acquisition and consumption models. This is the promise of policy.

New Age Investing

by

Carter Henderson

Not too long ago, after lecturing on the economic outlook at a Southern university, I had occasion to chat with two women: the first an affluent college professor with extensive investments who was visibly frightened by the future, and the second a younger woman with no financial assets who was looking forward to it with confidence and anticipation.

It seems incongruous that a person with a diversified portfolio of all the "right" investments should be afraid of America's economic future, while one without a stock, bond, Krugerrand, or bag of pre-1965 U.S. silver coins to her name should be so self-assured.

The answer is that the frightened college professor has heavily invested in America's mainstream cash economy, which is visibly rushing toward collapse, while the confident younger woman has invested in a self-reliant lifestyle that's largely immune to the money system's escalating agonies (i.e., she lives simply, enjoys doing things for herself, belongs to a sharing network of friends and acquaintances, is active in the creative life of her community, and spends what little money she does need with great care).

The college professor's fear, shared by millions of other Americans reliant on conventional investments in today's unconventional world, arises from her inability to conceptualize what's happening to the U.S. economy, or think through how she can achieve personal security within it. Barbara B. Brown, in her new book *Supermind: The Ultimate Energy*, says this kind of "Destructive worry occurs when the emotions escape the governing throttle of the intellect, and for a legitimate reason: the intellect lacks the information it needs to solve the problem it perceives."

During the Fabulous Fifties and Soaring Sixties, you could invest with confidence in stocks, bonds and other conventional paper because what you were really doing was investing in the vigorous U.S. economy itself, which was growing by a predictable 4% or so a year with low-level inflation.

You could buy equity or debt paper issued by IBM, Xerox, Walt Disney, Polaroid, or any of the other "Favorite Fifty" growth companies, for instance, and then sit back knowing that your appreciating investment

Carter Henderson is a writer and lecturer on financial and economic affairs. He lives in Gainesville, Florida. © Princeton Center for Alternative Futures Inc.

would be there when you needed it for your children's college education, a rainy day, or retirement.

All this changed during the Sobering Seventies when rocketing energy prices, diving productivity, billions of unwanted American dollars sloshing around on world money markets and other powerful forces—manifesting themselves as intractable inflation—slammed the U.S. economy against the wall—thus ending a generation of unprecedented material prosperity and inaugurating a New Age of more spartan lifestyles. "The days of 'high, wide and handsome' economic growth are probably over in the United States," Henry Ford II told a *New York Times* reporter in 1977, "and that is not all bad since we have been 'just outliving our means' in the past 20 years."

The only remedy economists have devised which is powerful enough to cure today's cancerous double-digit inflation is the chemotherapy of government-induced recessions which, if handled ineptly, could quickly deteriorate into a full-blown, 1930s-style depression, or into hyperinflation, which is worse since it could destroy the currency.

While Merrill Lynch Pierce Fenner & Smith may still be "bullish on America," Wall Street's stock and bond hustlers have little to offer which can protect investors against rampaging inflation's rotting of their money's purchasing power. Nor, for that matter, do purveyors of gold, silver, antiques, first editions of *Superman* comics, Fabergé Easter eggs, and other exotica whose wildly gyrating prices are scaring off all but the most intrepid crap-shooters.

Since it will take years to conquer high-level inflation if we are lucky (and decades if we are not), millions of investors, myself among them, are turning to a failsafe investment strategy—unknown to Wall Street and the Gnomes of Zurich—which can substantially increase their economic security as the nation enters a New Age of waning material affluence.

New Age investors see the United States at the beginning of a great economic transformation, similar in many ways to the rebuilding of war-torn Europe and Japan, during which it will have to literally clear away the rubble of its old disposable, drive-thru, buy-now-pay-later culture, and replace it with a more sustainable system geared to conservation, renewable resources and humanism.

New Age investors are taking command of their own economic destinies by reducing their need for cash incomes, learning to coax more purchasing power out of the money they do have to spend, becoming do-it-yourself experts, capitalizing on the untapped productive power of their homes and communities, frequently creating their own income-producing jobs, and discovering to their delight that people can be even more engrossing than products. In the argot of Wall Street, New Age investors are taking the contrary investing theory to its logical conclusion.

Conventional investments in selected securities will still be profitable in the future, and fortunes will undoubtedly be made and lost by professional speculators playing these markets with the dedication of card counters working the blackjack tables at Atlantic City.

But the historically brief interlude when investing in one's future

253

economic security meant stocks, bonds and other paper money-denominated securities is over for now, ended by the virulence of Latin American-style inflation and the unpredictability of Washington's hapless efforts to control it.

Work and Leisure in the Future

by

Fred Best

The balance between work and leisure has always been a topic for speculation. The questions are many: Will the time given to leisure grow relative to that given to work? What forms might future increases of leisure time take? What groups will seek more time off their jobs in coming years, and what are the prospects that institutions will make adjustments to human preferences? These issues will be reviewed from the standpoint of U.S. data, but much of this discussion should have international relevance.

Growing Desire for Worktime Reforms

A host of indications suggest that interest in institutional reform concerning worktime and the options for leisure have grown over the last decade and will continue to grow. Starting with the use of flexitime, a vast array of reforms have been proposed and applied. Some of these include "job splitting" in which two or more persons share the same job, compressed workweeks such as working 10 hours a day for 4 days a week, a sabbatical leave for federal civil servants, options to voluntarily exchange portions of one's annual earnings for added vacation time, and the rapid growth of permanent part-time jobs providing career opportunities. One indication that social pressures have grown and are likely to continue growing for more individual choice in balancing work and leisure come from two successive national surveys showing that the percent of American workers citing problems with "inconvenient or excessive hours" rose from 29.5% in 1969 to 33.6% in 1977.

This rising concern over worktime is rooted in a number of changes occurring within our society. Among the most important of these has been the rise of working women, many of whom are mothers who prefer less than full-time jobs and flexible work scheduling in order to jointly pursue careers and child-rearing activities. Along with working women has come the rise of dual-earner families and fewer children, at once tending to increase family income and reduce financial needs, thus allowing men to reduce their worktime and earnings. At the same time, there has been increasing interest in part-time and part-year work among

Fred Best is Director, Shared Work Evaluation Project, California Employment Development Department, Sacramento, California.

the younger student population and older workers near or past retirement age. In addition, persistently high levels of unemployment have increased interest in sharing available worktime—not only to spread available jobs among more persons, but also to share the limited number of desirable positions among an increasingly skilled work force. Finally, there are indications that American values may be moving away from materialistic goals in favor of less tangible aspirations for "quality of life." While these changes are not likely to foster revolutionary changes, they can be expected to create constant pressures over the next few decades for shorter work hours and more free time, as well as increased individual discretion in the scheduling of work.

Potentials for More Free Time

An updating of an earlier study conducted by Juanita Kreps and Joseph Spengler provides a framework for viewing the potentials for reducing and realigning worktime over the next few decades. Working from computations based on "slow recovery" projections of economic growth, this updating shows how much free time the average U.S. worker might expect to gain by the year 2000 if one-third of expected real economic growth was forgone for more leisure. The number of hours worked per year by the average worker would decline from 1,911 in 1976 to 1,598 in the year 2000 (see Figure 1). If individuals could have their choice of the form this gain in leisure might take, the average worker could have a 33-hour workweek, or an 11-week paid vacation every year, or a 13-month sabbatical every seven years, or retirement by age 56. Of course, workers might also take free-time gains as some combination of all the above options.

Worker Preferences for More Free Time

What indeed might we expect if individuals were given the freedom to choose the amount and scheduling of their worktime? The National Commission for Manpower Policy is now in the process of conducting an exploratory national survey on the issue of worktime preferences, but these data have not yet been released. However, one indication of worktime preferences comes from an exploratory survey of 791 varied employees of Alameda County in California which was conducted in late 1976.

Among other things, respondents were asked to choose among five equally costly time-income tradeoff options: a 2% pay increase, 10 minutes off each workday, 50 minutes off one workday a week (presumably Friday), one additional week of paid vacation, or earlier retirement. In response to this question, only 14% of the sample chose the pay increase while some 56% chose the one-week added vacation (see Figure 2).

In considering these responses, it should be noted that this type of question is biased against the expression of preferences for part-time work. Because the exchange of a 2% pay increase cannot buy much in the way of shorter workdays or workweeks, those concerned with such options are left with few choices representing their preferences.

256

FIGURE 1

ALTERNATIVE USES OF ECONOMIC GROWTH IN GNP PER CAPITA AND HOURS WORKED, 1976-2000

Based on Extrapolations of BLS "Slower Recovery" Economic Projections

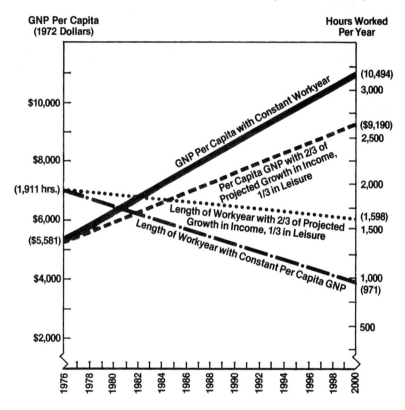

FIGURE 2

WORKER PREFERENCES AMONG EQUALLY COSTLY OPTIONS
FOR INCREASED INCOME OR FREE-TIME
(Percentage Breakdown. Cost of All Options Equal to 2 Percent Pay Increase)

2 Percent Time-Income Tradeoff Options	First Choice	Second Choice	Third Choice	Fourth Choice	Estimated Fifth Choice*
2 Percent Pay Increase	14.3	19.6	28.7	25.8	13.7
10 Min. Reduction of Ea. Wkday	.7	3.7	12.0	27.3	57.8
50 Min. Reduction of 1 Wkday/Week	12.2	29.7	28.9	22.7	5.7
5 Additional Days Paid Vacation	55.6	24.9	9.6	5.0	2.7
Earlier Retirement	17.2	22.2	20.8	19.3	20.2
Total	100.0	100.0	100.0	100.0	100.0
Number Respondents	746	731	726	722	703

QUESTION: Suppose that your employer gave you a choice of the following options: A. Pay increase of 2 percent (1/50th more than your current income), B. Each workday reduced 10 minutes, C. Shortening of Friday (or any other workday) by 50 minutes, D. 5 additional days (1 workweek) of paid vacation each year, E. Earlier retirement by accumulating 7 days each year until retirement. Mark the answer spaces with the letter of the option which best reflects your own preferences: Which option would be your first choice? (   )   Which option would be your second choice? (   )   Which option would be your third choice? (   )   Which option would be your fourth choice? (   )

* Remaining row percentage points adjusted for a 100 percent column total.

257

In response to this problem, another study revealed that when options for larger tradeoffs are provided, that about 10 percent of surveyed workers expressed a willingness to exchange large portions of their "current" income in order to reduce their workdays to 6 hours or less. While available data still indicates that a larger portion of workers are likely to exchange substantial amounts of their earnings for more vacation time, there is also a notable interest on the part of a significant proportion of interviewed workers for major reductions of the workweek.

There are two important implications to these survey findings. First, responses to these questions indicate that many workers may be willing to make notable exchanges of current and potential earnings for more free time. Second, individuals have different preferences concerning the forms of free time that are most valuable to them personally. As a result, worker willingness to forgo income for time is likely to increase as the options for alternative forms of leisure increase.

Worktime preferences vary in accord with social characteristics. As often hypothesized, preferences varied by sex, with women tending to be more willing than men to exchange earnings for time and expressing slightly more interest in shorter workweeks. Surprisingly, stated willingness to exchange pay for time did not vary greatly according to income. Finally, it should be emphasized that available data indicates that worktime preferences vary considerably by age and family cycle stage. Put differently, worktime arrangements that are highly suitable during one stage of life may be barely tolerable during another stage. As a broad generalization, I would hypothesize that the average person would prefer part-time and part-year work during school years, standard workweeks and longer vacations in early adulthood, shorter workweeks and part-time work during the early and middle child-rearing years, longer vacations and sabbatical leaves during post-child-rearing years, and part-time work in old age.

Worktime Trends and the Need for Reforms

A brief review of social problems associated with ongoing worktime trends suggests that future balances between work and leisure may come to better reflect the plurality of individual preferences expressed in survey studies.

What then have been the worktime trends of the past? As we all know, the average workweek has declined from about 60 hours to 39 hours over the last century. However, since the 1940s there has been only slight reduction in the workweek, and most of the reduction that has occurred has come from the effects of the increasing proportion of part-time workers on workweek averages. Since the 1940s there have been some increases in holidays and vacations, but these leisure gains have not been great.

While it might appear that there has been little in the way of increased leisure since the 1940s, a brief look at the lifetime distribution of work shows that there have been tremendous increases in non-work time in the form of years for education during youth and retirement in old age. As a result, the years spent on work have been compressed into an ever smaller portion of the total lifespan. The proportion of the average male's life given to work has declined from about 67% in 1900 to about 60% in 1970. If current trends persist, Bureau of Labor Statistics projections indicate that the portion of life given to work will decline to about 56% by 1990, leaving 44% of the average male's life spent on non-work activities, 10 years of which will be in the form of retirement (see Figure 3).

FIGURE 3

**U.S. MEN'S LIFETIME DISTRIBUTION OF EDUCATION, WORK AND LEISURE
BY PRIMARY ACTIVITY
(Projected for 1980 and 1990)**

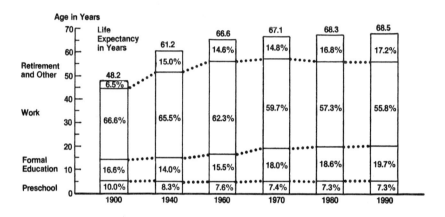

There are now growing indications that the continued compression of work into the middle years of life intensifies a number of pressing social problems. In an all-too-brief summary, this increasingly pronounced lock step progression from school to work and/or homekeeping to retirement is causing problems in the transition from school to work, fostering overextended schooling and underutilization of educational attainment, limiting opportunities for re-education and "second chances" at school after the traditional school years of youth, imposing harsh career penalties upon parents who choose to reduce work or leave the labor force for child-rearing, contributing to intense time pressure and family stress within dual-earner households, reducing chances for leisure during mid-life, contributing to a widespread inability to deal with prolonged free time during retirement years, forcing retirement upon unwilling elderly persons, creating long periods of inadequate income during youth and old age, and leading to fiscal depletion of public funds due to expenditures for income maintenance for the young and old.

The problems resulting from this compression of work into mid-life are likely to create pressures for a number of worktime reforms. First and foremost, it can be expected that future gains in free time will occur in the traditional "work years" of life, and that work activities may be increasingly extended on a part-time or part-year basis into

259

the early and later stages of life. Second, it is likely that there will be considerable effort to increase the diversity of worktime arrangements rather than move toward a monolithic reduction of the "standard work-week." Specifically, we can expect increased interest in innovations such as flexitime for days and weeks, compressed workweeks, staggered work hours, "job splitting," permanent part-time work, longer vacations, work sabbaticals, voluntary leaves without pay, and a number of voluntary time-income tradeoff programs such as the German "flexiyear contract" and the American "cafeteria plans" providing fringe benefit choices to employees.

Needless to say, the applicability of such innovations will vary greatly in accord with the specific constraints of different types of work organizations. Employers in both the public and private sectors must move cautiously to assess the costs and benefits of these proposals. Our work-time arrangements are part of the institutions and norms that we confront every day. They are changed or perpetuated by human choices. Options to make such choices are not always easy to gain, nor are the choices themselves without cost. Clearly, the extent of change in this area will depend on the priority we give such matters as we deal with the myriad of daily personal and collective decisions that will shape the world of tomorrow.

"Survival in the '80s"
or
How Technology Rescues Growth

by

W.H.C. Simmonds

Not so long ago we were told that, once started, economic growth could continue indefinitely and that the main problem left was one of "fine-tuning" the economy. This has not proved to be the case. Those that put it forward treat technology as a given, or exogenous variable, something always available to bail out the economic system whenever necessary. This may have been a reasonable assumption for a non-technologist to make based on the experience of World War II, the 1950s and the 1960s; but it is no longer valid today. It turns out on reflection that the situation may be almost exactly the opposite way round. It is economic growth which is self-limiting; left to itself (with constant population and no changes in technology) what would it do but grind slowly to a halt? And what is the major factor which has prevented it from doing this for the past two hundred years but the invention or discovery of new technology and its successful application in industry!

This paper presents first the reasons why economic growth was so successful in the '50s and '60s; some evidence on the self-limiting nature of economic growth; the new concept of sustainable growth; the new business situation developing in the '80s and beyond; and some ways in which the chemical and chemical process industries can adapt and "ride" the new world of continuing change successfully into the future.

The Old Ways of Thinking "Oldthunk!"

Why was economic growth so successful in the '50s and '60s and why was it not continuing to be so in the '70s? The reasons for its extraordinary success in the postwar era are summarized in Table 1 (Economic Growth 1945-70).

An enormous demand was generated through lost consumption during the (dirty) threadbare '30s and the war in the '40s, by the urgent

Walter H. C. Simmonds is a policy analyst with the Industrial Programs Office, National Research Council of Canada, Ottawa.

Table 1—Economic Growth 1945-1970

Why It Was So Big!

1. Lost consumption   War damage repair
   in '30s & '40s
2. Population increase
3. Harnessing of science and technology
4. Productivity increases through scale, cheap energy, labor shifts, and substitution of labor by machines
5. Decolonization
6. Acceptance of the growth ethic

and Why It Cannot Repeat!

need to repair war damage, and by population increase which began around 1938 in North America.

The war effort had already begun to confirm the workability of Keynesian economics based on demand. The necessities of war showed that science and technology, from the most fundamental scientific theory to practical know-how, could be harnessed and applied successfully to immediate practical problems. Subsequent experience showed that most of these advances could be transferred to the civilian sector—aircraft, jet engines, operations research, the computer, radar, electronics, petroleum-type and petroleum-based operations in the chemical and rubber industries, nuclear, penicillin, national nutrition, etc.

Productivity rose significantly due to increases in scale of operation which reduced unit costs; more energy became available at lower cost in gaseous and liquid form which helped promote the use of more energy-embodying, but people-displacing, machines; and people moved from lower productivity agricultural jobs in the country to higher productivity manufacturing jobs in the towns.

Abroad, colonies became nations in their own right competing with their resources and markets for world trade; and everywhere the growth ethic—the national goal of a high rate of economic growth—was gradually but increasingly accepted: by governments because it promised the best route to their goal of full employment; by business because growth promised power and profits to the successful; by the public and labor because economic growth paid off in higher real incomes. These in turn promoted the philosophy of materialism and possession and apparently vindicated Madison Avenue's portrayal of the consumer society as the ultimate good.

Economic growth can also be looked at in hindsight from the systems point of view, as shown in Table 2, for the Western industrial nations.

Table 2—System Characteristics of Economic Growth

1. Clearly defined goals
2. Equilibrium economic theory to deduce objectives
3. Rational criteria for performance
4. Highly visible results
5. Materialism and the consumer society reinforced

First, there was a clearly defined and increasingly accepted goal. Secondly, the development of Keynesian economic theory and Leontief's econometrics enabled the overall goal of growth to be translated into specific objectives: to name a few, a greatly improved and general system of national accounts, the Bretton Woods agreements on currencies, the General Agreement on Trade and Tariffs, and the creation of the International Monetary Fund and the World Bank. These agreements established the ground rules for international trade and commerce and for currency exchange. They in turn enabled technological and scientific advances to be built into new, larger, world-scale and world-oriented plants which helped produce the higher productivities needed to fuel economic growth.

Economic growth also established economic efficiency, based on the most efficient allocation of resources, as the primary criterion not only for business but subsequently for governments and even for individuals for their own decisions.

The feedback loop was closed positively when people realized that their incomes were rising with obviously greater real purchasing power. This in turn reinforced the goal of economic growth, the acceptance of new products, and the advent of the consumer society.

Thus, economic growth in the '50s and '60s comprised a well organized, uniquely integrated, positive feedback system producing remarkable results—so long as one did not look at the boundaries which a systems analysis must also include; and this is where the troubles began.

The Self-Limiting Nature of Economic Growth

During this period it was largely believed that economic growth was a process that could continue indefinitely, and that the main problem left was the "fine-tuning" of the economy. Unfortunately this belief has not been substantiated. Economic growth turns out to be no different from any other growth process; it creates conditions which ultimately limit its continuation. In other words, economic growth—like the growth of government, the growth of bureaucracy, even the growth of taxation and enterprise—is ultimately a self-limiting process. More accurately, these should be termed contingent, self-limiting processes. By this is meant that something else is required to maintain economic growth outside the economic frame of reference, if its growth is to continue. Examples of the limiting processes generated by continuing growth are shown in Table 3.

Table 3—The Limits to Economic Growth

1. Growth changes economic shares in society (Kuznets)
2. External constraints:
   pollution, safety, health, energy, planetary survival
3. Internal limitations (not dealt with in this paper):
   consumptions, satisfactions, moral order, household capitalization, GNP omissions

First, the well-known economist Simon Kuznets pointed out that economic growth alters the shares of wealth in society and can continue only so long as the political process can accommodate the changes produced. Tom Settle has shown further that, if economic growth based on individual self-interest were to continue indefinitely, it must logically destroy the society in which it takes place. (See his book *In Search of a Third Way: Is a Morally Principled Political Economy Possible?*, McLelland & Stewart, Toronto, 1976.)

Second, today's economic system is not the simple, theoretical model shown in Figure 1, with infinite sources of energy and materials and an infinite capacity for absorbing wastes. It is a finite system with a finite boundary (the earth), as shown in Figure 2.

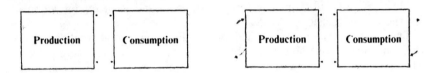

Fig. 1—Conventional Two-Sector Model of the Economy

Fig. 2—Systems Two-Sector Model of the Economy

The best example of this finiteness is Tokyo. The single-minded determination with which the Japanese pursued economic growth (10% a year for some 15 years) created such a deterioration of the atmosphere in some streets in Tokyo that police officers' had to be given oxygen to keep them going! The Japanese finally realized their mistake and have removed this limit to their growth by cleaning up the pollution in Tokyo at a cost of several billion dollars.

Sustainable Growth

The costs of pollution, safety and health can be looked at in two ways. They were often described publicly by industry executives as largely unnecessary, inflation-creating price increases to be passed on to consumers, forced on industry by governments panicked into action by a relative small number of activist individuals or groups. The point of view put forward here is quite different. The control of pollution is part of *the price payable to enable growth to continue.* This point of view gives us a clue how to evaluate what we mean by sustainable growth. If the price of removing existing limits to economic growth is too high, then the rate will fall; if we design our plants, processes and products so that they avoid the creation of such limits, then the rate can increase. If we improve the tax system, reward enterprise more, reduce the necessity for welfare payments, etc., we not only mitigate the limiting factors to growth but add positive motivation as well. Nor is the research and work done to reduce limits to growth such as pollution wasted. There may not have been much net gain industrially when biodegradable detergents replaced the non-degradable ones. But the development of synergistic chemical-biochemical-biological control systems for insects, pests, and diseases has considerable future potential, particularly in tropical countries; the loss of mercury is leading to a gain in knowledge about membranes, diaphragms, surface, catalytic and electrode behavior, all areas with major future potential. Pollution illustrates an old maxim: for every threat there is an implicit opportunity—if not for you, then for someone else. It is sound advice today to take any negative or threat statement and, as a mental discipline, deliberately recast it into positive or opportunity-creating form.

Sustainable growth then becomes that rate of growth which we can just sustain into the future: (i) by avoiding unrewarding, dead-end, or socially undesirable forms of growth; (ii) by controlling or removing the negative aspects of growth as they appear or as we become aware of them; and (iii) by turning our knowledge of what is unwanted into better processes to produce what is wanted. It is fascinating to watch the food industry's discoveries of what can be done with so-called food wastes; and the entire polymer industry sprang from the unwanted tars, gums, and gunk at the bottom of flasks and autoclaves, as everyone in the chemical industry is well aware.

"Newthink"

The above summary shows that the '50s and '60s were not the norm, but were abnormal or a-normal years which compensated for the deficiencies and losses in the '30s and '40s. They are not, therefore, a satisfactory basis for looking at the '80s and '90s. For those who are canoeists, kayakists, or rafters, the '50s and '60s can be compared to canoeing in smooth water where the aim was to see who could get the biggest canoe and paddle it fastest despite the shoals, sandbars, logs, fallen trees, etc. In the '70s the flow of the river downhill increased. We are now in white water. The name-of-the-game is to avoid the rocks ahead, to negotiate the small waterfalls, while at the same time positioning ourselves so that we can make the bend in the river safely which we can see just ahead. Hopefully we will not plunge over a nuclear waterfall. We do not know how long the white water will last—the maps in this region are fragmentary and often misleading—and we have never been down this river before. There may be a few stretches of open water here and there, but by-and-large it looks as if the white water is going to last for several decades to come, probably for about two generations, because the peaking out of the world population, the energy rearrangements, and their interactions can hardly be resolved much before 2040.

The first requirement in real life for such a situation of continuing and prolonged change is the development of a non-equilibrium theory dealing with economic transactions, which includes directly the factors producing change. The author believes that this is the most important single piece of research in the world today because of its potential impact on governments. Some chemical companies are already concerned that the current economic advice given to governments is based too

265

much on the concept of equilibrium and may be misleading. Such a concept is ill-adapted to an era of continuing change since it must specifically exclude the factors which produce change—for example, knowledge and information, and the creation and impact of technology.

A good starting point may well be the national accounts since estimates of economic growth are based on them.

First, the GNPs calculated by the labor productivity, gross domestic productivity, and tax return methods do not agree. The reasons for these disagreements are not yet fully understood. Thus we do not really know what our growth is at the moment, and published figures have often had to be revised. Secondly, the GNP does not include explicitly the major product of the economy—knowledge and information. Those engaged in national statistical studies might well, therefore, like to see some changes: data collected on stocks and flows of people as well as things; and then the assignment of value to products (by prices through the market system) and to knowledge/information (through the educational market system establishing the value of people and hence the cost of obtaining knowledge/information). We would then have two matrices representing the economy instead of one; one would show the flow of material and energy into products and the other the flow of knowledge/information through industry and the economy. The knowledge/information matrix could show, for example, the cost of meeting governments' demands for information. It could also show the dollars used to create new knowledge through research and development.

Given a statistical framework of this type, a dynamic, non-equilibrium picture can be put forward for the function of technology in the economy.

The Function of Technology

Since 1776, the function of technology has been to raise continuously the limits to growth of the economy. The other major factor for change has been population growth. Technology drives the economy in two basic ways: by utilizing existing knowledge/information to raise productivity primarily through what is now called innovation; and by creating new technology from new knowledge. New technology creates new economic *potential*. This only becomes actualized when an entrepreneur decides to risk investment of capital, land and labor in it in the hope of gain. In the public sector a similar situation exists except that the hoped-for pay-off is in the form of votes.

On the other side of the coin, obsolescence and foreign competition eliminate old technology (for example, the displacement of natural products by petrochemicals after World War II). The overall or net effect is therefore a dynamic, non-equilibrium outcome between three fluctuating processes—productivity gains plus new economic potential being generated through new technology versus loss of old technologies with some or all of their associated economic activity. With this picture of the behavior of technology in our minds, we can now look at what some of the likely coming changes in industry may be.

266

The Coming Changes in Industry

Table 4 summarizes the coming changes in industry as seen in the studies of the decade 1976-1986 made for the Joint Economic Committee of the U.S. Congress.

Table 4—The Microdynamics of Economic Change

1. Scarce-input industries
2. Income-elastic goods & services
3. Age-dependent industries
4. The replacement—maintenance shift
5. New growth industries
6. Technologies adaptive to people

The scarce-input industries are those using above-average amounts of energy and certain raw materials, such as housing and construction. Reduced use of materials, better design, and a halt to increases in size are evident. Social stress is likely to be greater if critical shortages are not anticipated by the market, but the problem of anticipating price increases has not yet been solved; for example, at what rate should oil—heating oil—prices rise in North America? The problems here are on the supply side.

In contrast, the luxury-type, income-elastic industries will encounter demand-type problems. Increasing food, heating, and gasoline costs leave the consumer with relatively less disposable income for these industries. Certain of these industries (sport, relaxation, pleasure in cities) may increase, but those in remoter areas are likely to experience difficulties.

The extraordinary changes in age structure in the population are by now well-known; they are the biggest ever experienced in North America. What may be less obvious is that they affect the supply of people to industry as well, with a reduction in the number of entrants to the labor force of 50% in Canada (where there were 3 persons in the '70s, there will be only 2 in the '80s) and 33% in the United States (from 4 persons to 3). These changes have important significance for industries with dirty, hazardous or night-shift operations.

Rising material and energy costs also imply a shift from replacement demand for products (the throw-away society) toward maintenance demand, (e.g., growth in the car and other repair businesses), plus a slow shift towards better-made products with energy efficiency and durability guarantees. The durable goods industry will be most affected here.

The same factors which act as threats to one group of industries produce opportunities for other industries. Housing may be threatened, but not insulation. Lighter cars travelling more miles per gallon make better news for plastic manufacturers than for makers of glass and steel. These same factors are expected to produce further changes in life-styles and to change the nature of jobs. These in turn will be fed by growth in microelectronics, solar energy, biomass, biochemistry, bioprocesses, etc. For materials it implies more composites in which the most advantageous property of each constituent is used to maximum effect. In overall terms the shift is from the quantity approach (tonnage, poundage, gallonage as the yardstick) to the quality approach (maximizing molecular architecture to minimize consumption of material). These are all areas in which the chemical industry has worked very successfully in the past and this trend will surely continue.

The final point is that we have to recognize that economic equilibrium does not occur through the interaction of large numbers of *identical* economic men, but of non-identical people. Hence there is a third axis to every equilibrium graph, an axis which measures the degree of human involvement. Keep all other factors constant, but just alienate your workers; which way does productivity go? If quality of life and quality of working life are to improve, then the human, social and cultural aspects of work must be treated equally with the technical, economic and environmental aspects. The newthink, holistic approach differs from the conventional motivational approach in that processes are designed from the start with full knowledge of their human implications. Technology can adapt to people instead of people having to adapt to technology, but we have not explored this possibility very far to date.

J.P. Blair and Gary Gappert comment that the changes summarized above would be enough to keep the U.S. economy fully occupied for the next 20 years. The situation that they portray implies, however, a change in management approach in the face of prolonged change. Grand designs, immaculate plans are out; a much more pragmatic, learning approach on a step-by-step basis seems more appropriate—an approach in which each step forward in the present is used to increase our options in the future, and our future plans and intentions help give guidance to our present actions.

Progress may not be fast; we may have to emulate the Japanese initially and learn to make haste slowly. But they have shown that, when a consensus can be achieved, action can then follow swiftly. Where there is a will there can be a way—in the United States and Canada as well as in Japan!

Conclusions

The conclusion is that we will still need the old ways of thinking in those areas of business where they continue to make sound business sense; but we will also need "newthink" for those areas where unsolved problems such as inflation, inertia, inaction, lost consumption and lost pride through under- and unemployment plague us. We are like players on a chessboard. In the past the palm went to the queen with her ability to move in straight lines all over the board; today we look at the knight, the only piece on the chessboard able to move around obstacles—forwards and sideways. The move forward indicates the continuation of the strengths of the past on which the chemical industry was founded and has continued; the move sideways portrays "newthink," the flexibility and adaptiveness in mind and body required to cope with continuing change, to remove limits, and to turn apparent threats into growing opportunities. Surely this is what the chemical industry has done so successfully in the past and will continue to do in the future. And to the extent that it succeeds, economic growth can continue also.

Human Values:
Personal, Social,
Religious

Reverential Thinking

Henryk Skolimowski

Words move, music moves
Only in time; but that which is only living
Can only die. Words, after speech, reach
Into the silence.

T.S. Eliot

Thinking has a colossal future. Of late, however, our thinking (the thinking that stems from our technological culture) has been showing the signs of stress, strain and exhaustion. As with everything else in nature, the idiom of our thinking must be continually renewed.

The dialectics of life are endlessly fascinating. And so are the cycles of nature which generate viable and radiant forms of growth. Our thinking of the recent past has suffered the effect which monocultures produce in nature. Homogeneity invariably brings in its wake unintended detrimental consequences. If you introduce one single crop within a given ecological habitat, be it coffee or rubber or maize, then at first your yields will be impressive. After a while all kinds of problems will start developing, not only with regard to the soil and the health of your corps, but also with regard to your economy, as an excessive specialization leads to excessive perils.

It has been so with our overspecialized linear thinking, which has been geared to the ideal of technological efficiency. At first this thinking brought about impressive increases in the productivity of labor; also an increased efficiency in our exploitation of nature; and also increases in our standards of material living. But then after a while, this specialized thinking has brought in its wake unintended negative consequences, of which the elimination of jobs on a massive scale is not the least important. There are other consequences, of course: the ecological and environmental devastations; our estrangement from nature, which has been deemed within our linear thinking to be a resource for our exploitation; an increasingly growing alienation of the individual from society and of the individual from other individuals and from himself.

Immanuel Kant has maintained that reason without action is impotent

Henryk Skolimowski is a professor of philosophy at the University of Michigan in Ann Arbor, Michigan.

and action without reason is blind. Action tied to a myopic reason brings about myopic results. Action tied to one-dimensional and over-specialized reason brings about unprecedented alienation and ecological devastations. Our one-dimensional overspecialized thinking has turned out to be thinking against nature and not with nature, thinking against human culture and not with culture, thinking against human happiness and not for human happiness.

We have perceived the limitations of our analytical, objective thinking for quite a while. As an antidote, all kinds of correctives have been devised. Among those correctives, cybernetic thinking and systems thinking are most striking examples. When we look into the scope and magnitude of our present problems, however, we realize that those correctives are clearly insufficient. They are insufficient because although they have overcome certain forms of one-sidedness, they still remain one-sided and overspecialized.

When we look at nature and nature's way of "thinking" and connecting things, we immediately realize that the connectedness occurs on all levels of nature's being. Nature does not recognize the kind of strictures and boundaries that we have devised in our systems of knowledge, whereby we separate various phenemona in strictly separated boxes. Nor does nature recognize the distinction between the descriptive and the normative, between the objective and the subjective. Nature is cease-lessly normative in its *modus operandi*. It continually transforms and connects its various levels of being for the sake of its *well-being*. The connectedness of nature cuts across categories and levels established in our descriptive sciences. It can be said without an exaggeration that goodness, truth and beauty are one and the same for nature; or aspects of each other.

If there is any clue to be taken from nature with regard to our thinking, it is this: Our most creative and therefore most viable thinking (as far as the future is concerned) is one that moves freely across all levels of our knowledge and understanding. It is the kind of thinking that can connect the most unexpected elements and layers; the kind of thinking that is not imprisoned by or regimented through existing categories and existing disciplines. Indeed, this kind of thinking (connecting unexpected elements from different levels of knowledge) has been one that has produced the most striking human inventions and the most original breakthroughs in human knowledge.

This new kind of connected thinking amounts to a new ecology of mind. Ecology, we should be aware, is not only a descriptive term standing for a specialized descriptive discipline. It is also a value term which postulates reverence for natural systems. Ecology also postulates that understanding of larger connections between parts and is more important than the understanding of mere parts. Understanding inter-connections is understanding wholes. Thinking in totalities, thinking in terms of wholes, is the beginning of wisdom, is normative thinking.

> *Who rightly with necessity complies*
> *In things divine we count him skilled and wise.*
> Euripides

The connected thinking which is required and, indeed, necessary, for a viable global future of the human family will have to recognize itself as normative thinking. One of the main deficiencies and, indeed, perils of our one-dimensional, overspecialized thinking (including cybernetic thinking and system thinking) has been the assumption that our thinking should be "clean," clinical, objective, neutral. In fact, it has never been that; for it has always been at the service of some normative purposes, and always laden with values.

What I am suggesting is that we explicitly recognize the normative character of our thinking, particularly when it involves multiple relationships with ecological habitats, and especially with cultural habitats. Moreover, I suggest that we should go one step further and not only recognize that our thinking is normative per se, but also recognize that reverence for life be a fundamental mode of our thinking. *Thinking reverentially* is an odd concept within our present categories. Yet, under a deeper reflection, it makes sense, for it enables us not only to understand things analytically and logically, but also compassionately and through this peculiar mode of understanding which is called empathy. Many problems and dilemmas concerning man's relationship with nature, as well as many agonizing human and social dilemmas, cannot be understood until and unless we comprehend them through empathy and compassion and not measurement and logic. Reverential thinking (and reverential reasoning) are more encompassing forms of human comprehension than merely analytical thinking.

Reverential thinking, when employed as a mode of our understanding on a large scale, will produce numerous and far-reaching consequences: it will affect and restructure our perception; our perception will no longer be a cold scanning of what material benefits we can derive from a given piece of physical universe but will become a celebration of life, without losing at the same time the facility of realizing that the universe around us can be used to our material advantage.

Reverential thinking will also influence our perception of other human beings and our perception of ourselves. Reverential thinking will also affect our ideas about economics and about management. Ultimately, reverential thinking is good economics, for it will inform and guide us how to take care of our entire well-being while preserving the integrity and viability of other beings, including large-scale ecological habitats, without which our well-being (even economic well-being) cannot be secured in the long run. Reverential thinking, when spelled out in detail and applied to our global problems, is not only justifiable, but makes good sense, for it is the kind of thinking that enables us to understand in depth the multiple facets of our physical and transphysical universe and the multiple aspects of our human, social and spiritual existence.

We should be aware that reverential thinking spelled out in detail will form a new philosophy. I call this philosophy *Eco-philosophy*. The idea of Eco-philosophy offers a new paradigm for our comprehension of reality and for our thinking in it.

To think reverentially is first of all to recognize human *life* as an intrinsic value; is to recognize *love* as an essential and indispensible modality of human existence; is to recognize *creative thinking* as an inalienable part of human nature; is to recognize *joy* as an inherent part of daily living; is to recognize the *brotherhood of all beings* as the basis of our epistemological paradigm. He who thinks these precepts "romantic" and "unrealistic" is subscribing to shallow and unworkable economics. For a truly workable economics is one which accounts for our physical existence as well as emotional and spiritual existence. A slice of a human being is a dead human being.

Thinking reverentially is not only using our gray cells in a new way; it is also embarking on a new set of values. If matter could think and assert judgements, it would no doubt confirm that objectivity and detachment are the suitable vehicles for expressing and handling its state of being. On further reflection, if matter could *think* it would probably desire to become something else than mere matter; if it had a choice it would probably want to acquire extra-physical sensitivity and then it would want to be accounted for in terms of compassion and not only in terms of cold objectivity. In order to express the states of being characteristic of human beings, we require an impressive repertoire of values: instrumental, ethical, aesthetic, eschatological, which reflect and recapitulate the variety of aspects of man's existence.

When American Indians thought and maintained that there is a spirit behind every tree, they did not mean to say that there is a ghost-like apparition roaming around every bush. This was their way of expressing their reverence for nature, of expressing the fact that, for them, all living things were of intrinsic value. This form of value and this form of reverence are acknowledged in the Orient in another way: there is a Buddha in a blade of grass.

Projecting alternative futures is projecting alternative values—and is also assuming alternative modes of thinking which convey, implement and safeguard these values. Reverential thinking is a vehicle for the restoration of intrinsic values without which we cannot have a meaningful future of any sort.

I have been alarmed of late by the profusion of "new algorithms" for futures thinking. No question: we have to evolve new modes of thinking in order to make our global future viable. What has struck me as odd and alarming is that too many people have attempted to monopolize futures thinking within rather confined schemata of their own. It strikes me as both premature and perilous to attempt to institutionalize futures thinking in the moulds which are, by and large, the epicycles of the past linear overspecialized thinking.

The potential of our mind is unfathomable. So is the potential for the new modes of thinking. Let us pay tribute to our creative thinking by creating new kinds of thinking, by not imprisoning it prematurely in a set of confined boxes. For thinking has a colossal future.

> *Science is a sense of curiosity about life,*
> *Religion is a sense of reverence for life,*
> *Literature is a sense of wonder at life,*
> *Art is a taste for life,*

Philosophy an attitude towards life—
Based on a comprehension of the universe
As far as we happen to know it.

Lin Yu-tang

Future Creativity: Inspiration for Peace

Alfred Bernhart

At this time when the most recent cultural phase, namely the industrial phase, ends for certain groupings of mankind, industrialization-mentality still exerts strong influences. Yet, with the fading of the industrial phase, new values emerge, which are consistent with the thinking of the evolving next cultural progress phase.

The clash between the two value constellations—old and new—causes the difficulties from which we now suffer. The alert observer notices many signs and signals of these ongoing changes. Declining in importance are values developed by the clock-dominated industrial society, such as time-"splitting" mass-production, fast "economical" transactions, time-"saving" processes, hectic movements, overrated material comforts. Ascending are values enhancing human life and its quality, as well as values related to human community and its interactions.

Mankind's future creativity will emphasize these new values, for example:

- Guiding the ethics of procreation of human life.
- Improving quality and duration of human life.
- Intensifying human life in community.
- Shaping urbia for stronger community interaction.
- Strengthening global understanding and sharing.
- Developing human multithought capacities.
- Unifying spiritual concepts.

It is my interpretation of the objective of this global thought exchange that, in keeping with a value constellation consistent with the new, now-evolving cultural phase, we all want to help to clarify the direction of future creativity for humanity's benefit.

Procreation of Life

The increasing respect for the value of human life demands that new human life be procreated only if a satisfying and pleasant life

Alfred P. Bernhart is a consultant on environmental planning and engineering. The ideas presented in this article are expanded upon in Bernhart's book Future Creativity: Inspiration for Peace, *which can be ordered directly from the author, whose address is 23 Cheritan Avenue, Toronto, Ontario, Canada M4R 1S3.*

can be secured for the newborn.

In the future, human creativity and intellectual awareness—governed by the growing respect for human life—will exert an increasing influence on sexual union, so that only wanted life will be procreated, and a high quality of life for future generations will be secured.

Quality of Life

The growing value of human life also demands, and has already resulted in, strong efforts to improve health and nutrition for people during their increasing life-span.

Future creativity will project towards further improvements of health, towards physical and mental well-being, towards extended life expectancy—for increasing contributions of older brains to mankind's progress.

Life in Community

In community with others, life becomes more rewarding. Community not only stimulates the human intellectual potential, but it also provides the essentials for physical survival of the individual.

As part of a community, individuals surrender some of their freedom of decision-making, and simultaneously gain from joint achievements. The framework of advantages and restrictions is laid down by codes of law that the community as a whole establishes and enforces.

In the future, human creativity will revise the rules of behavior in communities to make traditional laws compatible with newly found knowledge and newly evolving value concepts.

Community Environment

One of the physical expressions of community, shaped by human creativity, is the community's environmental forms.

The growing intensity of community life draws ever increasing numbers of people into *urbia,* in particular into inner urban areas. This is a desirable, culture-intensifying force; it is not, as is often said, an undesirable trend that must be counteracted by decentralization.

Future creativity will shape environmental forms for increasing togetherness—in particular in urban centers where high graceful buildings, interspaced with green areas, will stimulate intense community interaction and cultural progress.

Understanding and Sharing

Different groups of humanity have advanced at varying paces of progress and with somewhat different value constellations. While total egalité of all human beings is probably impossible to achieve and is perhaps not even desirable, the positive forces in humanity strive for a more equal distribution of mankind's achievements and benefits.

The understanding of the problems and difficulties between different human groupings is a prerequisite for effective help and sharing. Such understanding would be much easier if all people could exchange their thoughts in the same common language. Such language could either be the only language a particular group of people chooses to use, or, for another grouping, it could be a "second" language, which may be used for global thought exchange, while the "first" language would serve local discussions and preservation of heritage.

In the future, human creativity will lead to peaceful understanding between groupings of mankind—with consequent global sharing of material and intellectual achievements—by worldwide thought-exchange through a universal language.

Multi-Dimensional Thinking

Creativity is an amazing human gift. The human brain can develop many thoughts at the same time—the brain has simultaneous multidimensional thought-capacity.

It was, and still is, one of the shortcomings of the creative thrust during the industrial phase that creativity is mostly directed towards linear single-thought sequences—whereby one thought follows, rather than complements, the other. This thinking scheme, still affecting all of us, considers simultaneous multi-thoughts as "distractions."

Future creativity will apply the brain's full multi-thought potential to all thinking efforts, so that newly developed knowledge will serve for the benefit of not only a few, but for all of mankind.

Spiritual Concept

As mankind advanced through its cultural progress phases, religious concepts were formulated, which stressed the inherent human good (such as the desire to help others). While all great religions are based on a gradual but steady approach of the human mind towards the creator—which should have a strong unifying influence on humanity—the often minor differences between the various religions caused many conflicts.

In the future, human creativity will formulate a unified religious concept with all positive aspects of the great religions—a concept that will be flexible to incorporate newly-gained scientific knowledge into spiritual formulations.

With responsible procreation, enhanced vitality, intensified community, global sharing, extensive thought-exchange, multi-dimensional thinking, and renewed spiritual creativity, humanity's future will be inspiring.

Such a promising future will, however, not evolve by itself; rather the required re-direction of creativity depends on the active involvement of each of us—and needs the participation of all groups of mankind. We all will have to make our own singularly important contribution, be it ever so small or ever so significant.

Re-directed creativity, with contributions from all of us, will bring humanity a peaceful future—materially rewarding, intellectually inspiring, spiritually enlightening.

The Obsolescence of Modernism

by

Ervin Laszlo

The foundations of the contemporary world rest precariously on the values and practices of modernism. But modernism has become obsolete. This is not a contradiction in terms, for to be modern is not necessarily the same as being up to date; it is also being identified with the typical values, beliefs and practices of the Modern Age. And the Modern Age was not born yesterday: it is now over three centuries old and shows signs of wear. In the late twentieth century, modernism has become an unsafe foundation for any society. We have to face the fact that to be modern no longer means being up to date. Today, it means being increasingly out of date.

The aging of an age is not an unusual phenomenon. Mankind experienced many different ages in its long history. They came as breakthroughs in the existing patterns of living; they flowered as seemingly eternal blueprints of human existence; and they passed unmourned and almost unnoticed when conditions, values and beliefs changed beyond their reach.

The first great leap into a new age occurred in the shift from Paleolithic food-gathering to Neolithic food-producing societies. This "Neolithic Revolution" took centuries to accomplish; many generations came and went before the nomadic hunting and food-gathering tribes turned into settled villagers. As the revolution spread, more people came to be supported by the available lands, and more of them could devote their time and energies to specialized tasks other than the raising of crops and the caring for animals.

Cities came into being, and established trade routes criss-crossed the inhabited world. The taboos and mores of primitive agrarian and pastoral societies—gods and goddesses and rites of fertility and of the earth—came slowly to be replaced by new values, new symbols and new religions. The classical empires of Greece, Rome, and Constantinople arose, made their conquests, and ultimately fell. The tenor of existence varied from the opulence of emperors, the discipline of legionnaires, to the misery and hardship of slaves. But even as Europe lapsed into the Medieval

Ervin Laszlo is Special Fellow, United Nations Institute for Training and Research, New York City. He is the author of A Strategy for the Future: The Systems Approach to World Order *and other books. This paper is adapted from a forthcoming book* Leap Into the Future: Building Tomorrow's World Today.

Age, time stood almost still in many of the non-European civilizations, measured only by the fortunes of ruling houses and dynasties.

After the Plague, faith in eternal values and justice became foreshortened in Europe; people and societies became survivors of a natural catastrophe and became anxious to improve their chances of life and well-being. No longer was the spiritual health of man his only concern. Spiritual progress would follow in the wake of material progress. Four centuries after the Plague, the Marquis de Condorcet provided the clearest testimony of this shift toward materialism in his essay, *Sketch for a Historical Picture of the Progress of the Human Mind*, published in 1795.

But the veritable bible of the new emphasis on material progress was written by Adam Smith the economist, formerly a professor of moral philosophy in Glasgow. His *Inquiry Into the Nature and Causes of the Wealth of Nations* exalted materialistic selfishness on the part of all people, enterprises and nations. The consequences of such inventive egoism would be transformed by an "invisible hand" of economic balance into the greatest good for the greatest number.

The shift from concern with eternal values and spiritual well-being to temporal values and material progress was bolstered and brought to fruition by the birth of modern science and its subsequent marriage with practical skills and crafts. The laws of the earth and of the heavens were united by Newton, having been removed from the sphere of the metaphysical by Galileo and Copernicus. The skills of traditional handicrafts were later subjected to review by scientists who conceived the entire universe, including terrestrial nature, as basically a giant mechanism. They were concerned to wrest the secrets of nature from her for human benefit, and to apply their newly-won knowledge in making powerful tools and machines. After a period of some two centuries of ascendancy and expansion, modern science was fully liberated from bondage to medieval dogma. It gave birth to modern technology, and itself became the object of admiration, even veneration, for countless millions.

The Modern Age burst upon mankind with the force of an elemental flood. In Europe as well as in North America, modern technical civilization blossomed in diverse yet seemingly inexorable ways. Not only science and technology, but the institutions of society came to be divorced from religious authority. The shift from a feudal and other-worldly to an increasingly urban and secular pattern of life was more profound and more rapid than anything mankind had previously experienced. Its "side-effects"—the misery of farmers and the creation of the urban proletariat—bore witness to the severe lags and stresses that always accompany rapid and profound social change.

The social and political systems created in the process of the first industrial revolution are those in which we still live today. They have spread to the four corners of the earth, to peoples and civilizations that did not experience the intervening phases but which were first conquered by industrial civilization's military might, and later became captives of its economic power.

The typical values and practices of the Modern Age brought Western societies untold benefits: material comfort undreamt of in the Middle Ages, better working conditions, a longer life-span, travel and new forms of recreation, and information on anything and from anywhere at one's fingertips. But precisely because modernism gave us all these things, and because it enabled us to communicate with people in all parts of the world, all people began to want its fruits. Modernism spread readily to the tropics, to the deserts, and to the two poles. "Modernization" became synonymous with development. National leaders became anxious students of the Modern Age, trying to learn its ways and fighting to gain access to its technologies and imitate its life-styles.

Soon after the end of World War II, the tide of modernism came up against unexpected barriers. Cities grew to unforeseen and unmanageable proportions. The green revolution proved to be too energy and skill intensive to be of worldwide use. Merely a small percentage of people in developing countries could become part of the modern sector; the rest were condemned to live on the subsistence level, often in the shadow of modern enclaves. Developing countries felt themselves exploited; instead of acquiring the benefits of the Modern Age, they had become its suppliers. Only small elite groups benefited, and their sumptuous modern life-styles contrasted painfully with the misery of the rest. But even they became discontented. The more their countries oriented their economies to become competitive on world markets, the more they became dependent on the rich countries and on the transnational corporations on their soil. Frequent nationalization of industries and the quadrupling of the price of oil were among the countermeasures.

A number of developing countries began to question the value of modernism itself. A few—among them Tanzania, India, Burma, and Sri Lanka—took energetic steps to find, alternatives. They began to grope for national roads to development, development alternatives, the preservation of indigenous culture patterns, and appropriate technologies. Although industrialization and economic growth continue to be their main objectives, these countries no longer take the Western pattern as a panacea. Modernism, a brain-child of 17th and 18th century Europe and America, turned out to be a mixed blessing for the rest. The days of reckoning its true costs and benefits have begun.

Interestingly enough, some of the basic values of modernism have also come to be questioned in the advanced industrial societies of North America, Europe, and Japan. While there is still a deep split between the "establishment," made up of economic and material growth-oriented power groups, and the "counterculture" of youth groups, environmentalists, anti-nuclear groups, human potential enthusiasts and the like, the mainstream of industrial society itself has begun a cautious move toward post-modern values. In the U.S., for example, polls taken by Gallup, Roper, Harris, Yankelovich and others came up with these surprising findings:

- **Living with basic essentials.** By a margin of 79% to 17%, Americans wish to stress "teaching people to live with basic essentials" over "reaching a higher standard of living."

- **Living a more austere life.** 55% of the U.S. public thinks that "doing without something and living a more austere life would be a good thing."
- **Non-material experiences.** By a margin of 76% to 17%, Americans would rather learn to get pleasure out of non-material experiences than satisfy their need for more goods and services.
- **More human, less materialistic values.** By a respectable 63% to 29%, the people of the U.S. would rather learn to appreciate more human, less materialistic values than find ways to create more jobs for producing goods.

Some people even thought that the current shortages are a good thing since they will encourage them to use things more efficiently and less wastefully. Confronted with inflation, rising unemployment and uncertain advances in the quality of living, the people of the advanced industrial societies also grope for alternatives to the economic growth-ethic, and the materialism and egotism of the last decades. How fundamental the changes in public attitudes have been can be best seen if we compare the above new orientations with some of the "classical" values and beliefs of modernism, rampant still in the 1950s and 1960s:

- **The law of the jungle.** Life is a struggle for survival. Be aggressive or you perish.
- **A rising tide lifts all boats.** If as a nation we prosper, all our citizens prosper and even other nations will do better.
- **The trickle-down theory.** Another watery metaphor, it holds that wealth is bound to trickle down from the rich to the poor, and the more wealth there is at the top the more the trickle that reaches the bottom.
- **The invisible hand.** First formulated by Adam Smith, it holds that individual and social interests are automatically harmonized. If I do well for myself, I also benefit my community.
- **The self-regulating economy.** If we could only ensure perfect competition in a free-market system, benefits would be justly allocated by the system itself without need for intervention.
- **Efficiency cult.** We must get the maximum out of every person, every machine and every organization, regardless of what is produced, whether it is needed, and who can or cannot be employed in the process.
- **The technological imperative.** Anything that *can* be done *ought* to be done. If it can be made or performed, it can be sold, and if it's sold it's good for you and for the economy. If nobody wants it, then demand must be created for it.
- **The newer the better.** Anything new is better than (almost) anything old. If you cannot bring out a new product, call the old one "new and improved" and progress—and profits—will be yours.
- **The future is none of our business.** We love our children, but why should we worry about the fate of the next generation? After all, what did the next generation do for us?
- **Economic rationality.** The value of everything, including human beings, can be calculated in money. Everybody wants to get rich,

the rest is idle conversation or simple pretense.

- **My country, right or wrong.** We are sons and daughters of our great land; all others are foreigners, out to get our wealth, power and skills. We must be strong to defend our national interests, preferably stronger than any possible adversary.

As these values and beliefs, dominant 10-20 years ago but still with us today, indicate, *Homo modernus* is a curious species. He lives in a jungle, benefits mankind by his pursuit of material gain, trusts invisible forces to right wrongs, worships efficiency, is ready to make, sell and consume practically anything (especially if it is now), loves today's children but is indifferent to the fate of the next generation, dismisses things that do not have immediate payoffs or are not calculable in money, and is ready to go and fight for his country because his country, too, must fight for survival in the international jungle.

These curious traits of *Homo modernus* are now endangering his future. Belief in the law of the jungle encourages tooth-and-claw competitiveness which fails to make use of the benefits of cooperation—especially crucial in a period of reduced growth opportunities and frequent squeezes. Holding to the dogmas of the rising tide, the trickle-down effect, and the invisible hand promotes selfish behavior in the comforting—but no longer warranted—belief that this will be bound to benefit others. Faith in a perfectly self-regulating free-market system ignores the fact that in a laissez-faire situation those who hold the power and control the strings distort the operations of the market in their own favor and push the less powerful and clever partners into bankruptcy (a totally unacceptable situation when the less powerful and skilled comprise two-thirds of the world population). Efficiency without regard as to what is produced, by whom it is produced, and whom it will benefit can lead to mounting unemployment, a catering to the demands of the rich without regard to the needs of the poor, and a polarization of society in the "modern" ("efficient") and the "traditional" ("inefficient") sectors. The technological imperative becomes dangerous when economic growth curves are slackening, markets are becoming saturated, the environment is approaching the limits of its pollution absorption capacity, and certain energy and raw material resources are becoming scarce or expensive. Falling for the "newer the better" ploy is merely being gullible: One day a product is "improved" because it contains a certain ingredient (fluorocarbons, antihistamines, cyclamates, or whatever), and the next it is improved precisely because it does *not* contain it! Health and social benefit seem to get lost in the competition between artificially inculcated fads and desires.

Living without conscious forward-planning may have been fine in the days of rapid growth when the future could take care of itself, but is not a responsible option at a time when delicate choices have to be made with profound and far-reaching consequences for future generations. If today we would shrug and say *après moi le déluge* we would indeed bring about a flood—of overexploitation, overpopulation, inequality and chaos. The naive reduction of everything and everybody to economic value seemed rational in epochs when a great economic upswing turned all heads and pushed everything else into the background, but is foolhardy at a time when people in all parts of the globe are beginning to rediscover deep-rooted social and spiritual values and to cultivate life-styles of voluntary simplicity. And finally the simple chauvinistic assertion of "my country, right or wrong" can play untold havoc both domestically and internationally, calling for people to go and fight for causes which "their country" later repudiates, to espouse the values and worldviews of a small band of political leaders, and to ignore the great and growing ties of cultural solidarity and economic interdependence among the peoples of today's world.

Despite its obsolescence, modernism is not extinct today; *Homo modernus*, though far from well, is still alive. The people of the 1970s and 1980s are by no means the same as those of the 1950s and 1960s, but their ideas and ideals still lag behind the requirements of the times. No sunset laws have been passed for the spirit of the Modern Age. We have not yet decided whether we are ready to make the leap into a new age, or whether we just want to crawl uncertainly into an extended and increasingly crisis-prone present.

The Future of Religion in a Post-Industrial Society

by

Ted Peters

What is to become of religion as our society moves further and further into the post-industrial period? Certain trends are fairly easy to identify. For example, we expect an expansion of Islamic influence due primarily to the sudden expansion of wealth in Muslim hands. But in this article I would like to bypass trends of this type and focus on something else, namely, the potential interaction between religion and the current understanding of the human self which has developed during the now passing industrial period.

My thesis is that as our civilization becomes increasingly post-industrial, our preoccupation with consuming goods and services will most likely commoditize religion. There is now a strong trend—which I believe will continue—toward treating the moral and spiritual dimensions of life as a commodity to be acquired and disposed of according to the tastes and whims of shoppers in the religious marketplace. Excessive consumption, however, whether it be consumption of material goods or spiritual values, is the root of the crisis we call the "world problematique." In addition, as long as the consumer mentality prevails, we will be condemned to a prostitution of the essential religious vision, a vision of the transcendent unity of all things which requires a sacrifice of the human ego. It is just such a vision, however, which holds the greatest promise for resolving the world problematique.

The term "post-industrial society," as employed by futurists such as Daniel Bell and Herman Kahn, is to be contrasted with *pre-industrial society*, i.e., one still preoccupied with its battle to extract a living from nature through agriculture, fishing, and mining, and which is relatively low in its production of wealth; and to be contrasted also with *industrial society*, i.e., one centered on human-machine relationships, using natural sources of energy and material to manufacture and distribute

Ted Peters is a professor at Pacific Lutheran Seminary and the Graduate Theological Union in Berkeley, California. He is the author of Futures—Human and Divine *(John Knox, 1978) and* Fear, Faith, and the Future *(Augsburg, 1980).*

goods. *Post-industrial society* is the next phase. By the year 2000, less than one out of ten U.S. workers will be engaged in extraction or production. The post-industrial stage centers on relationships between persons: education, communication and service-oriented professions. It will be the age of full technology. With the battle for survival and dominance over nature behind us, we will be able to concentrate on the "higher things" in life and enjoy more fully what it means to be human. At the risk of overgeneralization, we might describe most of Asia, Africa, and Latin America as pre-industrial; Eastern Europe and the Soviet Union as industrial; and the United States, Canada, Japan, and Western Europe as emerging post-industrial.

The Culture of Consumerism

The central cultural characteristic of our present late stage in industrial development is the consumer mentality, which I believe derives from an excessive reverence for the autonomous human self. We used to call it "liberty;" sociologist Daniel Bell labels it "antinomianism;" and still others tag it with "egoism" or "narcissism."

It began with the Enlightenment and culminated in the revolutions of the 18th century, wherein we in the West rejected two kinds of authority: we rejected the authority of the king to tell us what to do, and we rejected the authority of the Church to tell us how to think. Freedom came to be understood in *laissez-faire* terms as the absence of external constraint. Added impetus was given in the 20th century by the all-pervasive influence of Sigmund Freud, wherein not only external constraints, but also the internal constraints of inhibiting moral codes are now seen as illicit restrictions upon the freedom of the self.

Anything that blocks the satisfaction of our desires is viewed as a restriction, as an oppressive force. Thus, as we move into the post-industrial era, we do so with loyalty to a concept of the human being as an autonomous and independent self, responsible for creating its own values and priorities, subject to no external authority, and charged only with the task of freely fulfilling its own self-defined potential for living. Should there arise no countervailing cultural tendencies, such unbridled egoism will eventually plunge society into uncontrolled anarchy.

What has thus far prevented us from falling into total anarchy? My hypothesis is that the powers of *industrial production* have been removed from the masses of people, leaving the autonomous self the opportunity for free expression only in the realm of *consumption*. On the assembly line the average worker can perform his or her task in only one way: the assigned way. It is at the shopping center, then, where we experience the freedom we revere. None of us can doubt that we are free, because while racing from store to store we are stimulated by choice if not overchoice. We create our own self-identities through choosing what to buy; how we consume determines who we are. Whether it is illusion or reality, we consumers believe we are the captains of our own soul and masters of our own fate.

The reason anarchy is avoided is that when self-oriented freedom is restricted to the realm of consumption, it is relatively harmless. It is harmless, that is, to those *within* the post-industrial society. But to those outside—to those Third-World citizens who are still struggling to survive in pre-industrial economies—the unbridled consumption of the affluent world is seen as a threat. The industrial and post-industrial economies are siphoning off the natural resources of the pre-industrial peoples; and futurists look forward with anxiety to the day when all of mother nature will be denuded of her life-nourishing potential.

Consumerist Religion

How will the advancing post-industrial culture influence the course of religion? It is my forecast that religion will become increasingly treated as a consumer item.

Because our economy produces so much wealth, we are free to consume and consume beyond the point of satiation. There is a limit to what we can consume in the way of material goods, e.g., new homes, new cars, new electronic gadgets, new brands of beer, new restaurants, etc. So we go beyond material wants to consume new personal experiences, e.g., broader travel, exotic vacations, continuing education, exciting conventions, psychotherapy, sky diving, etc. What will come next and is already on the horizon is the consumption of spiritual experiences, e.g., personal growth cults, drug-induced ecstasy, world traveling gurus, training in mystical meditation to make you feel better, etc. Once aware of this trend, religious entrepreneurs and mainline denominations alike will take to pandering their wares, advertising how much spiritual realities "can do for you." It will be subtle, and it will be cloaked in the noble language of personal growth, but nevertheless the pressure will be on between now and the year 2000 to treat religious experience as a commodity for consumption.

The Electronic Church

Mass media religion today may be signalling the consumerist religion of tomorrow. Because the television viewer is allegedly free to turn the on-off switch or the channel selector, each TV preacher must sell his or her product fast. It must be a simple, attractively packaged, hard-hitting religious message that appeals to the already established wants and desires of the viewers. Ambitious status seekers who are achieving less than they wish in life will want to buy "possibility thinking." The lonely person who lacks intimate friendship will want to become a "partner in faith" with the dynamic personality who is directing an important worldwide ministry.

The 1980s will bring a new stage in the development of television, namely, two-way or "interactive" cable television. Whether it will be done by mainline denominations, independent revivalists, or confederations of religious groups, we can forecast advances in the techniques of the electronic church. Members of the viewing public will soon be able to sit at home and watch the religion of their choice; and in addition, by pushing buttons on a hand-held console, they will be able to order a book being recommended or make a financial pledge. It

287

will be religion without geographical proximity, without eye-to-eye contact, without personal commitment, without fellowship. It will be religion totally at the consumer's disposal.

Touring the Church

As another example of things to come, let me compare touring a church today with how it might be done tomorrow.

Increased secularization of social institutions combined with increased demand for holistic personal growth may produce a new form of museum, i.e., the living museum. Entrepreneurs in the tourist industry will further develop and refine the ability to create the worlds of past eras. To walk through the British Museum today is to view the statues and friezes from the ancient Parthenon sitting atop plain unadorned tables in a room that could just as well hold metal lathes or dirty laundry. The great pieces of art have been ripped out of their original context of meaning and placed in the sterile atmosphere of detached or objectivist sightseeing.

To a large extent this has happened to churches as well. While living in Europe my wife and I visited the cathedrals of Germany and Italy. During Sunday morning *Gottesdienst*, a sign was posted on the cathedral doors in Cologne forbidding the taking of photographs during worship. There were so few actually worshipping the day we visited, however, that camera flash bulbs could disturb only a handful of pious souls. Some tourists snuck in, knelt down, and then unabashedly turned their eyes and craned their necks and nudged their neighbors and whispered loudly while examining the cathedral's art work. What is important to a tourist in a German church is its romanesque or gothic architecture, its high vaulted ceilings, its friezes and statuary; it is not the fact that it was built to glorify God. Our industrial and objective mentality—aimed at satisfying the aesthetic tastes of the consumer—removes the church from the body of tradition in which it once nourished the life of a culture.

What will happen in the future? Our tastes are becoming much more complicated. The present drive to get beyond secular and objectivist thinking to consume personal holism, I forecast, will have its effect on religious institutions, institutions which have been objectifying their past. Now, personal growth is not the same thing as worshipping God, to be sure, but it will lead to a much more holistic approach to religion.

I forecast that the trend to turn churches into museums will continue, but a new twist will be added sometime before the end of this century. An attempt will be made to retrieve and recapture the original world of meaning in which the Church had its life. The churches will become live-in museums, perhaps for weekends or two-week summer retreats.

The more highly educated and historically sophisticated will come to experience just what it was like to sit at the feet of teaching rabbis at Jamnia, to chant as a medieval monk, to receive the spirit while listening to the preaching of John Wesley, or to pray like a Quaker at meeting. But the motivation will not derive from pure antiquarian curiosity about the past. This will not be an uninvolved looking from the outside. Rather, it will derive from that desire of the individual to enhance his or her own personal being through a deep experience with the spiritual world of our forebearers. The psychic and emotional investment in our religious past will be genuine ... at least for the short time one is in attendance. After the weekend is concluded or the two-week vacation is over, then everyone will go home and return to the routine of post-industrial life. It will be sort of like the Monday after Sunday syndrome of our churches today.

This will not be an authentic expression of religious faith, however, because in this case the autonomous individual is still in control. Religion will be bought and sold to satisfy our desires for exciting experience just as conventioneering, continuing education, psychotherapy, summer camp, and amusement parks today.

This religious scenario alerts us to two rather serious problems. First, it is the consumption mentality of the wealthier nations that is usually designated as the primary source of the world problematique. Second, the consumer attitude toward religion fails to apprehend the true essence of the religious reality in life. We will look at these two problems in turn.

The World Problematique

The post-industrial societies are not the only societies in the world. And understanding the relationship between the various societies and economies is crucial for recognizing that future post-industrial nations will not be able to go it alone. All our destinies are tied together.

This has led the Club of Rome in its best-selling book, *The Limits to Growth*, and its other publications to examine the list of common predicaments that threaten humanity everywhere on earth: poverty in the midst of plenty; degradation of the environment; loss of faith in institutions; alienation of youth; rejection of traditional values; runaway inflation; and global insecurity. This combination constitutes the "world problematique." The dark clouds of the future get darker and darker as the gap between rich and poor continues to widen. And because there are limits—limits to how much wealth we can extract from nature, to how much food we can grow, to how many mouths we can feed, to how much longer our machines can run on diminishing supplies of energy, to how much pollution we can tolerate—the consumer-dominated post-industrial economies cannot continue indefinitely to leach wealth from their industrial and pre-industrial neighbors. The cultural mind-set that lives for unrestrained consumption is blind to the realities of life; it fails to perceive its own self-destructive course. It may, in the final analysis, produce the anarchy entailed in the doctrine of radical autonomy.

Self-Sacrifice

Neither the consumer mentality nor the doctrine of the autonomous human self which underlies it apprehends the essence of religion. In all of the higher religions at least two important things are taught which fly in the face of industrial narcissism. First, the self is not as autonomous or independent as we believe. Each one of us is part and parcel of something greater than we. We do not belong to ourselves alone. Somehow our very being is tied to the being of the divine, to the all. The meaning of our lives is not determined by the things we choose to buy, but rather it is determined by our role in the cosmic drama. Whether it be Dharma, Tao, The Great Spirit, or the will of Yahweh, who we are is determined by our relationship to a purpose greater than ourself.

Second, the road to salvation sooner or later requires self-sacrifice, the turning of oneself over to that which is greater. In Hinduism, for example, true liberation (*Moksha*) is found only when we surrender our separate and distinct selfhood (*Atman*) to the transcendent unity of all things (*Brahman*). In Buddhism we find the principle of "letting go." The very word "Islam" means "surrender." In Christianity, Jesus says the Kingdom of God is for those who give away everything to take up their cross and follow him; even God sacrifices. St. Francis closes his famous prayer: "Help me to learn that in giving I may receive; in forgetting myself I may find life eternal."

If we hold tenaciously to the belief in the autonomy of the human self, that the purpose of life is to satisfy one's desires, and that freedom consists in the unconstrained consumption of goods and experiences, then the depths of the religious insight will elude us. At best we will have a pseudo-religion, one we have fabricated and not one revealed to us by the divine.

The Central Project

If we allow our religious impulses to have the freedom to surface and take control of our lives, then we may find ourselves on the track toward resolving the world problematique. What is needed now is not the anarchy of autonomous individuals consuming whatever their hearts desire; rather, we need a sense of the unity of all things, a commitment to a destiny that is larger than our own private growth goals. The authentic religious vision can draw us out and beyond ourselves.

Futurists themselves—whether religious or non-religious—see the need for unity and are trying to cultivate a sense of global community. Georgetown University political scientist Victor Ferkiss advocates what he calls "ecological humanism," an "ism" that testifies to the unity we share with one another and with all of nature. (See his *The Future of Technological Civilization*, George Braziller, 1974.) Willis Harman of SRI International says that what our society requires now is a single "central project" to pull us together, to unify our goals, and to enlist worldwide cooperation in facing the challenges of the transindustrial era. (See his *An Incomplete Guide to the Future*, W.W. Norton, 1979.) Can religion in our advancing post-industrial society prompt us to seek out and support such a central project? A religion that is co-opted and prostituted by the consumer mentality cannot. Authentic religion just might be able to.

290

Two Scenarios

In conclusion, two scenarios seem apparent. If, on the one hand, the unbridled egoism bequeathed us from the industrial era continues unabated into the post-industrial, religion will become one more consumer item among others. By itself this may be harmless. But should there be no challenge or check upon accelerating First-World consumption, then we will continue down a track toward cultural breakdown and global anarchy.

If, on the other hand, the transcendent unity of all things makes itself definitively felt through authentic religious encounter, and if enough people surrender themselves in response, then our civilization may discover a new unifying heart, a new purpose, a renewed vitality, and we will find ourselves pulling together to write the next exciting chapter of our planet's ever more unified history.

Future Adolescent Values

by
Irving H. Buchen

Demographics fully used is not limited to numbers but possesses considerable conceptual power. Specifically, projections can be made not only of how many, but also of what kind; and how much of that kind may be new or nostalgic. A major case in point is the capacity to designate chronological cultures—cultures or subcultures that have an existence only through a band of time or age span. The first major chronological tribe to be identified in this century—in fact, in 1904—was that of adolescence. More recently, the chronological calipers have developed the classification of senior citizens. One ironic conclusion can be drawn from this juxtaposition of the categories: the senior citizens category may have more of a future than adolescence, at least in the United States; and, further, the United States may more resemble the Old World in age when set against the present and future global picture than the New World it embodied 200 and even 100 years ago. In any case, adolescence has been around long enough to support a history of adolescence. What that history would have to display, as Gary Gappert in *The Post-Affluent World* maintains, is simultaneous multiplicity. Namely, that at least five generations currently exist; and that by the year 2000 six to seven may coexist. That means in terms of our focus that there are at least five different age spans and sets of generational values that currently coexist. But my purpose here is less to profile the various pasts as to present a series of projections of what adolescence may be like in the future—by the proverbial 2000.

Providing a rationale for focusing on adolescence also begins the process of describing its particular power as a category. The most obvious value is that adolescence is prefigurative. By very definition it is a period of maximum transition—neither childhood nor maturity—hence adolescence or little adult; or even Kenneth Keniston's preferred substitute, youth. Indeed, as the most intensely ambiguous state of all stages of existence, one even might be able to predict the capacity of that generation for handling ambiguity and change by virtue of the way they handle adolescence. Another important factor is that the adolescents are impressionable and reflect the stamp of their age's difference.

Irving H. Buchen is Dean, School of Humanities, California State College, San Bernardino. He formerly was Director of the Division of the Future at Fairleigh Dickinson University.

Thus, the current generation of young people both in high school and in the first two years in college are frequently and accurately described as the TV generation in that their birth and upbringing are virtually coincidental with the beginning and evolution of TV. Equally as important, they are more of a visual and oral than a writing and arithmetic generation—hence deficiencies of basic skills—a process reinforced by the enormous visual influence TV has had on the production of textbooks and pedagogical materials. But perhaps the most important reason for projecting adolescent futures is that methodologically it strikes a neat balance between long range and precision. Specifically, if one limits, for example, the chronological spread of adolescence from 13 to 19, one can comfortably talk about adolescents in the year 2000 with a strong sense of realism; for the 19-year-old would be born next year in 1981 and the 13-year-old in 1987, or years before the end of the decade.

Factors Shaping Adolescents' Future

Here then in summary form are some of the major factors that will shape adolescents by the year 2000.

1. More Young People. Globally the bulk of the population will be younger. In Africa, one half of the population will be under 20 by the year 2000. In contrast, one third of the population in the U.S. may be over 60. Thus, the U.S. in the future may be viewed as one of the older countries, not unlike the way historically the U.S. viewed Europe in the 18th and 19th centuries. What will be critical—and the outcome is perhaps not known, let alone predictable—is what effect being young in a older country will have on the young; and what effect being perceived by the young of other countries as being part of the establishment will have on youth. In other words, it will not be enough for adolescents to undertake the conventional search for identity, they also will be engaged in justifying their identity as youth, globally.

2. Extended Youth, Extended Age: A related factor but too important not to be stated separately is the extension factor of modern science and civilization. When applied to the focus on adolescence, what this means is that young people will be young longer and older people will be older longer. All research documents the contributions of highly industrialized societies to the increase in length of adolescence. Specifically, puberty and physiological maturity have been occurring earlier and earlier, and those trends will continue in the future. At the opposite end, there will be perhaps a permanent increase from 22 years old for adult independence to between 24-26 years old. These extensions at both ends of the age spectrum suggest an increase in the marginality of young people for longer periods of time than ever before. If that marginality also characterizes the relationship of older people to the society, then the central drama of the year 2000 may be the relation between the generations, as the relation between the classes was the central social issue of the earlier part of the century.

3. Emergence of New Norms: Such a long period of transition or ambiguity may prove too intense for many adolescents and what probably will surface, especially in education, is a series of new norms, many of which are visible already now. The old norms in college, for example, are full-time students and part-time students. Full-time finished in four years of college, part-timers finished in eight. The new norms are full-time working students, some working full-time, others half-time, others one third-time; and part-time students carrying limited educational loads. The time it will take to finish is a total variable. There will still be colleges that will keep the old pattern of a basically young adult world intact but increasingly they will be in the minority as more veterans return to college (if the draft is restored that number will increase substantially) and as older people in general intermingle with young adults. In short, whatever forms it may take, the future generation of adolescents will be ingenious in finding ways of growing up and working out various forms of independence while they are contained in this now extended marginal period of their lives.

4. Impact of Divorce and Single Parenthood: The present generation of adolescents as well as the one immediately to follow are socially unique in that they contain more offspring from divorced homes raised by single parents than any previous generation. Lest one conclude that this pattern is limited to the U.S. and as such, is a sign of increasing decadence, a survey of the stability of marriage in forty non-European countries randomly selected in Asia, Africa, North and South America revealed that 24 of the 40 countries had divorce rates in excess of those of the U.S. and further that 30-40 of the countries showed no difference between men and women in initiating divorce. Although it is still too soon perhaps to know the full effects of divorce on the psychology of a future generation, one can reasonably conclude that a segment of those from divorced homes may avoid marriage altogether or marry without having children. That trend may be reinforced by the new and apparently nonpathological option of homosexuality on the one hand, and the life of the singles groups (a paradoxical coupling) on the other hand. That in turn may be undergirded by the general economic availability of apartments or condominiums. The singles thrust more than any other single factor has been largely responsible for the resurgence of urban living. The net result is that a substantial portion of the adolescents of the future will be seeking a life that is child-free, and their economic and political position will be to support those who recognize the value of zero population growth. At the same time, because of the tremendous increase (especially on the part of the young) of religious fervor and even evangelicism, a substantial portion of young people may return to large families. On this issue alone there is a very good possibility that uniformity, which has always been a reliable characteristic of adolescent culture, may not be operable in the future. Or that the only way such uniformity may remain is regionally. Such disparities between young people are already apparent in those young people who are against the nukes and those who are against the kooks who are against the nukes. To sum up the problem, the market researchers have their work cut out for them as far as future adolescent social patterns are concerned.

5. The Ideology of Scarcity: The next generation of adolescents, more intensely than the current one, will be exposed fully to the ideology of scarcity. In particular, they will have been raised on diminished and diminishing expectations—there may not be enough to go around for everyone; things may not last long enough for you to get your share. That generation already will have learned that they are being penalized for their fewer numbers; and they may not be able to understand why they should be penalized because there are fewer of them. What will particularly intensify their situation is that their generational span will be the terrible inbetween one—between dwindling natural resources on the one hand and no real big technological breakthroughs on the other hand. But whether or not things are used up, what is clear is that for the future generation of adolescents the days of the cornucopia and of unlimited growth are over, at least until the end of this century and probably into the first two decades of the 21st. What that means is that instant gratification will be replaced by delayed gratification pretty much the way delayed adulthood may be the extended norm. When and if that predominates then a current trend now may gain greater force and application—the trend of behavioral modification. B. F. Skinner in *Walden Two* indicated that the central malady of the modern world was the inability to tolerate and withstand frustration. What I am suggesting, therefore, especially in light of increasing emphasis on behavioral goals, is that the dominant psychology of the future may not be Freudian but Skinnerian; or that Skinner may turn out to minister to the many while Freud to the few, but that perhaps in either case the key adolescent need may be frustration management. The traditional form that delayed gratification took historically in the past is that of religion, which may account in part for its resurgence now.

6. Influence of Technology: No forecast can exclude the impact of technology. As noted, current adolescents are largely what the media has massaged them into being, which includes being more visual and oral than written and conceptual. That influence may still persist although the massive and often urgent efforts of back-to-basics to remedy the deficiencies created by television may be sufficient for redress of the imbalance. But the crucial new technology that will shape the current and especially the new generation of adolescents is that of the computer. It is already estimated that as many as 68% of the work force will use computers directly or indirectly in their work by the early 1980s. Computer-assisted instruction, especially under the new futuristic aegis of the autonomous learner, is steadily increasing in use, especially where productivity has had to become an educational as well as economic factor. The computer games—in particular, the computer learning toys like "Little Professor"—already are preparing the new generation of adolescents for a regular relationship with machines. The prediction then is that the future adolescent will have been raised in greater proximity to the computer than any generation of adolescents before him; that as an autonomous learner he will spend more time learning by himself; and that he may form better or equally significant relationships with machines than with human beings. In fact, Skinner would totally dominate if he could add to his behavioral modification techniques the psychology of human-machine symbiotic relationships, for the future adolescent may spend as much time with machines as with human beings.

In summary, what then are the over-all patterns of the planet of the young by the year 2000?

In the U.S. there will not be as many of them as there are in most countries of the globe. Nor will they command the visibility of numbers the way they used to. Although because of scarcity and other factors, they will not have as many opportunities as perhaps other generations have had—the planet appearing to be all used up—they will not be militant, at least in the U.S. They have virtually no knowledge of the student revolts of the 1960s; and they do not appear to be even interested in the movement, although their professors often seem obsessed by it. They will not mutiny because generally they will be a less revolutionary, more conservative group. They will be used to intense competition and conclude that mutiny only wrecks your chance at getting ahead. Many of the others will not revolt because of religious values. They will create all sorts of new and complicated arrangements with their education and with their spouses or girl friends or boy friends to the point where it may all be unclassifiably fluxy. But they will expect the institutions and the laws of the society to be responsive to their variety. They may truly be pluralistic and unclassifiable. The notion of lifelong learning as an enlightened position usually associated with increased leisure will not be the way things work out. There will be lifelong learning but that will be because of the necessities brought about by changing jobs and information obsolescence than by genuine love of learning. They will be assertive rather than aggressive—the days of revolution of the young are over—and use the system, tolerate it, but never seek to overthrow it. They will recognize that the system is basically civilized and civilizing, and they will develop a healthier respect for machines than any other generation before them. The prospect of voting for an IBM computer to be president of the U.S. in the year 2000 may be both more realistic and attractive than voting for a female minority figure; and offer more hope for sanity than any of the human candidates. In short, increasingly in the future and particularly with adolescence as a cutting-edge chronological culture, technology, like democracy, may turn out to be the last great hope for humanity.

The Future of the Family

by

Donald R. Raichle

"I remember Mama," Kathryn Forbes told us a generation ago. She also remembered Papa and her brother and her sisters and Uncle Chris and the others, of course, but most of all she remembered Mama. Kathryn Forbes's work is one of the widely known celebrations of the bonding between mother and child, the bonding that the historian Edward Shorter has seen as the hallmark of the modern family as it evolved out of medieval Europe. But Forbes's celebration of motherhood was also, however unintentionally, an act of farewell; it honored the past rather than delineated the future. Mother, God bless her, will still be with us in the future, but the overwhelming role she played in the family, dominating the emotional life of the child, rested on social conditions and attitudes that have already begun to erode and in all probability will continue to erode in the future.

In part that role rested on an increasingly unacceptable view of women which saw them as subordinate, not really equal to the role of work or the reins of power when compared to her helpmeet. Female intellect, it was thought, lagged in comparison to the male, although it was deemed of sufficient competence to manage the household and the children under the watchful eye of husband and father. Moreover, increasingly in the nineteenth century this creature with the insubstantial intellect was also seen as possessed of a loftier moral nature, purer than that of her male counterpart—even unencumbered with a sexual appetite—and more religious, closer to God, if not in understanding then in spirituality. That was the romantic gossamer that made up Mother's robes; it has little to do with the blue jeans or the pants suit that she wears today on Sunday if she won't be home until Monday.

If woman is not to be subordinate, she must be economically independent. It has taken two hundred years in our industrial societies to develop mass acceptance of the respectability of women in the work force, but that day is here and the home of Kathryn Forbes's childhood is no longer representative and grows increasingly less so. In the United States, for example, not even a fifth of the families are made up of

Donald R. Raichle is a professor of history at Kean College of New Jersey, Union, New Jersey. He has done much research on the history of the family and gives a course entitled "The Private Life of the American People."

the father who works, the mother who stays home and takes care of the children. And of that fifth, one-third of the mothers plan to enter the job market. Mother will be little more visible to the children than father has been in the past.

As mother, in her new role, shifts away from the family, father moves closer to it. It is no longer considered unmanly to push a baby carriage, take the two o'clock bottle-feeding, or change diapers. Fathers become increasingly supportive and nurturant. Papa intuitively makes his bid to be remembered by some future Kathryn Forbes equally with Mama. Even when he does not, Mama does not go back to her old role. She has a competing model: Nora, in Ibsen's *The Doll's House*, who determined that her first debt was to herself and that until she had herself sorted out, the children could go hang. The contrast between Forbes's Mama and Ibsen's Nora illustrates both the joys and the penalties of individualism. The heroic quality in the romantic conception of Mother derives not so much from her piety and her purity as from her selflessness, and the sure knowledge she gave her children that they were the center of the world. Remembering Mama is the remembrance of the one person who, more than any other, liberally and without stint, nurtures in the child the belief in his own importance. And, as Eugene O'Neill has so often reminded us, even when she failed to live up to those expectations the searing pain of her failure did nothing to diminish the vision of the Mother-that-ought-to-have-been.

If the burden of those giant expectations were not too great to bear in the past, they have become so. Modern woman is presently deep in a very human dilemma. To the extent that she devotes herself to her own individualism and her career, she becomes more like her husband and the father of her children, dividing her interests, her loyalties, and her time. This is not to say women cannot and do not and will not have careers and families; many can and do and, no doubt, more will. Women with outside interests may be far better capable of coping with child-rearing than those who are sheltered from the outside world. But the image of mother remembered will be quite different. Many women who now cope successfully with this problem pay the price in stress, and as more women flow into the job market there is little reason to expect that the stress will decrease, especially with the growing number of those who aspire to climb the career ladder, where the strain is most intense. As woman achieves egalitarian status with her man, among the heads that will lose their crowns is that of Mama herself. More powerful in the outer world, more independent as concerns her own destiny, she will not be described by the historian of the future as the center of the family.

Trends already in progress thus promise a sharply limited role for mother while others, no doubt, will take shape to reduce it further. The child-care center, the multiple or group marriages, the rising divorce rate take their toll already. Alvin Toffler sees, in addition, a weakening of motherhood through the development of advanced biological techniques. The implantation of the egg from one female to another—indeed, the development of the embryo *in vitro*—may shatter biological ties, raising complex questions about the very meaning of the word mother. Through implantation of the embryo, one woman may give birth to the child of another. Who is the mother in this case? Precisely what the emotional effects of such a practice may be would be difficult to predict, but there is little hope that it would intensify the attachment of the mother to the child. Should the development of embryos *in vitro* make birth itself unnecessary, then couples might have children at any age, postponing families until after retirement. These circumstances might bring some renaissance of mother, who with career behind her, may choose to make child or children a full-time occupation. Of course, even here, her sexagenarian husband (septuagenarian? octogenarian?) may choose the same thing, so mother may have a formidable rival.

Whatever the fate of mother in the future, we may be sure that the concept of family will become more diffuse, more wide-ranging as the family itself develops a multiplicity of both form and function. Nothing can be predicted about the family with more assurance than that the traditional view of father-the-breadwinner and mother-the-homebody-bringing-up-the-children has had its monopoly broken. Even the continental attempt to restore the pattern of large families via governmental subsidy may be seen as a last hurrah rather than as the shape of the future, although it may add another facet to the varying types of the family. Simply to run through these variations as they exist now marks the degree to which a single pattern has become obsolete as a model for the family. Married couples with children, married couples without children, unmarried couples, single-individual households, single-parent households, plural marriages, contain within themselves other patterns. Meanwhile, behavior equally shows variety. In addition to the ancient practice of clandestine adultery, there has been an increasing development of adultery known to the other partner, who may either tolerate or even approve it. "Swinging" is the boldest development along these lines. Here both parties to a marriage engage in violating what has been the most primal taboo in the Judaeo-Christian heritage, not only with the approval of the other, but perhaps under the family roof and in view of each other. Whatever view one may take of the desirability and of the morality of the recent trends, there can be no denying the exploration of new marital forms and behavior. Legal forms have already yielded to the new mores, so that law like religion no longer seeks a single standard in shaping the behavior of society.

Among those who take the view that sex is basically recreational, there are those who see the only bars to full enjoyment to be lack of technique and the Puritan predilection for not allowing anyone to have too good a time. If this were true, one might look forward to an end of anything like the monogamous family. But, of course, the matter is far more complex. Already, the campus, which in the last few years has surrendered its authority *in loco parentis*, has sent up warning signals received from the students themselves that thorough-going permissiveness works its own havoc on many of the young. Both recent psychology and ancient tradition caution that there are always limits—however they may vary from one people to another—within which the game can be played. History is constantly reorganizing the specific rules as well as the attitudes and the societal conditions on which these are based. In our time these rules change with lightning speed, leaving vast numbers reared in a more inflexible past in the trauma of inability and unwillingness to adjust. Yet the difficulties of adjustment should not blind us to the fact that what we are watching is a reordering of the rules, not an abandonment of rules. Once again it is being perceived in a new context that the psychic need for order in human relations has not been repealed by the sexual revolution of the 1960s. Marriage and the family are by no means in decline in our time. On the contrary, the twilight of authority has opened wider possibilities for people to demand of the marital and the familial situation more of personal fulfillment and mutual self-expression than could be hoped in an earlier, more rigid period. The increase of divorce has not reduced the number of marrieds; it has meant a movement to serial monogamy. The young woman who, filling out an application for employment, paused momentarily at the line which asked for marital status and then wrote "unremarried" pointed to one direction of the future.

We must not necessarily assume that divorces will continue to rise in a straight line, that sexual activity be increasingly promiscuous or casual, or that the family grows obsolescent. On the contrary, Lawrence F. Stone and others have shown that changes in the family are cyclical rather than linear. Wide though the range may be, there are limits to change. Despite the strains and the frustration of the monogamous life, the exploration of new ways does not necessarily lead to the conclusion that there are more rewarding alternatives. In addition to the needs of the psyche, in itself more demanding than the body, there are also the influences of the changing societal conditions that make new demands of institutions such as the family. Should there be a swing toward the strengthening of authority, a climate less hospitable to sexual freedom might well develop. This could take the form of political repression; there is no guarantee that democracy in the future is assured. But it also might come in the form of a social consensus, a folk wisdom, that the confrontation of the sexes fares better within some limits. Where this is left to voluntary compliance, freedom might still be reconciled with it.

Communications: Connecting Ourselves Together

FUTURECOM: The Human Future in Communications

by

Lane Jennings

Communication is a mind-linking process—the transfer or spread of ideas from one memory or consciousness into another. In the past century, a host of new technologies have been employed to help human minds communicate more easily across the barriers of time and space; and in the 1980s, even newer and more fantastic technologies will be widely available. But technology is only one part of the communication process—and not the most essential part at that.

The future of communication in the 1980s, and beyond, may depend far less on innovations in technology than on changes in *language*—in the sounds and symbols people use for conveying information; changes in *values*—in the range and subtlety of the information we regard as *worth* communicating; and changes in our choice of *communication partners*—in the other intelligences we wish to exchange ideas *with*.

The Changing World of Words

Change is the natural state of any living language. New words and expressions are constantly coming into fashion and going out of style. But the language changes that *last* are those that make communication easier or more effective for a significant group of language users. One way to approach the language of the future, then, is to look at the problem areas of language today—to ask where existing words and phrases are failing to convey ideas accurately, and consider what new ideas and experiences people may need to communicate in the years ahead.

Of the many consciousness-raising movements at work in American society today, none is having a more direct impact on language than the Women's Movement. Stereotypes embedded in the English language are among the prime targets of those who seek to bring an end to all forms of discrimination based on sex.

To avoid such potential linguistic mindtraps, a number of sexually neutral terms—particularly for job titles and forms of address—are

---

Lane Jennings is Research Director of the World Future Society and Editor of the World Future Society Bulletin.

302

coming into use. In the latest edition of the U.S. government's official *Dictionary of Occupational Titles*, for instance, many familiar but gender-specific job categories have been given new unisex labels: not *steward* or *stewardess*, but *flight attendant*; not *mailman* but *letter-carrier*; not *busboy*, but *diningroom attendant*, not *seamstress*, but *custom sewer*, not *governess*, but *child mentor*, etc.

Other sex-related vocabulary changes becoming increasingly common include "humanity" in place of "mankind," "artificial" not "manmade," and "husband and wife" rather than "man and wife" (soon, perhaps, simply "spouse and spouse").

One language innovation to look for in future English is a common gender pronoun to replace the awkward "he or she" in expressions that could apply equally to men and women. Such pronouns already exist in several other languages including Chinese, Japanese, and Hungarian. Suggestions for a unisex English pronoun include "e," "s/he," "hesh," "co," "tey," "ve," "he'er," "thon," and "jhe," with such possible possessive forms as "cos," and "his'er." None of these suggestions has yet gained any real popularity though, and unless some new standard is established soon (perhaps by a best-selling novel, or a popular television series) phrases such as "Will everyone please stand up and stretch *their* legs" will most likely become standard English by default.

New Words, New Language

Language, like nature, abhors a vacuum. Whenever a new invention or experience comes along, new words and expressions are devised or adopted to describe and analyze it in detail. Today, we need very few words to discuss outer space. But if the space program expands in the next two decades to include orbiting factories, permanent colonies, or settlements on the moon, many new words and phrases will be added to the language. For example, we can expect new words to describe the different sensations of varying degrees of weightlessness encountered by construction gangs in space, and new direction-descriptors like "sunward" or "starward" to replace the earth-linked terms "up and down," "east and west," etc. Other words and phrases may keep their form, but change in meaning. Today, "space-sickness" is used like "sea-sickness" to describe the nausea associated with rapid motion in three dimensions. But in another generation it could come to be used like "homesickness" to mean "nostalgia for space."

Just as new inventions and experiences create a need for new words and expressions, changing political and economic conditions on a global scale—including increased awareness of problems and opportunities that transcend national boundaries—produce growing incentives for the adoption of a world language. Several languages have been especially devised for this purpose. But even the most successful of these, Esperanto, is understood and used regularly by only a few hundred thousand people— a tiny minority of the earth's population of four billion plus.

True international languages do exist, however, and are used by millions of people every day. Music notation is one of these, mathematics is another. Each is useful, but can only express a limited range of information in a fairly specialized area.

Surprisingly perhaps, the closest thing to an all-purpose global language is English. With over 300 million native speakers worldwide, English ranks second (behind Chinese) in the number of people who use it as their principal medium of communication. Moreover, while most Chinese-speakers are found in and near mainland China itself, significant English-speaking population centers are located on every continent. The government of the People's Republic of China recently began a widespread campaign urging its citizens to study English as a second language. If, during the 1980s, a sizeable percentage of China's huge population were to swell the total of English speakers on the planet, it could prove decisive in making English the "language of Earth."

But the logic of numbers alone will not decide this issue. For political and cultural reasons many groups object to using English; and, indeed, the charge of "cultural imperialism" implied in the adoption of English as an international language cannot be ignored. Certainly, if English *does* emerge as the "language of Earth," it will not be the dialect spoken today in England or the United States, but a modified form incorporating many changes in grammar and pronunciation, as well as a much wider vocabulary.

English is already a composite language, built up of Greek, Latin, Germanic and Celtic root words, with additions from practically every other language on earth. In the past, the influence of French was particularly strong. In the future, we can expect a host of new additions to English from Arabic, Chinese, Spanish (particularly in the United States), and quite possibly from African and Southeast Asian languages, as the nations of the Third World increase their influence on world affairs. The adoption of a standard phonetic spelling (like the new Roman alphabetization of Chinese) would remove a major barrier to students of English, and could also serve to differentiate "global" English from the "native" dialects used in Britain, Canada, Australia, or the United States.

Body Talk

Moving away from words, there is the language of the body itself to be explored. Movements, posture, facial expressions, and hand gestures all contribute to communication; and the same movement may have very different meanings in different cultures. Recognition of such differences is already beginning to have an effect on the teaching of language. Laurence Wylie, who recently retired as Professor of French Civilization at Harvard University, has said: "I think of communication as a dance between two people. Sounds are often just the music to accompany the communication that takes place." Just as listening to audiotapes has helped students learn to reproduce the melody and cadence of a native speaker, videotapes may be used in the language labs of the 1980s to teach students the "dance" of hand gestures and facial expressions that individuals from a particular culture use to reenforce (or sometimes, to undercut) their words.

Even among speakers of the same language, such silent messages as a raised eyebrow or a worried look contribute a great deal to understanding. A major weakness of electronic communication media like the telephone and, more recently, the "on line" computer networks, is that they allow no possibility for direct eye contact, touch or smell—all of which do much to establish a framework for interpreting information received from another person. It is easier to lie on the telephone than face to face, and easier still to lie by computer. Despite rising travel costs, and widespread availability of electronic communications devices in the 1980s, the impersonality of "meeting by machine" combined with nagging doubts about who one is really talking to, and who else may be secretly "listening in," could prove a major stumbling block to public acceptance of computer conferencing, electronic banking, and other much heralded "advances" of the information age.

Protecting the Freedom to Lie

Deliberate confusion or ambiguity is something people seldom think of as a facet of communication. But in fact, it is often useful, and sometimes absolutely necessary, to be *imprecise* when we communicate.

Diplomacy, salesmanship, polite conversation, courtship, humor, and a great deal of poetry all rely on double meanings, puns, innuendo, sound effects, partial suppression of information and outright lies. Social critics from Confucius to Edwin Newman have inveighed against the *careless* use of language. But must one agree, with Plato, that *deliberate deception* is a criminal act?

Efforts to ban certain forms of advertising, or to limit public access to pornography, or to suppress inflammatory political tracts all represent attempts to improve communication by protecting people from being misled by distortions of reality—from mischievous or self-serving partial truths. But if we become too successful at protecting people against the possibility of being deceived by language, we risk denying them the chance to be surprised, delighted, or entertained by it as well.

Governmental and social limits to free expression will remain a major influence on the use (and misuse) of communication technologies such as television, satellite broadcasting, and international exchange of data by computer through the 1980s and probably well beyond. Language itself is vulnerable to censorship and implicit biases. But whatever the standards may be by which one nation or cultural group distinguishes "responsible" from "irresponsible" language use, genuine improvement in future *communication* (closer mind to mind contact as opposed to more efficient exchange of coded messages between machines) will require increased awareness of, and sensitivity to, the standards and expectations of other nations and cultures—and perhaps more emphasis in schools on learning how to evaluate and test for meaning what we read and hear.

Meeting Mind to Mind

Ultimately, sounds, symbols, and gestures are all nonessential to the basic goal of communication, which is: to get ideas out of one mind and into another. Experiments in telepathy—direct mind to mind com-

305

munication—have been conducted for many years now, with results that impress some researchers but not others. But whatever the state of the art may be today, no one projecting alternative futures for communication should overlook what enormous changes might occur if reliable methods of telepathic communication are perfected.

For example, if all human beings can be trained to communicate telepathically, spoken languages might rapidly disappear. If thoughts can be recorded, writing and sound recording too might be abandoned, and a new form of art, "dreamcasting," might emerge to take the place of literature and music as we know them. If telepathy can take place across great distances, what need will remain for elaborate electronic message relay systems such as the telephone?

On the other hand, it may be that only certain gifted individuals can communicate mind to mind on a regular basis. If so, they might become living transmitters, performing a function in tomorrow's society similar to that of the village scribe or local telegraph office in earlier days.

But human minds need not communicate only with one another. There are also animals. John Lilly's research with dolphins, porpoises, and whales since the 1960s has convinced him that these creatures have a brain capacity at least as great as that of humans, and possess a system of sound signals for communicating that deserves to be called a true language. The value of attempting to communicate with these intelligent sea mammals, Lilly believes, lies not only in what they can tell us about their impressions of human beings and their surroundings in the sea, but also what they remember of the past. As Lilly puts it: "They've been around for an estimated 25 million years with a brain size equal to . . . ours. I want to find out if they have sagas, teaching stories, histories. . . . It will take a lot of work of course before they can tell us stories we can understand. [And] they may laugh at us." Not all marine biologists share Lilly's confidence in the intelligence and language use of cetaceans; but research is still going on at several locations.

Less controversial (and, so far, more successful) experiments have been undertaken with apes and monkeys. In the mid 1960s, Allen and Beatrice Gardner, using Ameslan, the American sign language for the deaf, succeeded in teaching a chimpanzee named Washoe to recognize and use a vocabulary of some 150 different signs. Since then, more than a dozen other chimps have been taught Ameslan.

Francine Patterson of Stanford University has taught a gorilla named Koko to use a vocabulary of over 375 signs in ways that cover almost the entire range of human communication. Koko uses sign language to describe her emotional state (happy or sad), to refer to events in the past or the future, to make jokes, to rhyme, and even tells lies on occasion to avoid blame for misbehavior.

Despite these impressive achievements, communication between animals and humans may have its limits. Fictional characterizations of talking or thinking animals, from *Aesop's Fables* to *Watership Down*, generally assume that animals have the same emotions and values as civilized human beings. From what we know of nature, this seems doubtful. Suppose we could in some way exchange ideas with a giant squid, or a spider, or an ordinary house cat. At what level could we share or comprehend each other's life experience? Could we tolerate their attitudes and values without prejudice? Considering how easily "civilized" explorers have been shocked by the beliefs and practices of other human cultures, the outlook for a "peaceable kingdom" built on interspecies communication in the future is not entirely promising.

The Ultimate Future of Communication

With this sobering thought in mind, we must ask ourselves one final question: What would it be like to encounter a wholly alien intelligence? "Little green men" or space-suited invaders are one thing; but what if there are other races of intelligent beings in the universe vastly larger than ourselves, or so unlike us in other ways that we could not recognize them as "alive" at all? Science-fiction writers have scarcely begun to explore all the possibilities for a future involving human/alien contact.

For communication to be possible at all, some common system of signals or language must be found. Mathematics and music are two possible languages that have already been used for this purpose. The first message from earth was launched in 1972 aboard the spacecraft Pioneer 10. It consisted of a small metal plaque showing the outline of a man and a woman together with a schematic rendering of the spacecraft itself drawn to scale, and a symbolic diagram of the solar system. A second spacecraft of this type, designed to fly past the outer planets and then leave the solar system on an endless trajectory through deep space, was launched five years later in 1977. Called "Voyager 2," this craft carried a special recording of "the sounds of earth," which include animal and nature sounds, spoken greetings in 100 languages, and examples of music from many different ages and cultures.

The chances of either message being found are far smaller than those of a letter in a bottle, tossed overboard in mid-ocean, ever reaching shore. But if nothing else, these two space messages serve the purpose of protecting our past.

Whether humans foolishly destroy their own planet, or survive as a race until the sun expands to reabsorb the solar system six billion years from now, we can still boast of one small triumph for communication: using language, art, and music, we have left a memento of our passing in the universe.

The Emergence of Ethnotronic Systems in the 1980s

by

Earl C. Joseph and Arthur M. Harkins

Ethnotronics is the new field of studying and designing inorganic electronic devices that have interactive "cultural" characteristics, shared with people and/or other systems.

The core of ethnotronic systems is the unit that allows information to be learned and stored so that it can be put to use to amplify human (or other) system functions. Silicon "chips" or microprocessors are the most-used information units today.

Ethnotronic devices are already being marketed in many countries. While they are still at very early stages of evolution, they have already had significant impacts on people. In the years of the 1980s, the impacts of ethnotronic devices will grow exponentially.

Ethnotronic systems allow ordinary people to carry around with them low-cost data and information appliances in the form of calculators, language translators, timepieces, memo and reminder devices, music playing and composing machines, and game devices. Larger systems are also becoming available; these include home microcomputers, programmable or "smart" ovens and television recorders, and "convivial" intruder alert and discouragement systems. Automobiles are also becoming ethnotronic systems as they are designed to be more capable of self-diagnosis and fail-safe actions. Convivial, accident-avoiding cars may not be far off.

Such appliances, possessing communication capabilities meshed with computer intelligence, will establish an ethnotronic culture in which people will communicate with appliances, appliances will initiate conversations with people to make the person they are amplifying "currently aware," and appliances will "talk" with other machines in order to amplify the person they serve.

Further breakthroughs in mass storage technology in the coming decade will see the creation of very large data bases that will be within the

Earl C. Joseph is Staff Scientist-Futurist at Sperry Univac, St. Paul, Minnesota.

Arthur M. Harkins is Director of the Graduate Futures Program,University of Minnesota, Minneapolis, Minnesota. He is a sociologist and anthropologist.

308

economic reach of even small organizations. Decreases in mass storage costs of one or two orders of magnitude will profoundly affect business and society by providing faster movement into the ethnotronic society; greater economic productivity; a movement to the electronic office of the future; real-time, life-long educational systems; and ethnotronic systems based on knowledge, as distinct from data or information. Such advances are indisputably in store for the 1980s. These projections may, in fact, err on the side of being too conservative.

Changes in Technology and Hardware

The development of such revolutionary technology, measured in picoseconds and submicrons and characterized by embedded components, will accelerate in the 1980s. Low-cost, high-performance component computers will operate 10 to 100 times faster than today's fastest maxicomputer. With very high performance, multiple-component computers, computational speed will increase more than a thousand- to a millionfold. Not only will speed increase but, at the same time, cost will drop dramatically. Data communications costs will decrease to one to ten percent of current costs, and a large growth in use is forecast—with the result that a typical business may actually find itself spending more for data communications.

More important than any of the new hardware, however, will be the change in the way the average person perceives technology. Much of the technology that we deal with today is essentially problem-producing, but it need not always be like that. Science-fiction writers, stubborn optimists, have given us many descriptions of an era of convivial technology; that era will soon be a reality. By embedding component computers into factory and office machinery, automobiles, and so on, we will be able to make those machines ethnotronic and, therefore, easier and more comfortable to use. Technology is moving inexorably in that direction. The surface of tiny silicon chips will contain hundreds of thousands, even millions, of very fast circuits in submicron geometries. When we embed the tremendously complex logic of such microengines into everyday machinery in order to ease its interface with people, we will be bringing technology closer to convivial symbiosis with people and with their environment. The spread of convivial ethnotronic systems will lay the foundation for a world from which everyone—rich and poor, expert and nonexpert, highly educated and educationally deprived—can benefit.

The point at which we will see technology moving decisively toward this better world will occur in the 1980s. We can be sure of that by simply basing our projections on the leading edge of today's technology. Much of what we now perceive as steady, evolutionary development will in retrospect be seen as the radical, revolutionary change it really is.

The energy crisis, by raising fuel prices to hardship levels even in the U.S., will force us to seek every means, including ethnotronic technology, of using energy more efficiently. Chips will be installed in automobiles and other vehicles to wring the utmost value from every gallon of gasoline. Information and computing power will be rapidly dispersed in order to reduce the distances workers must travel to their places of employment. Although the dispersal of chips will favor the proliferation of micros in the 1980s, it would be rash to conclude that the days of the mainframe are numbered. By the 1990s, when multiple systems are integrated onto wafers, there could be a resurgence of macrocomputers (macro in the sense of power, not physical size). Studies show that as more computer power is dispersed to remote locations, more power is required at the central nodes to handle traditionally centralized functions and to support the remote systems and devices.

The Calculator's "Children"

In the last few years, the hand-held calculator has brought error-free mathematics within the reach of millions of reasonably nimble-fingered people. Consider how a set of four or five basic computing routines, added to the keyboard and simple electronic display of the calculator, could amplify the intelligence of its owner. Sets of basic computing routines could easily be provided for different professions or activities, giving us the ethnotronic manager machine, the ethnotronic doctor machine, or the ethnotronic artist machine. The possibilities are almost endless.

Each machine would evolve into an ever smarter version every three or four years with the addition of communications capabilities through an ordinary telephone, resulting in increased memory, more sophisticated display, and other technical advances. The next step for anyone enjoying the benefits of these ethnotronic machines in his or her work would be to acquire one or more of them to enrich his leisure-time activities.

Software Cast into Hardware, or Solid-State Culture

Throughout the history of computers, each new generation of machines has incorporated more programming problems into hardware architecture. Before the early 1950s, most computers did not have wired multiplication and division, and programmers toiled to code these primitives. In the 1960s, algorithmic primitives such as indexing, floating-point, and square root calculations were built into the architecture. The trend continued in the 1970s with the wiring of such language and control primitives as input-output, high-level, and system primitives. In the 1980s, we can expect to see such applications primitives as management and accounting built into computers. Looking ahead to the 1990s, we can predict the incorporation of robotic primitives.

Future primitives (or hard software) will either be incorporated into ethnotronic architecture, provided as optional adjuncts to computer systems, or offered as such special-purpose, stand-alone units as payroll machines or electronic filing systems.

The Ethnotronic Office of the Future

This concept has received a great deal of attention recently. Intelligent typewriters, filing systems, and data banks, as well as smart sales and accounting machines, will create an environment in which workers will become steadily more productive. In the mid-1980s, technology will make widespread real-time problem-solving possible through knowledge, query, and dialogue. The logical extension of this trend will, in the late 1980s, bring us energy- and knowledge-oriented processing with remote offices, offices of machines, management information systems on a wafer. We can expect, and must begin to plan for, sweeping changes in business and society by the end of the decade.

Conclusion

The computer population will greatly increase in the coming decade. Old computers will not fade away; they will be joined by many new ones. A significant part of this increase will be invisible and will consist of component computers embedded into other machines. Computers will be the nuts and bolts of other systems. Does this mean that data processing management will be a shrinking, perhaps even vanishing, profession? Certainly not—except for some application areas. For those applications that we can almost completely automate, and thus cast into hardware, data processing management will not be required. On the other hand (a phrase much favored by forecasters), as computers become smaller, less expensive, and more capable, they will be more widely used and will, therefore, need more support services—indicating a need for more data processing management.

As we have tried to show in this article, the ethnotronic developments of the next 10 years will immeasurably alter the structure and face of the office, the factory, and ultimately our entire society. It is not too soon to begin analyzing the probable social impact of these developments in order to ensure that ethnotronic systems are directed toward desirable ends and that their benefits are maximized. The decade we are now entering could be a Golden Age of humanitarian technology, a decade in which the quality of life for all the world's peoples is dramatically improved.

A Global
Voluntary Information Network:
The Most Hopeful Global Collective
Means

by

Yoneji Masuda

Introduction

The most fundamental causes of difficulties blocking the solution of various global issues are: (1) aggrandizement of state power and economic power of private enterprises; (2) failure of parliamentary democracy to function properly; (3) the widening gap between industrial countries and developing countries; and (4) diversification of human values and abuse of personal freedoms. Therefore, no conventional means are sufficient to solve global issues. For this purpose, three new transformational means are required to be created.

Principle of Synergetic Feed-forward

The first new transformational means is "synergetic feed-forward." Feedforward means control in moving toward a goal, and viewed from the standpoint of the subject of action, it means a controlled development of the current external environment to change it to a more desirable environment. There are two contrasting kinds of feed-forward systems, competitive and synergetic. The former is the most typical feed-forward system in the present industrial society. But in the future post-industrial society, the latter will become an essential and effective feed-forward system.

The competitive feed-forward means that the subject of action and the external environment compete with each other in the feed-forward process.

In industrial society, private enterprises carry on business activities freely. The result has been that this free competition has meant the development of the national economy as a whole, and provided national

Yoneji Masuda is President of the Institute for the Information Society, Tokyo, Japan.

economic welfare. This free competition in the micro-enterprise economy has functioned effectively, without conflicting, on the whole, with the orderless macro-national economy, because the law of price, Adam Smith's invisible hand, has guided and adjusted business activity. Behind Adam Smith's law of price, however, was the tacit economic assumption that resources are limitless and that, if demand expands, the production of goods will go on expanding indefinitely.

But this economic assumption is now proving to be invalid: Smith's invisible hand is not functioning as effectively as in the past, because we have begun to recognize that resources are finite.

The synergetic feed-forward means that the subject of action and the external environment are in a mutually complementary relationship and act together to reach a common goal. To support this synergistic feedforward in the post-industrial society, the fundamental factors will be globalism and spaceship thought.

The first basic characteristic of this synergestic feed-forward will be the common goal, based on common awareness and common group needs that do not conflict with the goals of individuals. The second is that action will be voluntary. There must be no coercion. The third is that individuals and groups will cooperate actively to attain their common goal; this cooperation must be dynamic, not static, in methods and organization. The fourth characteristic is self-control. Individuals and groups will voluntarily and continuously control their own action as they move toward the common goal. These are the basic principles of synergetic feed-forward.

The Call for Participatory Democracy

The second new transformational means is "participatory democracy." Present parliamentary democracies and international organizations already have the potential to make appropriate political decisions. The reason for encouraging participatory democracy is that many of the questions that we have to decide are matters that concern all mankind–global issues that know no national boundaries, and the settlement of which directly affects everyone.

Take two examples: the question of the population explosion, and shortages of natural resources and energy. These diverse global issues override national borders, and while the activities of the United Nations and other international organizations through international cooperation will have an important role to play in resolving them, by far the more important role will be the voluntary cooperation of all citizens in resolving such global questions. Citizens must exercise restraint in their own lives. The question of the population explosion is a problem that can only be democratically resolved if throughout the world there are voluntary restraints accepted in the people's way of life, by which they restrict themselves to a basic replacement rate averaging about two children per couple. The only way to get cooperation in adopting such a principle is to secure the participation and agreement of citizens in working for such solutions.

To enable this participatory democracy of citizens to function effectively, it will be necessary to set the following six basic principles, which would have to be strictly and faithfully observed.

First Principle: All citizens would have to participate in decision-making or at least, the maximum number.

All citizens interested directly or indirectly in any question proposed would have the right to participate directly in this system, irrespective of race, religion, age, sex or occupation. No democratic solution would be possible without the participation of the teen-age generation on such matters as smoking, education, sex, and others.

Second Principle: The spirit of synergy and mutual assistance should permeate the whole system.

To ensure the smooth management of the system of direct participation, and so that it may be fully effective, the basic attitude of all participating in this system should be inspired by the spirit of synergy and mutual assistance. "Synergy" means that each person cooperates and acts from his or her own standpoint in solving common problems, and "mutual assistance" implies readiness to voluntarily sacrifice one's own interests for the common good, to level out the disadvantages and sacrifices to other persons and/or groups.

Third Principle: All relevant information should be available to the public.

When a question is to be resolved with the participation of all the citizens, all relevant information must be made public.

It is necessary that the public be informed not only on factual information, but also on all the possible social, economic and other effects on the living of the people. Only in this way can each individual understand the problems in which one is interested, not one-sidedly or short-range, but with a broad, long-range perspective.

In addition, people will be expected to provide information voluntarily to contribute to a solution of any question. In the information society, it will be rather this kind of information provided by citizens that will play the major role as basic data for the solution of various problems.

Fourth Principle: All benefits received and sacrifices made by citizens should be distributed equitably among them.

All problems that require direct participation for their solution are complex by their nature, and the way they are solved would affect different people differently, depending on their place in life and the circumstances in which they live.

The balance to be maintained in such cases would be by combinations of the various benefits and sacrifices, determined by the nature and degree of effects on individuals and groups in different places and positions, a balanced combination achieved with a long-range perspective.

314

Fifth Principle: A solution should be sought by persuasion and agreement.

A decision on the solution of a problem should, in principle, be made by the general agreement of all citizens concerned. Patient efforts will be needed to lead opposing individuals or groups to reach agreement, employing persuasion.

In case there are individuals or groups that, even after tireless persuasion, are still opposed to a proposed solution, a second solution put up by such individuals or groups would have to be adopted, out of respect for a minority view, the condition being, however, that such a solution does not impose hardship on other individuals or groups.

Sixth Principle: Once decided, all citizens would be expected to co-operate in applying the solution.

The principle is that all citizens will be expected to cooperate in the implementation of a solution decided with their participation. This obligation is a corollary to the right to participate directly in policy-making, but it carries with it the expectation of voluntary self-restraint, and should not assume the form of compulsion accompanied by punishment by enforcement of law, as in the present industrial society. Participation in decision-making, and the observance of the decision through voluntary self-restraints are inseparable, and it is on this that a new policy-making system and a new social order will be based in the post-industrial society.

Establishment of Global Voluntary Information Network

The third new transformational means is the establishment of a "Global Voluntary Information Network" (GVIN). The GVIN is an informational network on a global scale formed with voluntary citizens as nodes.

The GVIN has three distinguishing features:
(1) It forms global supra-national informational space.
(2) It is based on voluntary citizens as nodes with common attitudes toward global issues.
(3) The three up-to-date media of information and communication, namely, communication satellites, communication lines (optical fiber cable), and personal computers, are integrated to provide a technical basis for this network.

The following method and procedures would be necessary to solve global issues using the GVIN:

The first step is the gathering of basic data on global issues through voluntary participation of citizens (nodes).

The second step is analysis by neutral specialists, presentation of projections, and early warning.

The third step is study of common solutions through participation of neutral specialists and citizens (nodes) and the reaching of decision on a joint action program.

The fourth step is persuasion work on ordinary citizens and development of global activities among citizens through participatory means.

The fifth step is voluntary joint action by broad sections of global citizens for the solution of global issues.

Four minimum conditions should be needed to realize the GVIN:

(1) Launching of a civil telecommunication satellite and opening of civil relay stations (public utilization at low cost of existing facilities and equipment as the second best means).

(2) Formation of nodes by voluntary citizens with a home computer.

(3) Establishment of regional sub-centers, each consisting of a rather small number of nodes (independent organizations or neutral universities, research institutes, etc.).

(4) Establishment of a global center for the integration of sub-centers (utilization of existing voluntary global institutions such as WFS as an alternative means).

Conclusion

These three new transformational means will bring about a systematic, orderly transformation from the present nationalistic authoritarian competitive society to a global voluntary synergetic society.

In this societal transformation, there will be an emergence of global communities. These will be quite new types of communities instead of traditional local communities. First, communities will be formed by citizens' voluntary action. In the second place, the fundamental bond to bring and bind people together globally will be their common philosophy and goals in day-to-day life; it is the technological base of computer communications networks that will make this possible.

If these principles and procedures are followed, global voluntary synergetic communities will cooperate in solving the problems and crises that are common to all mankind.

316

Computer-Based Human Communication Systems

by

Julian M. Scher

Computer-based human communication systems (CBHCS) have arrived! The 1970s saw their software development and evaluation take place in the research centers and laboratories, and as we embark on a new decade, we are already witnessing the commercialization and public availability of CBHCS. The visions we have had of "electronic cottages" and a "network nation" portend to become a reality within the coming decades. The EIES computerized conferencing system at New Jersey Institute of Technology is an example of such a system, supporting the information transfer and decision-making needs of close to 800 users nationwide and worldwide, as they participate in specialized structures involving task-oriented subsets of the EIES population. We can now enter the planning stages for the support of more specialized communication structures for different application groups of users. Temporal and spatial barriers which heretofore have guided our planning with ordinary communications need not influence our intentions. Our objective here is to examine how CBHCS could influence futuristic trends occurring in two very much intelligence-information-intensive areas:

    i) higher education.

    ii) management and organization.

Higher Education: Some Trends That Will Be Influenced by CBHCS

The dominant trend we shall witness, from the perspective of students who flow through our higher education system, will be the desire for increased student flexibility in merging educational objectives into individualized packages tailored to personal lifestyles and career-intellectual aspirations. The flextime work schedules that have popularized the business market-place in the past decade are making their impact felt in higher education planning. Perhaps the most prominent consequence of this has been the steady increase in external degree programs, which

Julian M. Scher is Associate Professor of Computer Science and Associate Director of the Computerized-Conferencing Center, New Jersey Institute of Technology, Newark, New Jersey.

permit students, through programs of self-study, testing and work-experience, to earn a college degree with minimal (or even zero) time spent physically on a "traditional" campus. While Great Britain's Open University program is probably the best known, other well-known ones include those of California State University, the State University of New York's Regents Program, and Thomas Edison College of New Jersey. So foreboding is the impending growth of external degree programs that one educator, Samuel Dunn, views these as a major contributor to "the case of the vanishing college."

Another consequence of flextime trends in higher education has been the new philosophy of bringing the "college" to a place convenient to the student, rather than bringing the student to a location convenient to the college. This has become a *modus operandi* for numerous graduate-level programs. Our noted colleges and universities are most often located within urban centers, while the student clientele they seek to serve today and in the future are situated in the outlying residential-commercial areas which were the cornfields and swamps of yesteryear. The response of the universities has been that of satellitization—the establishment of off-campus "satellites" in exurbia where the professor will teach on a "simulated" campus. An illustrative extreme of the satellitization phenomenon can be found at Adelphi University, which offers to qualified commuters on the Long Island Railroad numerous classes on the trains, leading to an MBA degree. (This is one instance where the classroom can be late for the student, rather than vice versa!)

A most interesting phenomenon that we may come to witness by the year 2000 will be the movement away from what has been termed the "linear life plan" by Fred Best. Our traditional linear life plan now finds the formal educational years bunched together at the beginning of a person's lifetime, with the middle years focused upon employment endeavors, and the later years consisting primarily of leisure. There are many futurists, such as Best, who believe that this pattern of linearization "is stifling the vibrance and productivity of our lives and perhaps even draining away the productive potential and financial solvency of our society." The alternative lifetime pattern to "linearization" is what Best refers to as a "cyclic life plan," where non-employment time is redistributed through the middle years to allow periods of formal education and leisure in mid-life. These mid-life "sabbaticals" could easily be supported by the general tax revenue base and the social security system, since we are merely redistributing education and retirement from the early and later years, respectively, to the middle years of one's life. The much-heralded mission of higher education as centers for life-long learning could thus become a reality, providing perhaps the salvation for colleges and universities from becoming, as Ronald E. Barnes forecasts, "museums or monuments of irrelevancy."

How does the advent of CBHCS impact these futuristic trends in higher education of flextime scheduling, external degree programs, satellitization and non-linear life-styles? As we examine alternatives to traditional professor-in-the-classroom-on-campus modes of instruction, we must pay careful attention to the dialogue between student and professor, and the multilogue between all the students. If we are to provide a meaningful education, and not just impersonalized training, then we must make each student aware of alternative value systems, thought processes, perspectives and experiences of other students, and seek to foster the inquiry systems of each student. In a nutshell, if higher educational trends lead us away from face-to-face dialogue, then we must be adamant in our support of telecommunication replacements, such as (but not limited to) CBHCS. We note that CBHCS, such as the EIES computerized conferencing system, supports the all-important flextime philosophy through its inherent general asynchronous communication structure. The most vehement criticisms of external degree programs and satellitization, we report, stress the loss of personal contact between professor and student as well as student-student contact; these criticisms, we feel, could best be satisfied through carefully designed CBHCS.

While some may view the non-linearization of higher education as overly idealistic, since parental and home responsibilities are also focused in the middle years, we note that CBHCS will allow the adult to remain home, albeit in his Tofflerian "electronic cottage," to pursue further education (and even continued part-time employment in an information-intensive industry). The movement towards non-linearization will, we suspect, be a slow process. But the satellitization and external degree programs are present-day phenomena, and we do see the need for CBHCS to support these trends and enhance the intellectual excitement that could, and should, occur for students studying in a non-campus mode.

We have focused upon educational trends, from the perspective of student desires. Will college administrators actively support them, and will they view CBHCS as a necessary component? To answer this, we must identify futures that university administrators are currently contemplating. We are all aware of the projected "flattening" of university enrollment in the '80s, due to the decline of the post-war baby boom clientele. But the decline will not be uniformly distributed amongst all colleges. As a consequence of escalating costs, the price of a four-year college education by the year 1990 has been projected at $82,000 for a private college and $47,000 at a publicly-supported college (these figures being based on a 6% inflation rate). Dunn forecasts that, by the year 2000, 25% of our currently existing liberal arts colleges will disappear. Even more dramatic are the forecasts of Pyke, who, using substitution analysis, shows that the substitution of publicly supported colleges for privately supported colleges is well under way and, by the turn of the century, the number of privately supported colleges could drop by a staggering 89%, while, at the same time, enrollment in publicly supported institutions could jump by 58%.

To counter these trends, university administrators will have to seek student clientele from non-traditional sources, and be more cognizant of, and supportive of, changing lifestyles. The concept of "bringing the college to the student" could very well become the key survival strategy for many colleges. Satellitization, flextime, external degrees and non-linearization could become the buzzwords of colleges as they react to projected enrollment trends. Smaller institutions could maintain viable Master's and Doctoral programs without the "critical mass" requirement by making productive use of CBHCS in linking together networks of scholars at different institutions. Such a linkage has already been demonstrated by the National Science Foundation-sponsored Operational Trials program on the EIES computerized conferencing system. Most critically, though, we shall see a greater emphasis on the part of higher education in becoming centers for life-long learning, a goal which, we maintain, implicitly mandates that CBHCS become more publicly accessible in the coming years.

Management and Organizations: Some Trends That CBHCS Will Impact

The buzzwords that one hears these days at management and organization conferences are "office automation," the "paperless office," and "decision support systems." A decade or so ago, the buzzwords then in place included "time-sharing systems" and "management information systems." Yes, the buzzwords have changed, but the changes, we maintain, are the result of a long-term evolutionary trend, whose realization could result in significantly dramatic changes in how we view our organizations and employment practices.

The advent of time-sharing systems and management information systems (MIS) in the late '60s brought forecasts of every manager having a computer terminal on his desk, with quick access to numerous data-based report-generating systems. During the '70s, time-sharing and MIS aptly demonstrated that we can enhance the *efficiency* of management and organizations by providing, on a real-time basis, automated access to information. The emphasis, however, has almost universally been on the automation and effectiveness component, i.e., systems were judged on how much time they saved and how they made individuals in organizations more efficient. In contrast, we believe that the '80s will see systems being judged on their *effectiveness* in bringing about better decision-making on the part of *groups* of people. Basic work in this area started in the '70s under the rubric of Decision Support Systems, whose design philosophy called for the in-depth examination of decision-making activities of the individual manager, and the identification of those actiities whose performance could be significantly enhanced through the introduction of interactive computer-based supportive tools. Present decision support systems focus on what are termed semi-structured decisional tasks of managers, i.e., decisions where neither the computer system/model alone or the intuition of the manager alone will produce as effective a decision as the two in a synergistic combination.

The advance we see taking place in the '80s is that of what we term Distributed Decision Support Systems. In such systems we have a *supportee* (decision-making group) aided by *supporters* (computer models plus data bases plus human information resources) whose *resident supporter base* will be a set of (distributed) computers and the *supporter-supportee interface* being a sophisticated CBHCS, such as the EIES computerized conferencing network. Distributed Decision Support Systems are aimed at the effectiveness of decision-making, and recognize

320

that the key to the entire spectrum of decisional tasks, from semi-structured to unstructured, is to have an active supportee base consisting of not only computer-based models and data bases, but the active input and dialogue of other human beings.

Office automation is a concept that means many things to many people. All generally acknowledge that it is a medium to enhance human capabilities in the office place. In an attempt to better focus the U.S. government's approach to office automation, the National Archives and Records Service (NARS), Office of Records and Information Management, recently proposed the following definition for office automation:

> *Office Automation is the use of information processing technology in an office environment to create, process, store, retrieve, use, and communicate information to improve the performance of managerial, professional, technical, administrative, and clerical tasks.*

Unfortunately, the current posture among most organizations that have made commitments in office automation is to view it in terms of the efficiency it provides to the office place. Word processing systems have attained a degree of synonymity with office automation, neglecting thereby not only the synergistic effect inherent in invoking all components of the NARS definition, but leading many to believe that office automation will primarily benefit secretarial and clerical staffs in their creation, storage, and retrieval functions of the electronic-paperless office. However, we can see changes taking place. Office automation in the coming years will place greater emphasis on the "use" and "communicate" verbs in the NARS definition, with the benefits going primarily to the managerial, professional, technical and administrative users in organizations. Moreover, as CBHCS becomes an integral part of what we now term office automation, we venture to guess that we will see the demise of this ill-termed notion of "office automation," as it gives way to what we shall term Organizational Support Systems. Indeed, CBHCS will show that the "office-place" is indeed a rather unwarranted spatial limitation, particularly in light of our envisioned "electronic cottages." Furthermore, our perspective of what is an "organization" will be significantly extended. Organizational Support Systems will provide management and organization with the connectivity and communication structures necessary to enhance the effectiveness of decision-making; in this sense, we see the Organizational Support System as a synthesis of the (Distributed) Decision Support System philosophy with that of Office Automation.

Education:
Learning to
Meet Tomorrow

Education in the '80s: An Appraisal

by

Jim Bowman, Fred D. Kierstead, and Christopher J. Dede

The Widening Gap

Although futures research has become a significant field over the last fifteen years, those studying educational futures have wondered if their work is having much effect on educational practice throughout the world. Many educators are concerned about the lack of long-range vision in how we approach instruction, but conservative and reactionary forces (as manifested in restrictive definitions of accountability, performance contracting, and "back-to-basics") still dominate teaching and learning.

Interestingly, the Third World has been more open to innovations in education than the developed countries. These developing countries understand that colonial, Western, industrial-era models of education are no longer appropriate for the overall evolution of civilization. "Appropriateness" is a mindset that is necessary for maintaining a healthy evolution in all social institutions.

Such an outlook on change, as well as historical assessment of the costs and benefits of industrialization, have been valuable tools for Third World conceptualizations of optimal education. Alternative thinking styles are emerging as an important problem-solving approach; one lesson which can be learned by developing countries is that problems have normative and conceptual components and therefore trend analysis is not a sufficient basis for planning.

With the exception of positive extrapolists, futurists have expended a great deal of energy trying to include normative and conceptual aspects of problem-solving in futures planning. Dennis Gabor, John Platt, O.W. Markley, John Pulliam, and Edward de Bono (to name just a few) have committed to paper their axiological and epistemological concerns. As Markley indicates, we too often see problems as substantive (needing only resources for solution) or process (needing a method of attack)

Jim Bowman, Fred Kierstead, and Chris Dede are Associate Professors of Education and Futures Studies at the University of Texas at Clear Lake City. They are the co-authors of The Far Side of the Future: Social Problems and Educational Reconstruction *and editors of* Educational Futures: Sourcebook I *(World Future Society, 1979).*

rather than as matters of conceptualization (misunderstanding the issue) or values (having contradictory goals). Pulliam's reminder that all problems are philosophical—requiring ontological, epistemological and axiological analysis—has gone generally unheeded. Educational practices in developed countries are unfortunate examples of this point.

The gaps between possibilities and probabilities, expectation and resignation, and innovation and retrenchment seem, therefore, to be most extreme in developed countries like America. The probability of economic malaise, the resignation felt toward 20-year cycles in educational practices, and recent retrenchment in favor of behavioralist objectives and "back-to-basics" are strong deterrents to innovative approaches to education. Educational institutions continue to assume reactive, rather than pro-active, roles. Trend analysis continues to dominate planning, as best suited for reactive participation, although most futurists in education recognize the danger of the assumptions made.

Signs of Progress

Despite the tremendous inertia of the U.S. educational system, some progress toward alternative approaches has been made. Futures research is itself a grassroots movement. Educators have generally understood that "teaching" values, truth, and realities reduces the meaning of education to a specified amount of knowledge. Many teachers recognize the intrinsic problem of educating for a world that doesn't exist. Value-free technological "advances," win-lose mindsets, and conformity to expected patterns of linear, deductive logic are only a few of the characteristics of industrial-era schooling now questioned by educators and others. Despite logical inconsistencies, educators are directed to screen for jobs and further education *plus* "mainstream"; socialize *and* develop individuality; entertain *and* discipline; educate with specific knowledge *and* educate for life; act as parent *and* develop valuing exercises. It is the authors' contention that only the first half of each of these requirements is being accomplished with any degree of success. It is no wonder that a growing number of educators believe they have not only been "sold down the river," but also have been asked to invest in the river (somewhat like buying the Brooklyn bridge) without getting much help from the rest of society looking on from the shore!

An overall sense of powerlessness pervades many educators today. Teachers are tired of trendy innovations; increasing responsibility without funding; low economic, political and social status; and an increasing sense that "others" are running the show. Those members of society who have power to affect educational policy (i.e., legislators, parents, the media, business interests, and the federal government) are seen by many educators as "externals." This we/they dichotomy must be resolved if any concerted action is to take place.

No one group of people in one occupational role can accomplish all that is expected of teachers. An educator must be viewed in a much broader sense, if the widening gap between expectation and actuality in education is to be closed. An educator could be viewed as someone who helps others realize human potential—one who helps others shape beliefs, aspirations and values within the cultural context. Educators, therefore, would be news reporters, media experts, community leaders, politicians, business executives, parents, the clergy, engineers, and teachers. Linking these and other groups together to discuss major goals and problems we have in common would be a major step in educating the public to take control over their futures.

Transcending the Industrial Era

Many futurists believe that America is transcending the industrial era, but the emerging alternative is not easily defined. Buckminster Fuller argues that we must perceive the world as "spaceship earth." Robert Theobald believes that the new era is best defined as the communications era and argues that home computers will create an information complex that will change all forms of work. John Platt reminds us that the 300,000 new titles per year listed by the Library of Congress will soon result in the creation of "2000 ordinary-sized books every day." In his analysis of the silicon revolution, Earl Joseph suggests that we will soon be able to put all information on small chips or wafers—imagine having the ability to carry one's teacher, medical practitioner or politician on a chip with one's library, hospital or school on a wafer! In a different area of change, Amitai Etzioni sees the current period as a genetic revolution and believes that it "will do to our genes and brain chemistry what the Industrial Revolution did to our muscle power."

Others assert that Americans are evolving beyond an industrial mindset of physical or material growth toward inner or psychological growth. This "consciousness era" depicts the movement toward altered states of consciousness (including meditation, hypnosis, experiential naturalism, drug-induced inner experience and the perception of the brain as a human biocomputer). Willis Harman, for example, believes that we are entering an evolutionary period in which leaders will be guided by supraconscious intuition.

The new era has also been characterized as a "world without borders" controlled by multinational corporations (MNC's) and supranational institutions. Lester Brown argues that economic stability requires interdependence of nations through the cooperative efforts of MNC's.

The above conceptions for transcending the industrial-era are brief in description, but establish the degree of diversity among futures theories. Also evident is a consensus that decision-making is becoming an increasingly interdependent process throughout the world. This is significant as global problems affect all individuals, institutions, and nation-states at a more rapid pace.

The Global Problematique

Blocking the emergence of a positive new era is the global problematique (the term *problematique* is borrowed from the Club of Rome to describe multiple, interrelated exponential problems). These substantive problems seem to be clearly defined. For example, population growth, food and water shortages, energy shortages, and resource depletion are substantive problems. The world population recently surpassed four billion and, unless a major negative trend occurs (perhaps through war, famine or disease), most forecasters predict a world population of eight billion in thirty-two to thirty-five years. Lester Brown, president of Worldwatch Institute, projects that world demand for food will double again in the final quarter (just as it doubled in the third quarter) of this century.

Brown also expects global inflation to increase. In 1967, it was 2.5%; in 1972, it was 4.8%; and by 1974, global inflation exeeded 10%. Double-digit inflation in a world of diminishing resources cannot be perceived as a temporary problem.

Double-digit unemployment also complicates the global problematique. Uncertainty about the dollar provides yet another example of the complexity of economic planning. Eurodollars and petrodollars (dollars outside U.S. control) are transferred without established standards pursuant to institutional reserves and interests.

The global problematique also contributes to psychological and social dilemmas. There is an increasing amount of anxiety and stress. Alienation is evident. Melvin Seeman defines "alienation" as one or more of the following: anomie, powerlessness, meaninglessness, self-estrangement, and isolation.

In an era of diminishing returns, industrial-era values may be losing their appeal. When, for example, the savings account erodes and reduces "real money," it is unlikely that the cherished value of deferred gratification will be retained by the "consumer." Christopher Lasch believes that, as the future becomes increasingly uncertain, more people will "buy now and pay later." He adds that, in the culture of narcissism, "the happy hooker stands in place of Horatio Alger as the prototype of personal success."

The increase in public seminars on assertiveness training, self-help, and success through intimidation and seduction further exemplifies the anxiety, loss of confidence, and loss of control experienced by many Americans. Other symptoms of the problematique are evidenced through increases in crime, racial tension, drug usage and abuse, mental clinics, and suicide. Threatening information has increased at an exponential rate. Bad news and violence in contemporary affairs are often random. This, too, contributes to the proposition that attempts to resolve substantive problems will necessitate more than technological innovation.

Compulsory Learning Through Recession or Depression?

The problematique goes to the core of internalized values and goals. It brings into question the desires and dreams of a world which is doubting its process for constructive change as well as its goals regarding "the good life." During the 1970s, all countries struggled to minimize the maximum loss. During the 1980s, the results of delay in decision-making will likely emerge as bad debts of the past are finally absorbed.

During the 1970s, the world adjusted to crises and misjudged an intensity in the crises. In the 1980s, the crises may provide their own compulsory education through the development of a severe recession or depression. (Here, as educators suggest, it is possible to learn from mistakes, even though we prefer to learn through success experiences.)

Progress is no longer viewed by developed nations as being inevitable. There is growing support for the argument that America is about to witness an economic catastrophe. Edward Cornish, president of the World Future Society, says: "My investigation into the possibility of a depression leaves me convinced that a depression during the 1980s is not only possible, but probable." Some of the reasons given by Cornish are lack of financial liquidity among individuals and corporations, heavy speculation in real estate, higher energy costs, and higher labor and capital costs.

When these American concerns are combined with the global problematique, the breakdown of the present system seems more obvious. Robert Theobald believes that the most frightening trend in recent years has been a general refusal to admit that there is a problem: "Reality is just too disastrous to contemplate, so we refuse to look at it." This repression of reality may be slowly changing as more information filters down to the general public.

Harry Browne's best seller, *New Profits from the Monetary Crisis*, exemplifies recent concerns of the public about the possibility of a depression. This material, like that of Howard Ruff (*How to Prosper During the Coming Bad Years*), suggests a "buy guns and gold" perspective which is not strongly supported in academic circles. It does suggest, however, that the layman is considering the consequences of the present crises.

Higher Education in the 1980s

Given even the most optimistic of projections, institutions of higher education will have less money during the 1980s. The substantive problems discussed earlier will continue to reduce budgets (for example, rising energy costs will increase utility bills and paper expenditures) and will reduce the number of students who can afford higher education. There has also been a decrease in births, so the number of college students should decrease by 20% from 1980-1985 (assuming no major changes in adult or continuing education programs). Many universities are suffering inflation rates from 10% to 15% per year with revenues of approximately 5% to 8% per year. This results in a "real dollar" loss of 5% to 7% per year.

At a time when universities and colleges are struggling with financial problems and trying to survive, further demands are being placed upon the schools. Demands for "quality" in the learning/teaching process are coming from Up (legislators), Out (society at random), and In (students and faculty). "Quality," of course, depends upon what various groups interpret as important. Quality education is defined by some as the development of skills for a particular job (the meal-ticket theory). It may also be defined as liberal education for life in a democratic country where everyone is educated as a ruler (the educated vote theory).

In this highly disruptive period, there are many perspectives of quality. With Sputnik, in 1957, society demanded engineers and scientists. Today, however, society is less confident about what is needed from education.

Educators are being asked to satisfy far more ambiguous demands couched in such terms as "performance-based education," "competency objectives," and "accountability."

Through a loss in financial resources (5% is conservative) and increasing societal demands, higher education will make some profound changes in its delivery systems. Many educational institutions will not survive the transition. It is reasonable to speculate that approximately 25% of the liberal arts colleges will disappear by 1990 (assuming that a recession-type economy prevails rather than a depression). Some of the changes that will take place in the remaining institutions will be an increase in educational technology; external learning programs; and interdisciplinary, cross-generational planning structures.

Education will become more capital intensive (rather than labor intensive) as computers become less expensive and more available. Educational use of the computer has been held back partially by poor quality software and high hardware costs, but these constraints are changing. The state of Minnesota now utilizes 2,200 educational computer terminals. Computer games are in toy stores and will certainly change Christmas as well as education. Within the next ten years, 70% of American homes may have video cable. Samuel Dunn believes that these systems will be interactive—facilitating entry and retrieval of information by the customers. The technology is available for some 500 program options at any given time.

Numerous universities are presently offering external degree programs. There are forceful debates about the quality of education being provided through correspondence courses and external degrees. Economic considerations, however, make such approaches a tempting option for education during a time of diminishing returns on all forms of consumption (including education). External degrees in conjunction with home computers and video cables make "external education" increasingly probable in the next decade. It is possible that college students will spend at least two years in studies at home. Eventually, it may be economically necessary for the bachelor's degree to be an external achievement altogether.

The concept of life-long learning has come of age. In the 1980s, education will be cross-generational, as people of all ages strive to develop new skills and knowledge. The problematique that society faces will require everyone to become more interdisciplinary—rather than specialized—in their knowledge. Higher education will serve as an integrating source of information, problem analysis and planning.

Institutions of learning should expect to offer a process for change in the coming turbulent decade. In *The Far Side of the Future*, we suggested that educational institutions will serve as "problem analysis/futures planning centers." Here, educators will function as change-agents through the facilitation of problem-solving groups. Today's problems are interdisciplinary and impact related. Education, during an extended recession, will have to address this framework of crises.

These projections are based upon a recessionary period coupled with conservative advances in technology and information exchange systems.

In the event of a depression in the next few years, it is our opinion that only a few institutions of higher education will be operational in each region. Such schools will function in a problem-analysis service pursuant to concerns in energy, food, employment, et cetera. Hopefully, some scholars will be involved in plans for appropriate technology, sustainable growth, re-allocation plans for world resources, and quality-of-life futures planning. This optimistically assumes that warfare is limited.

Pre-College Education in the 1980s

Public schools will face many of the same problems outlined in the preceding section on higher education. One crucial difference is that kindergarten to high school instruction will continue to be mandatory worldwide. As a result, the market mechanisms that compel colleges to close in times of financial difficulty will not operate in formal education to the same extent, and the strategies which schools use to cope with a changing context will be more limited by societal regulation of instruction.

Two important trends that will affect education in the developed countries can be mentioned in the brief space available.

First, the roles which formal education plays in different types of communities may become quite disparate by the 1990s. Communities with a large percentage of two-wage families will expect schools to provide much higher levels of supervision and socialization than areas with a predominance of one-income households. In metropolitan areas, demographic concentration of minority groups and immigrants (many non-English-speaking) will create a set of educational needs quite different from those of suburban, upper-income areas. Schools (mostly private) that convert quickly to capital-intensive instructional approaches will have a very different classroom environment than the traditional, as will schools which respond to pressures for a meritocratic, high-powered system of gifted/talented education to train an elite capable of reversing the problematique.

High population mobility will ensure the need to smooth transitions among these diverse environments. Moreover, the uniformly high degree of socialization requisite for functioning in high technology societies will require some degree of national standardization and coordination. Substantial challenges in equity and practice will result from these emerging, diverging educational roles.

Second, the financial constraints which trouble formal schooling in the 1980s may be augmented by several other major problems. "Here and now" concerns will become so dominant in society that planning and leadership will become very demanding roles in education, as multiple, continual crises drain time and resources. The strains which students experience in their lives will make maintenance of traditional academic standards very difficult. A pervasive sense of lack of control will cause disillusionment, apathy, and cynicism about the possibility of preserving the current schooling system.

National priorities and local mandates will continually be in conflict,

329

posing grave problems for educational decision-makers. Demands for documented accountability and competence will badly reduce the ability of educators to accomplish their basic duties. The current lack of consensus on what the basic content of education should be will widen.

In short, the existing model for formal education will become almost unworkable. Education will be cited as an example of a crisis area in the struggle between those who feel the "post-industrial dream" is still possible to reach and those who argue for a radical shift to a new approach. The challenge for educators will be to shift from a reactive to a proactive, reconstructionist position and to take a united, professional global stand on the future of schooling.

Summary

The preceding discussion makes clear that an objective appraisal of education in the 1980s reveals a grim context in which some hopeful signs of change are beginning to emerge. The global problematique with its concomitant problems of inflation and alienation exemplifies the terrible dilemmas posed by the present. The grassroots movements in response to these threats illustrate how educators can find methods to help the world reverse its slide toward barbarism and decay.

As the beginning of this article discusses, the developing countries have, in many ways, more insight in how best to achieve a positive future. Ironically, the resources necessary to actualize these insights are largely controlled by the developed nations, who are squandering them in a fruitless effort to forestall the eventual bankruptcy of industrial values. Hopefully, the '80s can mark the beginning of a collaboration in education to reconstruct a good civilization from the mistakes of the past.

Appropriate Education for the '80s

by

Walter G. Pitman

North America is obsessed with the drastic changes facing the universities—changes which have already swept through elementary and secondary schools. We know that there will be a decline in enrollment over the next decade, one which could undermine the financial viability of some institutions and will ultimately threaten the jobs of a great many faculty and staff. We are aware also that these circumstances will place severe restrictions on the universities' capacity to hire bright, young people, and the implications for scholarly activity in our institutions are serious indeed. The continued decline in the commitment of governments and the public to post-secondary education gives little hope that immediate resources are on the way to assist in finding any long-term solutions.

However, I would suggest that these issues are only symptoms of a much more pervasive sickness which involves the total educational system. I think it is not unfair to suggest that post-secondary educational problems can be addressed only in the context of the way in which society must deal with the learning of all of its citizens. Further, I think it can only be addressed within an understanding of the total environment within which our schools, colleges, polytechnics and universities find their reality. I would like to assess our educational problems from a comprehensive perspective and within a broad perception of the economic and social trends our society must understand and be prepared to face in the days ahead.

What is that environment? It is an economic situation which is in the short-term very depressing. We know that North America has a problem of inflation, of unemployment, a weak dollar, a trade balance which is a continuing concern, a balance of payment pattern which worries all of us. We seem to be falling behind many of the other industrial nations in our capacity to cope with new trade arrangements, with new expectations of productivity, with more imaginative mechanisms for solving labor-management relationships.

Yet there is one sense in which even these problems appear to be only an immediate indication of an overall shift in our 20th century from a growth/production/consumer/waste/pollution society to a more

Walter G. Pitman is President of Ryerson Polytechnical Institute in Toronto.

restrained/efficient/conserver society. History exhibits high levels of continuity and one can trace the threads of change back through the centuries. But history also exhibits changes of pace in human affairs—periods when the thrust of new patterns of development speeds up and provides the circumstances which one author has called "future shock." The 1980s appear to have the capacity to see implemented many of the much-heralded prognostications which in the '60s and '70s were perceived only in part. We are trying to comprehend the implications of a major shift from a perception of our planet as virtually unlimited in resources to a concept of a very finite globe, a spaceship earth of quite limited resources, many of which are non-renewable and must support an increased population in the years ahead. In that sense, the end of cheap energy is but a forerunner of a decade in which the reality of "limits to growth" will be worked out.

Thus, many of the options which we had during the '50s and '60s no longer exist. We cannot create economic growth and full employment by heating up the economy—the cheap energy resources are not available. Nor are we prepared to see the environment savaged in order to encourage a major upswing in economic activity. Seeing these doors closing, our politicians can predict only dark days and "tough decisions."

I would like to suggest that just as our unemployment/inflation problems represent a small part of the overall economic problem of shifting to the new paradigm—in the same way focussing on declining enrollment and limited resources for schools, colleges and universities represents a very fragmented and inadequate base of concern from which to assess the needs of our educational system. I would suggest that we are in need of a more complete holistic perception of both our economy and our educational system. It would seem to me that we need to be asking some very basic questions.

- Are we looking at our local situations when we should be considering the total picture of education and the economy throughout the world?
- Are we prepared to create an educational system which will accommodate the realities of a vastly changed society?
- Are we stressing the responsibility of our educational institutions to provide young people with skills and capacities to cope with change and make an important contribution to that society both as participants in the economic order and as human beings trying to understand themselves and that new environment?

I would like to suggest that our society will demand responses that are "appropriate." The word "appropriate" will be much used in what follows. I realize that the adjective has already been over-used and also recognize that there is really no other word which expresses very precisely the quality and nature of the response that our society will demand as we move into the conserver world of different values and behavior patterns.

We speak of appropriate technology—a technology which tends to be less violent and much more gentle with the environment, which corresponds to the needs of people, which tends to be smaller in scale, which conserves rather than consumes energy and resources, both human and natural.

We speak of appropriate lifestyle—a lifestyle less consumer-oriented, less obsessed with acquisition of goods, more concerned about human potential, more aware of the quality of personal relationships, more sensitive to societal issues.

In the same way can we not talk about appropriate education—education associated with individual need, rather than highly structured collective expectations, based on psychological realities rather than mindless traditional practices—an educational style less costly, less wasteful in terms of personal energy, materials and resources; education which stresses the outcomes of individual growth as well as skills related to the needs of the economy, emphasizing attitudes and behaviors leading to effective citizenship.

Inappropriate Education

Under these circumstances what is *in*appropriate? First of all, I think our citizens are convinced that there is a great deal which goes on in our educational system which represents a heavy investment of tax revenues with minimal effect upon the well-being of the society. I think there is a sense that there is a great amount of duplication and that very expensive resources are being ineffectively utilized. Most of all I think there is a feeling that a confusion of education with custodial services has been allowed to develop and that this lack of clear purpose is detrimental to the learning of young people.

A number of further questions arise—is full-time continuous schooling necessary or desirable for many young people who are now in our schools? Can we make use of existing services in our society—our libraries, television and radio services—to provide opportunities for educational development? Have we made use of the most important educational device—the family as a learning unit? There are those who would say that schools are essentially rehabilitative operations for children whose curiosity and desire to learn have been stifled or left undeveloped during the early years within their own families. If so, how should we make use of teachers in the community instead of so concentrating their efforts in classrooms.

We are learning a great deal about children and there is a large body of opinion which would suggest that much of the academic activity carried out with children up to the age of eight is virtually counter-productive. There are those who say that we have taken young children and placed them in restrained classroom situations much earlier than their physical and mental needs would suggest. It is extremely costly to provide inappropriate services of an academic nature when in fact more physical activity and recreation would be, on the whole, a better investment in future health and psychological well-being of young children.

Secondly, we have confused qualification with learning. The greatest pressure to continuous schooling is that of achieving higher levels of qualification which may or may not be related to the needs of either the individual or society. We have a tendency to over-train and to under-educate. Over-training people is extremely costly in terms of public resources and is costly in terms of human frustration. It would seem strange that in my own country, Canada, for example, we should produce five engineers for every technologist when, in many industrial lands, the reverse is the case.

It is patently inappropriate to set up unnecessary hurdles of vocational skill or information acquisition which are quite irrelevant to the level of employment which the individual may find useful in the job market. We have used very little imagination in breaking down career pyramids and assessing the component parts which will make valuable careers for individuals possessing fewer skills and capacities or serve as stepping stones to higher levels of responsibility and services for those with greater gifts. The strength of an economy is determined by the appropriateness of the response to the needs of all the various levels of skill and information from the very base of largely unskilled to that of the fully qualified professional. We tend to make use of people with higher qualifications to carry out functions which are less sophisticated and thus can be carried out by people who have adequate, though less costly training.

I want to stress that I am not talking about "over-education"—that is virtually impossible. At the same time I would like to make it perfectly clear that I do not regard training and education as two isolations. I would hope that any effective training would have a very high quota of liberal arts and social sciences and humanities so that, in fact, our educational system will be producing what E. F. Schumacher called "technologists with a human face" or businessmen with a high sense of ethics and social responsibility.

In fact, I would suggest that making a clear definition of "appropriate" education would be a great boon to the liberal arts and sciences. I fear that in our efforts to provide "relevant" educational offerings we may very well find ourselves undermining those qualities of our universities which must be preserved. The university should not be expected to provide vocational skills. This is an essential point associated with the question, "Are we producing young people capable of coping with the ambiguity and rapid shift of perception that the future appears to hold?" Any stifling of the liberal arts emphasis in our universities will cause untold damage to our public life. Gordon Allport put it well when he said:

> Today we are witnessing the frightening things that political leaders with one-channeled minds can do. What alarms us is their simplistic view of social and political reality. They know only one solution and this solution is totalitarian and spurious. Their lack of tolerance and fear of dissent reflect their own lack of freedom. One-channeled minds can never comprehend that truth may have many channels.

Thirdly, I would suggest that it is inappropriate to place virtually the entire resources for education in the direction of children and youth and thereby provide quite insufficient opportunities for adults. There are few people who would disagree that learning can be much more efficiently and therefore less costly accomplished if the client is anxious

334

to learn, is ready to learn and sees the relevance of the learning. What may take several weeks for an indifferent adolescent to learn can be grasped in a few hours by a highly-motivated adult. This tremendous appropriation of resources to youth education has had deleterious effects upon adults of all ages. We still have adults who are illiterate and whose productivity as participants in the economic sphere, to say nothing of their role as citizens, is damaged as a result. We have not been very anxious to place adequate educational resources in the hands of adult women. We are now beginning to realize the extent to which we have provided virtually no resources for those who are the more mature and can be designated as "senior citizens."

Ivan Illich, in his analysis of his own experience, points out that schooling has actually deprived many people of education. His experience was largely in the Third World and most certainly in those countries where schooling is reserved for the well-to-do. Nevertheless, it means that the great majority in those lands received no services at all. Until very recently, we could assume that with our capacity in the rich industrial West there was an infinite supply of money which could be invested in education. All could be served—there would be no "losers." Now, in the context of restraint we find it is no longer possible to throw money at problems and to misappropriate funds. To put it simply, the entire planet must begin to adopt the style of Third World countries and must husband resources carefully. It will be perceived to be totally "inappropriate" to waste human potential as it is to waste physical and non-renewable resources by force-feeding learning to young people at too early an age or to keep young people in school when they would be better doing something else. And I hope to suggest that "something else" very soon. If these are perceived to be *in*appropriate then what would be appropriate education?

Appropriate Education: Its Characteristics

First, it would seem appropriate to accept that life-long learning or continuous education is the most appropriate style of learning in a world of limited resources in which the fulfillment of human potential becomes the essential issue. It is obvious that in a society which must make best use of its people a style of interrupted education from the "cradle to grave" would best address the needs of both individuals and society. It is obvious that I am suggesting an approach which coordinates the roles of both traditional, institution-based learning institutions as well as non-traditional, informal opportunities for learning. Most important, it would allow people to move up the career ladder, step by step, through a combination of work-learning experiences at the secondary level with perhaps a full-time experience in the world of business, industry or the helping professions at the end of the secondary school. Later, a "normal" experience might include attendance at college—then a period back in a work situation at a higher level—perhaps to attendance in a polytechnic—back to an experience in the world of work—to a further experience in a university setting. It would mean an intense commitment to education on the part of business, industry and service professions.

This style would make the best use of our educational resources, and the client would be learning when he was ready to learn and when he had some sense of the appropriate things that were needed to learn (on a shorter-term decision basis) rather than depending on the long-term hopes and expectations of employment, remuneration and status encouraged by the present style of continuous uninterrupted learning. That "appropriateness" would relate both to individual need as well as the collective need of the society to have a changing industry and business provided with skilled people on short notice.

It would seem to me that appropriate education would be concerned with balance—a balance of emphasis on education for work as well as education for living. There is a large gap between the educational system and the hopes and expectations of the people that the system serves. There seems to be no linkage of the needs of the economy and the society with the learning that is going on in the elementary, secondary and post-secondary institutions.

The situation in Ontario, Canada, at the moment is quite dramatic. We have come to realize that we cannot possibly replace the tool and die makers who will retire from our factories in the next decade. In the past we have imported people with those skills but that is no longer possible. Although the Ontario government appears to be obsessed with that particular problem, one could say that there are comparable, if somewhat lesser, unaddressed manpower needs in many other areas of the economy as well. There are not enough highly-skilled technologists and technicians and not enough people skilled in middle management positions. Strangely enough, this lack of people to carry out crucial activities which will affect the well-being of our economy has been blamed on the universities. I would suggest that probably our colonial past has had a great influence upon our unwillingness to have our young people move into blue-collar positions. (Fleeing the farm and manual labor seems a pattern of behavior not unlike the French Canadians who after the conquest insisted that bright young people should move either into the clergy or law). In Ontario there seems pressure to move into the professions or clerical jobs. Of course, in recent years, research and development has been carried on in the United States by multi-national corporations rather than in Canada. It is hard to attract young people to the manufacturing sector when the most exciting aspects of technical activity have so little emphasis in Canadian industry.

There must be a willingness to fund the period of transition to an appropriate style of education and this means funding existing institutions "appropriately."

As the president of the University of Windsor, Ontario, has pointed out, providing resources for the university, college or polytechnic is an investment in the future, and we fail to make that investment at our peril.

It is not merely a comprehending of the present. If the term "learning society" accurately describes the new value of "learning" over "productivity and growth," then we must have a population which can understand and cope with this new concept. If "learning a living" is also (as Marshall McLuhan suggests) the process of the future, then our institutions must adapt.

The appropriate educational system will force specific changes in our social policy. Nothing can be more devastating and destructive to personal morale than to continue the system of lack of portability of our pension schemes while at the same time providing interrupted educational opportunities which will encourage people to move much more flexibly from job to job in order to make use of new skills and information. Nor will it be possible to operate a factory or office if there is little opportunity for collective decision-making—industrial democracy will become more than a catch-phrase if there is a blurring of human development and employment at the workplace.

"Educational Leaves" in Industry

There will no doubt be a major emphasis on paid educational leave as one of the ways by which business and industry and the trade union movement can encourage the work force to improve its capacity to contribute to the economy and to accept expanded responsibilities for participation in decisions which affect the quality of the workplace.

Finally, "appropriate educational system" must be translated as a process of involving the entire community in learning.

North America has not been as successful in encouraging business and industry and the caring professions to regard themselves as a part of the educational scene. It is quite evident that in the United Kingdom, in Europe, and even in the United States, there is a greater commitment on the part of business and industry to ensure that resources are provided for training young people. There are certain kinds of training which can only be carried out in business and industry. There is no doubt that schools, colleges, the polytechnic and universities cannot possibly keep up with the changes in equipment and the increasing sophistication of process that can be found in the up-to-date local industry.

Investment in Education

Essentially, we are driven to take a look at the degree to which investment in people is where we must put our attention in view of the fact we cannot depend on cheap oil, unlimited sources of capital, or concessions to industries allowing them to reduce their commitment to a clean environment.

I would suggest that we would *not* need more total investment of tax dollars in education if we had an "appropriate" dispensation of those resources. It is paramount that we develop an educational style which will allow us to make the best use of our community resources to the benefit of the human growth of both old and young. However, we must begin to coordinate our efforts. It is not particularly reassuring to know that there is a great deal of activity going on which seems to have a decided lack of direction. In one part of the Ontario Ministry of Education, for example, we have a new and rather exciting development—Employer-Sponsored Training, with advisory councils all over

Ontario prepared to encourage the development of work-learning activities within private industry. Of course, the colleges of applied arts and technology are also involved in a degree of manpower training. The senior and continuing education branch of the Ministry has a commitment to job training, particularly as it is carried on in our formal institutions at the secondary level. There is an industrial training council which is attempting to devise policy in the area of creating skills for our manufacturing sector. In the Department of Labour, a Manpower Commission has begun its work in assessing the manpower needs of Ontario for the years ahead. Although there is a commendable degree of commitment and activity, one does not sense that there is any coordination of all this activity. To put it bluntly, it is an inappropriate response to the kinds of problems we face.

I would conclude that we need to see a concept of ecodevelopment of our educational system—educational activities which must be capable of being sustained, which must be environmentally responsible, restrained in cost, effective in results. If our educational system is to be ecologically sane in the widest sense of that term, then it must be precise in its aims and there must be coordinated a relationship of institutions, both formal and informal, both private and public committed to the concept of continuing educational opportunity for all citizens. Each year makes coping with transition more difficult. Unless we make decisions, we face increasing difficulties ahead.

Someone has said of the '80s that the "new society is fundamentally different, more difficult, more dangerous, more honest and more helpful." Surely all of us can share in the excitement and delight of the positive aspects of this "new age" instead of our present concentration on deprivation and disaster ahead. Our institutions must change along with our values and ultimately our behavior.

John Kennedy stated that "those who make evolution impossible make revolution inevitable." Those who have seen revolutions in the past cannot be filled with much assurance that revolutions will really change the world around us. Normally they simply place a different group of people in power and they may not be as wise and thoughtful as those whom they have replaced.

The challenge to produce appropriate education is full of difficulty, ambiguity and contradiction. However, one must suggest that continuing to massage an inappropriate North American educational system can only lead to personal hardship and collective unhappiness on a continent with the greatest opportunity for well-being.

The 1980s As a Decade of Learning

by

James W. Botkin

There is little doubt that the 1980s will be a decade of learning. Global issues—especially diminishing resources and increasing demands—are not only challenging collective conventional wisdom but also rendering fundamental changes in human understanding inevitable. The question is not so much *whether* a renewed emphasis on learning will characterize the 1980s, but more significantly *what kind* of learning the 1980s will bring. Will it be "learning by shock," the historically familiar, costly, and regressive procedure often used by societies to face new challenges? Or can some alternative be encouraged, such as innovative learning that stresses conscious renewal and restructuring and that prepares people to act in new, possibly unprecedented, situations?

The reasons why learning by shock bodes disaster in the context of global issues and how innovative learning could serve as an alternative are spelled out in a report to The Club of Rome entitled *No Limits to Learning.* Here I will try to summarize some of the main ideas in the Club of Rome report, and then describe the Forum Humanum, a rather extraordinary initiative towards implementing some of these ideas.

Key Ideas in "No Limits to Learning"

Science and technology have stimulated unparalleled advances in knowledge and accomplishment. Sufficient economic means exist, though unevenly distributed, to provide the basic needs of all members of the human community. Yet despite the fact that humanity is at a peak of scientific knowledge and economic power, the human condition continues to deteriorate. Whether this deteriorating situation can be reversed will depend on another major—and decisive—factor: human learning.

"Learning" in this sense has to be understood broadly. It is taken to signify a whole approach, both to knowledge and to life, that emphasizes human initiative. It may occur consciously, or often unconsciously, usually

James W. Botkin, co-author of the Club of Rome report No Limits to Learning: Bridging the Human Gap *(Pergamon Press, 1979), is now associated with the International Center for Integrative Studies, 45 West 18th Street, New York, New York. Previously Academic Director of the Salzburg Seminar in Salzburg, Austria, he co-authored the Club report while an Associate in Education at the Harvard Graduate School of Education.*

from experiencing real-life situations, although simulated or imagined situations can also induce learning. Probably every individual in the world, whether schooled or not, experiences the process of learning—and probably none of us at present are learning at the levels, intensities, and speeds needed to cope with the complexities of modern life. Thus, learning goes beyond what conventional terms like education and schooling imply. This is not to ignore formal education but to stress the important, sometimes predominant, role of other factors inherent to the learning process.

Those concerned with the future of learning and education face hard choices. Conventional schooling—a huge enterprise which directly occupies one of every six inhabitants of the planet and is supported by over $400 billion annually—has failed to prepare people for the complexity of global issues and indeed is thereby contributing to further deterioration of the human condition. The communications media, one of the most significant factors in generating the information and images whereby entire societies learn, continue to dispense "business as usual" programs, largely rejecting their *de facto* role as educators and remaining remarkably immune from public policy. And family and work life, two important elements in learning, remain based on the values of a world that is rapidly disappearing.

What is likely to occur under these conditions is a repeat of a historical pattern of continuous *maintenance learning* interrupted by short periods of innovation stimulated largely by the shock of external events. Maintenance learning is the acquisition of fixed rules for dealing with known and recurring situations. It enhances our problem-solving ability for problems that are given. It is the type of learning designed to maintain an existing system or an established way of life. Maintenance learning is, and will continue to be, indispensable to the functioning and stability of every society.

But for long-term survival, particularly in times of turbulence, change, or discontinuity, another type of learning is equally essential. It is the type of learning that can bring renewal, restructuring, and problem reformulation—and which can be called *innovative learning*.

Throughout history, the conventional formula used to stimulate innovative learning has been to rely on the shock of events. Sudden scarcity or catastrophe have interrupted the flow of maintenance learning and acted—painfully but effectively—as ultimate teachers. Even now, humanity continues to wait for crises that would catalyze or impose this primitive *learning by shock*. But under current conditions of global uncertainty, learning by shock is a formula for disaster.

The conventional pattern of maintenance/shock learning is likely, if unchecked, to lead to one or more of the following consequences:

1. The loss of control over events and crises will lead to extremely costly shocks, one of which could possibly be fatal.

2. The long lag times of maintenance learning virtually guarantee the sacrificing of options needed to avert recurring crises with long lead times.

3. Over-reliance on over-specialized expertise, typical in times of

crisis, will alienate and marginalize more and more people.

4. The incapacity to quickly reconcile value conflicts under crisis conditions will lead to the loss of human dignity and individual fulfillment.

The net result of taking any one of these paths is that humanity persistently will lag behind events and be subjected to the whims of crisis. The fundamental question that this prospect raises is whether humanity can learn to guide its own destiny, or whether events and crises will determine the human condition.

Innovative Learning

The main purpose of *No Limits to Learning* is to initiate debate on learning and the future of humanity, centered around the concept of innovative learning and its chief features. The thesis is not that innovative learning *per se* will solve pressing world problems. What is argued is that innovative learning is an indispensable prerequisite to resolving any of the global issues, especially those that have been, and continue to be, created by humanity itself. Innovative learning is the process of preparing individuals and societies to act in concert in new situations. This is not to ignore that other actions involving political power, science and technology, and economic policies and programs will not also be instrumental—although innovative learning needs to underlie and penetrate these and other actions as well.

Two key elements comprise innovative learning: *anticipation* and *participation.*

Anticipation is the capacity to face new situations; it is the acid test for innovative learning processes. Anticipatory learning stresses preparation for future alternatives, not adaptation to the present. It goes beyond foreseeing or choosing among desirable trends and averting catastrophic ones: it also enhances the ability to create new alternatives. Its opposite is adaptive, reactive learning, where one responds only to given changes in the environment, delaying the search for answers until it may be too late to implement solutions. Under the influence of maintenance learning, those who should be alarmed are not moved by gradual deterioration. It is only when shock occurs and events roll like thunder that people suddenly look up for the lightning that has already passed.

Participation is a term that powerfully and controversially evokes the aspirations of individuals and their groups to be partners in decision-making, to strive for equality, and to reject unduly limiting roles. The demand for participation has become nearly universal, and is being felt on every level from local to global. Groups of every definition are asserting themselves and renouncing marginal positions or subordinated status: Rural populations are aspiring to urban-like facilities; factory workers seek participation in management; students demand a voice in administering important school policy; and women are demanding equality with men. It is the age of *rights*—and rightfully so—but it is also not yet the age of *responsibilities.* An intrinsic goal of effective participation will have to be an interweaving of the demand for rights with an offer to fulfill obligations that such rights entail.

A major task of learning in the next decade will be learning how to participate effectively. In too many instances, "participation" as we know it today is in crisis. Many special interest groups are practicing "participation by veto," showing more skill in blocking proposed plans than in formulating constructive alternatives. Some participation is too short-sighted, which may produce counter-productive results when anticipation is lacking.

If participation is to be effective, it will be essential that those who hold power do not block innovative learning. The time has ended when decisions could be handed from the top down. A critical mass of people on an unparalleled world scale will have to work together, not so much to "solve" global issues as to generate a common understanding of them and a shared willpower to address them. Activating the latent potential of innovative learning present in the world system hinges largely on the degree of effective participation at international, national and local levels.

The aims of innovative learning are *survival* and *human dignity*. To put human survival in the forefront signifies that this is not a metaphysical issue; rather, learning has become a life and death matter. But survival at any price is not a sufficient ideal or cause. One must go beyond "submitting in order to survive." Human dignity, a wide term with many meanings, is designated as the "beyond survival" goal. It is taken here to stand for self-respect, for mutual respect among individuals in culturally diverse societies, and for the respect accorded to humanity as a whole.

Initiatives Toward Implementation

No Limits to Learning does not recommend any world blueprint for action—indeed, it has been criticized for not spelling out pragmatic steps for action. The present-day reality is, however, that learning and education are, and should remain, as decentralized as possible. While the analysis about learning is global, most actions concerning learning must and ought to be an individual, local, or at best societal matter. Several such attempts to implement innovative learning are presented here:

Forum Humanum: An international project of a new Swiss foundation of the same name, Forum Humanum attempts to support teams of people presently in their 20s or early 30s to work on global issues of significance beyond the year 2000. The project has two purposes: to give its participants genuine global experience in dealing with global issues and to increase public awareness about the need to act now to improve the future. The plan is to establish at appropriate institutions several work teams linked around the world for the study of selected global issues. The Forum Humanum will be based in Switzerland and will start with study teams in a limited number of locations in Europe, Latin America, North America, Asia, and Africa.

The subjects of study will include material concerns such as food, energy, environment, and an accelerating arms race as well as human and ethical issues such as rising cynicism, untapped learning potential, threats to cultural identity, and the changing status of women. These issues encompass both developing and developed countries. As the 1980s begin, not only are these and other problems growing worse, but too little is being done to educate and train people to deal with them. Forum Humanum is one response, initiated globally and acted out locally, towards the creation of a network of young people with the capacity and commitment to cope with future global issues.

It is a dramatic and bold initiative. It will stress anticipatory learning and will be built on participation from many countries, with only a minimal structure for administrative coordination. Participants in Forum Humanum will receive support for up to three or four years, and will have sufficient means to travel, to work closely with one another, and to consult with people of all ages in government, business, labor, and academic life. As one output of their work, they will be expected to produce joint reports—written, audio-visual, or otherwise—aimed primarily at influencing policy makers and world public opinion.

UNESCO—New Initiatives in Learning Research: At the urging of the Deputy Director General, UNESCO officials have been considering whether and how some of the innovative learning principles could be translated into practice. Discussions and planning to date have encompassed, among others, the following sorts of issues:

There is a need for an interdisciplinary, international project on learning research. Not only is remarkably little known about how individuals and especially about how societies learn, but what is known is highly fragmented into competing and often contradictory theories.

Most research about learning undertaken to date has occurred in the developed countries; yet the need for applied theory harmonious to cultures in the Third World is pressing. A focus on *learning for development* would be valuable, carried out through regional cooperation with the initiative coming from the local level. A special effort is needed to examine, in specific cases, what elements in traditional practices of learning could be preserved and utilized as effective and more appropriate alternatives to the Western model of education.

Three areas of relatively new research were mentioned: the role of communications in learning, the development of new curricula for anticipatory learning, and "societal learning"—what it is and whether it could provide a useful concept to help explain how and why societies change or fail to change.

Toward a Systemic Education

by

Michele Geslin Small

The education we offer our youngsters seems in many respects irrelevant and hopelessly outmoded when one considers the nerve-racking pace with which change has been occurring in the last few decades and the pervasive emergence of new values, characterized by a keener awareness of the relationships between man and man, man and nature, and man and his future, as well as the new desires for pluralism, personalization, responsibility, and participation which are emerging in our society.

As Edward T. Clark points out, "Historically, the primary starting point for structuring knowledge in Western thought has been to begin with the smallest self-evident part and proceed from these parts to incrementally build the whole. This approach is based on the Cartesian assumption that the whole can be predicated and thus extrapolated from its parts."

The result of the method is all too obvious in higher education. In the sciences, the Cartesian approach led to the sharp, unequivocal distinction between the mind (soul substance) and the natural world (physical substance), and was responsible for the enormous successes of physical science from Newton onward. Yet, at the same time, all those aspects of human experience which did not fit into the mechanical picture were set aside as non-empirical, non-scientific, or just not fit for genuine scientific study. Consequently, the tendency of the scientific worldview is to exclude all consideration of mankind's traditional spiritual and psychic notions. It is sad to conclude that the nature of scientific education is such that there seems to be a direct correlation between success in science courses and lack of awareness of wider human issues.

In the humanities, which traditionally have been dedicated to the notion of the whole man, the same splintering has occurred. It is ironic that even though they feel separated from their scientific counterparts, the humanists, impressed by the little-understood scientific method, have adopted the reductionist approach so ill-suited to the subject matter. For the sake of "managing" the constantly mounting mass of material,

Michele Geslin Small teaches in the University of Minnesota's Department of Social, Psychological and Philosophical Foundations of Education, Minneapolis, Minnesota.

time has been conveniently divided into eras, periods, and centuries. Those digestible slices are thus compartmentalized and neatly labelled and become the focus for areas of specialization, thus providing the chance for accuracy and the comfort of self-confidence. The students, limited to the study of a very precise slice of history, fail to perceive the role of precursors and forerunners.

Finally, not only have the humanists become "idolaters of the past" but they provide very scanty references to the broader context. Can we really understand anything about Shakespeare's works unless we are infused with the understanding of the political, social, philosophical, aesthetic, and economic background of the period? Deprived of an understanding of the spiraling process of the flow of ideas and of the meaning inherent in a broader context, the students are left to their own devices to integrate the disparate bits and pieces they have collected all along, a far cry from the concept of the well-rounded man.

The social sciences, a field less burdened by the load of past knowledge, have taken present-day contemporary civilization as their primary orientation. Their concerns focus on the immediate issues and the problem-centered studies of man and society. There again the approach is analytic. Unfortunately, they are so anxious to ape their "hard science" counterparts in order to give solidity and prestige to their discipline that they get entrapped in a morass of meaningless data, methodologies, and measurements, losing touch with the ineffable qualities of man and carefully avoiding the "non-scientific" issues or values.

In addition, not only is the approach to knowledge severely stunted in our educational system, but the management of students' lives in our schools is a caricature of the principles and methods adopted in factories and reflects once more the fragmentation that pervades the fabric of our lives, especially in the primary and secondary schools.

Basic Principles of Today's Education

The French futurist Joel de Rosnay has schematized satirically and somewhat cynically the basic principles on which our traditional education is based:

- *Basics*: What we have to master even though we have no idea how we are going to benefit from them.
- *Subjects*: What we have to know in order to acquire a "minimal knowledge" (whatever that is!).
- *Curriculum*: The organization of subjects in time so that there is more efficiency in the acquisition of knowledge (obviously what is not included in the curriculum has very little educational value!).
- *Time*: An arbitrary time limit is assigned to each class which should allow anyone to assimilate a given amount of information (never mind the unique learning modes of the individual!).
- *Equality*: A principle according to which all must receive the same kind of information in the same period of time (too bad for the slow students or the very bright ones!).
- *Tracking*: A specialization which starts early even though it might entail potentially drastic consequences over a lifetime.

- *Exams*: A ritual invented by the adults in the process of which the student regurgitates what has been crammed into his head (and which will be promptly forgotten).
- *Degree*: A passport to finally enter active life.

[See Joel de Rosnay, *Le macroscope: Vers une vision globale (The Macroscope: Towards a Global Vision),* Editions du Seuil, Paris, 1975.]

Obviously, our education system is suffering from a deep-seated malaise which we seem to feel but do not know how to handle adequately. Too often in the past, attempts have been made to solve the basic problem by plugging in "stop-gap" solutions, generally products of our technology, such as audio-visual materials, teaching machines, and computers . . . but subsequently we have realized that the audio-visual by itself is nothing but a pictorial representation of words, that teaching machines are too expensive to be used on a large scale and do not always fit the students' working habits, and that even the well known computer-assisted instruction—which has shown tremendous potential for controlling a multi-media environment, teaching hundreds of students at a time, testing their retention of knowledge and suggesting supplementary sources of information, while providing individualized instruction—has proven too costly with very modest results.

As for interdisciplinary programs, in most cases they have proven to be nothing more than the juxtaposition of discrete fields which are not truly integrated. Consequently, the courses offered under the auspices of these programs are too often a succession of modular units, presented in turn by professors who are never really "collaborating," even though they happen to share the same building.

The relative failure of these new methods shows that curing the symptoms is not sufficient when the body is sick. Any "band-aid" approach will continue to fail unless we are ready to tackle the problem at the core.

What do we learn from this look at our educational system, a microcosm of the larger societal system that surrounds it? The logical conclusion is that Western thought, based on a materialistic model, has served us very well in the area of science, both pure and applied, particularly in the wondrous creations of technology. However, its failure has been precisely in the areas having to do with human beings. It is but an incomplete worldview, a one-sided approach to reality.

Fortunately, we are not alone. Parallel to the development of the Western scientific "cline," there has been an evolution of Eastern thought, whose conception of the world as a living evolutionary process is different from ours and essentially holistic, and in which the distinction of mind and body never exists since they are one and the same.

The advent of the new discoveries in the fields of information and communication, which tend to reduce the world to what McLuhan called the "global village," have sped up the process of exchange of influences between the two clines—the Western and the Eastern—especially in the fields of medicine and psychology.

Acupuncture, biofeedback, transcendental meditation, and Zen have been introduced to us as "techniques," all related to the well-being of man. Behind them lies another worldview, another map for the territory of reality, very different from ours since it is unitary and does not establish any distinction between the observer and the observed.

Current research on the brain has indicated the distinctive roles played by the two hemispheres. The left side is the seat of the cognitive, analytic, language-oriented, rational mode of thought; the right side, the seat of the artistic, metaphoric, and intuitive mode. This is an apt analogy to demonstrate that our Western culture seems to have overemphasized the role of the left brain to the detriment of the right side and that a more profound knowledge and understanding of the Eastern worldview (the right-brain approach) could give us valuable insight to revitalize and integrate our divided selves.

Since we have shown that our education system has favored in a disproportionate manner the analytic over the synthetic, the rational over the intuitive, we would like at this point to suggest that a more holistic, systemic education would overcome the problems that we have pointed out. However, we cannot afford to repeat the mistake by replacing the stereotyped left-lobe linear culture with the one-sidedness of the stereotyped mystic right-lobe approach. This in effect would be arguing whether one should only go on the left foot or only on the right foot. It is only in the interaction between both of these uniquely human endowments, the analytic and the synthetic, that a healthy balance can be reached to cure our educational malaise.

What can we do, then, to develop our stunted holistic perception and infuse it into our educational system? As defined by Clark, the systemic approach "begins with the whole in order to provide a context within which the parts, as they are learned, can be understood in a different perspective, that is, in relation to each other and to the whole."

Guidelines for a New Education

For a more concrete application of this principle, we now return to Joel de Rosnay who, in his book *Le Macroscope*, establishes some guidelines for a new systemic education, according to which, we should:

1. Avoid the traditional linear or sequential approach and favor one which consists of coming back many times, but at different levels, over the material which must be understood and assimilated. The material is thus covered in successive touches following the pattern of a spiral: first the subject is seen as a whole in order to delineate its boundaries, and evaluate its complexity; then it is reconsidered later in a more detailed fashion.

This approach, for example, would proscribe the chapter-by-chapter method of teaching too common in our schools. Only when the work under study has been read, discussed, and evaluated *in toto* should the slow, analytical process start. It is only when we see the total picture of the proverbial jig-saw puzzle that we can appreciate its discrete components and their interrelations. In addition, we might well want to teach our students some helpful "tricks of the trade," such as the importance of the preface, the introduction, the conclusion and particularly the table of contents where, in one glance, one can catch the subject matter of the book, its subsystems, and their interrelations.

2. Avoid definitions which are so precise that they either polarize us or limit the play of imaginations. A concept or a new law must be studied from different angles and integrated into different contexts. This avoids the mechanical application of any definition.

For example, the concept of "progress" should not be reduced to the standard mechanistic definition of "more and bigger." It should be examined in a historical perspective, its development traced through the periods of industrialization and new technological discoveries to our present time where the global context, especially that of the environmental and natural resources, demands new definitions and a mapping out of alternatives. Can we live better with "less"? What do we mean by "the quality of life"? Such questions should be posed to our students and they, in turn, should be led to exercise their creative imaginations, so that they can come up with new, more realistic, and more appropriate definitions.

3. Stress the importance of the concepts of limits, mutual causality, interdependence, and dynamic equilibrium in the study of complex systems, taking as examples the disciplines which integrate the notions of time and irreversibility, such as biology, ecology, and economics.

At the elementary level, the basic concepts of a systemic education can be pictorially described and the intellectual processes illustrated through examples chosen in everyday life. What better example than the thermostat to illustrate the concept of "negative feedback"? What are the animals which live in a symbiotic relationship besides the remora and the shark? What about the water-cycle on the earth? Have we not been re-using the same water since the beginning of time?

4. Use a thematic approach at the vertical level which can integrate many disciplines and different levels of complexity around a central core.

For example, in the sciences, the theme of "the origins of life" involves astrophysics, physics, chemistry, geology, molecular biology, and the theories of evolution and ecology. In the humanities, the themes of "love," "death," and "childhood" could bring together works written by authors from many countries over centuries of time.

5. Never separate the knowledge of facts from the understanding of the relations which link them.

This principle is valid for all levels of the educational system and is a *sine qua non* if we want to prepare the younger generations for the global problems as well as the challenging prospects of life in the 21st century.

In addition, teachers should also:

- **Emphasize the notion of Heisenberg's "principle of uncertainty," which debunks the myth of objectivity and shows that the observer is irrevocably bound to the observed, a concept inherent in the Eastern worldview.** As Clark points out, "The best way to be 'objective' in any given situation is to recognize one's subjectivity and always take it into account in any decision."

- **Stress the multiplicity of individual and cultural values and the relativism of worldviews.** Students should be exposed to writings from authors who come from different countries and different cultures. Let's consider some nature poetry from Japan and India: How do these poems compare with those written by American poets? How similar are they? How different? What do they indicate about the life of these people and their values towards the land? What about the concept of justice in an Islamic country, contrasted with the principles of the American constitution?
- **Allow for, and encourage, an intuitive, creative, and non-rational approach to problem-solving.** A flash of insight can be as valid as a solution arrived at by the slow and methodical analytical process.

When those fundamental directions have been established, the technological hardware mentioned earlier can be utilized to its fullest potential and smoothly integrated within the new education as a useful support system instead of remaining as a collection of haphazard, uncoordinated, stop-gap measures. Students will be encouraged to work at their own pace with the mode which is most appropriate for them. This might mean audiovisual aids, programmed learning, games, simulation kits, and computer modeling.

In addition, the present information explosion, supported by continuous refinements in the computer and microprocessor industries, is helping to break down the fictitious barriers which have been erected between schools and society. We can facilitate this process and help make education a true learning experience related to the world outside by pursuing and implementing a variety of alternative modes: open education in preschool and the elementary grades, schools without walls at the secondary and college level (including cooperative education, work-study programs, and internships, which get students into the real world and back to the school again), and, for adult and senior citizens, the opportunity of life-long education which would allow them to either retrain themselves for new jobs and new careers or simply to pursue their special interests so that they can be happier and feel more at ease in our fast-changing society.

If the structure of the traditional education can be compared to a tree (the trunk represents basic knowledge, the branches the multiple areas of specialization), systemic education will be like an inverted cone. One would start with the most general and successively, in broader and broader circles, one could reach an essential knowledge which could be applied through life in multiple ways.

This systemic education will produce an osmosis between life and school and a re-discovery of the fundamental meaning of education: *to communicate man's experience.* On the personal level, learning will become a real life-long activity where every action will be a way of feeling, enjoying, producing, and contributing, as well as an opportunity for a deeper awareness of man's relation with his world. On the societal level, we can hope to form multi-dimensional people who, because they will think through the broader implications of the particular actions they advocate, will be able to tackle the increasingly complex world where each area is inextricably connected to others.

We can hope that these well-educated and joyous men and women—able to ask the right questions in order to implement the correct solution to the right problem—will achieve real maturity, defined by C. West Churchman as the ability to hold conflicting worldviews simultaneously and be enriched thereby.

Health:
New Approaches
to Staying Fit

The Soft Health Path: An Alternative Future for Health in the '80s

by

Trevor Hancock

When considering the future of health and health care in the 1980s, it is necessary to begin by looking back at the decade we have just left, in an attempt to discern the "wrinkles," the discontinuities which suggest that the future for health and health care will not be simply an extension of the past. Undoubtedly the "medical-industrial complex," which includes the pharmaceutical companies, the medical equipment and supply companies, the hospital industry and the professional associations, and which employs one in every twelve workers in the USA is not an easy monolith to either dislodge from its present powerful position or divert from its present technological course. Nonetheless, there are enough straws in the winds of the '70s to suggest that the '80s might witness a major transformation in health and health care.

Straws in the Wind

In the 1970s we saw a radical reappraisal of the concept of health and its determinants throughout the world. Among the more significant developments was the "rediscovery" of the importance of environment and lifestyle and the recognition that man is part of and not apart from the planetary eco-system. In the developing world this led to an increasing recognition of the place of health in the development process, as well as some of the adverse health effects of development. The World Health Organizaiton pledged itself to achieving the goal of "health for all by the year 2000" and promoted the Primary Health Care concept as the means of achieving this.

In the industrialized world, the reappraisal was perhaps best seen in the document *A New Perspective on the Health of Canadians* (the Lalonde Report, 1974) and its imitators in the United Kingdom (*Prevention and Health: Everybody's Business*, 1976), the United States

Trevor Hancock is a community physician and works as a public health planner for the City of Toronto Public Health Department. He served as the coordinator of the health and medicine track for the First Global Conference on the Future.

(*Healthy People*, 1979) and elsewhere. The increasing emphasis on environmental sensitivity and personal responsibility has been popularized by Ardell and others, and there has been a growing recognition that our present values and systems built around them (e.g., economic growth) may not be conducive to health. Increasingly, the social and political roots of health and disease were being recognized during the '70s.

The scientific and technological aspects of medical care have continued to grow apace throughout the '70s, though their relevance to health is no more apparent now than before. What is more, the '70s saw the emergence of serious opposition to the medicalization of society, as exemplified in Ivan Illich's *Medical Nemesis* (1975), and an increasing demand by patients, and particularly by women, to be treated with more concern and to reassume more personal responsibility for their own health.

One reaction to scientific medicine has been the emergence in the Western world of the holistic health movement, with its emphasis upon the appreciation of the whole person and the reaffirmation of the importance of the psyche and the spirit in health and healing. The development of theories and observations demonstrating a "scientific" basis for such approaches has been of great significance, and has served to confirm for Western minds truths which have been accepted for centuries in the East.

The relative unimportance of medicine, and by implication of physicians, in creating health has been noted; one response to this has been a move towards de-professionalization, and the increased interest, in both developed and developing worlds, in the deployment of paramedics and community aides is a further recognition of this issue.

Environmental sensitivity, recognition of the need for social change on the one hand and personal responsibility for health on the other, and the growing use of non-physicians and community aides will mean an increasingly important role for public health, which has languished for some decades. We are perhaps witnessing the birth of a second public health revolution, one that will be more global in its outlook and yet more based in local community action than the first.

Thus have the seeds been sown in the '70s for a very different approach to health and health care through the '80s.

Soft Health Paths for the '80s

In his book *Soft Energy Paths* (1978), Amory Lovins defines "soft" as meaning flexible, resilient, sustainable and benign, and he describes five characteristics of soft-energy technologies: they are renewable; they are diverse; they are flexible and relatively easy to use (and therefore accessible to the general population); they are matched both in scale and in geographic distribution to end-use needs, and they are matched in energy quality to end-use needs. He concludes:

> The distinction between hard and soft energy paths rests not on how much energy is used, but on the technological and socio-political *structure* of the energy system, thus focusing our attention on consequent and crucial political differences.

It is not hard to see the parallels between soft energy technologies and many of the changes in the health field that began in the '70s. At the most profound level, the questioning of the givens of our present technological and socio-political structures, Draper has noted that the allies of the renaissance of public health are to be found in three broad groups: those concerned with ecological and conservation issues and the socially responsible use of global resources; those concerned with Third World development and international responsibility and those concerned primarily with the philosophical and yet practical examination of social goals and values. In this respect, the development by Henryk Skolimowski of an eco-philosophy which is, among other things, life-oriented, environmentally and ecologically conscious, politically aware, socially concerned, and health mindful, will contribute greatly to our rethinking of, and understanding of, health. What could be more in tune with the Soft Health Path than Skolimowski's comments that "taking care of one's health is taking responsibility for the fragment of the universe which is closest to one, expressing a reverence towards life through oneself," and that "to be in a state of positive health is to be on good terms with the cosmos." Elsewhere, I have expressed the view that the Conserver Society, as an alternative technological and socio-political structure, holds out a healthier prospect for our future. The Soft Health Path, as it emerges in the 1980s, will increasingly lead those concerned with the creation and maintenance of health to focus their attention upon the crucial political differences betwen a hyper-expansion (HE) future and a sane, humane and ecological (SHE) future, as envisioned by James Robertson in *The Sane Alternative* (1978).

There are many other analogies between soft technology and what I have chosen to call the Soft Health Path. The need for flexible, resilient and diverse "technologies" is surely mirrored by the emergence of the holistic health movement, with its emphasis upon multiple healing modalities, the importance of body, mind and spirit, the ability to integrate and utilize both our right and left brains, and the power and possibility of voluntary control of bodily functions. Robert Ornstein first synthesized much of this in his book *The Psychology of Consciousness* (1972), and the development of this approach to health has implications far beyond the health field. In his book *Person/Planet* (1978), Theodore Roszak noted that "the road to wholeness leads through the feminine," a thought closely paralleled by Carl Sagan, who noted in *The Dragons of Eden* (1977) that we need to use both cerebral hemispheres to solve complex problems in changing circumstances: "The path to the future lies through the corpus callosum." Indeed, it may be that voluntary control, necessitating as it does a greater appreciation of the oneness of the universe, of the interrelationships of matter, energy and spirit and of the interdependence of person and planet, may prove to be a necessary precursor of a Voluntary Simplicity lifestyle.

The need for sustainable and renewable technologies is paralleled in the health field by the need for self-sustaining and self-renewing means of becoming and remaining healthy, reducing the dependence of individuals upon professionals and the system for their state of health.

This can be seen in the growth, the veritable explosion, of the self-care movements, patients rights groups, mutual support groups and community aides programmes. The need for readily understandable and easily usable "technologies" also underlies the emergence of such groups and movements, and the same need is related to the growing involvement of the community in the planning, running, and evaluating of its health-care systems.

In the global context, the Primary Health Care concept is undoubtedly a recognition of the need to match health resources to end-use both in terms of scale and geographic distribution and in terms of the quality of the health technology. Thus the improvement of health in many parts of the underdeveloped world does not require a few highly qualified doctors using sophisticated technology in large city hospitals, but rather requires many paraprofessionals and community aides using simple and appropriate technology in a multitude of rural and urban community settings. Nor should it be thought that this approach applies only to developing countries: many of the industrial world's health problems might be more effectively dealt with by community-based preventive measures.

Finally, soft technologies are benign, and one only has to read the current medical literature on iatrogenesis, or more especially Illich's *Medical Nemesis,* to recognize the extent to which our present hard technology medical care can be malignant.

To sum up, there is evidence that a new approach to health care is emerging. This new approach can be described as the Soft Health Path. It is a synthesis of environmental health, community-based public health, the primary health-care concept, the holistic health movement and the self-care movement. This Soft Health Path is compatible with and leads towards a sane, humane and ecological future.

Health in the '80s: Toward Optimum Human Existence

by

Russell M. Jaffe

The perimeter or boundary of how we view and define health is under fundamental reexamination. While this process has not occurred (significantly) in over 30 years, such examinations have occurred in the United States every 30 years or so since its founding. Each re-examination has been stimulated from outside the mainstream of medical practice and medical education. An alliance of consumers and health innovators has traditionally formed to initiate discussion which precedes this change. While each change has been resisted by the prevailing health lobbies, change has occurred. This change has usually expanded the usefulness of health-care professionals and has been beneficial to our social fabric and community life.

The issues which usually stimulate change in health are:

1. We do not have enough scientific and technological bases for our medical and health strategies, or,

2. We do not have enough relevant, personal, and communal health services.

In addition, when viewed from a broad (200 years or more) perspective, we discern a pendulum moving from option 1 to option 2 and back.

At present, we find ourselves poised at the extreme of one expression of option 1 (more technology) yet a rising voice is heard for option 2 (more emphasis on personal and environmental health) by those who are developing new approaches to health. In essence, then, we are at the extreme of one swing of the pendulum; the return of the pendulum may well characterize new approaches to health for the 1980s. Another way of expressing the views that seem to predominate the "alternating force" within the world of health is the classic Pasteur versus Beauchamp debate. Pasteurians hold the view that disease derives primarily from factors outside the person. These factors include:

Russell M. Jaffe is a wellness practitioner; Research Associate of Commonweal, Bolinas, California; assistant professor, Uniformed Services University of the Health Sciences, Bethesda, Maryland; and is also associated with NOVUS (New Options for a Vital U.S.) and the Health Audit, Washington, D.C.

356

1. infectious agents
2. environmental toxins
3. sugar or cholesterol
4. lack of vaccination
5. allergens, pollens, etc.

The Beauchampists hold an alternative view—that an individual's susceptibility or intrinsic resistance determines his susceptibility to disease. The factors which are the major determinants of health according to this view are:

1. the body's intrinsic immune systems
2. the neuroendocrine system—especially the thyroid, thymus and adrenal glands
3. alternating periods of rest and activity
4. the harmony or balance in one's life
5. life purpose, satisfaction and joy

The Pasteurian view is that molecular biology research and technology can improve personal health quality. In contrast, Beauchampists would hold that life-style and personal attitudinal integrity are the primary determinants of personal health quality.

The Pasteurians tend to hold that the objective scientific facts will lead the way to the eradication of disease; the Beauchampists lean toward a reliance on subjective experience as the more direct route to avoiding disease. This debate began during the mid-19th century when Pasteur and Beauchamp led respective medical research institutes in France.

The approach of Pasteur dominated overwhelmingly during the 1950s and 60s. Within the last decade, the debate has become heated and enlivened again. We stand poised for new work in health. A consensus conceptualization of what some of this work may contain is the focal point for the rest of this essay.

New work in health usually arises to meet some perceived need. Among today's perceived needs in health are:

1. Slowing the escalation of health costs (which rise twice as fast as the GNP as a whole and will exceed $240 billion in 1980).

2. Reducing chronic illness among teenagers (which doubled in the last decade).

3. Re-discovering the primary importance of fulfilling relationships and their relation to health.

4. Developing strategies for attaining optimum human health and reducing our bio-social decline.

5. Working toward voluntary and conscious control of autonomic function.

6. Exploring contemplation, meditation and spiritual inspiration in relation to health attainment and maintenance.

7. Investigating genetic engineering to produce complex biological products—like the proteins insulin, growth hormone, and interferon (which specially-produced bacteria were first induced to synthesize during 1979).

8. Investigating the role of laughter and pleasure in health attainment

and maintenance.

9. Emphasizing the importance of self-care in health.

10. Learning to recognize subtle signals which the body gives when it is in balance, distress, or disease.

11. Exploring the role of the electromagnetic field in health, medical diagnosis, medical treatment and health optimization.

12. Investigating the bio-chemical, environmental and social causes for ecologic sensitivity (such as food "allergy") and "executive fatigue syndrome."

13. Studying the impact of environmental lighting, air, electricity, sound, water quality, and synthetic materials on the body's natural defenses and the manner in which these factors predispose people to be susceptible to or resist illness.

14. Extending our concept of human growth and development to its broadest demonstratable limit.

15. Investigating other cultures; and the utilization of efficacious approaches toward health maintenance and disease reduction.

In essence, we are examining the fundamental assumptions upon which our health and research strategies have rested for the last generation.

We may have the extraordinary fortune to be participatory witnesses of a shift from a narrow view of health (which focuses primarily on disease treatment and prevention) toward a broad view which defines health in terms of the positive quality in soil, water, atmosphere, energy, and industrial output and which leads to healthy food, healthy environments and healthy people.

We are reaping the fruits of an intensive and productive generation of molecular biology research in medicine. Ushered in by the Salk-Enders-Sabin polio vaccine (in the early 1950s), this work is bringing noninvasive analysis of blood flow to the heart; monitoring of the heartbeat and muscular tone of the infant *before* delivery (thereby alerting the doctor to "fetal distress," should it occur); and long-term total intravenous feeding of the chronically ill or seriously disabled.

Medical information doubles every five years. Among the most important results of our rapidly expanding body of scientific and medical knowledge is the recognition that previous medical "fact" is now clearly seen as "fiction." For instance, our attention to dietary cholesterol as a significant risk factor in our epidemic of cardiovascular disease is now known to be based on a misinterpretation of the facts. Indeed, except in the tiny fraction of people (less than ½ of 1%) who have a genetic inability to metabolize blood fat, there is no direct relationship between dietary cholesterol and blood cholesterol. Rather, we are coming to recognize that abnormal laboratory results—for instance, an elevated blood cholesterol—are a reflection of some *imbalance* in the body. When the cause of the imbalance is discerned and balance re-established, the abnormal laboratory result usually normalizes on its own. On the other hand, when the imbalance is allowed to persist, medications are often ineffective. Until recently, this anomaly has been mysterious. Today it is an exciting frontier in medicine.

Another myth which is now disproven is the concept that much chronic illness is genetic. By chronic illness is meant arthritis, heart disease, arteriosclerosis, stroke, obesity, diabetes, etc. While it is still sometimes taught that these conditions "run in families" and are *therefore* genetic, an accumulating body of wisdom suggests that families perpetuate certain life-styles and environments which are more directly responsible for these diseases of modern civilization than is the genetic material or DNA. An extension of this concept is the recognition that these "genetic" disabilities should remit and disappear if the life-style or environmental conditions responsible for their persistence are removed. Such is the case. Atherosclerosis—a cardiovascular condition leading to hardened blood vessels—is now increasingly recognized as a reversible condition. Were this a principally genetic expression, reversibility would be most unlikely. The fact that reversal or regression of arteriosclerosis, arthritis, diabetes, etc., does occur, in some cases, is a favorable prognosis for the future of our health and that of our children if we implement the proper life-styles and healthy environments. On the other hand, it is understandable that these chronic disabilities continue to afflict increasing numbers of Americans—and all those who lead our environmental life-style—because most health professionals do not yet have the benefit of being taught what to do in light of the insight alluded to above. Specifically, we can expect more emphasis on healthy food, nutrition, air and water quality, attitudinal maturity, and self-responsibility for health as the biomedical research of the '80s yields fruit.

Another frontier of biomedicine in the '80s is the recognition that each of us is our own laboratory control. In other words, it is increasingly clear that comparing individuals to laboratory results obtained on a "similar" population is, at best, a deceptively crude approximation. Just as our fingerprints and faces are unique, so is our metabolic personality. Hence, it is wise to profile us during times when we are healthy. Subsequently, we can be compared to our own prior "control" values to determine impending or present disability. This approach can yield premonitory evidence of illness—sometimes years before any gross symptoms appear. Obviously, the earlier an imbalance is detected, the easier is its remediation. What is now known for a few thousand fortunate Americans may become the standard of care for all of us in the near future.

New work in health includes psychology, psychiatry, and the emerging sciences of psychobiology and transpersonal humanistic psychology. As the last two terms imply, they represent syntheses and logical/experiential extensions of earlier conceptual frameworks—notably by Freud, Adler, Jung, Sullivan, and Rogers.

Psychobiology explores the functioning of mind through interactive tools of psychologic evaluation complemented by biochemistry. Perhaps the most notable example of this domain is the recognition that truly new learning and brain sprouting can take place in the fully mature and adult brain—given optimum conditions. Notable in this field is Gary Lynch, who shows that at high potassium concentrations, mature brain cells can develop new interconnections. Potassium is the salt which cells concentrate inside. This is in contrast to sodium, which is generally excluded from cells and exists in high concentration in the circulatory system. Foods rich in potassium (and other nutrients) are traditional "brain foods" of indigenous cultures. These "brain foods" include bananas, similar fruits, and fresh vegetable juices. We are just beginning to rediscover the importance of nutrition in life-long learning. In a similar fashion, we are discovering that optimum learning takes place in an atmosphere of relaxed, comfortable informality. Remember what your classrooms were like? This approach, called superlearning or suggestology, derives from Bulgarian physician George Lazanov and is being extended by innovative educators in the U.S. Both learning-disabled and gifted children (and adults) show accelerated learning curves and improved retention under these conditions. A similar approach, known as neuro-linguistic reprogramming—an extension of Erichsonian hypnosis with a liberal admixture of practical spirituality and suggestology—is a promising application to human growth and psychological maturation.

New approaches in the fields of education, psychobiology, psychology, and biochemistry, to name a few, characterize the present examination of the way in which we view health. We are rediscovering that each individual can serve as his or her own control so that an imbalance in his or her system is readily detected; that many diseases which "run in families" may be related more to similar life-styles than to similar genetic materials; and that fulfilling relationships, contemplation, laughter and attitudinal integrity all relate to health attainment and maintenance. Instead of focusing on disease prevention and treatment, our definition of health is now broadening to include the positive qualities in soil, water, atmosphere, energy, industrial output, and life-style which lead to healthy food, healthy environment, and healthy people.

The Impact of Industrialization on World Health

by

Jennie Popay, Jenny Griffiths, Peter Draper, and John Dennis

Industrialization is, of course, an extremely complex phenomenon. On the one hand, it has clearly been accompanied by numerous benefits. In health terms, the older industrialized nations have certainly seen a reduction in the massive toll of suffering, disease and death associated with the infectious epidemics such as cholera, polio and tuberculosis which ravaged populations in the earlier stages of urbanization. Equally, it cannot be denied that life expectancy improved around the turn of the 19th century and for the next 50 years or so in countries like Britain. On the other hand, it must also be acknowledged that many industrialized countries have recently been experiencing an unfavorable change in the burden of disease from infections to conditions such as coronary heart disease and the cancers. Some of these justify the description of "modern epidemics," and their origins lie at least in part in the very process of development that has brought so many blessings.

The Greek myths of Hygieia and Asclepius symbolize contrasting philosophies of health which, though well over 2000 years old, are very much alive today and of direct relevence to any discussion of industrialization on health. At the risk of oversimplification, contemporary followers of Asclepius can be said to be concerned with the relief of suffering and the treatment of disease. The doctor is seen rather as a mechanic repairing and occasionally servicing a machine. Followers of Hygieia, in contrast, are concerned more with the effects of the immediate and wider environments on the health of individuals and societies. Concern here is with preventing unnecessary suffering, disease and death. The debate, however, is not about choosing between Hygieian or Asclepian approaches; rather it is about whether and how advanced industrial societies can strike a more appropriate balance between the

The authors are with the Unit for the Study of Health Policy, Department of Community Medicine, Guy's Hospital Medical School, London, England. Two former members of the unit, Gordon Best and James Partridge, also contributed to the development of this paper.

two. It is a central thesis of this paper that, at present, most countries have the balance sadly wrong—even those that extol "prevention."

Despite powerful criticisms about the costs and effectiveness of modern medicine, it is still widely believed that progress in health will be achieved in the main by the provision of more and more hospital-based health services. Hats are occasionally doffed towards primary care and the caring and residential services in the community, but current preventive policies, at least in the United Kingdom, are emaciated and unrecognizable decendents of Hygieia. They contrast with the public health activities of the past which have paid serious attention to the effects of the wider environment on health—from sewage in the drinking water to a concern with "unwholesome trades." An equivalent movement today would need to look very seriously not so much at the health implications of industrialization per se, but at the largely indiscriminate nature of present economic growth—that is, at much of what is ironically termed wealth-creation. (See Table 1.)

TABLE 1

Economic Conventions, Health, and Wealth

	Convention or Assumption	Principle	Example
Indices of economic value	1. In general, the economic value of a good or service produced in the economy is equated with the price it fetches in the market place.	If one good or service is sold for X and a second is sold for 2X, then the contribution of the second to society's economic "welfare" is conventionally taken to be twice that of the first.	In terms of national accounts, if £1m. is spent on anti-smoking educational measures and £83m is spent on advertising and promoting tobacco, then tobacco advertising is viewed as over eighty times as valuable—in economic terms— as are the educational measures.
Indices of economic progress	2. In general, the health of the economy is seen to depend in part on increases in the aggregate sales value of the goods and services that exchange in the market place.	Measures such as GNP or national income measure the *level* of economic activity: that is, they increase (or decrease) as the total (price-corrected) sales value of goods and services increases (or decreases).	£1,000 pounds spent on frozen vegetables (and their packaging, retailing, etc) has a positive effect on GNP; £1000 "worth" of home-grown vegetables that are consumed (or informally exchanged) by the growers do not enter national accounts (and therefore GNP).
Indices of welfare	3. In general, many unintended side effects of market activities (e.g. noise, pollution) are omitted from measures of economic welfare. Moreover, measures of economic welfare are often confused with measures of social or general welfare.	The production and consumption of goods and services are conventionally viewed as the *primary* activities of the economy: the unintended "production" of, for example, air or water pollution or occupational "stress" or accidents are viewed as "external effects," the costs of which are rarely reflected in measures such as GNP. Indeed, they sometimes are viewed as benefits.	"Defensive" expenditures such as those incurred in cleaning up the air or water, or in "repairing" people following preventable accidents, are added to rather than subtracted from measures such as GNP. Many "external" outputs of the economy for which no "defensive" arrangements exist do not enter national accounts at all. Measures of economic welfare can increase therefore

Convention or Assumption	Principle	Example
		even in situations where general welfare may be in decline.
Distinctions between productive and non-productive	4. In general, the production of many "public" goods and services is viewed as a "drain" on the wealth-producing (marketed) sector of the economy.	The economic value of many goods and services that are central to the quality of life but which are not, in general, marketed (e.g., health, education, etc), is regarded as proportional to the market value of the productive "inputs" they consume: they are therefore viewed as "non-productive" (i.e., marketed) resources.	Marketing health, education, etc., renders them productive in terms of national accounts. In the extreme, putting health care "on the market" can be seen as a measure that might well improve "economic welfare" despite the fact, that again, general welfare may decline.
Distinctions between economic and non-economic	5. Many essential productive activities that are important not only to the economy but to social welfare are not counted as contributions to society's economic welfare.	Much work that is undertaken without monetary remuneration has no economic value.	Child-rearing, housework, voluntary activities (e.g., blood donations) and any other charitable or benevolent activities, the outcomes of which do not enter into national accounts, have no economic value and therefore do not contribute to economic welfare.

Note:

There are a variety of assumptions as well as accounting and linguistic conventions that are commonly adopted in discussions of policy when attempts are made to try and understand the "state of the economy," or, for example, the nation's rate of economic progress. Although such conventions and assumptions have been frequently criticized by economists and others, they are still used as primary "benchmarks" in the formulation and implementation of national economic policy and as such, severely restrict the range of policy options considered and seriously discussed. Amongst other objections, these conventions—or perhaps more accurately, habits of thought—serve to obscure the antithetical relationship between many of the goals of conventional economic policy and the desire to promote human health and well-being. The table summarizes some of these conventions and gives examples of the ways in which they serve to conceal many of the health and wealth conflicts mentioned in the text.

Source: From a paper by members of the Unit for the Study of Health Policy, Royal Society of Health Journal, June 1977.

Enemies of Hygieia: "Health versus Wealth"

To pursue social and economic policies that largely neglect a variety of health hazards, and often actually increase such hazards, is to pursue a form of development that is in total conflict with the Hygieian idea. Yet in advanced industrial societies today, this is in many ways exactly what we seem to be doing. More specifically, apart from attempts to control inflation, the pursuit of social progress in industrialized societies is often reduced to the pursuit of a single goal: economic growth. And despite the fact that increasingly this goal is not achieved, the pursuit in itself conditions a number of critically important economic and social policies and practices. Indeed, many of our prevailing ideas of social progress can be seen to reflect a fundamental desire to effect what can fairly be called indiscriminate increases in the total output of material goods and marketed services. Typically, for example, industrial, agricultural and trade policies make no distinction between measures that might increase the production of socially useful products (such as nutritionally wise foods) and measures likely to increase the output of socially damaging and health-damaging products such as cigarettes. Our goal seems to be purely quantitative—increased productive output: what we produce, how we produce it and how we distribute it are of secondary importance.

There is a fundamental conflict between the "production of wealth"—as it is commonly defined—and the promotion of health. For example, the higher the level of transport activity, the greater the number of cars, trucks and lorries which can be sold, the more fuel will be consumed and so in economic terms (at least on paper) things will be better: but other things being equal, the more transport, the more accident and emergency resources that will have to be devoted to traffic accidents. Similarly, cigarettes and alcohol production are "wealth producing" from an economic perspective, but from a health perspective they are "ill-health producing." It is not only the nature of the products, however; the ways in which they are produced, marketed, distributed, and consumed can also generate health problems.

To be critical of the pursuit of simplistically-measured economic growth is not, however, to argue that considerations of health should be paramount in our quest for social progress. Rather, it is to argue that a more reasonable balance between Asclepian and Hygieian approaches cannot be struck if the very processes whereby our society produces "wealth" are at the same time a significant source of the conditions that jeopardize health. To clarify the issues we are raising, we have attempted to group such conditions and their associated accident, disease and health problems in relation to a broad classification of many of the economic processes involved in the pursuit of indiscriminate economic growth (Table 2).

TABLE 2

Conflicts between health and wealth: A grouping of accidents and diseases (mainly as experienced in the United Kingdom in the 1980s) by economic, rather than biological, categories

Economic category	Examples: Source of risk	Specific diseases, problems of risk
PRODUCTION i. Conditions primarily related to the *nature* or *organization* of production	the use of various chemical and other toxic materials in mining, industry and agriculture.	occupational diseases and injuries, e.g., asbestos diseases; numerous skin, lung, bladder and other cancers; radiation diseases.
	the careless use of capital-intensive productive methods	industrial injuries and deaths; capital-labor substitution leading to unemployment and thereby to anxiety states, de-

Economic category	Examples: Source of risk	Specific diseases, problems of risk
PRODUCTION		pression, alcoholism and the cigarette diseases such as bronchitis and lung cancer.
	increases use of human-beings in passive, repetitive or machine-like roles.	obesity; industrial accidents; cigarette diseases; alcoholism; boredom and stress-related diseases and conditions.
	industrial pollution	affects not only workers but also rest of our society, and other societies (e.g., lead pollution locally; sulphur dioxide and other pollution problems in Norway which are created in the UK).
	multinational operations in the Third World	malnutrition resulting from cash cropping and distortion of the agricultural base.
ii. Conditions primarily related to the *level* of production.	pressures leading to damaging rapidity in the production process	increased risks of accidents, e.g., diving accidents; executive stress leading to cigarette diseases, road accidents, alcoholism and over-eating (obesity).
	pressures related to frenzied and damaging marketing	results in various conditions as indicated in "executive stress" above and where domestic life significantly disrupted, to increased risk of mental illness.
	pressures to utilize new and inadequately tested forms of energy inputs.	nuclear power radiation hazards and deaths.
	pressures to adopt damaging levels of goods transport and labor mobility.	road traffic accidents affecting not only lorries but involving cars, coaches and buses; disrupted domestic life as above.
CONSUMPTION i. Conditions primarily related to the *nature* or *organization* of consumption.	the consumption of disease and accident linked products.	cigarette diseases; dental caries and the sweets and chocolate (and other sugar) diseases—including obesity and some diabetes; road accidents secondary to alcohol, hypnotic or tranquilizer consumption; poisoning from weed-killers and pesticides; aerosol sprays.
	the consumption of nutritionally deficient products	refined flour and sugar, i.e., fibre-deficient carbohydrates leading to diverticulitis, some cancer of the colon, etc.
	waste pollution hazards	poisoning from heavy metal or other chemical and radioactive wastes, e.g., to workers on waste tips or to others through water contamination, etc.
	bottle-feeding of babies in the Third World	increased nutritional and infectious disease problems in infancy
ii. Conditions primarily related to the *level* of consumption	pressures to consume more in an absolute sense, e.g., advertising of the form "eat more, drink more."	advertising which contributes to over-eating and therefore to our major nutritional problem, obesity and associated diseases, e.g., heart disease.
	pressures to replace/update consumer durables and	anxiety states and depression which arise from financial and other pressures

(cont. on next page)

365

Conflicts between health and wealth: A grouping of accidents and diseases (mainly as experienced in the United Kingdom in the 1980s) by economic, rather than biological, categories *(continued)*

Economic category	Examples: Source of risk	Specific diseases, problems of risk
CONSUMPTION	other products at an ever-increasing pace (including "planned obsolescence").	to "keep up with the Joneses."
DISTRIBUTION i. Conditions primarily related to the maldistribution of economic opportunities or resources	global inequalities	persistence of diseases of poverty in the Third World; diseases of affluence in the West
	chronic persistence of shortages and inadequacies in housing and basic amenities despite ever increasing levels of productive output and energy consumption.	hypothermia; respiratory and gastro-intestinal conditions which arise from grossly inadequate housing and sanitation, overcrowding and homelessness; accidents to children from the lack of safe and attractive play facilities, e.g., the special problems of high-rise flats.
	chronic problems of unemployment and poverty amongst specific sub-groups of the population.	many single-parent families; immigrants living in over-crowded and decaying urban areas with high unemployment; middle-aged and older unskilled workers whose physical fitness has been lost; agricultural workers who have little or no land of their own for vegetables, chickens, etc. Generally, poverty and unemployment effects such as malnutrition or subnutrition, anxiety and depression and associated cigarette diseases, methyl alcohol drinking, etc.

Source: Adapted from a paper by members of the Unit for the Study of Health Policy, Royal Society of Health Journal, June 1977

A practical implication of this kind of classification is that attention is focussed on the diverse range of causal—or conditioning—influences that originate in the functioning of the economy and that contribute to what René Dubos and others have called "diseases of civilization." Such an economic grouping (as opposed to the more conventional biological classifications) suggests directions for fruitful research and action.

A second set of problems, however, is at least equally important to the development of a better understanding of the health-versus-wealth conflict. Essentially, this second set of problems relates to the various linguistic and conceptual conventions that characterize most practical discussions of economic and social policy objectives and that serve to obscure or mark many of these conflicts. Table 1 has attempted to illustrate the nature of these conventions by giving examples of them and illustrating some of the ways in which they tend to conceal important health (and other social) questions in the consideration of national policies.

These examples and illustrations of the health-versus-wealth conflict suggest that the thoughtless pursuit of indiscriminate economic growth can best be understood as a contemporary *religion*, the worship of the god Economic Growth. Ironically, the very idea of health has also been conditioned by the growth imperative. The activities undertaken to ameliorate this situation constitute a significant proportion of what we call "health services" and these services have come to be equated with the idea of health. We need, it is argued, to create more "wealth" in order to be able to afford more "health services." But is that really how we make progress in health?

We need to get out of the habit of thinking that treatment service policies constitute adequate health policies. We must develop economic policy, social policy and health policy in an integrated way rather than putting economic considerations first and thus creating health and social problems. Industrial and transport policies, for example, are partly health (or anti-health) policies. We need to make sure that prevention is directed at underlying causes. Apparently desirable preventively-oriented activities can mistakenly focus on symptoms and amount to useless exhortations. For example, the essentially moralistic and puritanical appeals to the individual—"pull yourself together, change your personal lifestyle, stop smoking, stop overeating, take regular exercise, drive carefully" and so on—achieve little and distract attention from the policies and practices that mould lifestyles and that generate the stresses and risks. As the tables suggest, attention has to be directed to removing or reducing the conditions that pressure people to lead unhealthy lives.

The solutions to many of these problems lie, for example, in the creation of appropriate technology rather than technology which so often squanders energy and creates unemployment as well as pollution. They lie also in a biological and ecological, rather than a narrowly chemical and engineering, approach to agriculture, nutrition and medicine. Most important, we must recognize that current economic behavior, whether for industrialized or developing countries, is generating accidents, illnesses and deaths on a massive scale as well as creating resource and pollution problems. With these points in mind, Table 3 gives examples of the health implications of a much more selective form of economic growth in the UK. But is there a good chance that such strategic objectives will find wide support?

TABLE 3

Some specific policy areas: The health implications of more selective form of growth

Area of Policy	Strategic Objectives	Examples of Policy Measures	Typical Health Implications
1. Transport	i) *Less overall long-distance travel*; greater reliance on shared forms of transport.	Selective goods movement taxes to encourage local distribution of goods.	Less community disruption, noise, dirt, etc. Fewer road accidents, injuries and deaths.
		Local "vehicle pools" and incentives for the shared use of private cars.	
	ii) *Shift away from high-*	Investment in rail, water-	Less lead and other forms

(cont. on next page)

Some specific policy areas: The health implications of more selective form of growth *(continued)*

Area of Policy	Strategic Objectives	Examples of Policy Measures	Typical Health Implications
1. Transport	*energy consuming forms of travel.*	ways, etc., and in better pedestrian and cycling facilities for short-distance travel.	of air pollution; more physical exercise.
	iii) *Fewer, longer-lasting road vehicles.*	inducements for the production of longer-lasting vehicles and taxes on non-durability.	Improvements in safety through less "testing in use."
2. Energy	i) *Overall reduction in energy consumption* including the use of less wasteful and more efficient forms of electricity generation.	Incentives to develop and invest in more energy-efficient forms of technology and production.	
		Increased use of district heating.	Less risk of serious industrial accidents (e.g., mining accidents, nuclear accidents, etc).
		Increased use of energy conserving forms of building technology, insulation, etc.	
	ii) *Shift away from capital-intensive, extractive forms of energy production* toward lower technology, "income" forms of energy production (e.g., solar, wind and other non-depletable energy sources).	Investment in research into alternative energy sources.	Less risk of climatic and other unknown changes due to over-heating of the atmosphere.
	iii) *Less energy-related pollution* and waste disposal.	Stricter pollution and waste disposal regulations.	Less air, water and other forms of pollution (e.g., sulphur).
3. Nutrition and Agriculture.	1) *Greater national, regional and local self-reliance* in food production; more employment in agricultural production.	Import restrictions on animal food grains and incentives to "local holdings."	Better diet and fewer diet-related health problems (e.g., less diverticulitis and obesity).
	ii) *Less reliance on capital-intensive, high energy forms of agricultural production* (e.g., reduced utilization of nitrogen fertilizers, herbicides and pesticides and intensive animal rearing). This leading to: Greater reliance on cereals, vegetables and fruits. Less consumption of highly refined foods and their associated dyes, preservatives and other additives.	Incentives to producers of "home-grown" cereals, vegetables and fruits. Pricing and subsidy policies to favor home-produced foods as above. Consumer nutritional education.	Less land and water pollution risks (e.g., nitrate pollution of water). Less exposure to fertilizer and pesticide products and by-products.

Source: From work done at Unit for the Study of Health Policy by Gordon Best, John Dennis, and Peter Draper

It is worth noting that there is a remarkable and encouraging consistency between economic policies that are sound in environmental and ecological terms and economic policies that promote public health. There may also be support for such policies in industrialized countries from those who are concerned about the division of resources between North and South. Thus, those whose primary concerns are health, the ecosphere and the Third World might find themselves sharing a global perspective on the process we call "industrialization."

Futurism As a
Way of Life

Sociopolitical Forecasting:
Managing the Black Hole of the Future

by

Raymond P. Ewing

Some would like to know what the future holds out of a mere sense of curiosity, others out of a simple desire for profit or power, and a few out of a responsibility for foresight, planning, and management. Conventional wisdom, however, has always sought to dash all hopes for knowing the future.

Indeed, most people view the future as if it were a black hole in space, a place from which no information—not even light or X-rays—can escape to reach us on planet Earth. This negative attitude was best expressed by the Greek playwright, Aeschylus, who wrote, "The future you shall know when it has come. Before then, forget it."

Despite this attitude of contemporary cognoscenti, there have always been those who have refused to accept a categorical denial of the possibility of knowing the future. They have sought to know the future through whatever consultants, techniques, or technologies were available to them—from oracles, fortune tellers and witches to religious divinations, drug-induced trances, and mathematics.

All of these efforts had one thing in common: the foretelling of a fixed future through some human power of precognition. It was not until the opening of this century that another possibility was suggested: an inductive knowledge of the future, indeed, a science of an open future!

This startling proposal was made by H. G. Wells in 1902 in a talk before the Royal Institution in England, entitled, "The Discovery of the Future":

> I believe that an inductive knowledge of a great number of things in the future is becoming a human possibility. I believe that the time is drawing near when it will be possible to suggest a systematic exploration of the future. And you must not judge the practicability of this enterprise by the failures of the past . . . but suppose the laws of social and political development, for example, were given as many brains, were given as much attention, criticism, and discussion

Raymond P. Ewing is Issues Management Director, Allstate Insurance Companies, Northbrook, Illinois.

as we have given the laws of chemical combination during the last fifty years, what might we not expect?

Wells went on to say:

Until a scientific theory yields confident forecasts you know it is unsound and tentative; it is mere theorizing, as evanescent as art talk or the phantoms politicians talk about. . . .

And if I am right in saying that science aims at prophecy, and if the specialist in each science is in fact doing his best now to prophesy within the limits of his field, what is there to stand in the way of our building up this growing body of forecasts into an ordered picture of the future that will be just as certain, just as strictly science, and perhaps just as detailed as the picture that has been built up within the last hundred years to make the geological past? Well, so far and until we bring prophecy down to the affairs of man and his children, it is just as possible to carry induction forward as back; it is just as simple and sure to work out the changing orbit of the earth in the future until the tidal drag hauls one unchanging face at last toward the sun as it is to work back to the blazing molten past.

In the 78 years since Wells issued his call, several generations of researchers have sought out the laws of social and political development, firmly establishing the social and behaviorial sciences in the process. One of their major contributions to sociopolitical forecasting is their analysis of the public policy process in a democracy, which permits a free press, freedom of speech and the peaceful assembly of voluntary associations.

The public policy process is the mechanism by which the public's dreams and dissatisfactions work their way up through public issue debates into law and regulation.

The Yankelovich, Skelly and White public policy process model is the one preferred by my associates and myself who are concerned with public affairs and issues management at the Allstate Insurance Company. In simplified form it begins with the public feeling dissatisfaction, concern over a real or imagined wrong, or the belief that a right is being ignored. Not much happens until it gets a name—a label.

Once it gets a name—welfare rights, fair housing, redlining, etc.—the media can pick it up and start to talk about it. The media don't create these issues, but they do play a role in issue development.

After the news media take the issue to a broader audience, nothing really happens until a pressure group takes note of the issue and decides to add it to its agenda. After the activist group takes it up and begins to create pressure, its ultimate effectiveness is determined by how well it can mobilize political force beyond its own membership. The media, of course, are a critical part of this process.

When the action gets churned up enough, government officials begin paying attention. They become concerned because of their regulatory responsibility, rule-making authority under existing law, or role in the writing of new legislation.

Finally, the elected legislative officials stand at the vortex of this process, brokering the conflicting demands, bending in the end to their key publics.

PUBLIC POLICY PROCESS MODEL
(Social Control of Business)

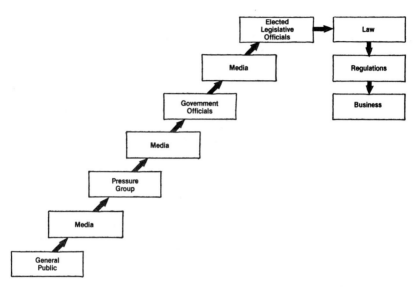

Ray Ewing interpretation of
Yankelovich, Skelly & White
and other models.

Of course an issue does not have to travel the whole route from the general public to legislative consideration, but can emerge and start to move at any point on the process model—at the pressure group level, the government officials level or at the legislative level. Also, every issue is not resolved by the enactment of a law: many are not capable of legislative solutions or legislators are not willing to subject society to legislative solutions. In some of those cases, extra-judicial solutions are frequently sought through direct pressure by citizen associations, peer pressure within groups, and voluntary agreements between conflicting groups or voluntary codes of conduct within an industry, profession or civic association.

This process model is real and accounts for most of the good and bad changes that have happened in the business world during the past few decades. Unfortunately, the business world has had a sorry history in this process. According to Chairman Harold Williams, of the U.S. Securities and Exchange Commission, we ignore the developing process until it is too late. We leap in at the legislative enactment stage, when we can do little more than hope to moderate the dire consequences of the legislation.

Common sense tells us that we must intervene in the process well before the legislative confrontation stage if possible. We then have the

373

hope of helping guide the process with the other participants. However, this hope is possible only if we work at early recognition of issues on the local and national levels as they emerge and resolve to participate in the developing process.

Although business has had a minor role, there has literally been an explosion of citizen participation in the process as public interest groups, consumer groups, environmental groups, neighborhood organizations and thousands of special interest groups awoke to its possibilities.

Although the forces bringing about the democratic or social control of business seem to have sprung up only recently, the process has been underway in the United States for over a century. Commencing with the effective control of railroads and public utilities, the social control of business has been developing at an accelerated pace.

As one business commentator said about the process during the first half of this century, "It may be guided and directed, its movement made more informed and enlightened, but it cannot be stopped, and no one group can dictate its course."

It is important to note at this point that the term "issues management" refers not to an effort to "manage" the public policy process, which is patently impossible as noted above, but to manage the corporation's or other institution's efforts to participate in the process. Thus the use of sociopolitical forecasting is an important tool in an institution's effort to help create and fit itself into the future, as Allstate's Chairman Archie R. Boe has pointed out.

Use of the public policy process model depicted here involves regular opinion sampling of the general public, pressure group leaders, governmental officials and state and federal legislative officials. Additionally, private discussions with selected leaders as well as a careful monitoring of newsletters, books and reports of public interest orgnizations, foundations and government agencies are also necessary. Likewise, a content analysis of leading newspapers must be performed, both to identify the early appearance of emerging issues and to evaluate the progress of matured issues. Independent research and consulting organizations exist to provide these services in the United States. (However, there is none that monitors radio and TV news programs or attempts to evaluate the trends emerging in popular entertainment—movies, plays, novels, TV shows, etc.)

John Naisbitt, publisher of *The Trend Report*, which contains content analyses of 200 daily newspapers, believes there are five bellweather states in the United States. These states are California, Colorado, Washington, Connecticut and Florida. Graham Molitor, president of Public Policy Forecasting, Inc., has identified seven domestic jurisdictions which he cites as early innovators and adoptors of sociopolitical change: New York City; New York State; Dade County, Fla.; Massachusetts; Boston; California; and Illinois.

Molitor's research has revealed that on the international scene certain countries can be studied as precursors of changes that will eventually work their way through most countries over several decades. These early innovators are Sweden, Norway, Denmark, the Netherlands, Switzerland, West Germany, Great Britain, the United States, and Canada, in that order.

As for the United States, policy analyst Molitor, Steve Nowlan of Human Resources Network, Inc., and William Renfro of the Library of Congress have seldom found issues emerging at the public level in the above process model that reached final enactment into law at the federal level in less than six years. Thus a careful scanning for emerging issues plus consistent monitoring of them thereafter affords ample opportunity for a concerned institution to develop policy and supporting programs in time for it to participate in the process well before such issues reach their final legislative stages.

Since sociopolitical forecasting permits one to view the lineaments of alternative futures, it follows that proper foresight, planning and execution will also permit the management of what actually goes into the black hole of the future.

This foresight and planning will move one from the usual crisis or post-crisis posture most institutions find themselves in to a pre-crisis posture of thoughtful preparation for events. This permits self-management of one's role in history.

Prospective: Decision and Action

by

Hugues de Jouvenel

Prospective studies aim at enlarging our capacity to invent and to establish a new social system which will facilitate human development—that is to say, a system which will offer to individuals the optimum opportunities for freely exercising their capacities.

Prospective studies are characterized by three postulates: the first of which I will call the postulate of freedom, the second the postulate of power, and the third the postulate of choice.

The postulate of freedom is the conviction that the future is not predetermined or fixed, but remains open to a plurality of possible futures. To assert that the future is not predetermined is to state that it cannot be known and hence that prophecies—even when established by using the most powerful computers—can never be more than prophecies, just a few of innumerable possible views of the future.

To state that the future is the field of freedom is to state, at the same time, that it is the field of power. To claim that it can never be the field of predetermined events is to assert that it is the field of what is desired, not of what must be suffered. By making these statements I want to affirm our new desire to intervene in the forward march of history, to shape for ourselves the pattern of progress rather than to leave fundamental relations to the action of obscure forces.

Do we, in fact, still have any choice? Our freedom in respect to the future is mortgaged by past developments and by underlying trends. In my view this means that we no longer have a choice between the policies of laisser-faire and the policy of voluntary intervention.

By saying that we no longer have a choice I am implicitly stating that there was perhaps a time when we still had a choice. I would like to look at this for a moment, because when it is stated that the rate of change is accelerating, this means that the pressure exerted by questions demanding answers on those who have to make the decisions is increasing as time goes on. In such a case it appears to be reasonable that such questions should be considered in order of their urgency. Each problem only appears on the agenda, therefore, when it has become a burning question and when, in chess terms, the move is forced. There

Hugues de Jouvenel is General Delegate and Secretary-General of the Association Internationale Futuribles in Paris.

is no longer any possibility of choice between different actions which could modify a situation when it was still flexible. Decision-makers then justify their actions by saying that they had no choice. It is certainly true that they *no longer* had any choice, but that is another matter. While they can be exempted from blame in respect of a decision which had in effect become inevitable, they cannot be exempted from blame for having allowed the situation to develop to the point where they were denied any freedom of choice. To avoid such a situation it is necessary to ask questions about situations as they develop, and when they can still be influenced.

Freedom Requires Forecasting

I began by saying that there could be no discussion on the future without freedom; I will now say that there is no freedom of decision without forecasting activities.

The freedom to think and to dream, the pleasures of conjecture and of discussions directed towards the future, only form one aspect of prospective studies. Another aspect is that of action. Prospective studies invite us to consider the future not only as a field of uncertainties but also as a field of power. It is based on our conviction that the future will result, more or less, from the actions of man on his history. The postulate of power is the faith that we can influence the course of events.

This obviously does not mean that every person or every organization has the power to realize what they design or hope for. It is a problem of complexity, a problem of means and a problem of social structure.

The complexity problem arises from the coexistence of various actors and the simultaneous exercise of their various powers, of greater or lesser effect, and coming into conflict to a greater or lesser extent. To state that the future will depend on the interplay of these actors is to recognize that each possesses a unit of power but that also it is necessary that each person should have a forecast enabling him to inform himself on the direction imparted to the complex by the acts of others.

To this distribution of powers is added the problem of means, which raises the questions: Do the means exist? Who is able to exercise them? I will merely recall two obvious points: One relates to the question of physical limits, which, despite the impressive technological progress we have experienced, still largely limit the range of possible futures; the other has to do with the concentration of means—and hence of power—in the hands of a small number of men and organizations.

We will have occasion to return to this point, but first I would like to say a few words about the third postulate, which I have called the *postulate of choice*, because the exercise of power assumes the existence of a driving reason, of a system of ideas and of values by which we are able to discern and to choose, from the range of possible futures, those which appear to us to be desirable and those which appear to be undesirable. On what basis are we to establish our scale of priorities? On what basis will certain persons, rather than others, exercise these choices on behalf of the collectivity?

Let us look for a moment at an extremely simple example. Several surveys have shown that, when a choice is offered between an increase in wages and an improvement in the setting of everyday life, the decision is always in favor of an increase in purchasing power. If, however, we heed the warnings of a number of ecologists, it will soon be too late to save the world if we do not take heed immediately. So, if the value "employment" seems to be more important today than the value "standard of living," perhaps because the first seems to be more immediately threatened than the second, can one perhaps reverse the popular choice in an authoritarian manner in the name of the alarmist doctrines of a "new elite of enlightened futurologists"?

Such examples could be multiplied indefinitely. They raise, in effect, two kinds of questions relating on the one hand to the criteria for decision-making and, on the other, to those institutional arrangements which are most propitious for the exercise of a true democracy.

It is commonplace to point out that the criteria which control decisions today are essentially of the political and economic kind. They can be summed up in the form of two questions: What must I be seen to have done between now and the end of my term of office if I am to encourage the electors to re-elect me? What measures should I take to achieve the maximum immediate economic profit? Just as long as these two types of criteria are the only ones involved in decision-making, so long will it be futile to try to induce in the mind of the decision-maker any qualitative and long-term preoccupations. By that I do not mean to say that we are confronted by an insoluble conflict between quantitative and qualitative or between short-term and long-term. Many examples make it possible to demonstrate the absence of such conflicts. But it is nevertheless a fact that the cost of eliminating pollution is not negligible and that the existing economic system does not encourage taking external costs into local account. It is also the fact that nothing encourages the forester to plant oaks rather than fast-growing poplars.

Industrial society is today compromised by the increasing dissatisfaction it engenders and also by its physical limits, which present an obstacle to the continued advance of growth. Decision-makers will be increasingly constrained to take qualitative factors and the long-term dimension into account.

Planning Pontiffs? Exports in Utopia?

I do not believe that the solution is to replace classical economists by planning pontiffs and experts in utopia. But it is not to be doubted that those responsible for decisions will increasingly have to seek the assistance of experts in prospective studies; they will need to appoint staff officers who are experts in the setting of everyday life. On the evidence, this trend could be very dangerous since it would tend to entrust to an isolated corps of "wise men" the monopoly in respect of prospective activities, that is to say, in respect of freedom, choice and power. One must beware of such staff officers working confidentially for their own superiors, since the latter, always inclined to demand that blind confidence be placed in their judgment, would not fail to point out that they had consulted the auguries or read the auspices.

This danger is even greater today since the uncertainty in regard to the future is engendering a demand for comforting statements and guarantees in respect of the future. It is even greater since the expert now is a cult figure, crowned with the prestige of the computer. What is involved therefore is the relationship between three kinds of agents:
- a public inclined towards disengagement and allegiance.
- a group of experts carefully cultivating the myth of an absolute and universal science.
- a group of governments which ask only to retain and develop their powers by profiting at the same time from the vanity of the oracles and the paralysis of the citizen.

If I point out that the situation is reflected in this relationship it is also because I am convinced that this forecast, valid for some five years, should now also be questioned. I believe, in fact, that we are now involved in a radical questioning both of science and of democracy by delegation.

I believe that the individual is tired of the monopoly of an administration which wants to foresee everything, claiming always to be more in touch with every problem of the citizen than the citizen himself. He is tired of a system characterized by the absolute primacy of ideas of standardization, uniformity and homogeneity which in turn accompany the centralization of power and false rationality: what is in question is not just the satisfaction or dissatisfaction of the citizen but his increasing refusal to lend his support to a crusade in which he no longer believes. What is involved therefore is the invention of a new social system: the defining of a new ethos and a new democratic process.

Comments on Current Revolution

I will close this rather extended essay by making three comments which, in my opinion, characterize this revolution.

My first comment concerns the questioning of science in the widest sense of the term, that is to say the formation of bodies where those magical verities which have so far remained without answer could be openly discussed. In this context I will merely recall the concept of a surmising forum which was put forward at the time the Association Internationale Futuribles was formed: "It is already being pointed out that it is necessary to create a surmising forum where 'advanced' opinions may be put forward on what may happen and on what can be done. Since the passage of time throws up new situations and new seeds of change it is clear that such a forum must remain in continuous operation: there is no question of envisaging the future once and for all, but of maintaining an ongoing discussion."

My second comment concerns the institutional arrangements which would be most propitious for the exercise of a true democracy which would permit the active exercise of citizenship and of human development. What is involved here is a political system allowing the more extensive expression of the wishes of the citizen. In this respect it is important to emphasize that the questioning of the power of divine right and the declaration of the sovereignty of the people were immediately accompanied by the installation of a democracy of delegation. Scarcely has the Nation snatched power from the hands of the Lord than the Nation delegates it to its elected members. The sovereignty of the people was discovered only to be handed over. Today we are involved in the questioning of this system which, based on the available evidence, cannot permit citizens to be fully responsible. This system of delegation is accompanied by increasing dissatisfaction, and we can see today the growing desire of individuals to take their destiny back into their own hands. This is leading to the development of the concept of participation. The fundamental question, therefore, is one of knowing whether the *democracy of participation* will replace the *democracy of delegation.* My feeling is that we will have to undergo a revolution in our political systems, the objective of which will be to find a fair balance between these two forms of government.

My third comment concerns *social innovation* since what is fundamentally involved is our capacity to free human energies and to invent a free market for ideas and wishes. But a free market for ideas will not be enough: it is also necessary to create a free market in experience.

It will undoubtedly be a delicate task for our societies, characterized as they are by the desire for order and power, to accept the disorganized emergence of initiatives which will sometimes be of a contestant character. But it is time to have done with the concentration of power, of simplistic rationalism and the illusion of convergence and of progress. The decentralization of initiatives is without doubt the most important step forward. Its political importance is immense since it will return autonomy to the citizen so as to allow each, by his personal support, to contribute to invention and to the development of new solutions at all levels. This implies a profound questioning of the traditional centralism and the deliberate development of pluralism in all its forms. It is necessary to give back to men the greater part of those decisions which forge their own destiny and to allow the free confrontation of ideas and experiences.

A Good Futurist Is Fully Present

by

Marilyn Saunders

What Do You Mean by "Fully Present"?

You are fully present right now to the extent that you are reading this article without being distracted by the thoughts of your own mind, the noises in your environment, the feelings and sensations in your body, and whatever else you happen to be distracted by.

Being fully present means the ability to give one's attention to what's happening right now. Not what happened last year or five minutes ago or what you think may happen at two o'clock or next week. It might be that what's happening for you right now is that you are planning a trip for next month or a policy study for next year. To the extent that you can be fully with that planning (rather than requiring that the trip be a certain way or that the study have a certain outcome) you are fully present.

Being fully present also means the ability to quiet the mind and stop figuring things out—to stop doing and become quiet and receptive in order to take in. Being quiet and receptive is a powerful learning stance. For me, it's a wonderful time when I allow myself to forget everything I "know" and create empty spaces for new things to come into—or to leave empty for a while. It's a time when looking at a tree can tell me how to teach tomorrow's class or holding a stone can help me understand what's happening with a particular client. It's a time when I learn more about how much I trust myself and when I learn that I have access to a source of very great wisdom and love. It's a time when I learn that I am not alone in this universe and that I am very much connected to everything else that exists. And to the extent that I do trust myself—my deeper, higher, wiser self—it's a time of grace and beauty and clarity.

It's also my experience that to the extent I can be fully present, I can let go of my fear of the future, and it is then that my actions in the present help to create a desirable future. This is true even when I'm experiencing pain or anger or frustration. To the extent that I can be fully present and experience these states, I lose my fear of them, which frees me to let go of them. What I am afraid to experience

Marilyn Saunders is Founder and Executive Director of the Center for Conscious Evolution, Washington, D.C.

I hang onto and drag around with me. Then those pieces of the past prevent me from being open to the present and color my view of the future. I find this true also of more pleasurable states. To the extent I am carrying around yesterday's high I am not open to experiencing the present and I am prevented from receiving new information which could help me create the future.

A View of the Present

One of the things that happened to me when I began to work toward being fully present was that I began to ask: What's happening? Where are we now? How can I make sense of the present? How does it all fit together? And I began to look for the forces which are pushing and pulling us toward change. Following are the major categories which I found. First, the breakdown of beliefs, assumptions, values, and institutions which are no longer working. For example, the traditional concepts of family, church, educational system, government, and business are all being questioned and challenged. For many people, the accumulation of material goods is no longer a satisfying life goal. The role of the expert is being questioned; alternatives to hierarchical organization are being sought.

Next, we have developed enormous scientific and technological knowledge and power. We have the ability to destroy ourselves and to recreate ourselves in new ways. We are exploring on both the microcosmic and the macrocosmic levels, from the atom to the universe. Our capacities in bio-engineering are increasing and pushing us into new ethical areas. We can communicate around the globe in seconds. And along with these new capacities we have developed a love/hate relationship with science and technology.

Further, we are placing increasing attention on the human potential. We are studying the human brain, meditating, becoming conscious of consciousness. We are developing new therapies and increasing our interpersonal communications skills. We are beginning to take responsibility for our own thoughts, for our own actions, and for our own health. We are developing our psychic capacities, and more and more "ordinary" people are having mystical experiences. And as we look deeper into ourselves we are discovering each other and also the universe and we are recognizing that we are all one. In caring for ourselves we are learning to care for each other and for the planet and for its other life forms. And we are realizing that we still know very little about the human potential.

In addition, we're beginning to realize that we live on a finite planet. We're learning that it is one ecological system: that food, population, resources, and pollution are interconnected and that we are all interdependent. A few have the vision that we're all planetary citizens and urge us to think globally while we act locally. As we become familiar with the finiteness of the planet, we're beginning to look beyond it. We call it Spaceship Earth and wonder if there are others. We visit our own moon and send probes deep into space. We're talking about living in space and wrestling over what priority we want to give to realizing that possibility.

And finally, there is the hunger and the search for a new guiding mythos and the emergence of new images of reality and new values. We make new attempts to find a workable ethic which values the general good more than private profit and we make demands for increased participation and inclusion of ethnic minorities, of women, of the old, the young, the poor, the rich. We place new emphasis on perceiving and understanding whole systems and we have new regard for the gentle strength of feminine energy which is in all of us.

What all this means for me is that we live in a very challenging and exciting time of change where our task is to understand what's happening from the broadest perspective possible, to get in there and participate in whatever ways are meaningful, and to stay fully present to what we are doing.

Evolution—Ready or Not

More on the hunger and the search for a new guiding mythos: As I went through my own period of mid-life crisis and transition I heard others saying that what was lacking in Western culture was a guiding mythos—a story, a perspective—which would give meaning to our lives. That resonated within me and I realized that I was looking for a meaningful personal mythos as well. Then I found what I like to call the evolutionary mythos, based on the work of Teilhard de Chardin and Barbara Hubbard. I began to view what we're going through now as part of a larger process and I began to experience a deep sense of meaning and purpose.

The evolutionary mythos states that what is happening now is part of a process that has been going on for billions of years (somewhere between seven and twenty billion years depending on which scientists you ask when). This process has included several major transformations including the creation of the physical universe, the development of earth and the solar system, the emergence of life, of multi-cellular life, and of humanity. This process is still very much in progress and perhaps on the brink of another major transformation. Chardin states in *The Phenomenon of Man* that evolution is a process of increasingly complex whole systems and he emphasizes the occurrence of synthesis—the creation of new forms out of the old. At each step, whatever is happening eventually reaches a state of overcomplexity which leads to crisis which leads to a higher synthesis.

As I became more familiar with this evolutionary mythos I realized that it not only gave me a meaningful perspective to view the world around me—it also described what was happening in my own life. I began to see patterns in my own personal process that were the same as the patterns in our social process, and I began to make sense for myself out of what I saw happening both around me and within me. At the same time, the more fully present I became in my own life, the more I realized that I was learning about a larger process also. I had glimpses of what the mystics mean when they tell us we are all microcosms of the macrocosm.

I now look at our social crises (and our personal crises) as what Barbara Hubbard calls "evolutionary drivers"—forces which push us toward our next steps. Crises are evolutionary events which occur when more of the same doesn't work. They are signals which tell us that we need to change, that we need to grow—signals which remind us that the evolutionary process is continuing and that it's time to go to the next stage.

However, to the extent that we are aware that we are part of an evolutionary process and that growth and change are natural and normal, we may be able to avert crisis. Often it is crisis that forces us to find new ways. An alternative is to allow the forces of attraction and excitement to lead us to the new. In my own personal experience, I find that to the extent that I listen to my own growth needs and pay attention to the things which attract me, which interest me, which excite me, I don't need to experience crisis. However, when it's time to evolve further and I stay too long in a place of comfort and ease, ignoring the voices of attraction, I stagnate and then often a crisis occurs which tells me I need to evolve further.

I believe that the process is the same on the social level—that to the extent that we pay attention to the attractive forces rather than digging our heels in and resisting change we can avert crises. The catch is that sometimes it's difficult to find the attractions and sometimes they seem to involve tremendous risks. Following one's attractions often involves doing something new and different and, of course, that's what evolution is all about. Evolution is the creation of new forms out of the old. When we evolve we get to places we haven't been before. The risks are real. Evolution offers no guarantees that a particular attempt will work. Often it's only through multiple attempts that a new form breaks through.

To what extent at this point in this multi-billion year evolutionary process do we, humanity, have control over this process and to what extent are we merely vehicles or pawns of it? I think we need to realize that the process has involved an increase of consciousness with each phase and maybe we're at a point of co-creation where we are becoming partners with higher forces which many people have experienced and very few understand. If this is true, we have tremendous responsibility in terms of how we view our capacities—scientific, technological, human—and how we use them so that we can become increasingly able to respond to the crises which have been developing and are becoming more visible in the 1980s.

There is no going back—evolution will continue whether we are ready or not. I believe, however, that we still have the option of evolution by attraction, that we can choose to move through the present period of change by listening and paying attention to the alternatives that excite us. But to do this we need to be fully present; the signals of attraction are often quiet and gentle and cannot be heard unless we are receptive, and it's very difficult to be receptive without being present. So to the extent that we can be fully present I believe that we can evolve through attraction rather than crisis. However, my sense is that we're getting close on time for exercising this option, and that is why I state that a good futurist needs to be fully present.

Senior Citizens As Futurists

by

Frank Snowden Hopkins

Many young and middle-aged Americans immersed in their current careers and professional interests think of their elders as men and women who are mired in the past and not well-equipped to understand the contemporary world. They were born and brought up in a simpler time, according to this view, and do not understand the enormous promise of all the new scientific ideas and technologies that have significance for the human future.

My own view is quite a different one. Older people may not excel at understanding all the newest ideas and how they may cause revolutionary changes in the years ahead, but what they do have is tremendous experience in observing the changes that have already occurred and are still going on. It is because they have been through so much change already and witnessed its results that they possess a historical perspective that is lacking in many younger people.

I would argue, then, that it is not the younger members of our contemporary society, excited by the promise of new discoveries and new technological developments, who are best fitted to plan the future, but our older people who have already seen so much happen on a very broad front. And it may well be that the younger people, who are admittedly the experts on a lot of new accomplishments, are the *least* fitted to work out in their minds how all the changes now in prospect will affect the century ahead in which today's children will live their entire adult lives.

Let's look at the evidence of what our more thoughtful senior citizens have to offer. The twentieth century, experienced by all of us who have now reached retirement years, has been a period of turbulent events and revolutionary changes. If an individual has lived through this turbulent period, he has acquired perspective on the meaning of social and historical change. But if he has been born recently, he may be too young and too inexperienced to understand in a deeper sense what is now going on in our late-twentieth-century world.

In defining who is a senior citizen for the purposes of this paper, I have set 60 as my minimum age because only the persons born in

Frank Snowden Hopkins, who spent many years as a journalist and diplomat, is Vice-President of the World Future Society.

1920 or earlier have grown up in and experienced the most rapidly changing society in all of human history. Their experience has been particularly vivid if they were born in a rural area but have lived their adult lives in urban America.

Some of us are much older than 60. Some of us were born before 1915, before 1910, before 1905, even before 1900. Some of us have experienced the entire twentieth century. One of the wisest friends I have—the author of more than thirty books on twentieth-century subjects—was born in 1888 and has a perspective on the twentieth century which almost all of us can envy. I am speaking of Stuart Chase of Connecticut, who at 92 is still writing; he is a futurist and a very thoughtful one, whose thinking is projected far, far ahead. He is the author of a splendid recent book, *The Most Probable Future*, and has written an article within the past few years for our Society's journal, THE FUTURIST ("A Modest Utopia," October 1975).

By a remarkable coincidence Stuart Chase and I share the same birthday, twenty years apart. I envy him his perspective and his ability to simplify complex issues and focus on what is most essential to our future lives. Alongside my friend Stuart, I am a Johnny-come-lately, but at least I have lived in all our century's decades and witnessed many changes and many achievements. What Stuart Chase and I have in common is a sense of historical onward movement and a deep concern as to the direction it is taking. It seems to us that every thoughtful, well-read observer of the contemporary scene must share this sense of history and this feeling of concern. I would also add that those of us who have lived longest have a deep moral obligation to share with our younger contemporaries what we think about the present century, what we believe should be done to prepare for the next one, and what we want our society to do for today's children—children who can benefit from our generation's accomplishments, but who also must live with our mistakes and the damage we have done to our planetary environment through heedless materialism and reckless mismanagement of many precious natural resources. We who are senior citizens have a moral obligation to speak out and tell others what we have learned over many decades. We have witnessed more social and technological changes in our life spans than any generation which has ever existed.

Many generations in human history have experienced change—sometimes slow and gradual, sometimes sudden and dramatic. But ours, surely, is the generation which, on a worldwide basis, has experienced the most change. We have seen how changes occur, what they signify for the years ahead, and what they are likely to do to us if we do not deal with them. Since we not only experienced this change but also contributed heavily to it, our generation has, in my opinion, a sacred obligation to try to guide change in such a way that it contributes to a better management of our national society and our international community, and not to their mismanagement.

To illustrate more graphically the points I am trying to make, let me tell you about a book I am trying to write. It covers a period of 150 years, beginning in the past and extending into the future. I am not sure yet of the title, but it will be something like *The Auto-biography of a Sesquicentenarian* or *The Sesquicentennial of a Rural American*, and it will deal with the 150 years from 1845 to 1995. I start with the year 1845 because that was the birth year of my maternal grandfather, the Rev. Sewell S. Hepburn, D.D., a prominent clergyman of his era who lived to be 87 years old and died in 1932. The significance of 1995 is that it is the year when I myself will be 87, if I should live that long. What I am trying to do is to put two lives together, end to end, my grandfather's and my own. Since I was born in 1908, my life overlapped my grandfather's by 24 years, and I knew the old gentleman intimately, listening to many of his anecdotes and autobiographic stories during my early years. He was an educated man, who was one of the few college graduates of his generation, and he left copious written memoirs. All in all, I feel as if I know almost as much about his life career as I do of my own.

If I put my grandfather's life and my own together, I get a 150-year period in which many astonishing changes took place. By a trick of the imagination, I merge two personalities into a single person, with a single historical memory and a single historical experience and perspective. I shall call this merged, composite personality Hepburn-Hopkins, and in his long lifetime he will have lived from deep in the horse-and-buggy phase of American rural life, when the first trains were beginning to run and U.S. industry was just getting under way, to a period at the end of the present century when some new developments will have occurred than even in 1980 we cannot yet clearly foresee. All I can promise is that the fifteen years from 1980 to 1995 will be projected as plausibly as an experienced futurist can accomplish it. Whether I myself actually live to the year 1995 is irrelevant.

Let me start with the birth of Grandfather Hepburn and tell you of all the changes which my composite character, Hepburn-Hopkins, will have witnessed and experienced during his lifetime. The Rev. Sewell S. Hepburn was born on a Missouri farm in 1845 at a time when the population of the United States was only about 20 million and when hardly half the present fifty states of the Union had yet been established. Our national territory in 1845 included the Louisiana Purchase and the newly admitted state of Texas, but we did not yet have California and other Southwestern states, we had not yet legally validated our claim to the Pacific Northwest, and of course neither Alaska nor Hawaii had yet been acquired.

Our country was almost entirely agricultural in 1845, but we had some growing industries such as lumber mills, shipbuilding, textile factories, and iron and steel furnaces. The age of steam had begun, and we had steamboats on our inland waterways, steam locomotives pulling our trains, and steam power in our factories. When my great-grandfather Hepburn migrated from Maryland to Missouri in 1837, he took his family and his slaves with him in two covered wagons, but in 1853 when he returned to Maryland his group traveled on river steamers from Hannibal to Cairo on the Mississippi, then up the Ohio to Wheeling—at that time in Virginia, since West Virginia was not yet a state.

From Wheeling the travelers continued to Baltimore on the infant Baltimore & Ohio Railroad, an eighteen-hour trip which my eight-year-old grandfather remembered vividly in his memoirs. It has been said jokingly that railroads are run by "jerks," but that was literally true in 1853, for the cars were fastened together by rigid steel link-bars and every time the train stopped or started Grandpa and his younger brother suffered painful yanks which almost threw them out of their seats. From Baltimore a bay steamboat took the group across Chesapeake Bay to Chestertown, where they were met by relatives in horse-drawn buggies and wagons.

My composite character Hepburn-Hopkins experienced the entire second half of the nineteenth century, an era in which our empty country was rapidly filling up and our cities were becoming industrial centers. Millions of immigrants arrived from Europe and helped to settle the farmlands of the West and to provide labor for America's mines, factories, and building construction. My generation was brought up on stories about how naive many of the new immigrants were. One Irish boy is supposed to have written back to his parents, for example, that he was getting rich making a dollar a day as a hod-carrier. "All I have to do is carry bricks up to the fourth floor," he wrote. "The men up there do all the work!"

Anyway, the country prospered, even though the Civil War was a great disaster in the South and left the defeated states of the Confederacy economically prostrate for a generation. Hepburn-Hopkins saw a magnificent network of railroads and steamship lines link up the continental nation internally and connect it with the outside world. When my character was born in 1845, houses were lighted with whale-oil lamps and heated with wood fires, but he lived to see kerosene lamps, gas lights, and then electricity. He saw coal mines dug and exploited and then oil wells, to furnish fuel for home heating and for factories and transportation. He saw the invention of the telegraph, the telephone, and eventually, in the next century, wireless telegraphy. He saw the development of photography and then of motion pictures. He saw the early ocean steamships develop into ocean liners and into powerful navies with battleships and submarines and eventually aircraft carriers.

As the nineteenth century turned into the twentieth, most local transportation was still by horse-drawn vehicles—buggies, carriages, road-carts, farm wagons, huge drays used on the streets of cities—but the automobile age arrived with the invention of internal combustion engines fueled by gasoline. When Grandfather Hepburn was 63, Grandson Hopkins was born in 1908. It was still the horse-and-buggy era in my childhood, and I doubt if there were a dozen automobiles in my rural Virginia county when I can first remember. We drove horses and were always terrified lest our frightened animals run away with us when we met an early Model T Ford rattling around a bend in the road. Soon after automobiles came airplanes, and I well remember the primitive bi-planes which used to fly over our farm in the years of World War I.

Hepburn-Hopkins saw several wars. In his infancy our country fought the war with Mexico, and I knew people in my youth who could remember it—the oldest an old lady born in 1828 who as a girl of 16 in Alexandria, Virginia, remembered going to balls at which she danced with young army officers with brass buttons on their uniforms, getting ready to leave for the fighting. Then came the Civil War of 1861-65, to be followed by the Spanish-American War of 1898. Hepburn-Hopkins saw the great new industrial capacity of America applied to World War I in 1914-18 and become the decisive factor in victory after the United States became a combatant in 1917. This war, often in my youth simply called the Great War because it was unprecedentedly vast, was a struggle in which millions were killed, in which great nations were torn apart or changed in character, and in which frightening new political forces were turned loose on the international community. The Rev. Sewell S. Hepburn remembered the Civil War of his youth and was saddened by the struggle of 1914-18, wondering what its long-range effects might be. His grandson, six years old in 1914, ten years old in 1918, was less aware of the war itself than of its troubled aftermath in the 1920s and 1930s.

There were great social changes during this period. Grandpa Hepburn saw his horse-and-buggy world crumbling around him in the 1920s. All his life, from 1869 on, he had been a country parson, riding or driving horses in the performance of his church and parish duties. He felt that he understood country people and the rural life which they led on farms and in small villages, and he trembled with anxiety as the automobile penetrated even to his rural parish on Maryland's Eastern Shore and began to replace the animal he most dearly loved, the horse. He observed with anguish the changing life styles of the twenties as women shortened their skirts, bobbed their hair, colored their faces with cosmetics, and, to his special horror, began to smoke cigarettes—a custom he thought no true lady could ever adopt. He saw family life begin to weaken and decay while church attendance and religious zeal went into a decline. His last years were sad ones, lived in a new age whose values he could not accept. His grandson, on the other hand, went into the 1920s with eagerness and enjoyed growing up in the new freedom and tearing along dirt roads in an old Model T jalopy at thirty miles an hour, stirring up a cloud of dust. For the Hopkins half of my composite character wasted no regrets on the passing of the Victorian order and looked toward the future with rosy expectations. He wanted to become a professional writer and all his early years were directed toward this ambition.

In the field of social and political events, our composite Hepburn-Hopkins was aware both of gains and losses. Twentieth-century America was rapidly maturing and changing. Great cities were growing rapidly, and rural Americans were deserting farms and small towns and swarming into the centers of business and industry where the action seemed to be. During the earliest years of the century, immigrants continued to swarm into the United States, sometimes as many as two million a year. Masses of new Americans filled the city slums and seemed to many older citizens to be unassimilable into traditional American life. A worried Congress in 1924 clapped on immigration restrictions to curtail population growth and to try to maintain the primacy of the older ethnic stocks from the British Isles and the countries of northwestern Europe. Nevertheless, the agricultural republic into which Hepburn-Hopkins had been born in 1845 had become by 1930 a huge urbanized nation of 122,000,000.

The younger half of our composite person had been born into a simple life on a farm. He grew up knowing how to milk cows, to harness horses, to butcher hogs, to hoe potatoes and tomatoes, to shuck corn, to shoot rats and crows, to trap and skin muskrats, and to perform all the other skills which American farmboys learned. He went to college and university in the 1920s and became a city boy living in the heart of New York's Manhattan. He went through the economic miseries of his generation in the depression of the 1930s and took part in the huge war effort of the 1940s. Journalistic ambitions were shelved after years spent with newspapers in Minneapolis, Richmond, and Baltimore, and Hopkins went into a Baltimore shipyard to engage in industrial relations and personnel work. By an accident of fate, he found himself organizing and directing a program in which thousands of men and women were trained to be shipyard mechanics, and then in 1945 was employed by the U.S. Department of State to organize programs of training for the men and women of the American Foreign Service.

From this beginning in 1945, the Hopkins half of Hepburn-Hopkins spent the next twenty-three years performing a series of duties for the State Department, first helping to plan and develop the Foreign Service and equip it for the postwar world. Emphasis was on learning languages, studying the histories and traditions of foreign countries and areas, and learning how best to understand and communicate with foreign peoples, but much attention was given also to international economic and political problems and the need to bring about a more effectively organized world community. In 1952 Hopkins became a career Foreign Service officer himself and for the next sixteen years spent most of his time in foreign countries, acquiring familiarity with the peoples and problems of the twentieth-century world. By the time he retired in 1968 at the age of sixty, he was a long-range planner writing think-pieces for the Department's Policy Planning Council, focussing on America's foreign policy objectives for the twenty-first century.

During these years from 1945 to 1968, major technological and social developments were taking place in the postwar world. The old European colonial empires fell apart after World War II, with the exception that Communist Russia by the use of military power retained and added to the subject territories of the old Czarist Empire. But in the place of the old British, French, Dutch, Belgian, Italian, and Portuguese empires there were now scores of newly independent countries. Most of the new nations were overpopulated, under-educated, and poorly equipped to make their own way in a developing but highly complicated world economy. The already industrialized countries were applying modern science and technology and moving rapidly ahead, and a growing gap was developing between the countries of high educational standards and those which were lagging badly both in education and in economic development. The United States and other advanced countries sought to help the Less Developed Countries (LDCs) of Asia, Africa, and Latin America but their applied health technologies reduced death rates so rapidly that the population increases of the LDCs tended to outrun improvements in schooling and in economic productivity.

In his years with the U.S. Department of State, Hepburn-Hopkins witnessed extraordinary technological advances. The invention of atomic weapons led to the development of enormous nuclear capabilities by the two superpowers. Each country built up a stock of long-range nuclear missiles so enormous that it could bring down in ruins the entire civilized world. The development of rocketry and space technology enabled the Soviet Union to put its cosmonauts into space orbit and the United States to land its astronauts on the moon. Both countries explored the solar system's other planets by sending out instrumented rockets to Venus, Mars, Jupiter, and Saturn. There were phenomenal developments in air-space aviation, in satellite television, in under-sea exploration, in computer technology, and in many other fields.

But Hepburn-Hopkins also witnessed social, economic, and political disappointments. He saw the civilized countries of the world band together to form the United Nations and the UN's related specialized agencies, but then fail to transform this system into an effective form of planetary government. He saw the world split into two kinds of nation-states, one Communist, and the other non-Communist, and many dangerous rivalries develop between them. Along with this East-West conflict, he also saw a North-South confrontation develop between the rich nations of high technology and the poor nations struggling to feed, clothe, house, and school their people. He saw seething political dissatisfactions develop as populations increased more and more dangerously. And he saw the growth of more and more violence, terrorism, and criminal blackmail. The world was becoming steadily more turbulent.

As world population soared out of control in the LDCs, world food production lagged badly behind. Famines and starvation seemed to threaten in many areas. Many essential minerals became scarcer and more expensive to mine and process as the demands of modern industry seemed always to increase. An energy crisis loomed as petroleum, urgently needed by the industrialized countries, became steadily more costly. Conflicts over food and energy threatened much of the world. Another great planetary problem also menaced much of the globe—the pollution and despoliation of large areas of the Earth's biosphere, that thin layer of land, water, and air in which plant and animal life are possible. The man-made world which we call civilization was impinging ever more heavily on mankind's Garden of Eden, the world of nature in which human life first developed. Among the problems were deforestation, soil erosion, the over-fishing of oceans, seas, and inland waters, and the poisoning with noxious gases of the once-pure atmosphere over the Earth's urban communities.

Noting all these developments in 1980, Hepburn-Hopkins, looking at the sweep of history from the viewpoint of his 135 years, wondered what the final fifteen years of his sesquicentennial might bring. He

392

had deep roots in the nineteenth century, but had seen its peacefulness shattered by two world wars and many political conflicts in the twentieth. Would civilization endure, or was it on its last legs? Would the children of 1980, with life expectancies into the 2050s and beyond, have a fighting chance for happiness in the twenty-first century? Hepburn-Hopkins was not yet ready to despair, but his thoughts were filled with anxieties as he looked ahead to 1995. Nuclear war might break out and devastate the civilized world. Population increases might bring about widespread famines and epidemics. The energy crisis might remain unresolved and bring down sharply the standard of living. Pollution and the despoliation of the environment might continue in such a way that the world would be much less livable in another fifteen years.

Some scientists and technologists say that they have answers to each of these dangers. But human nature is the great imponderable. Is there any answer to man's selfishness, his drive for power, his capacity for self-indulgence, his emotional immaturity, his limited intellectual understanding? Man's worst enemy is himself; we have met the enemy and he is us, as a cartoonist has told us. Solutions are in sight for many problems, but meanwhile the problems themselves worsen. World political order is deteriorating, not improving. So as Hepburn-Hopkins tries in 1980 to project the events of his lifetime another fifteen years into the future, he is not at all confident that he will find much joy in his 150th birthday celebration. He has come a long way since his birth in 1845, but a period of moral and spiritual regeneration, a Great Transformation of all our value systems, is needed, and it is urgently necessary that it be under way by 1995.

So this writer, the junior part of Hepburn-Hopkins, feels very uncertain what the future holds for mankind. He looks at his children and finds them mature and responsible individuals of good character who will contribute their best efforts to any meaningful movement of regeneration. He looks at his grandchildren and sees in them promising youngsters with bright minds and favorable attitudes. He reads about the research that is going on into the human brain and into psychic phenomena, and hopes that it will bear important fruit. He realizes that he is not alone in his concern for the future of our species, for thoughtful people all around him are also worrying and trying to help improve our national and world societies. He dares to hope for the successful completion of his sesquicentennial, but although our society should hold together for another fifteen years, a lot of reforms are urgently needed now for the future to hold real promise.

So much for Hepburn-Hopkins, the 135-year-old composite man to whom I have introduced you. Let me now get back to the subject of this discussion, which is the responsibilities of senior citizens as futurists.

I shall not claim that senior citizens are the only generation with wisdom, or the only ones among us who feel concern about the fate of our descendants. I do think, however, that some of us have arrived at that stage of life when men and women tend to reflect more than they used to about the meaning of things. Most serious people are busy people, working hard at their personal careers to try to make a success of whatever they are working at. Politicians are absorbed in politics, economists are absorbed in economic problems, engineers in engineering projects, business men in running their businesses, and so on. Most such people don't have much time to devote to fields of activity in which they are not personally engaged, so most of us through most of our lives have a rather narrow focus. This tendency toward concentration is the characteristic of most of us until we reach retirement age and are able to broaden out and engage in reflection. It is at that stage, it seems to me, that we are able best to put together in a meaningful way all that we have seen and done and experienced over a busy lifetime. Many of us who are serious, well-educated professionals, very knowledgeable in our special fields, are so busy doing whatever we're doing that we tend to look at the future with one eye rather than two. We aren't blind, but neither do we see and understand everything that we should see and understand and put everything around us in our world in a complete perspective. It is when we reach senior years that we overcome some of this lack of perspective and therefore have special qualities and capabilities to contribute.

If we can see the future clearly with one eye, then of course we're a lot more knowledgeable than those who can't see at all, or at any rate not clearly, or may not even bother to look. There is an old saying that in the kingdom of the blind, the one-eyed man is king, so obviously it is better to have one good eye than no vision at all. But there is also another part of that old saying. It is to the effect that in the world of one-eyed men, the two-eyed man is a pretty special character. You don't have to have lived a long time and experienced many decades to be a two-eyed man, but it appears to me that wisdom is often accumulated through experience. So I would like to see those of us who have lived the longest, who have seen the most of our change-laden modern world, and who have experienced the most try to figure out what we have learned and what we can pass on to our younger contemporaries. Let us do our best to be two-eyed men in a one-eyed world.

There remains one final question to discuss, which is that of the moral obligation which our generation has to all the generations which follow us. A good many senior citizens seem to have the feeling that in their retirement they have earned the right to relax and just enjoy their remaining years. You hear it said, "I've paid my dues and done my duty. Now let younger people pick up the burdens of leadership." I myself don't agree with this attitude. To me it seems that our generation has made a lot of mistakes and along with its accomplishments it has created many problems for our descendants. We have been selfish, materialistic, and heedless. We have been guilty of complacency, of neglect, and of mismanagement of human affairs. We are passing on to our descendants a much more troubled world than we inherited from our ancestors. If there is any way we can help provide our children and grandchildren with a better set of options for the twenty-first century, if there is any way we can share with them what we have learned in the course of our long lives, then I would argue that we have a

394

sacred responsibility to do our very best for just as long as we can keep our health, our energy, and our mental activity.

The Futurist As Ethicist

by

Robert B. Mellert

The United States, Canada, Japan, and most of Western Europe presently enjoy a standard of living which is beyond what they can wish to become the standard for the rest of the world. What has become the accepted status quo in these nations is so high that, if all the developing nations of the world suddenly approached this same life style, the results would be critical shortages of food, energy and raw materials, as well as unmanageable problems of water, land and air pollution. We might ask ourselves about the morality of enjoying a standard of living beyond what we can even *wish* others to achieve for themselves.

This kind of moral problem may seem somewhat artificial to those of us in the advantaged group, but there are some real, practical corollaries to it which are now facing us and which will probably become more urgent later in this decade. They may be summarized into two questions, as follows:

1. In situations where voluntary modification of our standard of living would benefit the needs and aspirations of other people, is there a moral responsibility for those who enjoy the better life to undertake these modifications?

2. In situations where the use of the world's resources to improve living standards in the developing world is in competition with the need to conserve those same resources for our own future generations, where does our primary responsibility lie?

Let us look at these two questions in more detail, beginning with the problem of modifying aspects of our life style for the sake of others. In an expanding economic environment, it is easy to be generous. One simply gives from his abundance. Frequently even the act of giving can be used to promote the expansion of one's economic efforts. The free samples or large discounts given customers to try a new product illustrates this point, and the same principle is used in international trade to build new markets before raising prices to make those markets profitable.

However, in a static or contracting economic environment, such largesse is unprofitable. There are no free samples. What is given is the result of charity and/or voluntary restraint. People who helped unemployed friends

Robert B. Mellert is Associate Professor, Interdisciplinary Studies, Brookdale College, Lincroft, New Jersey.

and relatives during the Great Depression, even though it required considerable belt-tightening of their own, are examples of this principle. Parents who do without so their children can go to college illustrate this point, too.

Today many futurists are suggesting that the Western world may be shifting from an economy of expansion to one of restraint. In such an environment some have already begun to ask the question, "Who comes first, they or we?" Unless we can all agree to reply conjunctively (both they and we) rather than disjunctively (either they or we—and it won't be "they"!), there is no need to proceed further in our discussion. By a disjunctive answer in which we choose ourselves at the expense of all other claims, we would deny any responsibility beyond what we owe ourselves, and global concerns (e.g., towards the developing world) as well as futurist concerns (towards our own posterity) would become meaningless.

Let me stress the very real possibility that the Western world will respond to this issue selfishly and ignore the needs of others whenever their accustomed standard of living seems threatened. The possibility was illustrated by the apathetic and even hostile public response to the call for voluntary restraint during the recent gasoline shortage in the U.S.

If we can surmount the temptation to personal and immediate gratification and recognize the moral imperative of restraint in those situations where there would be benefit to others, we can then confront the second question stated above. It concerns our responsibility to the poorer areas of the world versus our responsibility to our own offspring.

A closer look at this issue may reveal why it is stated in the form of a dilemma. To the extent that we from the wealthier nations support the efforts of the less developed nations to move towards the standards of life that we enjoy, we reduce certain limited material resources which might otherwise be still available for our own offspring. In other words, presuming that we take the moral position favoring restraint for the sake of others, who are those others? Are they those people already born and striving for a more equitable share of the goods of this world, or are they those people not yet born but who represent our own posterity and the continuance of our way of life? How do we direct our moral efforts between these two competing groups? If faced with a genuine dilemma where one alternative excludes the other, will we be acting morally when we bequeath an adequate inheritance to the future or when we share the benefits of the earth with those presently trying to improve their lives?

Fortunately, this dilemma does not apply to our usage of all resources. In most cases, there is an adequate supply or adequate alternatives, both for the present aspirations of other cultures and for the future needs of our own culture's posterity. But there are sufficient examples to indicate that we do indeed face some moral dilemmas, and that these dilemmas will be more apparent during the next decade as the upper limits of certain resources are reached.

Situations where a modification of our present habits might make a difference to both present aspirations and future needs occur in two ways: by the rate we use certain scarce resources and by the way we waste reserves potentially but not currently useful. An example of this first situation is petroleum, which has become somewhat of a *cause celebre* during the last decade. At the present usage rate, the known reserves of oil that can be drilled in the conventional manner will run out during the first half of the next century. This will leave for our offspring only oil reserves that are considerably more costly to extract. Since petroleum is necessary for many purposes other than heating and transportation, we can be sure that they will have to pay the price to extract oil from shale, sand and "heavy oil" deposits. Meanwhile, if industrialization spreads rapidly to the developing world, the most accessible of these alternate sources of petroleum will already be exploited. The more that is used now, the more costly will be future production efforts.

Here, we clearly find the demands of the present in conflict with the needs of the future. If we in the Western world do choose to exercise the restraint that has been urged on us, the savings we generate will raise the question, To whose benefit? Shall it be used to improve the standard of living of the nations trying to enter the technological age, or shall it be guarded for the descendants of those already habituated to technological living?

A second example, this one concerning the waste of a potentially valuable resource, is the case of helium and natural gas. There is a limited supply of helium on the planet which is not replaceable by any human technology. Until recently helium has been of limited concern in our planning because it has few uses, the best known of which is to fill the balloons of children at the circus. So, in extracting natural gas from the earth for use as fuel, helium has been allowed to escape into the upper atmosphere.

Recently, scientists have been experimenting with liquid helium as a superconductor of electricity, and this could make helium a most important resource for communications and storage batteries. But today there is no commercial demand for helium, and so this limited and potentially precious resource is still left to escape into the atmosphere in our race to extract natural gas for fuel. If superconductivity lives up to scientific expectations, will there be enough helium left? What other potentially valuable resources are being squandered and thus kept from future generations in our attempt to continue development in the present?

These are only two examples, one illustrating the effects of scarcity and the other of waste, regarding the unconscious competition between the present aspirations of other lands and the probable needs of our future progeny. There are many, many more, especially regarding scarcity. Our best silver, tin and zinc are in short supply and could be exhausted in the decades ahead. Who should benefit from an active campaign to conserve and to recycle such materials—those who, alive now, strive to improve their standard of living, or those who, not yet born, will need these same resources to continue the civilization we have bequeathed to them? Which group ought to be given moral priority in the decisions we make today?

Traditionally, Western moral teaching has stressed the obligation to help others. By this is generally meant those already present, even though physically distant from us. Note, for example, how the word "neighbor" in Christian morality has been interpreted to include every *living* person. Until recently there has been little ethical stress on our moral responsibility to future people, even though they may represent our own posterity. This is probably because the world used to seem large and fecund enough to allow the future to take care of its own needs. Today, as we become more aware of the finitude of our planet and as we begin to adopt some restraints in our lives, we find that the hopes of the present in developing nations are coming into competition with what will in all probability be the needs of the future in our own civilization.

How can we resolve this dilemma? How much moral responsibility do we have to those presently alive but physically distant and unrelated to us? How much responsibility do we have to those not yet born, but who will (and must be) generated if the best of human life as we know it is to continue?

In order to shed light on this dilemma, let us first take note of the ways in which we know these two groups of people. Neither is immediately present to us. One group is not spacially present because they live in parts of the world we rarely visit or even think about. The other group is not temporally present because they do not yet exist. However, neither group is totally absent from our awareness either. The former group, the present/distant, are brought to our attention frequently by television, radio, newspapers and magazines. We do get an occasional glimpse, via the media, of those anonymous faces whose abject poverty inspires compassion in even the most hardened soul. In addition, these peoples do have advocates among religious groups, charitable agencies, and international organizations. So, even though our concerns for them are not as vital as perhaps they ought to be, they do speak to us in a variety of indirect ways.

The knowledge we have of the latter group, the future/proximate, is obtained somewhat differently. Because the subjects of this group do not yet exist, the source of our knowledge can only be from our projections about the future and from our imagination of them. Those of us who have children or grandchildren surely stop to wonder, from time to time, what the world will be like for them when they are our age. But what about *their* children and grandchildren? Surely the world will be much different, but will the standard of living three or four generations hence continue the upward climb we have experienced, or will our offspring be forced to adapt to a less appealing life style as the earth becomes a less habitable place to live? Ought we assume a moral responsibility now in their regard?

The basis of moral responsibility for the future can best be illustrated from an analysis of the obligation of parenting. We are responsible for what we procreate. But this principle extends further. Even non-parents, who by choice or circumstance will leave no heirs of their own upon this planet, share this responsibility for the future. For surely they would not wish that the earth some day be unpeopled. The very idea of the world without any rational life looms as the ultimate human tragedy for parent and non-parent alike. If, therefore, the idea of a lifeless planet is abhorrent to all of us, then the responsibility to maintain life is a duty common to all of us, too.

The problem, I believe, is not that we dispute our obligation in this respect; it is that we ignore it. It takes a conscious effort to accept moral responsibility for a situation that does not yet exist. There are no TV documentaries giving us visual images and no international agencies making appeals.

Now the first condition for the fulfillment of duty is the acknowledgement of responsibility. And we cannot acknowledge what we do not know. Therefore, in the competition between the present/distant and the future/proximate, even the limited awareness we have of the former gives them a definite advantage. Actual wants are always more persuasive than future wants. Who, then, will speak for the future?

The answer, of course, is the futurist. Consciously or not, the futurist is and must be the chief advocate for future generations. Whether working with graphs or charts, with printouts or Delphi projections, with scenarios or science fiction, the futurist functions as an ethicist by revealing new insights about the future and by reminding us what it may be like for the people who will live then. The futurist is the agent who brings knowledge and awareness of what will be, and what may be, so that we can all better choose what should be. By publicizing his projections, he makes it possible for all of us in society to think about future generations and to assume our moral responsibility towards them. The very nature of his work gives to society the data from which moral choices must be made. Thus, perhaps even despite his intent, the futurist assumes an essential role in the enterprise of moral decision-making.

The basic task of the ethicist is to provide the groundwork for a rational deliberation of moral issues. Depending on his particular philosophical orientation, he may perceive that groundwork in a variety of ways. For example, teleological ethicists look to some ultimate goal or end as the determinant of moral actions, and this generally involves an analysis of what we as human beings naturally strive for. Deontologists, on the other hand, seek to relate specific moral issues to an inner sense of duty that is defined by human reason. Some ethicists stress the practical consequences of a particular moral decision, while others look to the nature of the action itself to determine its morality. Finally, some argue that nature and the environment provide us ethical data which we must internalize in our moral decision-making; others say that the sense of morality comes totally from within oneself; and still others are persuaded that God has revealed a moral code for us to follow.

In very general terms, we might explain the basic task of the ethicist as follows: Our actions must tend towards some good if they are to be moral. The knowledge of what is truly good comes from our experiences of the world and from our inner sense of conscience, or reason. Our duty is to choose what is good and to reject what is evil. In so doing, we act morally.

Clearly, the task of the ethicist overlaps that of the futurist. The ethicist acts as a futurist by the very fact that he prepares the ground for moral decisions which, by their very nature, look to the attainment of future goals or the accomplishment of duty for the sake of the future. Ethics is always the consideration of what should be, but is not yet. Thus, the ethicist's field of concern is necessarily that of the future.

Just as evidently, the work of the futurist overlaps that of the ethicist. In suggesting what kinds of futures are possible and/or probable, the futurist narrows and illuminates the options available to us. Like the ethicist, he provides the groundwork for our rational deliberation of the issues. The issues raised by studying the future are nearly always in the context of which possible future we *should* strive to attain. And this is patently the same question asked by the ethicist.

Note carefully that neither the ethicist nor the futurist is charged with the responsibility of making the actual moral decision. Whether we choose to conserve our oil resources by voluntary restraint or to save our helium rather than let it escape are moral choices which must be made by all of us—futurist, ethicist and the public at large. The role of both futurist and ethicist is to provide the awareness and the knowledge so that these choices can be made. Whether we, the general public, choose to act morally or not is our responsibility, not merely that of futurist or ethicist.

In conclusion, let us return briefly to the moral questions we posed at the outset in order to illustrate the role of the futurist as ethicist.

The first question was, "In situations where voluntary modification of our standard of living would benefit the needs and aspirations of other people, is there a moral responsibility for those who enjoy the better life to undertake these modifications?"

By taking the future seriously, as futurists do, we can infer that there is some responsibility to concern ourselves with what is yet to come. This concern, for most futurists, carries beyond their own personal lives (or else older futurists would consider only short-range projections and younger futurists would do all the long-range forecasting!). As to whether the hypothetical part of the question is true, i.e., whether voluntary restraint would benefit others, the futurist again has a contribution: his analysis of the probable future is the best estimate we have regarding whether and in what specific ways a modification of our standard of living might have an impact on future generations. In this question, then, the futurist functions as an essential part of any ethical discussion.

The second question was, "In situations where the use of the world's resources to improve living standards in the developing world is in competition with the need to conserve those same resources for our future generations, where does our primary responsibility lie?"

Here the futurist makes the case for the offspring. Since most of us understand fairly well our own wants, and since the aspirations of the poorer nations are kept in our awareness by the media, data regarding the future is essential if any kind of comparison is possible. This is what the futurist is uniquely able to provide. Consequently, for this question as well, the futurist also assumes a role as ethicist. And it is probably fortunate for our progeny that he does!

Dreams into Action:
Methods and Real-Life
Experience

Community Decision-Making
in the Future

by

M. Susan Linderman

Alvin Toffler has described two problems facing contemporary democratic political systems: lack of future-consciousness and lack of participation. The remedy, he maintained, was development of "anticipatory democracy." As he defined it, "The term *anticipatory* stresses the need for greater attention to the long-range future. The term *democracy* stresses the need for vastly increased popular participation and feedback." Although he suggested eleven general actions that would aid in achievement of this objective, it was only recently that a specific system was developed to make it feasible. A device known as the *Consensor* enables community decision-makers to focus on long-range planning and simultaneously elicit increased public participation. In a decade devoted to "Thinking Globally, Acting Locally" it seems appropriate to consider how the Consensor can realize the goal of anticipatory democracy.

The failure of governments to engage in long-range planning is hardly a new phenomenon. Toffler (in THE FUTURIST, October 1975) notes the results of such a situation: "The energy shortage, runaway inflation, ecological problems—all reflect the failure of our political leaders at federal, state, and local levels to look beyond the next election." In a rapidly changing society a myopic political system can be devastating. Problems, unanticipated, fester and soon outgrow any remedy.

The tendency to try to cure existing ills rather than creatively prevent new ones reflects political reality—constituents are usually more concerned with here-and-now than hereafter. Since the goal of most legislators is to remain in office, they cater to their constituents' concern with the present. It is highly unlikely that legislators will commit electoral suicide by changing tactics and focusing on the future. It therefore becomes necessary for citizens concerned with long-range planning to have impact on community decision-making.

Lack of participation is not so much due to indifference as to impotence. Traditional methods of voicing opinions to representatives, such as writing letters, phoning, or signing petitions, have limited impact due to the

M. Susan Linderman is Director of Consensor Research and Development, Applied Futures, Inc., Greenwich, Connecticut.

small numbers received. Media stories and editorials are more influential but atypical, due to the desire for newsworthy articles. Most powerful of all are the lobbies of special interest groups which make sure their position is acknowledged through physical presence and political pressure. But these lobbies do not represent the views of most constituents—indeed, their whole reason for existence is to ensure that the minority viewpoint is heard. So what recourse does the "silent majority" have in providing input to elected representatives? The voting machine seems to be the only viable alternative, where citizens can register their (dis)approval of a representative's prior performance. But elections take place infrequently and then the opinions are *ex post facto*. The poor decisions have been made; the opportunities have been lost. What is needed is a mechanism to provide input from local constituents *before* decisions are made, not to provide feedback after.

Modern communications technologies now offer communities a readily available way to achieve "anticipatory democracy." The traditional town meeting, where all citizens engage in the community's decision-making, has by necessity been replaced with systems of elected delegates representing the burgeoning populations. But through synthesis of three communications systems—television, telephone, and the Consensor—a new form of town meeting emerges where elected delegates receive both *pre-facto* input and *post-facto* feedback. Telecommunications enable large numbers of constituents to participate, and the Consensor enables these constituents to instantaneously voice their opinions in a quantified, anonymous manner. Rather than being limited to the infrequent "Yes/No" response of the voting machine, the Consensor offers citizens a continual avenue for expression of qualified preferences, which can be immediately communicated to representatives.

The system consists of a series of individual "voter" terminals and a CRT display that reveals the collective results of a given series of votes or selections.

The hand-held voter's terminal has two small radial multi-switches: The first—*Selection*—offers eleven alternative values or shades of opinion ranging from "no" to "yes." The second—*Weighting*—enables each participant to apply various degrees of intensity to the opinion expressed on the first switch. This intensity depends upon that individual's self-adjudged confidence or personal familiarity with the issues under discussion.

Once these two controls have been set by each participant, the group's aggregate position is displayed as a histogram, on a television screen. The height of the bars indicate the cumulative input to each of the eleven selection alternatives, and both the average weight and the average weighted opinion are automatically calculated and displayed. A sample display is discussed in the following case study, which demonstrates how the three tools—television, telephone, and the Consensor—can help alleviate the problems of lack of future planning and lack of participation.

An Experiment in Alaska

The state of Alaska, in conjunction with the Media Group, recently undertook an ambitious project whose goal was "to maximize participation of the Alaskan people in decision-making in government." The specific task was to determine the best allocation of the state's large budget surplus. Alaskan state law requires legislators to attend town meetings around the state and gather opinions of the citizenry before making such an allocation. While it is a commendable policy, the process is costly in terms of time and money, and as one legislator noted, it is not truly representative, since the same few people show up at these meetings time after time. Considering the vagaries of weather, it seemed preferable to make the opinion-gathering process accessible to citizens at home through use of the telephone and television. In addition, there was a desire for quantifiable objective data, instead of subjective comments. This led to their use of the Consensor.

The procedure that was designed for this "experiment in communication between citizens and government" involved gathering opinions from the people in two basic ways. First, town meetings in Anchorage, Fairbanks, Sitka, Juneau, Kenai and Ketchikan were arranged over a period of nine nights. Each town meeting was set up for ninety participants, who were statistically representative of the population. Each participant was provided with a Consensor voting terminal for recording opinions. Secondly, citizens watching the proceedings at home on TV could register their opinions by dialing a number on the telephone which would record their votes on the computer.

The "Town Meeting in the Air" was conducted by satellite with two-way transmission between Daniel Schorr, who was located in Anchorage, and the participants at each night's particular town meeting. Schorr would give background on a specific issue, and then ask a series of questions concerning that issue. Citizens in each town meeting would respond to the questions by turning the selection dial on their Consensor terminals either to the left or to the right. This two-position response represented a variety of scales—Yes/No, Alternative 1/Alternative 2, Decrease Funding/Increase Funding. Citizens at home simultaneously voted over the phone. Within one minute, the telephone responses were displayed in percentages on the home TV screen, immediately followed by the results of the town meeting's Consensor vote. The Consensor readout was in the form of a bar graph which normalized the vote to 100%. After the votes were in, Daniel Schorr would address questions and solicit comments from a select panel of legislators, government administrators, and experts on certain issues.

An example of one issue concerned future transportation developments. One question asked was, "Are you more interested in developing a carpooling system *or* in seeing road improvements?" Participants voted to the left if they were in favor of carpooling and to the right if they were in favor of road improvements. The telephoned results in Juneau showed 58% in favor of carpooling and 42% in favor of road improvements. Then, Representative Jim Duncan asked for a preferential vote between the development of carpooling through incentives and development of mass transit. The results showed 17% for carpooling and 83% for mass transit on the right.

Other issues addressed included the desirability of increased employment through capital improvements; development of permanent funds; establishment of mass transit and ferry service among cities; improved jail facilities, roads, and bridges; exploration and use of oil and gas reserves; and distribution of Alaska's wealth. All told, one hundred twenty-two questions were addressed in the seven town meetings, with access to the opinions of over 80% of Alaskan citizenry. Forty-four panel members from all parts of society participated and they felt the new procedure to be a definite step forward in improving the legislative decision-making process. The final question asked was, "Do you favor TV town meetings in the future?" The Consensor showed that an overwhelming 94% answered "Yes."

A Connecticut Community

Another community using the Consensor to gauge public opinion is Bridgeport, Connecticut. Through the efforts of the United Way of Eastern Fairfield County, a Community Decision Laboratory was opened earlier this year as a public service. Any group of citizens wishing to discuss issues of concern merely requests a time to use the lab, with a minimal charge for use of the facilities. The Community Decision Lab is unique in providing citizens with a constant avenue for expression of views. Their input and feedback, by being made available to local representatives, can enable community members to contribute to the decision-making process on a regular basis. The lab's manual points out that "As we enter the eighties there will be more demands to meet in less time; fewer problems will be remedied with simple solutions; there will be more needs and less resources to meet them; there will be a growing challenge to improve the decisions that shape our future; and there will be increasing demands by citizens to engage in the planning and decisions that affect our lives." In order to meet these demands, the Community Decision Laboratory has been established, and "To facilitate community decision-making, the United Way is making available a new technological system called Consensor." Sherry Horosko, current director of the lab, feels that group and community decision-making can be enhanced by using meeting time more efficiently, preserving anonymity, crystallizing ambiguous statements, achieving 100% participation and "surfacing the *full range* of opinions on an issue." The Consensor system, designed specifically with these goals in mind, represents a tremendous advance over the present systems used for communicating with elected delegates.

The two examples cited above are but the first step in achieving "anticipatory democracy." The Alaskan experience demonstrates the workability of periodic, large-scale surveys of public opinion on long-range state planning issues. It is vivid illustration that anticipatory democracy can be achieved. The Bridgeport Community Decision Lab is a paradigm for localities that want a system able to continuously monitor public opinion and provide the input and feedback of citizens in community decision-making. The ultimate goal is a synthesis of the two systems, where public opinion can be made manifest on a large-scale, continuing basis. The technological capability is there. It only requires imagination and initiative to inaugurate it.

Lack of future-consciousness and public participation, Toffler warned, "endanger the stability and survival of our political system today." Through use of communications technologies now available on a large scale, however, it is seen that anticipatory democracy can be realized, and that these dangers can be mitigated. The mandate is clear. In a decade devoted to "Thinking Globally, Acting Locally," the opportunity to effect such an end can ill afford to be lost.

Shaping Urban Futures Through Public Participation

by

Louis J. D'Amore and Sheila Rittenberg

The decade of the 1960s will be recorded in social history as a decade of renewed awareness regarding the rights of citizenship. During that time, efforts were organized across the North American continent to improve, for the poor, the young, and the minorities amongst us, the distribution of benefits derived from being a member of society. Citizens' groups attacking a variety of "causes" flourished at all levels of society, and "people power" was in vogue.

While accomplishments as a result of these efforts have been significant, the period will also be marked as a time of confrontations, violence, and a parting of the ways between and amongst sectors of society. Participation in the '60s was largely expressed in protest; protest against discrepancies in our society that served to finally release frustrations that have been pent up for years.

The activity wavered, however, and finally died in many respects as the "angered" were forced to increasingly concentrate on going about the business of daily living. And so the '70s began to see the need for a new kind of participation to evolve—one that could be relevant to all interest groups and citizens; one that aims at achieving planned social change improving the very nature of our institutions, social agencies, and political structures.

Although this type of participation, and the very term "citizen participation," have become popularized in our present decade, its real meaning, and its implications for how we manage our cities, have yet to be sorted out. Left to a variety of interpretations, then, more recent efforts have resulted in a multiplicity of approaches at generating citizen participation which in their lack of clear directions and goals have often confused and immobilized the public.

Louis J. D'Amore was Project Director of the Saint John Human Development Project. He is President of L.J. D'Amore and Associates, a Montreal-based firm specializing in social planning, and is also President of the Canadian Futures Society.

Sheila Rittenberg is a consultant with L.J. D'Amore and Associates and was Project Coordinator of the Saint John Human Development Project.

Increasing the difficulty of achieving effective participation approaches, the '60s left us with as many failures in social change as it did successes. Idealism, optimism, and remarkable energy were often lost in the wake of lost causes. Emanating out of the style of "protest participation," cynicism and a sense of bitterness grew amongst protestors and "establishment" alike.

Compounding these losses and increasing the complexity of our society have been certain trends that emerged in the '70s. Economic instability, environmental overload, growing bureaucracies, and disenchantment with the poliitical process are illustrative of those trends and have often resulted in a change from a '60s concern for justice to a '70s concern for survival.

If a participative society, an informed citizenry active in shared decision-making efforts throughout all levels of society, was difficult to achieve through the almost exclusive form of participation of the '60s, its achievement has become that much more difficult throughout the '70s. Apathy, and alienation from community, have become common-term in recent years and, unlike the disenchanted of the '60s, they reflect a much larger cross-section of the population. Where anger and protest were typical of certain sectors of the '60s society, a sense of hopelessness and lack of belief in one's own sense of worth to society seem at work now within lower, middle, and upper income levels; different ethnic, language, and age groups; men and women.

Participation of a new order is called for to reverse these trends; it should embrace the commitment and emotion of the '60s while ensuring a collaborative, cooperative model of involvement for all sectors of society; it should recognize the importance of *equal responsibility* amongst all sectors of citizens to bring about positive change while adhering to the respect for *equal rights* that was generated by the '60s; it should be directed at broad social principles that do not change over time, while at the same time remaining flexible and responsive to changing needs, issues, and goals.

In the *Transformation of Man* (1956), Lewis Mumford has noted that there have probably not been more than a half dozen profound transformations in Western society since primitive man. Willis W. Harman, past Director of the Center for the Study of Social Policy, Stanford Research Institute, believes we are currently in the midst of such a transformation and that it is proceeding with extreme rapidity, such that the most critical period will be passed through within a decade. In the April 1977 edition of THE FUTURIST, Harman states that, "Our research leads me to the conclusion that the industrialized world is simultaneously undergoing a conceptual revolution as thorough-going in its effects as the Copernican Revolution, and an institutional revolution as profound as the Industrial Revolution.

Part of his argument rests on various "lead indicators" that have preceded other periods of historic cultural change and can be observed in today's society. These include:
- Decreased sense of community.
- Increased sense of alienation and purposelessness.

- Increased frequency of personal disorders and mental illness.
- Increased rate of violent crime.
- Increased frequency and severity of social disruptions.
- Increased public acceptance of hedonistic behavior (particularly sexual), of symbols of degradation, and of lax public morality.
- Increased interest in non-instituionalized religious activities (e.g., cults, rituals, secret practices).
- Signs of specific and conscious anxiety about the future.
- In some cases, economic inflation.

While the use of social indicators has not been sufficiently developed to measure these variables in Canada or elsewhere in Western society, it would appear that these advance indicators can be observed currently in Canadian society.

The current paradigm of Big Government, Big Business, and Big Labor appears less and less capable of resolving these issues. In fact, one could argue that they are a major part of the cause of the above trends. The combination of greater centralized control, emphasis on growth and profit, increased wages and fringe benefits, a five-fold increase in government spending in the last ten years and a concomitant increase in bureaucracy have created a situation where collectively and individually we are taking more from society than we have been giving. We have reached the point now where society can no longer sustain this imbalance—economically, socially, environmentally, and in terms of our available resource base, both man-made and natural.

Just as there are leading indicators regarding the requirement for a new socio-cultural paradigm, so too are there leading indicators that a shift towards a new paradigm is occurring.

The new paradigm is one seeking definition on three inter-related planes:

Self-realization and inner harmony with one's self.

Harmony with fellow man from one-to-one relationships of intimacy, to group relationships, to new definitions of community, to a concern for the well-being of disadvantaged persons throughout the world.

Ecological harmony with our natural environment on both a micro and macro scale.

Table A, "Shifts Towards a New Society," is a further elaboration of some of the leading indicators that can be perceived in a shift towards a new paradigm.

As we are a society in a state of rapid transition, it is more important now than ever before that people from all walks of life have an opportunity to voice their concern and have their say in decisions affecting their neighborhood, community, city, province, and nation. A vote every three or four years for an individual and/or party platform that is seldom achieved is no longer adequate democratic participation.

Successful public participation in a new social paradigm must be continuous and therefore requires adequate channels and information sharing so that all aspects of an issue can be considered by those participating. Further, it must be *genuine;* there must be sincerity, integrty, and trust on the part of all parties in the process. Only if these pre-

410

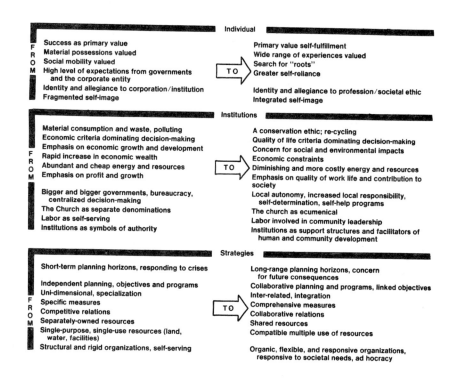

conditions are met can public participation rise above the tokenism of past efforts.

Let us now look at a specific example of how a community—in this case a Canadian city—can shape its future through citizen participation.

The Saint John Human Development Project

In 1973, the City of Saint John, located in the Province of New Brunswick, Canada, adopted a Comprehensive Community Plan to guide physical growth of the city. A number of concerned citizens and agencies believed at the time that it was important to give the same kind of guidance to the "non-physical" components of a city—the people, their needs, opportunities, and problems.

Indeed, the Comprehensive Community Plan itself stressed the need of a parallel social planning study to be undertaken so that attention could be given to the needs of people that are not manifested in physical terms.

This concern grew initially out of the rapid transition and growth in Saint John, spurred on by a construction "boom." Social impacts and needs were felt to be emerging from the city's growth, and human

411

development services were being faced with new demands and more complex problems to deal with.

Concern grew as additional industrial developments were projected for Saint John. Further, Saint John had been designated as one of the growth centers in the country, and the likelihood of accelerated and continued growth and change was introduced.

It was agreed that these and other social impacts of growth and physical development should be assessed. Further, that coordinated planning and delivery of human development services was necessary for both public and private agencies to respond to the increasing and changing needs of the people in Saint John. Most important, if the project was to have any significance, it was essential that the citizens of Saint John be involved in assessing current conditions and setting future goals and directions; and participate in the achievement of those goals.

The Saint John Human Development Project is a national demonstration project sponsored by the Social Services Council, United Way, and City of Saint John; the Provincial Social Services Department; National Health and Welfare and Ministry of State for Urban Affairs. Together, they commissioned the firm of L.J. D'Amore and Associates to design and conduct the project.

The Saint John Human Development Project focuses on a future consciousness—the kind of city Saint John citizens want to live in by 1986. That year is particularly significant as it is the first year of Saint John's third century. The event is of national significance as well since Saint John is Canada's first incorporated city and therefore the first to celebrate a bicentennial.

The project also focuses on an extensive base of citizen participation. It is believed to be the most comprehensive and extended process of citizen participation on a city-wide scale achieved to date in Canada.

It has in fact reached out to the blue-collar workers, poor people, the elderly, the youth—and also to the handicapped, single parents, juvenile delinquents, ethnic groups, families with alcohol problems, special interest groups, and yes, the middle class and affluent as well. The results of this collective effort are:

• A complete and detailed inventory of issues to be addressed over the next ten years.

• An inventory of resources—human, financial, and physical—available for human development.

• A comprehensive set of goals to be achieved by 1986. These goals fall into three general categories: environment, the system for human development services, and people.

• An organizational framework (referred to as the "Model") for the coordinated delivery of human development services and the continued participation of citizens in decision-making and self-help programs.

In the simple but eloquent terms of one participant in the process, the project provides answers to:

Where are we now?

Where are we going?

How are we going to get there?

The Approach to Change

The approach taken in the Saint John Human Development Project was based on the premise that the various publics of the Saint John community in reality constitute the "client," rather than simply those sponsors who had commissioned the study. Further, that each of these publics has the right and indeed the responsibility to participate in the research that is being done as part of a social change process. The objective of the project was not simply the accumulation of data, facts, and information for the eventual preparation of a report; but rather the initiation of action by the *involvement* of people from all segments of the community in what can best be described as an *action research process.*

Planning that prepares a program and then tries to "sell" it to the affected publics is no longer effective in our society. Equally inappropriate is planning that asks the publics to choose between alternatives that they have not had a role in formulating. Participation and mutual learning must start at the very beginning of the process, so that over time, understanding and commitment will grow, resulting in decisive implementation and actions towards mutually agreed-upon goals and objectives.

The concept of involvement therefore was one which embraced citizens and receivers of services; professionals and providers of services; governments at each level and policy makers, private agencies and their executives. It also sought and obtained the involvement of labor, the business community, churches, the University, and a wide range of associations. The project attempted to generate participation in a spirit of respect, mutual trust, adaptation, and open cooperation.

Any approach that involved only one or two of the above would not have achieved what we have come to call a sufficient "critical mass" of interest and involvement to achieve implementation of any significant social innovation.

Involvement had to occur in each of these sectors in a positive way in order to reinforce the involvement in each of the other sectors. In effect, the challenge was to try to "turn on" the city. The intent was to create an overall positive environment–an "umbrella effect" within which social innovation could be conceived, nourished, and made to happen.

The Design for Participation

The design for participation was actually an adaptation of a futures forecasting technique called *Delphi.* The Delphi has two basic characteristics:

- It seeks out "expert" opinion.
- It provides synthesis and feedback of information to participants over two or more phases.

A third key aspect of the design was a recognition that a successful public process must recognize that there are several "audiences" or publics that it is trying to reach, just as a fundamental principle used by every successful marketing executive is the principle of market segmentation. Further, if the involvement of these various audiences or publics is desired, it must be in a medium with which they are comfortable. An agency such as Family Services, for example, might be comfortable with preparing a formal brief. A group of single parents, on the other hand, might prefer a small discussion among themselves.

Therefore, the design comprised several "vehicles" of participation including: briefs, letters, personal interviews, group discussions, seminars, conferences, public meetings, ad hoc committees, self-study efforts, task groups, research projects.

The variety of "vehicles" for participation reaching out to diverse audiences created what can be called a "synergistic" effect. That is, each of the vehicles reinforced the others, and in turn was reinforced by them. Therefore, the extent of participation and the quality of participation, in total, was a quantum level higher than what might be anticipated from the simple additive results of each form of participation taken singularly.

By having each audience reflect in depth on those issues it knew best and was most familiar with, the first characteristic of Delphi, "expert" opinion, was achieved.

After each phase, or "round," of participation, all information was completely classified and synthesized. Feedback was tailored to each particular audience to avoid information overload and also to get response and further probing in the knowledge and interest area of each group. Therefore, opportunities were given for unhurried and repeated reflection and dialogue as the style for participation, rather than a one-time glance and response format. This accomplished the second characteristic of Delphi—synthesis and feedback.

In this manner, the project moved through four phases:

I		Awareness
II	(A)	Issue Identification
	(B)	Issue Verification and Expansion
III		Goal Formulation
IV		Organizational Design

The process described above resulted in the gradual building of a "participation momentum." As momentum began to build, people, the media, agencies and "the establishment" could begin to see the seriousness of the effort and credibility began to develop.

As the above description would suggest, the timing of hundreds of tasks and events had to be governed by the build-up and flow of participation. Critical path scheduling was used to accomplish this and to assure the proper orchestration of output and activities.

The policy adhered to in the study process was one of complete sharing of all information obtained among all those participating in the study and others who had a desire "to know." In this context, eleven interim reports were prepared during the conduct of the project and their contents disseminated to participants.

Figure 1 illustrates the basic overall flow of the public participation process. Broad awareness of the project was created in Phase I by the distribution of over 500 brochures describing the purpose and ob-

414

FIGURE 1
BASIC FLOW OF PARTICIPATIVE PROCESS

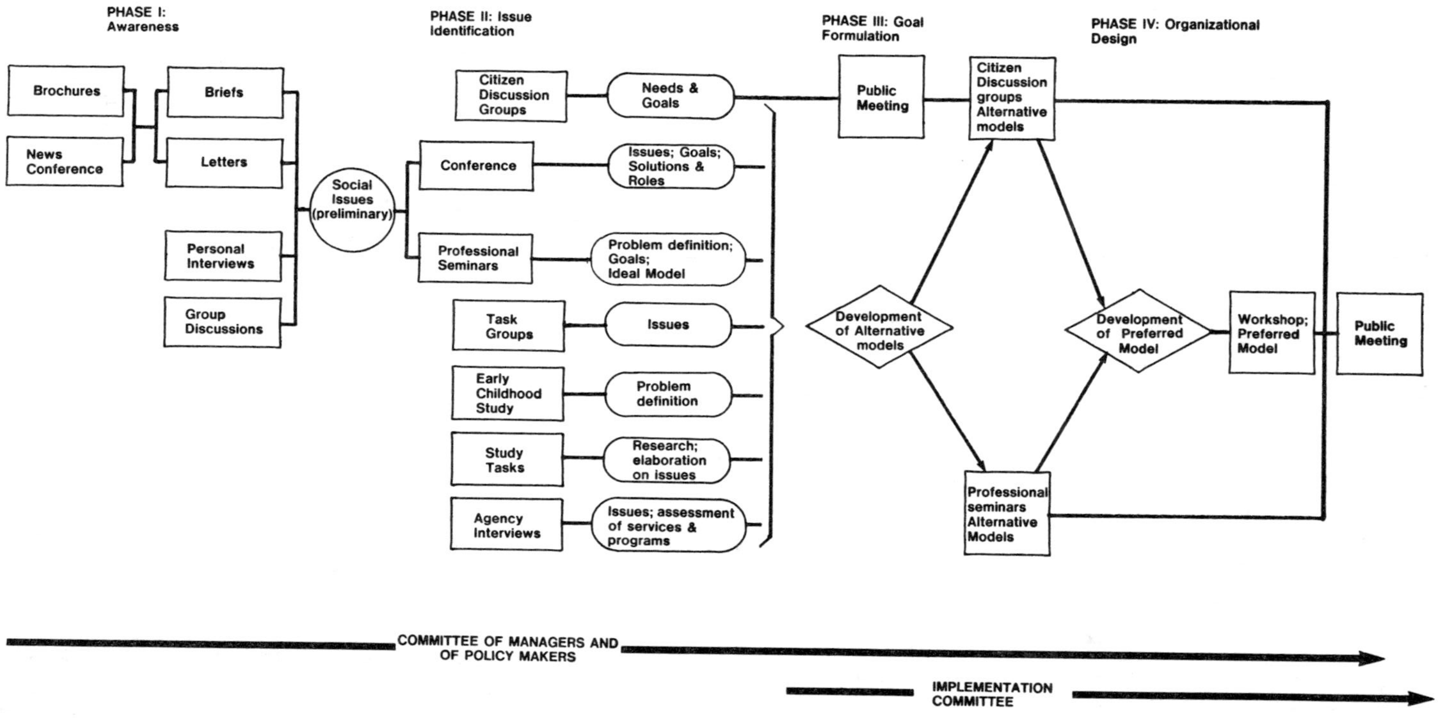

PHASE I:
Awareness

Brochures

News
Conference

Briefs

Letters

Personal
Interviews

Group
Discussions

Social
Issues
(preliminary)

PHASE II: Issue
Identification

Citizen
Discussion
Groups

Needs &
Goals

Conference

Issues; Goals;
Solutions &
Roles

Professional
Seminars

Problem definition;
Goals;
Ideal Model

Task Groups

Issues

Early
Childhood
Study

Problem
definition

Study
Tasks

Research;
elaboration
on issues

Agency
Interviews

Issues; assessment
of services &
programs

PHASE III: Goal
Formulation

Public
Meeting

Development
of Alternative
models

Citizen
Discussion
groups
Alternative
models

Professional
seminars
Alternative
Models

PHASE IV: Organizational
Design

Development
of Preferred
Model

Workshop;
Preferred
Model

Public
Meeting

COMMITTEE OF MANAGERS AND
OF POLICY MAKERS

IMPLEMENTATION
COMMITTEE

415

jectives of the project and suggesting various ways for persons, citizen groups, agencies, associations, companies, unions, and institutions to participate. This was timed to coincide with a news conference on the project. Some 100 briefs and letters were received as a result of this effort.

Participation during Phase I also occurred in the form of personal interviews and group discussions. These were unstructured and exploratory in nature and designed to complement the briefs and letters in identifying issues.

Participation in subsequent phases took various forms, including:

• Over 50 citizen discussion groups, including "special" groups such as youth, handicapped, senior citizens, consumer advocates, single parents, inmates, young offenders, and environmentalists.

• Eighteen conferences with various associations and societies such as dentists, lawyers, principals, teachers, labor, Board of Trade, home economists, etc.

• Professional seminars with persons involved in the delivery of human development services. A first round was on a functional basis, i.e., health, social services, recreation, education, culture, justice, and spiritual services. The second round was on an interdisciplinary basis.

• Think sessions in which models were explored, designed, and refined.

• Task Groups on housing, economic development, physical development.

• Several study tasks undertaken by students of the Urban Studies Workshop at the University of New Brunswick at Saint John, including: research on young offenders; study of the social costs of vandalism, theft, and alcoholism in Saint John; inventory of facilities for human development.

• Projects undertaken by high school students, including a Sight and Sound Presentation of "Life in Saint John." This was presented at the project's first public meeting.

• Panel discussions among junior high school students on social issues in Saint John.

• Drawings by elementary school students with the theme "Saint' John—1986," displayed at the first public meeting.

• Two public meetings, each attended by approximately 300 persons.

• A variety of ad hoc and working committees during all phases of the project.

Participation of ministers of relevant departments in the provincial government as well as other recognized leaders of the community such as the president of the District Labor Council, the president of the Board of Trade, the president of the United Way, etc., was secured through their membership on a Policy Committee to which the consulting team reported at key junctures in the project. This committee was chaired by the mayor of Saint John.

Participation of senior administrators of key human development agencies was secured by their membership on a Management and Advisory Committee. This committee met once or twice a month, giving guidance to the project and monitoring its progress.

416

An Implementation Committee, formed within the last three months of the project, was made up of community leaders, senior administrators, and professionals and was charged with the implementation of the proposed framework for human development.

In addition to the process described above, a survey was conducted of the 22 key human development agencies in the city. These provided the basis for a general assessment of services and programs.

A review of available literature on social planning and innovations in the delivery of human development services was conducted and informed the process, which led first to the design of alternative models for human development and eventually to the final proposed model put forward by the project.

This was also the case with information derived in on-site visits and interviews with innovative projects in four other Canadian cities.

Finally, meetings were held with social development policy advisers in both the provincial and federal governments to ascertain future directions of these senior levels of government. The intent of the proposed framework is to move in synchrony with these directions, and we believe that this has been accomplished.

Method of Information Processing

It was important for "feedback and reaction" at different stages of the project to be smoothly timed so that there was an almost rhythmic flow to the overall participation of the entire project. The method of processing information became a key dimension to ensuring the success of this approach.

Certain activity had to be organized at key junctures so that second and third rounds of participation had sufficient material to work with. Information had to be processed, organized, and presented on time to merge with the flow and timing of different "streams" of activity.

The method of information processing is illustrated by the manner in which material on social issues was handled. Figure 2 conveys how

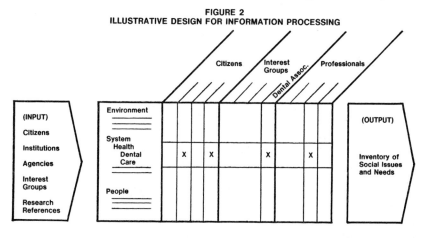

FIGURE 2
ILLUSTRATIVE DESIGN FOR INFORMATION PROCESSING

PROCESSING AND CLASSIFICATION

information was processed in Phase II with regards to identification and verification of issues. As the diagram indicates, the process is described in an "input/output" framework.

As information was received in Phase I, every viewpoint, regardless of source, was captured and organized in the major categories of Environment, System, and People. Sub-categories such as Health, within "System," were delineated as well as sub-sub-categories, e.g., dental care.

The horizontal axis at the top of the diagram represents the participating groups, or "audiences," of Phase II. In preparation for meetings with these groups, all categorized issues were reviewed. Issues specifically relevant to each group were extracted, and a "mini-report" was prepared specifically tailored to the knowledge and interest of each group.

As an illustration, the diagram shows that all issues relating to dental care in the "system" category were presented for review to a series of diverse audiences. An "X" is indicated where dental-related needs or issues would be pertinent to various groups meeting in discussion groups, conferences, or professional seminars. Citizens would have reviewed these issues in a discussion group or at the public meeting; the Dental Association in the Conference of Dentists; health professionals in their professional seminar.

With all issues handled in this manner, there is a high degree of confidence with regard to the validity of the issue. Also, the full range of issues can eventually be explored in depth by compiling the special knowledge of each particular group as it relates to the various issues.

Implementation Strategy

The process of implementation of a comprehensive framework for human development services began in fact prior to the project itself. It began with the sponsoring bodies and their commitment to improve the delivery of services in Saint John.

The participative nature of the project was also designed with a focus on implementation from the very first phase. Through the involvement of citizens, professionals, senior administrators, and policy makers, the model that has evolved over the course of the project is one that they have collectively shaped, structured, and tailored. Therefore it is a model that is "theirs"—they have a sense of "ownership" of the model.

Implementation took more concrete forms in the last few months of the project. An Implementation Committee was formed and a chairman appointed. The mandate of the committee is to ensure implementation and to provide a smooth transition from the consulting team to the core organizational components of the model.

The implementation strategy envisioned has four basic dimensions, which are as follows:

1. Continued high profiling of the Human Development Project in a positive way by all sectors of the media—this to set a receptive and positive atmosphere with regards to the project among citizens generally, citizen groups, institutions, and political leaders.

418

2. Community development work to make ready the base of citizen participation required and leading to the formation of Neighborhood Resource Boards. In this context, community development workers will give particular attention to those segments of the population who are difficult to reach but who often have the greatest needs.

3. Organizational development activity at the city level sustaining efforts towards, for example: a Council of Churches, a Service Clubs Council, revitalization of the Saint John Arts Council, programs of community leadership within organized labor, and developing further the collaborative roles of the Board of Trade, Law Society, dentists, etc.

4. The decentralization of human development services into four Community Service Centers in a manner consistent with the principles and organizational framework arrived at in the participation process. This dimension will require parallel in-service training to prepare professionals for interdisciplinary team functioning.

These dimensions are planned to evolve concurrently and in an "orchestrated" manner so that they are each mutually reinforcing.

The Saint John Human Development Project has the potential to provide a successful example of a city shaping its future through public participation. We wish the people of Saint John success in the challenge they have accepted.

Conclusion

What We Must Do:
An Agenda for Futurists

by

Edward Cornish

Interest in the future has accelerated in recent years because people have increasingly realized that they must look ahead if they want to survive and prosper in a fast-changing world. A major expression of this increased interest in the future is futurism itself, which emerged as an international movement during the 1960s. In that exuberant decade, when the world's economy surged to new triumphs and man literally reached for the moon, futurists came out of their closets and joined in organizations involving thousands of scholars, scientists, government officials, and others around the world.

Times have changed since the 1960s and so have futurists. The change has been reflected in the big meetings of the World Future Society, which was founded in Washington in October 1966 and now has 50,000 members in 80 nations. The Society's earliest meetings were small local gatherings, but as early as 1968 thought was given to holding a large meeting to which all Society members would be invited. This meeting—the first General Assembly of the World Future Society—was held in May 1971 and attracted more than 1,000 registrants. The Assembly had the theme "Dimensions of the Future," and the participants provided a wide-ranging exploration of the future in all its aspects. Most futurists seemed to see the future in rather glowing terms: A many-splendored universe lay before them, and with advancing technology they would take possession of it. Futurists were free to do whatever they wished, because nobody expected anything of them. The future was, for futurists, an exciting hobby; for non-futurists, an idle pastime. Thus the meeting was a visionary and optimistic affair, with much talk about realizing the human potential throughout the universe and little thought about the shadows that already had begun to darken the future.

The mood changed as the 1970s wore on. By the time the second General Assembly was being organized, futurists were expressing in-

Edward Cornish is President of the World Future Society and Editor of its magazine THE FUTURIST. *He is the author of* The Study of the Future: An Introduction to the Art and Science of Understanding and Shaping Tomorrow's World *(World Future Society, Washington, D.C., 1977).*

creased concern about the future and had begun to feel more strongly that they might have a real responsibility for it. The disappearance of the bubbly enthusiasm of the first Assembly was perhaps inevitable as the world moved through a period of intensifying shortages of resources, stagnating economies, increasingly dangerous population growth, political instability, and renewed fears of world war. Of course, thoughtful futurists had discussed these sobering possibilities in the 1960s (and earlier), but such concerns tended to be brushed aside by futurists excited by new technological possibilities and dreams of utopian communities.

The committee planning the second General Assembly held four meetings before agreeing on a theme that suggested the new focus of futurist concern: "The Next 25 Years: Crisis and Opportunity." The theme expressed a consensus on two points:

1. Futurists should focus special attention on the nearer-term future because this period would be critical for the long-term future of the human race and futurists might be able to help with the difficult decisions that needed to be made during this period.

2. The years ahead may be dangerous, but they also hold promise of many enormous triumphs in every field of human endeavor. Therefore, the proper attitude toward the future is neither pessimism nor optimism, but rather hopeful realism—a clear-headed appreciation of the problems and risks that lie ahead, but also a recognition of the emerging solutions and opportunities.

By June 1975, when the second Assembly was held, futurists could no longer be dismissed as idle hobbyists or demented votaries of some weird religious cult. Many world-renowned scholars and scientists spoke at the meeting along with three U.S. senators and four congressmen. What's more, the sitting President of the United States, Gerald Ford, had spoken at a Society meeting only a year earlier. This recognition from the larger community gratified futurists, but also reinforced their somewhat reluctant recognition that they could not be sidewalk superintendents during the construction of the future; the world expected them to participate actively in the effort—if not as workers at least as consultants providing thoughtful, helpful, and timely guidance.

Futurists had learned to tolerate the gentle ridicule that they experienced in the 1960s and early 1970s—and perhaps even to enjoy it, because it gave them a sense of being part of an elite coterie that could live in quiet exclusivity without any need to prove itself. In fact, many futurists enjoyed the future as a way of relaxing from the cares and troubles of the present; they could escape into the future just as others escaped into the past by reading history.

But as the 1970s wore on, futurists discovered that they were increasingly being sought out by people who genuinely wanted help in understanding the future. Nobody expected historians to be responsible for what happened in the past, but ·people did expect futurists to be responsible—at least in some measure—for what would happen in the future. Increasingly, futurists were regarded not as useless monomaniacs, but as forecasters whose help was desperately needed in a rapidly changing world. Instead of being dismissed as idle dreamers, futurists now found themselves being treated as oracles. For serious futurists, this was a mixed blessing. It is bad to talk about the future and find that nobody is listening, but it is worse to talk about the future and find that everybody is listening and believing every word.

Intensifying our discomfiture is the constant acceleration of change, which has had the effect of reducing the horizon of our vision. No longer can we confidently prognosticate for 50 or more years ahead in the happy realization that no one will take us seriously; now when the increasingly anxious world presses us for predictions, we find that peering even 10 years ahead seems dangerously beyond our capacities. Many of the telescopes through which we peered so perspicaciously in the 1960s now are exposed as kaleidoscopes—trick optical devices that obscure and confuse more than they reveal. And many of us have experienced the ignominy of seeing events occur with callous disregard for our forecasts. We did not always fail—indeed, on the whole, I think our record was reasonably good—but we erred often enough to feel a healthy degree of humility.

Chastened and cautious, futurists chose a very modest theme for the third General Assembly, held in Toronto in conjunction with the Canadian Futures Society. It would be the biggest meeting of futurists ever held, but the new theme—"Through the 80s: Thinking Globally, Acting Locally"—clearly indicated the growing modesty of futurists as they shifted from a long-term to a short-term time perspective—and also reflected their growing awareness that it is not enough to think about the future, they must play an active role in shaping it. Futurists could no longer regard the future as a playtime activity; they had to assume a responsible role in creating the future. The outside world would no longer allow them to do otherwise. The childhood of futurism has ended.

But can we really become leaders in the creation of a better future? Most of us, I think, feel overwhelmed by the responsibilities that are forced upon us. We would prefer to be "consumers" rather than "producers" of the future. We would like to watch the future develop the way we watch the news on television—sitting in a comfortable living room and having a pleasant drink with friends while the future world is created out of the sweat, blood, and tears of other people. But we can't, because we ourselves are part of the future we are creating and somehow we must try to fulfill, as best we can, the responsibilities that are thrust upon us.

What are the special tasks of futurists in the construction of the future world? Let me suggest three:

1. We need to develop a World Future Network that will serve as an interactive communication system for all those people everywhere who are seriously concerned about the future.

2. We need to create new visions of a better future world—visions that will inspire people everywhere to bury their differences and move on with the task of achieving the better world.

3. We need to disseminate the futurist perspective, which sees the future world as being created by what we do—or don't do—rather

than being imposed on us by mysterious external forces.

Let me explain a little about each of these tasks.

Building the World Future Network

The first task of futurists is to move rapidly forward in the construction of a World Future Network, which will link up futurists—and others—in all nations and in all walks of life. This network will welcome the participation of everyone and anyone who is interested in creating a better future.

The World Future Network will enable millions of people around the world to discuss—by means of a multimedia global forum—the basic issues of steering our little planet during a period of momentous change. By means of this network, people can gradually come to agreement on an increasing number of goals and programs for solving our most pressing problems. The Network is not, of course, a physical object, but rather a way of conceptualizing a communications system that will link up human beings everywhere and focus their thinking on common problems. The physical means of doing this may include a wide variety of technologies—from mimeograph machines and typewriters to videotapes, computer conferences, and satellite-cable television. What is important is that they provide interactive channels for communication among people all over the world. Before we can really get to work on building a future world, we need to talk things over in a kind of round-the-clock, never-ending Town Meeting. Not everyone needs to be talking all the time—God forbid!—but everyone who wants to say something should have an opportunity to provide input. I believe that such a Network is a necessary preliminary to the development of the global consensus that is required to cope with the challenges of the 1980s and 1990s.

The Network is not just a dream; it is actually being constructed now by the World Future Society and other groups. Today it consists of publications, conferences, and audiotapes that are shared by people around the world; tomorrow the Network will employ a wide variety of other means such as computer conferencing and videodiscs. As communications technology improves, so will the Network. Many people will object that the world's problems are urgent and demand immediate solution, and we haven't got time to wait while the Network is being built. Unfortunately, the world's pressing problems cannot be solved overnight any more than an adult man can be produced overnight; to suggest otherwise is to disregard the slow but real solutions that can actually help create a better future world. We can't take effective action on a global basis until there is some kind of global agreement, and we can't have global agreement until we have the means of communication with each other so that we can work out an agreement. Thus, a World Future Network—that is, a communications system open to all people who are concerned about the problems the world faces—is a necessary step. The United Nations is a useful organism, but another communications system of a different sort is required. It may be true that the Network cannot be built rapidly enough to forestall a third

World War, but the punishment for assuming that may be to convert World War III from a possibility into a certainty. There is, I believe, simply no other way to begin addressing effectively our great global dilemma.

Just what is this dilemma? The world is engulfed in a maelstrom of change due to the accumulation of technical knowledge that has enabled us to do more and more things, but we have not found the wisdom to manage our new powers without hurting or even destroying ourselves. We do not know how to live peacefully with each other, and our new technological prowess means that we can kill each other with remarkable efficiency. Somehow we need to work out a general worldwide consensus on how to manage the planet earth, but we cannot have consensus until we have effective communication among the people concerned about the future of the planet, and that means we must build the Network.

The need for the Network may perhaps be clarified if we imagine that some very brilliant fellow has devised a Master Plan for the world—and unlike all the other Master Plans, which are constantly being cooked up by cranks, this particular Master Plan is absolutely perfect: It really will solve all human problems immediately and permanently just as soon as it is adopted.

You will, of course, object that the plan could not possibly be perfect—and you will not be the only one who will raise such objections. People quite rightfully distrust all plans—especially Master Plans—because most plans are characterized more by megalomania and romanticism than by practical wisdom. People everywhere will raise objections and the perfect Master Plan will never be adopted. And that is precisely the point. We cannot solve problems with perfect solutions that are never implemented! What we need is *imperfect* solutions that *will* be implemented. We need to bring together: (1) people with knowledge about problems that are developing; (2) people who may have solutions to problems; and (3) people who will have to implement the solutions if the solutions are going to work. In other words, we need a communications system that will link up these three types of people (who are, of course, really the same people at different times). By bringing together problem-identifiers, solution-developers, and implementers, the Network will enable people everywhere to share both their problems and their solutions, and, when there is a match, to join together in collaborative efforts to realize solutions.

Building the World Future Network will be extremely difficult. There will be political obstacles, cultural barriers, language problems. There will be failures, big and small; but eventually, I believe, the Network will be built. And long before the Network is completed—if there ever is a point where we can say that the Network is finished—people will reach consensus on many, many problems, and the solutions will be adopted and the world will move forward peacefully. The many little defeats we will encounter in trying to build the Network will be more than matched by the victories we will achieve.

New Dreams for Man

The second thing we must do, in addition to building the World Future Network, is to create new dreams for mankind. Today countless millions of people lack any hopeful vision of the future. They believe that if human civilization does not self-destruct the best we can look forward to is something on the lines of George Orwell's *1984* or Aldous Huxley's *Brave New World*. This negative view of the future is extremely dangerous, because if people believe they do not have an attractive future, they are likely to act in such a way as to bring about the nightmare or oblivion that they anticipate; as King Solomon warned, many centuries ago, "where there is no vision, the people perish." Solomon's words should not be viewed simply as a gloomy judgment on our world, but rather as a prescription: we futurists must create new dreams. Great dreams that will inspire great deeds. Dreams that will help us to build the great future that we all know is possible.

Because we now lack a great dream of the future, we have governments that can't think beyond the next election . . . businesses that can't think beyond making profits in the current quarter . . . and schools and universities that can't think beyond surviving the budget cut planned for the next semester.

But if we can build the World Future Network, we can also dream of a better future, in fact, even an ideal future, for we live in an age when the creation of a peaceful, prosperous, and happy world is a genuine possibility.

When I talk about a happy future world, I find that many people become a bit uneasy. People who have learned to contemplate a thermonuclear armageddon with composure are horrified by the thought of utopia. They cannot imagine a society in which everyone is happy. For that reason, they tend to reassure themselves that utopia is only an idle dream.

And so there are a lot of anti-utopians wandering around who say that if real peace were to break out, life would become boring. If everybody had plenty to eat, no one would be willing to work—at least for a reasonable wage. If everyone were happy, human existence would be meaningless. For many of these anti-utopians, the thought that the human race is inevitably headed for collapse and barbarism (if not total destruction) is much more comforting than the thought that we might actually be headed toward utopia. Now why is this? One reason that utopia unsettles people is the widespread belief that utopia requires conformity if not uniformity. In a utopia, everyone behaves like a robot so as not to mess up the perfect social order. Individuality, freedom, and creativity are banned, and people lose their souls. What many people fail to realize is that they have come to confuse utopia with its opposite, dystopia. Dystopian novels like *1984* and *Brave ·New World* so dominate our thinking about the future that a dystopian novel now passes for a utopian novel, and utopia is thought to be a repressive police state or a robotized dream factory run by mad planners.

The first task in rehabilitating utopia is to recognize that a utopia is a person's concept of a *desirable* community or state, and not just any sort of future society, much less the sort of society he deplores. But even when we have straightened out that point about utopia, we still face the fact that people have different values and that one man's utopia is likely to look like another man's dystopia. Furthermore, our demands on utopia have escalated even more rapidly than our standard of living. Plato and Thomas More saw nothing wrong with having slavery in their utopias; today people will find things to criticize in even the most perfect utopia. A utopia in which peace is universal is usually a utopia in which nations and localities have yielded some of their ability to make war and individuals have given up their freedom to use bombs and guns. But any restrictions on freedom are offensive to people who insist upon freedom as an absolute value. All the residents of a utopia may be happy people, but if that happiness results from chemicals or electrical stimulation of the brain some people will be horrified.

Thus we must recognize that it is impossible to describe an ideal world that would satisfy everyone's criteria of perfection. As soon as we go beyond generalities like "peaceful," "prosperous," etc., we inevitably offend some people's sensibilities. And so when I think about the future I prefer to think about the world not as a single utopia but as a world in which hundreds, thousands, perhaps even millions of utopias are allowed to flourish. These utopias might range in size from large nations down to single individuals living their own lives alone according to their own privately held concepts of the good life.

A world divided into many communities—as interlinked or as interdependent as each chose to be—could provide scope for individual freedom and at the same time offer the means for testing out all sorts of living arrangements, technologies, art forms, etc. It would be possible to create communities modeled not only according to visions of the future but also according to dreams of the past. We could have Athens in the age of Pericles, Imperial Rome, Venice in the days of Marco Polo, or Florence at the height of the Renaissance. Such communities are foreshadowed by the Williamsburgs and Mystic Seaports of today, and would provide living museums for people who wanted a respite from change. And the people of the world tomorrow might live in many of these different communities during the course of their lifetime, moving on whenever they felt they could be happier or more productive somewhere else.

Other futurists will develop other dreams, and through the World Future Network we can share them.

The Futurist Perspective

Our third great task, in addition to building the Network and creating visions of a positive future, is to disseminate the basic philosophy of the futurist movement. If there is one key idea in today's futurism it is this: The future does not just happen to us; we ourselves create it by what we do and what we fail to do. It is we who are making tomorrow what tomorrow will be. For that reason, we futurists now think less in terms of predicting the future and more in terms of trying to decide more wisely what we want the future to be.

People everywhere must understand that the future does not just unfold according to a pre-arranged and unalterable script. They—and we—will make the future by what we decide to do in the years ahead. Of course, this is not an idea that we are completely comfortable with. Most of us like to think that other people run the world while we ourselves are innocent victims. We like to see ourselves as powerless to do anything about world conditions because that excuses us from taking responsibility and making an effort.

But the world of tomorrow will arise from the cumulative acts of several billions of little people who feel that they have no influence whatsoever. The most powerful statesmen will struggle with the huge problems created when individuals have babies or build houses or do their gardening. Yet when we make our decision we normally consider no one's interests but our own. In a vague way, we may recognize that the child adds to the world's population, and the house almost always means that there will be a slightly larger expenditure of the earth's limited and irreplaceable resources of coal, gas, or oil, and more pollution added to the atmosphere. But the impact of our actions seems so trivial as not to be worth considering.

By our actions, we little people are carrying forward the great revolutions of our time, and for decades to come the potentates will wrestle with the consequences of what we "impotentates" have done. We little people are the real shapers of history, and the fact that the world is not what we would like it to be is not due to our lack of power, but to our inability to exercise our very real power in a concerted, intelligent, and responsible manner. Whether or not we accept our responsibility, each of us is, in a very real sense, a legislator determining what mankind shall become in the years ahead.

As we begin to think about our role as legislators for mankind and the real creators of history, we confront a curious fact about actions: They can have impact only on the future, and that impact widens with the passage of time like the ripples on a pond. The past is fixed forever, and the present is a result of what has been done—or not done—in the past. Furthermore, we can have only the most limited influence on the immediate future, because that, too, is largely determined by what happened in the past. But when we look to the longer-range future we begin to discover a huge region where our seemingly puny efforts can have gigantic effects.

Frustrated government officials have reported that their bureaucracy seems impervious to the changes that they are trying to effect, yet that same "immobile" bureaucracy is changing very rapidly as a result of actions taken by previous administrations. The reason is simple: time—often many years—for a policy to be translated into programs, projects, and people. A human system, like a plant, requires time to develop. With sufficient time, a small seed of change can grow into deep-rooted traditions and enormous institutions. Our task as futurists is to explore the possibilities of the future, so that people can know better what seeds to plant.

428

We human beings have it within our power to create a civilization so vastly superior to anything known in history that we cannot even imagine its character. I have no doubts about that. Nor do I have any doubt that we can feed and clothe and house every person on this planet. We can eliminate poverty; we can wipe out disease; we can put an end to war. We can, in short, create a comfortable and happy world for all human beings everywhere. That is well within our power; in fact, I think we could do the job in 20 years if we really go to work. But that happy future will not necessarily happen; it will depend on whether people all over the world make the decisions that will move us forward to achieve that happy world. If they do, we will move into a brilliant new era of human history. We will see the transformation of mankind into a global civilization of happy people working productively in thousands of creative ways to build a world that today we can only dream about.

Postscript

The Challenge of the '80s

by

Aurelio Peccei

It is my perception that the world is in worse shape now than it was 10 years ago—and is getting worse.

Ten years ago, we at the Club of Rome predicted that bad social management, the wasting of resources, widespread pollution, and rapid overpopulation would eventually strangle our civilization. Few people listened. We now have increasing violence, fewer energy resources, military buildups, more economic difficulties, and continuing overpopulation.

At the annual conference of the Canadian Futures Society in Ottawa in 1978, I defied anyone to indicate any major front of human advance where things were going better than they were 10 years ago. Today, the world begins more and more to resemble a ricocheting bullet as it careens from disaster to disaster.

We are now heading into an even more complex and difficult decade. I have pretty well given up predicting what will happen unless we act. The Club of Rome now concentrates instead on what may happen if present circumstances prevail.

In the following key areas, it is relatively easy to see what will happen.

1. Population. This is the worst problem we face and it affects all of us. Today there are 4.5 billion people in the world. Projections show that between now and the end of the century there will be two billion more people. There are not enough resources on this planet to care for them. So if population is not controlled, we will not be able to control anything else. We are heading for a desperate situation here. We cannot even take care of the world's population today. One quarter of the globe's population now lives below the poverty line. When people's basic needs are not being met, there will be increased social tension, more civil and military violence, more unemployment, less food and less shelter. Because of this, practically everything will be unmanageable.

2. Economic Affairs. The economy will take slight up and down curves, but the overall projection is a downward trend in the next decade. The world economy will be under greater stress as prices continue to

Aurelio Peccei, inspirer and co-founder of the Club of Rome, is the author of such books as The Chasm Ahead *(1969) and* The Human Quality *(1977).*

increase in the area of foodstuffs, transportation, energy supplies, and raw materials. Because of this, economic enterprise will become harder.

3. Military Activities. There will be larger arsenals in the world; they will be more powerful; and there will be more occasions to use them. Because of this, the picture is becoming more worrisome. Right now, it is estimated that each person in the world is sitting on the nuclear equivalent of 10 tons of explosives. And every day around the globe, a total of $1.5 billion is being spent on the military. With the arms race heating up, fueled by Iran and Afghanistan, we are on the threshold of a new era of destruction.

4. Science and Technology. The problem here is that 40% of the world's scientists are working on military preparations rather than producing technology for the betterment of the world. And the scientific gains that we've made—in areas such as genetics and microelectronics—aren't being handled well by people. We still retain values our forefathers gave us, which are no longer valid in our civilization.

5. Eco-systems. Four ecological areas necessary to sustain life—ocean fisheries, forests, pastures, croplands—are under great stress today. This does not mean much in countries like Canada where there are vast spaces and policies of reforestation, but in other parts of the world, tropical rain forests are being destroyed and deserts are advancing. If we continue to burn tropical forests down to make way for highways and settlements, and to cut them down to produce lumber, we will be destroying the very basis of life and food. In 40 years, almost all the forests will be used up. Yet it takes 100 years for a tropical forest to grow back. And in 40 years, when the population has doubled, each citizen will have only one-tenth of the natural goods he has today.

Governance Is the Solution

What is to be done? The new project of the Club of Rome is to work to make the world more governable. By this, we mean a more regional approach to the new international order.

Today the world is a fragmentation of more than 150 nations. Each is fiercely nationalistic, but we must realize how much interdependence there is. For example, the Iranian crisis affects everyone—not just Americans.

I think it is impossible for 150 states to continue to be selfish.

What the Club of Rome is proposing is a plan to try to make the south of the globe as governable as the north.

In the north there are five giant communities: Western Europe, the Soviet bloc, North America, China, and Japan. In the south, however, there are 120 nation-states without any community.

We are therefore suggesting that in areas such as East Africa, West Africa, Latin America, and Southeast Asia, they should get together and try to speak with one voice.

Such a process will no doubt be long, tortuous, and painful. But it is certainly within the realm of possibility if we all accept the basic principles involved. Indeed, I consider it essential if a true sense of global community is to evolve.

World Future Society
An Association for the Study of Alternative Futures

The World Future Society is an association of people who are interested in how social and technological developments will shape the future. It is chartered as a nonprofit scientific and educational organization in Washington, D.C., U.S.A.

The Society was founded in 1966 by a group of private citizens who felt that people need to anticipate coming developments to make wise personal and professional decisions. In our turbulent era of change, the Society strives to be an unbiased and reliable clearinghouse for a broad range of scholarly forecasts, analyses, and ideas.

As outlined in its charter, the Society's objectives are:

1. To contribute to a reasoned awareness of the future and of the importance of its study.

2. To advance responsible and serious investigation of the future.

3. To promote the development and improvement of methodologies for the study of the future.

4. To increase public understanding of future-oriented activities and studies.

5. To facilitate communication and cooperation among organizations and individuals interested in studying or planning for the future.

Since its inception, the Society has grown to include more than 50,000 members in over 80 countries. Society members come from all professions and have a wide range of interests, and the Society counts many distinguished scientists, businessmen, and government leaders among its ranks.

The Society publishes a number of future-oriented periodicals, including:

• THE FUTURIST: A Journal of Forecasts, Trends, and Ideas About the Future. This exciting bimonthly magazine, which is sent to all members, explores all aspects of the future—technology, life-styles, government, economics, values, environmental issues, religion, etc. Written in clear, informative prose by experts, THE FUTURIST gives every member an advance look at what may happen in the years ahead.

• The World Future Society Bulletin. This bimonthly journal is intended for professional futurists, forecasters, planners, and others with an intense interest in the field. The Bulletin carries articles on forecasting methods, news of special interest in the field, book reviews, etc.

• Future Survey is a monthly abstract journal reporting on recent books and articles about the future. Each 16- to 24-page issue contains more than 100 summaries of the most significant futures-relevant literature.

• Three newsletters—Business Tomorrow, Education Tomorrow, and

Technology Tomorrow—each specializing in the future of a key aspect of modern society.

Recent books published by the Society include *The Future: A Guide to Information Sources, The Study of the Future,* and *Education and the Future.*

The Society's "bookstore of the future" stocks hundreds of books, and also a number of audiotapes, games, and films.

One of the principal activities of the World Future Society is the planning of a variety of futures conferences—both large and small—at which participants can exchange ideas and keep up to date on the latest futuristic developments in their field of interest. The Society's large General Assemblies have been held in Washington, D.C. (1971 and 1975) and, most recently, in Toronto, Canada (1980). The Society also has sponsored annual conferences on education (beginning in 1978) and special meetings on energy, business, and communications.

At the local level, the Society has active chapters in a growing number of cities scattered throughout the United States and around the world. These chapters offer speakers, educational courses, seminars, discussion groups, and other opportunities for members to get to know each other in their local communities.

Membership in the World Future Society is open to anyone seriously interested in the future. For further information, write to:

World Future Society
4916 St. Elmo Avenue
Washington, D.C. 20014, U.S.A.
Telephone: (301) 656-8274

World Future Society Publications

Cornish, Edward, ed. *The Future: A Guide to Information Sources.* Revised 2nd edition. Washington, D.C.: World Future Society. 1979. 722 pages. Paperback. $25.00. The revised and expanded second edition of this indispensable guide to the futures field contains even more information than the highly-praised first edition.

Cornish, Edward, ed. *1999: The World of Tomorrow.* Washington, D.C.: World Future Society. 1978. 160 pages. Paperback. $4.95. This first anthology of articles from THE FUTURIST is divided into four sections: "The Future as History," "The Future as Progress," "The Future as Challenge," and "The Future as Invention."

Cornish, Edward. *The Study of the Future: An Introduction to the Art and Science of Understanding and Shaping Tomorrow's World.* Washington, D.C.: World Future Society. 1977. 320 pages. Paperback. $9.50. A general introduction to futurism and future studies. Chapters discuss the history of the futurist movement, ways to introduce future-oriented thinking into organizations, the philosophical assumptions underlying studies of the future, methods of forecasting, current thinking about what may happen as a result of the current revolutionary changes in human society, etc. The volume also includes detailed descriptions of the lives and thinking of certain prominent futurists and an annotated guide to further reading.

Didsbury, Howard F., ed. *Student Handbook for The Study of the Future.* Washington, D.C.: World Future Society. 1979. 180 pages. Paperback. $5.95. This supplement to *The Study of the Future* is designed to help students develop a basic understanding of the field of futuristics. Much of the material has been "classroom-tested" by students in futures courses at Kean College of New Jersey.

Didsbury, Howard F., ed. *Instructor's Manual for The Study of the Future.* Washington, D.C.: World Future Society. 1979. 24 pages. Paperback. $2.00. A brief complementary volume to the *Student Handbook for The Study of the Future*, containing course outlines, research suggestions, teaching aids, bibliographical additions, and more.

Jennings, Lane, and Sally Cornish, eds. *Education and the Future.* Washington, D.C.: World Future Society. 1980. 120 pages. Paperback. $4.95. Contains selections from THE FUTURIST and the *World Future Society Bulletin* on the future of education. Packed with ideas for the classroom.

Kierstead, Fred, Jim Bowman, and Christopher Dede, eds. *Educational Futures Sourcebook.* Washington, D.C.: World Future Society. 1979. 254 pages. Paperback. $5.95. This book contains selected papers from the first conference of the Education Section of the World Future Society, held in Houston, Texas, in October, 1978.

Martin, Marie. *Films on the Future.* Washington, D.C.: World Future Society. 1977. 70 pages. Paperback. $3.00. This is the third revised and expanded version of the film guide first produced in 1971. The films are grouped by major subject areas (Education, Technology, etc.). A brief description of each film is supplemented by information about length, source, and rental costs.

THE STUDY OF THE FUTURE

An Introduction to the Art and Science of Understanding and Shaping Tomorrow's World

By Edward Cornish with members and staff of the World Future Society
World Future Society, Washington, D.C. 1977.
320 pages. Paperback. **Price: $9.50**

This exciting and unique volume is the Society's answer to the hundreds of inquiries it has received from people who want an easy-to-read, but authoritative and comprehensive introduction to futurism and future studies. The book includes:

- A concise history of futurism, from ancient times to today.
- A description of the philosophy of futurism.
- A discussion of the various scenarios developed by scholars for the future of our civilization.
- A detailed explanation of how organizations carry out futures research and how teachers give courses on the future.
- An annotated bibliography of selected books about the future.

—and much much more...

You'll meet the men and women whose contrasting viewpoints and informed perceptions have helped shape our visions of tomorrow's world—figures like Herman Kahn, Daniel Bell, John McHale, Alvin Toffler, Bertrand de Jouvenel, and Arthur C. Clarke.

You'll learn from non-technical summaries about the methods being used to make and test technological and social forecasts—methods such as Delphi studies, simulation gaming and computer model-building.

You'll examine how and why Big Business, Government, the Universities, and even Church and public service agencies are making future studies an essential part of their operations.

You'll discover ways to put futuristics to work for *you* in your own business, school and family environments.

We think you'll agree that *The Study of the Future* is a very special book. Here for the first time is a clear but authoritative introduction to the individuals, institutions and ideas at the cutting edge of humanity's never-ending exploration of the not-yet-known.

Order from:
Book Service
WORLD
FUTURE SOCIETY
4916 St. Elmo Avenue
Washington, D.C.
20014 U.S.A.

WORLD FUTURE SOCIETY

An Association for the Study of Alternative Futures

The Society is an association of people interested in future social and technological developments. It is chartered as a non-profit scientific and educational organization in Washington, D.C., and is recognized as tax-exempt by the U.S. Internal Revenue Service. The World Future Society is independent, non-political and non-ideological.

The purpose of the World Future Society is to serve as an unbiased forum and clearinghouse for scientific and scholarly forecasts, investigations and intellectual explorations of the future. The Society's objectives, as stated in its charter, are as follows:

1. To contribute to a reasoned awareness of the future and the importance of its study, without advocating particular ideologies or engaging in political activities.
2. To advance responsible and serious investigation of the future.
3. To promote the development and improvement of methodologies for the study of the future.
4. To increase public understanding of future-oriented activities and studies.
5. To facilitate communication and cooperation among organizations and individuals interested in studying or planning for the future.

Membership is open to anyone seriously interested in the future. Since its founding in 1966, the Society has grown to more than 50,000 members in over 80 countries. Most members are U.S. residents, with growing numbers in Canada, Europe, Japan, and other countries. Members include many of the world's most distinguished scientists, scholars, business leaders and government officials.

SOCIETY PROGRAMS

THE FUTURIST: A Journal of Forecasts, Trends, and Ideas About the Future.
This unique bimonthly journal reports the forecasts made by scientists and others concerning the coming years. It explores the possible consequences of these developments on the individual, institutions and society,

and discusses actions people may take to improve the future.

Publications
The Society publishes books, reports, films, and other specialized documents on future-related areas, including works such as *The Study of the Future, The Future: A Guide to Information Sources, Through the '80s: Thinking Globally, Acting Locally,* and many other stimulating, useful guides to the future.

Book Service
World Future Society members can purchase books, audio tapes, games and other educational materials dealing with the future, at substantial savings. The Society's unique "Bookstore of the Future" carries about 300 titles.

Tape Recordings
The Society has a growing inventory of audio tapes, which are available at low cost to members. This cassette series includes coverage of most major areas and issues of the future, including science and technology, government, education, environment, and human values.

Chapter and Local Activities
Society chapters and local activities in many cities offer speakers, educational courses, seminars, discussion groups and other opportunities for members to get to know each other. They provide personal contacts with people interested in alternative futures.

Meetings
Meetings offer special opportunities for participation and interaction. The *General Assemblies* are large, multi-disciplinary convocations where Society members can hear and meet frontier thinkers and doers. The Third General Assembly (The First Global Conference on the Future), held in Toronto, Canada, in July 1980, drew 5,000 participants. Specialized conferences are also held, such as a conference on "Communications and Society" in November 1977 and annual conferences on education since 1978.

Future Times
This informative publication covers meetings, activities, new books, tapes, films, and other information of interest to members. It is sent to all members regularly at no charge.